Rev Fr Dr Robert Afayori

CHRISTOLOGY
IN CHRISTIAN-MUSLIM
DIALOGUE

The Hermeneutics of Interreligious Learning
for the Promotion of Common Values

novum 🔺 pro

www.novum-publishing.co.uk

© 2020 novum publishing

ISBN 978-3-99107-293-5
Editing: Hugo Chandler, BA
Cover photo:
Valerii Brozhinskii | Dreamstime.com
Cover design, layout & typesetting:
novum publishing

www.novum-publishing.co.uk

CONTENTS

DEDICATION

In Memory of my late father Philip B. Afayori
(June 1945 to April 2019)

ACKNOWLEDGEMENTS

I wish to use this opportunity to express my sincere gratitude and appreciation to all who have in many and diverse ways contributed to helping me complete this work. I particularly want to thank Aid to Church in Need (ACN) for helping me pay part of my tuition fees. I would like to thank the School of Divinity scholarship committee for paying the substantial part of my tuition fees. The Ian Baillie Grant through Mrs Sheila Baillie and the family were equally of great support in my fee payments. Your immense support is deeply appreciated.

I wish to also thank my supervisors: Dr Nicholas Adams and Prof. Brian Stanley who provided the needed guidance and encouragement over my period of studies at the University of Edinburgh. The work was begun by Dr Michael Purcell (RIP) and completed by Dr Adams and Prof. Stanley. Thus, I am truly grateful to them for their wealth of knowledge, the academic resources they provided, and their constructive criticisms which contributed tremendously to giving shape to this study.

I equally want to thank my Bishop Most Rev. Alfred Agyenta who tacitly supported me during this journey. His Eminence, Keith Patrick Cardinal O'Brien (RIP) who provided me with accommodation and maintenance support during my studies. While remaining grateful to him, may the Lord grant him eternal rest in His kingdom. Here too, I cannot possibly forget the Parishioners of Our Lady Immaculate and St Margaret's Parish, Duns and St Joseph's Parish, Selkirk. With them I lived, worked and studied, deriving support and encouragement to push on.

Hence, I am particularly grateful to Mrs Patricia Julia Scott for all the support in helping me to get this book published. Immense gratitude to Mrs Christine Jobson for proofreading the work. Last but not least, thanks to my family for their prayers and moral support during this academic odyssey.

PREFACE: AN EXECUTIVE SUMMARY

Christology is one of the most contentious subjects in Christian-Muslim relations. While Jesus of Nazareth is construed as Christ, the "Son of God" and the "Saviour of the World" in Christianity, Islam conceives him as a "Prophet" or as the "Messenger" of Allah without divine connotations. Thus, Islam categorically rejects the Christian position on the identity and mission of Jesus and invites Christians to rethink their faith and jettison their claims on the incarnation, the divine sonship, and the death and the resurrection of Jesus Christ. Whereas these Muslim claims and rebuttals undercut the essential content of the Christian faith, the Christian church from the onset viewed the Islamic image of Jesus as a "new form of heresy" which needed to be sanitized by force, if need be. For the Muslim world too, the Christology of the Christian Church was born out of pure distortions and falsifications. This context of claim and counterclaim gave rise to polemical relationships between the much older Christian church (first century) and the newcomer, the much younger Islamic or Muslim world (seventh century).

Through the centuries, while the Christian Church initially reacted to the Islamic claims by adopting an aggressive and defiant policy of propagating the faith regardless of the views and confutations of Islam, Muslims too continued to accentuate their perceived concerns about the Christian stance, by underlining the Qur'anic position on the identity and the mission of Jesus, and the Qur'anic Jesus' own rejection of the Christian claims to his divine sonship. Realising over the years that its policy of defiant faith propagation was not that successful, the Christian church resorted to another policy of protective withdrawal from real contacts and communication with Muslims on the subject of Christology. When this calculative avoidance tactic was not very successful in shirking off what was then considered as the "new heresy", the church decided to take Muslims seriously by listening to them and making sense to Muslims the Christian position on the mission and the identity of Jesus. This gave birth to the most cherish twentieth century concept of dialogue between Christians and Muslims and interreligious dialogue in general. Yet, still unresolved, is the question on the identity and the mission of Jesus Christ – a historical person common to both religions, nevertheless divided between them.

While some scholars think that Christian–Muslim dialogue on Christology is altogether impossible because of the stark differences in their Christological understandings, this book shows that dialogue is possible depending on its nature and goal. The persistent lack of success in Christian–Muslim dialogues on Christology is because much of these dialogues have often centred on various versions of the tripartite traditional models of *exclusivism, inclusivism* and *pluralism*. While *exclusivism* categorically rejects the belief-systems of the other as inauthentic, *inclusivism* patronises other's belief-systems as less or partial versions of what is realized in only one, however, *pluralism* and its associate versions end up caricaturing the religions by its declaration of a limitless playfield of openness for all religions. In this way, not only do these traditional paradigms fail to adequately preserve the integrity and the identity of the *other,* they also fail to maintain the commitment of the *self* to its religious beliefs and practices. Throughout the history of Christian–Muslim relations, applications of these traditional models of dialogue have failed to meet the tripartite goals of interreligious dialogue: that is, (1) the profound knowledge of oneself; (2) the authentic knowledge of the other; and (3) living more accordingly as oneself as another.

It is in response to this difficult lack that this current study proposes a *new turn* to Christian–Muslim dialogue as "an exercise in learning". This model of dialogue traverses the weaknesses of the three traditional paradigms and creates the appropriate context for constructive engagements between Christian and Muslims on Christology. By its emphasis on "learning from and about the other", dialogue as "an exercise in learning" effectively negotiates the contentions that characterized the "claim and counterclaim" polemics in Christian–Muslim relations over centuries. What is significant in this form of dialogue is the interest to learn from and about the other's beliefs on the identity and the mission of Jesus Christ within their tradition-specific contexts, and how this learning contributes to enriching the relationship between the *self* and the *other* in contexts where they are considered estranged. The *self* and the *other* here can either be the Muslim and the Islamic understanding of Christology, or the Christian and the Christian understanding of the identity and the mission of Jesus Christ.

The relationship between the *self* and the *other* is a complex one, which is today, described as a hermeneutic relationship. This is because it encompasses the difficult and complex nature of the relationships that were established between the *self* and *other* in the past, and the perceptions, the attitudes and the concerns that they each bring into this relationship today. It is often said that for dialogue to be successful, it is essential that the dialogical partners perceive each as *equal-partners-in-dialogue* and unite their attitude of faith *commitment* to their beliefs and *openness* to the beliefs of the other. Here, Christians and Muslims are expected to open themselves to each other without losing their religious identities. This dialectic of *openness* and *commitment* raises hermeneutic questions such as: (1) What is *openness* and *commitment* in interreligious dialogue? (2) Are there limits to *openness*, and if so, how is this determined? (3) How is the dialogical call to *openness* related to *commitment*? (4) What is religious identity? (5) Is dialogue with the religious *other* (be they Muslim or Christian) a *threat* to one's identity or an *enrichment*? (6) If the latter pertains, what is the nature of this *enrichment*? (7) Is religious identity the *same* in respect of one's religious tradition, or is it a matter of *becoming, growing, change* and *transformation*? (8) If the latter pertains, how does *change* and *transformation* occur without the *self*-losing itself?

A response to the above hermeneutic questions within the context of dialogue as an exercise in learning, recourse is made to Paul Ricoeur's hermeneutics of the *self* which provides the framework within which the questions on religious identity, and the attitudes on *commitment* and *openness* are addressed. Ricoeur is a philosopher of mediation who never gives up on the *space-between* the *self* and the *other*. In terms of establishing the relationship between the *self* and the *other* in contexts where they are considered estranged, Ricoeur's asserts that *selfhood and otherness* are so interconnected such that *selfhood* and *otherness* cannot be separated. Through his concept of *attestation*, Ricoeur demonstrates that in narrating the story of our lives, we find that others contribute to our narratives and we theirs. These narrative *intertwinements* provide the hermeneutic fingerprints for the fruitful engagements between the *self* and the *other*, and the enrichment it manifests. Following the Ricoeurean hermeneutics of the *self*, the study demonstrates on the one hand, how Islam and Christianity possess symmetrical and dissymmetrical narrative discourses on Christology, and on the *other*, how these discourses serve as contexts for learning and enrichment.

Christianity and Islam hold similar Christological themes and titles such as: *the Virginal Conception, the miracles Jesus performed, the ascension and the Second Coming, Jesus as the Messiah, Jesus as the Word of God*, and as *the Spirit of God*, among others. Islam however denies the truthfulness of the *Holy Trinity*, the *Incarnation*, the *Crucifixion*, the *Death* and the *Resurrection*. Whereas learning from the other helps to unravel the deeper meanings of the similitudes and the dissimilarities between their Christological understandings, dialogue as an exercise in learning also leads to the profound knowledge of oneself (Christian or Muslim), the authentic knowledge of the *other* (Christian or Muslim), and the mutual enrichment this evinces. A significant aspect of the enrichments that is inaugurated by dialogue as an exercise in learning is on how it leads Christians and Muslims to the discovery and to the promotion of common values that are inspired by Jesus the *Messiah*. Some of these values which we shall discuss include *prayer and submission to God, peace and peaceful co-existence* and *solidarity with the poor and the marginalized*. These values are considered common to Christians and Muslims because they are inspired by the message, the life and the mission of Jesus Christ the "Prophet" and the "Messenger" of Allah and the "Son of God".

Key Words: *Christology, Interreligious Dialogue, Learning, Hermeneutics,* and *Interfaith Action.*

It is good to indicate at this stage that this book entitled "Christology in Christian-Muslim Dialogue: The Hermeneutics of Dialogue for the Promotion of Common Values" is composed from the work undertaken as part of the fulfilment for a PhD at the University of Edinburgh (2010–2015). The work presented here is substantially the same as contained in the thesis, although more research has been done to establish the clarity and the robustness that is required to strengthen some of the identified weak joints of the chain of arguments present in the thesis. In this way, what the readers find is the novelty that this study brings to the whole arena of Christian-Muslim dialogue on Christology. It is academically insightful and very engaging by its rich rigorous content and coherency in arguments and presentation. It provides the reader with something to hold unto, which in turn, grips the reader's insatiable curiosity in desiring to know what lies in the next pages, in the way it constantly provides fresh impetus on what is possible, and how this can be achieved through dialogue in general and Christian-Muslim dialogue on Christology in particular.

INTRODUCTION

1 The Background

In the world today most of the religious clashes, confusions and conflicts according to Douglas Pratt, are born from unexamined conflicting religious ideologies and unresolved mutual misunderstandings and thinking.[1] If an ideology can simply be understood as a set of beliefs, values and opinions which shape the way a person or a group of persons act, behave, interpret and understand the world, then unexamined conflicting ideologies that precipitate religious conflicts need to be critically examined and clarified. Conflicts between religions as a consequence of ideological differences are a well-known phenomenon in our world today. For instance, the 1994 tribal conflict in Ghana between the Konkombas and the Chumburus (largely Christian) on one the hand and the Dagombas, the Nanumbas and the Gonjas (largely Muslim) on the other is a sad story to recount. This tribal conflict which arose as a result of disagreements between two people from two different tribes, soon metamorphosed into a religious conflict between Christians and Muslims in the area; leading to the loss of thousands of people.[2] Peace, which is an essential value

---

1 Douglas Pratt. *The Challenge of Islam: Encounters in Interfaith Dialogue.* 2005, p.189–190. George Dardess and Krier Mich also indicate that the tensions that often characterize Christian–Muslim relations perpetuate a hopeless sense of doom and gloom (see, Dardess, G. and Mich, M.K. *In the Spirit of St Francis and the Sultan,* 2011).

2 Tsikata and Wayo report that 2,600 lives were lost, not counting those unregistered and the properties involved in this conflict (see, Tsikata, Dzodzi & Sein Wayo. "Identities, Inequalities and Conflicts in Ghana." 2004, p.46).

of every meaningful religion was jettisoned in place of war. The observed religious conflicts in Nigeria, Sudan, Iraq, Pakistan, India and Indonesia are but few examples. Religious conflicts have devastative effects on life, property and development.

Overcoming the ideological differences that trigger religious conflicts in our world today through interreligious dialogue is therefore a dire necessity. As Pratt put it, "for dialogue to proceed in the hope, if not the expectation, of a productive outcome, then the misapprehensions of the past, together with the prejudice of the present, must be addressed in a climate of mutual and reciprocal correction."[3] If interreligious dialogue is to succeed in this area, then there is the need for the development of constructive theological paradigms which support meaningful dialogues between them. Such paradigms need to provide context whereby the religions can creatively engage each other in conversations where shared religious experiences and theological exchanges can lead to the dialogue of life and the dialogue of common action.[4]

Within the context of Christian-Muslim relations, "Christology" is one of the most contentious Theologica-doctrinal constructs that places the two religions in diametrical opposition to each other. Whereas Muslims believes that Jesus was only a "Prophet" or the "Messenger" of Allah, Christians maintain that Jesus Christ is the "Son of God." Islam has constantly refuted this Christian perspective on Christology both in the Qur'an (Surah 4: 171) and in the Hadiths as blasphemy. For the Christian Church, the Islamic perception of Jesus Christ as

---

3 Pratt, Douglas. *The Challenge of Islam.* 2005, p.191.

4 *In the Spirit of St Francis and the Sultan* (2011), George Dardess and Marvin Krier Mich propose the fruitful encounter between Sultan Malik al Kamil and Saint Francis in Damietta (Egypt) in 1219 as the framework for Christian-Muslim interfaith relations. For them, Francis' openness to the possibility of spiritual companionship with the Sultan provides the roadmap for Christian-Muslim interfaith dialogues (p.17).

a "Prophet" or as a "Messenger" of Allah is heretical and must be condemned. Consequently, the contours of their relations have been one of claim and counterclaim. As a result, Gaudeul intimated that Islam and Christianity shared the same universe at a point, "but mentally they lived in different worlds and, as time went on, the mental universe of each society grew more impervious to the thinking, the values ... and indeed the whole universe of the other."[5]

Today, dialogue between Christians and Muslims has contributed to establishing openness between them to some extent. Part of the fruits of these forms of dialogues is demonstrated by the way Islam is no longer exclusively perceived as a "Christian heresy" but a religion in its own right.[6] Despite the Qur'anic rebuttal of the Christian belief in Jesus Christ as the "Son of God" (Surah 4: 171), there is growing openness between Christians and Muslims who view dialogue as the effective means to establishing a mutual understanding between the two religions on Christology. These dialogues are possible because the Qur'an has its own narratives about Jesus Christ and his mission in the entire divine plan of Allah. These Christological underpinnings in the Qur'an could be brought in conversation with the Christian accounts of the identity and the mission of Jesus Christ. Besides, Jesus Christ plays distinctive roles within Christianity and Islam as the "Son of God" and the "Prophet of Allah" respectively. His distinct identity and significance in these two traditions presents him both as a *bridge* and a *barrier* between them. Here, what is needed is the formulation of a dialogical framework which supports the effective negotiation of this dialectic of a *bridge* and a *barrier* to

---

5 Jean-Marie Gaudeul. *Encounter and Clashes: Islam and Christianity in History.* 1990, p.191.

6 "The Church has a high regard for Muslims. They worship God, who is one, living and subsistent, merciful and almighty, the creator of heaven and earth, who has also spoken to men" (*Nostra Aetate #3*).

allow for Christian-Muslim "dialogue of life" and the "dialogue of common action".[7]

It must be admitted that although significant scholarly work has been done in this area,[8] most of these do not specifically address the subject of Christology as a context for Christian-Muslim dialogue. Even in the few studies that tangentially address the subject of Christology in Christian-Muslim relations, none of them do so for the promotion of common values. For instance, Mark Beaumont's work on *Christology in Dialogue with Muslims* focuses on the critical analysis of the Christian presentation of Christ to Muslims in the nineth and in the twentieth centuries. Beaumont acknowledges the contentious nature of Christian-Muslim relations within these two epochs. He indicates that at the heart of these contentions is the Christian belief in the divinity of Christ and the Islamic denial of it.[9] Beaumont asserts that the Muslim denials of the Christian understanding of the identity and the mission of Jesus Christ brought about three forms of Christian reactions: firstly, Islam was regarded as a false ideology which had to be silenced by an aggressive policy of propagating Christian truths without considering the views of Muslims. Secondly, Christians distanced themselves from Muslims to avoid any communication with them; and thirdly, the Church attempted to, "take Muslims seriously as people of faith whose views on Christ need to be understood and related to in

---

7 The "dialogue of life" creates the context where people of different faiths strive to live in an atmosphere of openness, sharing together their joys, sorrows and their problems and preoccupations. However, the "dialogue of common action" involves an interfaith collective in response to issues of human flourishing (see, Dardess, G. and Mich, M.K. *In the Spirit of St Francis and the Sultan,* 2011, p.13).

8 See Küng et al. *Christianity and World Religions; Paths to Dialogue.* 1993, p.109–127; Jacque Dupuis. *Christianity and the Religions: From Confrontation to Dialogue.* 2002; Ayoub, Mahmoud. *A Muslim View of Christianity: Essays on Dialogue.* 2007, p.187–243; Siddiqui, Mona. *Christians, Muslims & Jesus.* 2013; Oddbjørn Leirvik. *The Image of Jesus Christ in Islam.* 2010.

9 Mark Beaumont. *Christology in Dialogue with Muslims.* 2005, p.1, 7-8.

genuine attempts to make sense of the Christian faith to them."[10] Beaumont's approach therefore follows this third response; the interest to avoid defiant proclamation and complete indifference by presenting the Christian Christ in a way that Muslims will understand.[11] However, does dialogue not build on mutual sharing with the goal to mutually understand the dialogical other? What about presenting an "Islamic Christology" in ways that Christians will understand? Beaumont's work lacks this side of the dialogue.

In his work on "The Portrait of Jesus in the Qur'an",[12] Hans Küng underscores the fact that the Qur'anic portrayal of Jesus as a Prophet must be understood independently from all Christian sources and interpretations and is situated within the Qur'an's overall theological vision. According to Küng, "from whatever source the information about Jesus may be derived, all the texts have been unmistakably stamped by Muhammad's intensive prophetic experience of the one God."[13] So, the Qur'anic' portrayal of Jesus should be interpreted against the stand-point of the Qur'an and not from the New Testament or the council of Nicaea. He emphasized that Christians should not try to either co-opt Muhammad or Muslims as "anonymous Christians" against the Muslim self-understanding of the uniqueness of their Islamic identity.[14] Whereas Küng's views here are considered laudable, he however advocates for a functional Christology – one *from below*[15] as the best approach to Christian–Muslim dialogue.

---

10 Mark Beaumont. *Christology in Dialogue with Muslims*. 2005, p.2.
11 Mark Beaumont. *Christology in Dialogue with Muslims*. 2005, p.2.
12 Hans Küng et al. *Christianity and World Religions; Paths to Dialogue*. 1993.
13 Hans Küng et al. *Christianity and World Religions; Paths to Dialogue*. 1993, p.110.
14 Hans Küng et al. *Christianity and World Religions; Paths to Dialogue*. 1993, p.110.
15 A Christology *from below* is one that emphasizes on the humanity of Jesus Christ as the starting point for understanding Christology. It is also referred to as "low Christology" and it stands at the opposite end of the spectrum to Christology from above or a high Christology.

For Küng, a functional Christology that views Jesus as elevated to a position of divine authority should be the theme of modern Christology rather than an ontological Christology, that is Christology *from above*. As Beaumont put it, Küng considers that, "the incarnation was an apostolic overlay of the much more modest claims of Jesus of Nazareth, who was proclaimed as the "Son of God" only after his death and resurrection."[16] Consequently, Küng argues that the Gospels reveal Jesus not as a man who promoted his "own person, role or dignity, but God's kingdom, God's name, God's will, which man is to fulfil through service to his fellow men and women."[17] In this way, Küng forgets that just as the image of Jesus in Islam needs to be understood within the overall context of Muhammad's religious experience, so also the Christian perspective on Christology has to be understood against the background of the overall experience of Jesus by the Apostles who believed in him as the "Son of God" and the "Saviour of the World". Christian-Muslim dialogue on Christology must not forget this tradition-specific understanding of Jesus Christ.

In his 1972 scholarly essays on "The Dialogical Relationship between Christianity and Islam",[18] Hassan Askari (an Indian Shiite writer) also presents an interesting contribution to the debate on Christian-Muslim dialogue on Jesus Christ. Here, Askari sees Christ as a "common sign" for both Christians and Muslims.[19] As a *sign*, Jesus directs both Muslims and Christians to the true God they seek to serve. As a person, he reveals the deep relational character of religion, liberating man from his dead circle of monological religion and restores unto him his genuine

---

16 Mark Beaumont. *Christology in Dialogue with Muslims.* 2005, p.191.

17 Hans Küng et al. *Christianity and World Religions; Paths to Dialogue.*1993, p.116.

18 Hasan Askari. "The Dialogical Relationship between Christianity and Islam" in the *Journal of Ecumenical Studies.* Vol. 8 (1972).

19 Hasan Askari. "The Dialogical Relationship between Christianity and Islam." 1972, p.483.

dialogical relation.[20] Thus, Askari suggests that dialogue between Christianity and Islam is the best way to resolve their monological impasse. Although he acknowledges that the process may involve anxiety and pain, he nonetheless believes that dialogue is the best way to a better understanding of God and meaningful relations between them. Askari's approach to Jesus Christ as a "common sign" between Christians and Muslims appears to be laudable from a glance. This is because the identification of Jesus Christ as a "common sign" between Muslims and Christians is likely to create the sort of common ground which support fruitful relationships between the two faith communities. However, a careful consideration on Askari's appeal reveals significantly attenuates the Christian understanding of the identity and the mission of Jesus Christ. To say that Jesus is a "sign directing Christians and Muslims to God" also presupposes that Jesus Christ is not God in himself, because a "sign" always points to something beyond itself. But for Christians, Jesus Christ is a concrete manifestation of God and hence points to himself as the ultimate and definitive revelation of God to humanity. This side of the Christian story must not be overlooked, muffed or fluffed when exploring issues relating to Christian-Muslim dialogue on Christology.[21]

In his book *The Muslim Jesus: Sayings and stories in Islamic Literature*,[22] Tarif Khalidi (a Palestinian historian and a professor of Arabic and Islamic studies) made historical and critical

---

20 Hasan Askari. "The Dialogical Relationship between Christianity and Islam." 1972, p.486. (See also Leirvik, Oddbjøørn. *Images of Jesus Christ in Islam*. 2010, p.12).

21 Hasan Askari's model of Jesus as a "common sign" for Christians and Muslims fits into what Walter Kasper describes as "patchworks of identity" the desire to form common grounds for interreligious engagement is undertaken without careful consideration of the definitive differences that set the religions apart (see, Walter Kasper. "Uniqueness and Universality of Jesus Christ". 2004, p.7).

22 Tarif Khalidi. *The Muslim Jesus: Sayings and stories in Islamic Literature*. 2001.

research into the Muslim Jesus. His work is entitled "Muslim gospel"[23] – a compilation of stories and sayings associated with Jesus in Islamic tradition. For Tarif Khalidi, "the totality of this gospel is the story of a love affair between Islam and Jesus ... a unique record of how a one world religion chose to adopt the central figure of another, coming to recognize him as constitutive of its own identity."[24] In this gospel, Khalidi further asserts that the wealth of tradition found in Islamic literature about Jesus reveals the deep religious and theological complementarity between Islam and Christianity. The question however remains whether Muslims will accept Khalidi's claim that the Qur'anic portrayals of Jesus are adaptations from Christian sources. In Islamic faith consciousness, Jesus is part of the line of prophecy revealed to Muhammed by Allah. To see the Qur'anic Jesus as an adaptation from Christian sources poses a difficult challenge both for Christians and Muslims alike. This is because while the Qur'anic portrayal of Jesus as a prophet does not resonate in Cristian faith and theology, many traditional Muslims too do not accept the Christian scriptures (especially the New Testament) as authentic sources for an understanding of the identity and the mission of Jesus Christ.[25] Ironically, many Islamic scholars rather affirm apocryphal writings like the "Gospel of Barnabas" or the "Shepherd of Hermas" as the authentic Christian sources for

---

23 Tarif Khalif. *The Muslim Jesus: Sayings and stories in Islamic Literature.* 2001, p.3.
24 Tarif Khalif. *The Muslim Jesus: Sayings and stories in Islamic Literature.* 2001, p.5-6.
25 See, Muhammad Ata ur-Rahim. *Jesus: A Prophet of Islam.* 1979, p.19; Louay Fatoohi. *The Mystery of the Historical Jesus.* 2007.

reaching a better understanding of Jesus Christ.[26] In this way, Khalidi's Jesus is an isolated personality who stands between Muslims and Christians, and is owned by none. Mahmoud Ayoub's contribution to the Christological discourse cannot be overlooked. According to Ayoub, earlier research on the subject of Jesus in Islam has been comparative and usually judgemental, the yardstick being the New Testaments account of the life, the teaching and the significance of Jesus, the Christ. "Useful as this research may have been for the wealth of information it had uncovered on Christian–Muslim relations, it had often harboured old prejudices and fostered new hostilities."[27] For Ayoub, enough work has been done on the comparative study of Jesus in Islam in response to questions of similarities and differences. "It is time for both Christian and Muslim scholars to go beyond this cataloguing on points of differences, similarities and drawing on old conclusions."[28] For Ayoub, "to go beyond" such comparative lines of theologising demands that the Islamic view of Jesus Christ is respected and accepted as authentic to the tradition of Islam. This is because, "no matter how different the Qur'anic and later Islamic view of Jesus may be, it is nonetheless the view which Muslims have to struggle with and understand and which Christians must take as Muslim views and accept them as such."[29]

---

26 The "Gospel of Barnabas" contains an account of the life of Jesus supposedly written by the Apostle Barnabas who was a missionary companion to the Apostle Paul. This body of work harmonizes very well with the Islamic interpretations of the identity of Jesus and contradicts much of the New Testament Gospels' account of Jesus. While it is debatable that Hermas of Rome (see Romans 16: 14) is the author of "The Shepherd of Hermas," the book is a Christian literary work which dates back to the second century. From a Christological point of view, it asserts that Jesus was seen as the "Son of God" because he was a virtuous man whom God adopted as a son by filling him with a Holy 'pre-existent' Spirit (Adoptionism).

27 Mahmoud Ayoub. "Towards an Islamic Christology." 1976, p.165.

28 Mahmoud Ayoub. "Towards an Islamic Christology." 1976, p.165.

29 Mahmoud Ayoub. "Towards An Islamic Christology." 1976, p.165-166.

From the above scholarly contributions, one can first of all assert that while much of the scholarly work on Christology in Christian-Muslim dialogue has been treated tangentially in the effort to explore the wider perspectives of the world religions and the possibilities of dialogue among them, some scholars who even focus on Christology proper tend to undermine the Islamic view or more so, jettison the Christian perspective on the identity and the mission of Jesus Christ (Reductionist Christologies) for the purpose of dialogue (Tariq Khalidi or Küng, 1993). Secondly, other scholarly approaches to Christian-Muslim dialogue on Christology focus either on the Christian presentation of Christ to Muslims' (Beaumont, 2005) or the Muslim views about Jesus and Christianity (Ayoub, 1976 & 2007). These approaches form part of what might be conceptualised as "the faltering attempts" at creatively engaging Christians and Muslims in dialogue on Christology. These approaches are considered inadequate for the dialogue on Christology because most of them fail to engage the religions in theological dialogues that recognise the alterity of the religious other, and yet, seek mutuality of understanding and co-existence.

This study asserts that an authentic Christian-Muslim dialogue on Christology must be structured within a framework which supports the mutual listening and the critical questioning of the narratives that have formed and shaped the Christological worldviews of the dialogical interlocutors. Such dialogues will need to negotiate the claim and the counterclaim monologues which have often bedevilled the history of Christian-Muslim relations over two centuries. To negotiate these dialogical impasses, this study proposes the structuring of Christian-Muslim dialogue on Christology as "an exercise in learning from and about the *other*". The *other* here refers to either Christians or Muslims and their respective tradition-specific understandings of Christology. If one desires to learn from the *other* about their stories of the life and the mission of Jesus as construed in their religious tradition, one must be open to listen to and ask questions about the other's narratives. On the part of the other, if they are to be able to authentically communicate these narratives, they must learn and know these narratives as they pertain to their tradition-specific contexts. In this way, the dialectics of *commitment* to one's tradition and the *openness* to learn from the other's tradition are seen as essential qualities for the understanding of dialogue as an exercise in learning. Furthermore, it is known that learning something always has a transformational dimension to it because in learning, the learners comprehend and acquire something new which they hitherto did not know.

Hence, structuring Christian-Muslim dialogue on Christology as an exercise in learning may help Christians and Muslims to learn from each other's narratives about the identity and the mission of Jesus Christ as they pertain to their respective classic texts, and how these are articulated in their theologies. This work demonstrates how these forms of dialogue could also lead Christians and Muslims to the discovery of "common values" inspired by the Qur'anic Jesus (the Prophet of Allah) and the Jesus of the Christian Scriptures (Christ, the "Son of God"). However, for dialogues of this nature to succeed, they need to be guided by appropriate conceptual and hermeneutic tools which support the practice of dialogue as an *exercise in learning from and about the other*; be they Christian or Muslim. Christianity and Islam have different belief-systems whose meanings can only be measured by their internal coherence.[30]

Consequently, against the pluralist theological approach which purports that, "all religions constitute different ways of experiencing, conceiving and living in relation to an ultimate divine

---

30 Catherine Cornille explains that the unique and distinctive belief-systems which define and set apart the various religions pose challenges of understanding across religious traditions because of the inexhaustibility of meaning within each belief-system, the complexity of religious life and the impossibility of penetrating all the dimensions of the belief-systems of a particular religion by an outsider (see, Cornille, Catherine. *Interreligious Hermeneutics*. 2010, p. xv).

reality which transcends all our varied vision of it."[31] This work advances a theological position which reaffirms the particularity and the incommensurability of the religions. Christianity and Islam have unique and all-encompassing interpretive schemas on the basis of which the reality, the identity and the mission of Jesus Christ are clearly defined. [32] While emphasizing the need to observe and to respect the religious particularity of the other, and that each religious tradition has the capacity to account for its Christological stance, dialogue between them then focuses on learning from and about the Christological accounts of the other. This explains why Christian–Muslim dialogue on Christology should be structured on the paradigm of *learning from and about the other's* narratives about the reality, the identity and the mission of Jesus Christ.

The goal of this form of dialogue is neither an attempt to forcefully fit each narrative account into "some supposedly independent communicative system" nor one that seeks to establish common grounds at the expense of alterity.[33] On the contrary, dialogue as an exercise in learning focuses on reaching the authentic knowledge of the other's account on Christology. While this knowledge may lead to a better understanding of the other's Christological viewpoint, it could also lead to a better appreciation of one's own account on Christology. In this way, dialogue as an exercise in learning operates within a carefully defined hermeneutic of *commitment* and *openness* between oneself and another. That is, it is structured on a hermeneutic framework which

---

31 John Hick. *An Interpretation of Reality: Human Responses to the Transcendent.* 1989, p.235–236. (See also Marianne Moyaert. "Absorption or Hospitality: Two Approaches to the Tension between Identity and Alterity". In: C. Cornille. and C. Conway. *Interreligious Hermeneutics.* 2010, p.70).

32 Marianne Moyaert. "Absorption or Hospitality: Two Approaches to the Tension between Identity and Alterity". In: Cornille, C. and Conway, C. *Interreligious Hermeneutics.* 2010, p.66.

33 Marianne Moyaert. "Absorption or Hospitality". 2010, p.67.

supports the dialectic interplay between *commitment* and *openness* in the dialogical relations between the self and the other by re-opening the *space-between* them for meaningful engagement of their respective Christologies. It provides an effective response to the question: "can we account for the identity that does not trap us in a polarity between identity and otherness; sameness and difference; insiders and outsiders?"[34]

So, in response to the question above, *dialogue as an exercise in learning* turns to Paul Ricoeur's hermeneutics of the *self*. Paul Ricoeur is a philosopher of mediation who never gives up on the *space-between*. Even though Ricoeur never set out to deal specifically with issues relating to interreligious dialogue or the impossibility of it, his hermeneutics of the *self* consistently explores or negotiates the *space-between* the *self* and the *other* to find some interrelationship between them, especially, in contexts where they are considered estranged. As a consequence, his hermeneutic philosophy takes on a "tensive" style which pays attention to the tensions which occur in human experiences and encounters. To mediate these tensions, he weaves together heterogeneous discourses to form composite ones in which new meanings are formed without diminishing their specificity and their difference.[35] As Marianne Moyaert put it, in the context of religious pluralism Ricoeur would ask, "how can we bring people who belong to different religious traditions together? How can we overcome the threat of incommunicability? The answer to these questions lies in the definition of identity in a context of change, difference and pluralism."[36]

So, by recourse to Paul Ricoeur's hermeneutics, the purpose is to see how his work provides the context for a systematic reflection on the challenges presented by the encounter between people

---

34 Marianne Moyaert. "Absorption or Hospitality". 2010, p.74.
35 See Kim Atkins. "Internet Encyclopedia of Philosophy: Paul Ricoeur (1913–2005)." http://www.iep.utm.edu/ricoeur/ (17/04/2015).
36 Marianne Moyaert. "Absorption or Hospitality." 2010, p.75.

from diverse religious backgrounds like Christians and Muslims. It is acknowledged that Ricoeur is a Christian philosopher whose works on theology are well known and acknowledged, but his philosophical writings here do not rely so much on his theological concepts. Much of Ricoeur's hermeneutics focuses on the human person in an attempt to comprehend the human situation. This explains why his works such as *The Rule of Metaphor*, *From Text to Action*, *Oneself as Another* and the three volumes of *Time and Narrative* are appreciated by Christians and non-Christians alike. In this way, by taking Ricoeur as our competent guide, it is hoped that Christians and Muslims would find themselves at home with his unique style – especially the style outlined *Oneself as Another* and the three volumes of *Time and Narrative*.

2 Stating the Problem

Douglas Pratt cites Charles Kimball as asking the questions: "Why do Christianity and Islam often clash so vigorously through the centuries? What informs the mistrust that pervades the history of Christian-Muslim relations and skews attempts to relate more constructively today?"[37] For Pratt, the reason for this phenomenon is partly because "Islam and Christianity are pre-eminently religions of belief. Each has struggled to define its own orthodoxy against variant heterodoxies and heresies from within and each has a history of self-proclamation as a universal truth against any other claimant of truth from without."[38] Within this context of claim and counterclaim is the reality, the identity and the mission of Jesus Christ often conceptualised as Christology.

As a theological construct, Christology is a Theologica-doctrinal that is problematic in the relationship between Christianity and

---

37 Douglas Pratt. *The Challenge of Islam*. 2005, p.102.
38 Douglas Pratt. *The Challenge of Islam*. 2005, p.102.

Islam. This stems from the fact that Christian faith and theology professes Jesus Christ as the "Son of God" and the "Saviour of the World". As Walter Kasper put it, "the assertion that 'Jesus is 'the Christ' is the basic statement of the Christian belief and Christology is no more than the conscientious elucidation of that proposition."[39] Against the above Christological understanding is the Islamic view of Jesus as a "Prophet" or as the "Messenger of Allah" without divine attributions. As Ata ur-Rahim put it, "Jesus was a Prophet who had been sent to the people of this earth; that he was a Messenger whose guidance and teaching were a reaffirmation and extension of the guidance which the prophets before him had brought and were a preparation for the guidance which the prophet coming after him would bring."[40] This Islamic depiction of Jesus is bereft of divine attributions.

How to properly negotiate this problematic to allow Christian-Muslim dialogue to occur has been the question many scholars have wrestled with over the years. Since both religions have struggled to define their orthodoxy against variant heterodoxies and heresies, how can one engage these traditions in constructive and positive dialogues on Christology for the promotion of common values? This study seeks to explore this relevant question. When one critically examines the creedal elements of Christianity and Islam – especially those that relate to Jesus Christ, one discovers that both the communities of faith share certain theological affirmations and beliefs on the reality, the identity and the mission of Jesus Christ. For instance, the Qur'an and the Synoptic Gospels reflect on common Christological themes such as the *immaculate conception* (Surah 3: 35-41), the *virginal conception* of Jesus (Surah 19: 16-21), the *miraculous powers of Jesus Christ* (Surah 5: 109-110), the *ascension* (Surah 4: 157-158) and the *second coming* (Surah 43: 57-67). Despite the fact that the Qur'an does not give divine interpretations to these theological themes, these theological and

---

39 Walter Kasper. *Jesus The Christ*. 1976, p.15–16.
40 Muhammad Ata ur-Rahim. *Jesus a Prophet of Islam*. 1999, p.206.

doctrinal concepts demonstrate that Islam and Christianity have something more to say about Jesus Christ than any other religion in the world.

Consequently, this study seeks to draw on these themes within an interreligious hermeneutic framework of dialogue which support the constructive engagements between the two faith communities in a dialogue as an exercise in learning. While reciprocal learning is the motivation for engaging the two traditions in this form of dialogue, its primary goal will be how this learning can lead to the discernment and to the promotion of common values inspired by Jesus Christ as perceived in each tradition. While the emphasis is on learning from and about the other, where issues of similarities and differences are made, they will all the more be directed towards laying the foundations for achieving the stated purpose: that is, "dialogue for the promotion of common values." In this way, the study is guided by the following relevant questions:

What theological and hermeneutic approach to dialogue is best suited for constructive Christian-Muslim dialogue on Christology?
How can Christian-Muslim dialogue on Christology lead to the discernment and to the promotion of common values between them?

The book is therefore developed in eight chapters in response to the above stated questions on Christian-Muslim dialogue on Christology. Derived from the above stated questions is the purpose of the book. That is, the interest to provide a new dialogical approach which supports the constructive engagement between Christians and Muslims in dialogue on Christology for the promotion of common values.

Chapter One focuses on the theology of the dialogue as an exercise in learning. It reviews various definitions of interreligious dialogue by bringing clarity to the meaning and to the understanding of interreligious dialogue which characterises the concept in the book. It proceeds from there to examine the tripartite traditional models of dialogue such as *exclusivism, inclusivism* and *pluralism*. Within the context of dialogue where interlocutors are expected to be committed to their religious beliefs and practices at the same time that they are open to listen to and learn from the other as equal partners-in-dialogue, the book asserts that not only do these traditional paradigms fail to adequately preserve the integrity and identity of the *other,* they also fail to maintain the commitment of the *self* to its religious beliefs and practices.

Thus, dialogue as *an exercise in learning* is proposed in this book as a better alternative to these models. This is because it traverses the weaknesses of the traditional models to allow for an effective engagement between the *self* and the *other* by its emphasis on *learning from and about them.* The complex relationship between the *self* and the *other* is often described as a hermeneutic one. This is because, it involves questions on the epistemological and on the ethical validity for this relationship.

So, to provide a hermeneutic framework which supports the intersubjective relationship between the *self* and the *other* within the context of dialogue as an exercise in learning, Chapter Two focuses on Paul Ricoeur's hermeneutics of the *self.* Ricoeur establishes the *intersubjective* dimension of *narrative identity* through his two poles of identity: *idem-identity* and *ipse-identity.* Ricoeur indicates that in narrating the stories of our lives, we find that others contribute to our narratives and we to theirs. Narrative identity is not only *static, sameness* and *seamless.* It involves others and changes as we change. Thus, Ricoeur discovers that *self*hood and *other*ness are so interconnected that *self*hood and *other*ness cannot be separated. By re-engaging the *self* and the *other* in this way, dialogue as an exercise in learning builds on this epistemological validity and proceeds with this confidence to re-engage Christians and Muslims in dialogue on Christology where they are considered to be irreconcilably divided.

Chapter Three focuses on the ethical and the moral implications of *narrative identity* for dialogue as an exercise in learning. Here, Ricoeur's "little ethics" provides the framework for critical reflections on the necessary conditions for interreligious dialogue such as *commitment, openness, respect for the other* and *equality.*

These necessary conditions for dialogue often raise challenges such as: the meaning of *openness* and *commitment* in dialogue; limits to *openness* and *commitment*; the meaning of religious identity and the threats to it. In other words, these challenges pose questions such as: "what is *commitment* and *openness* in dialogue? How is *commitment* related to *openness*? Are there limits to *openness*? What is identity? Is dialogue with the other a *threat* to one's identity or an *enrichment*? What is the nature of this *enrichment* if the latter pertains?" Ricoeur's ethical aim defined in "the aim of the good life, with and for others in just institutions" provided the context for reflecting on *openness, commitment, respect for others. and equality* as the necessary conditions for dialogue. These reflections provided the ethical legitimacy for engaging the self and the other in dialogue, and the warrant for engaging Christians and Muslim in dialogue on Christology.

Chapter Four focuses on the Christian tradition-specific understanding of Christology. It is emphasised in this chapter that for meaningful and constructive Christian-Muslim dialogue on Christology as an exercise in learning to succeed, it must begin from the Christian and the Muslim tradition-specific understandings of the life and the mission of Jesus Christ. It is from these tradition-specific perspectives of Christology so that learning can take place. Hence, Chapter Four addresses the question of Christology from the Christian perspective. While the Christian stance on Christology contains a vast array of theological issues which can never be comprehensively addressed in a chapter, the temptation may be to attempt a summary. Yet, such summaries are in danger of failing to do justice to the all-important theological subject at the heart of Christianity and the Christian life, which Christology encapsulates. So, to avoid these dangers, this chapter focuses on a theological reading of the Christology of the Gospel of Mark. It is said that while the synoptic Gospels "see Jesus Christ with the same eye", and so, tell similar stories about him; our interest in Mark's Gospel is informed by how Mark presents the identity of Jesus Christ through his the "Son of God" and the "Son of Man" motifs. This two-nature Christology represents the authentic Christian perspective on the identity and the mission of Jesus Christ. For Christian faith and theology, Jesus Christ is both God and man, one person, two natures, consubstantial with God the Father. It is this Christian commitment to Christology that must be brought to the dialogical table.

Chapter Five is the development of an "Islamic Christology" based on the Qur'an and some Hadiths. Thus, this chapter justifies the view that though "Christology" seems to be heavily loaded with Christian theological overtones; there are justifiable grounds on which one can establish a Christology that is specifically Islamic. This is because both the Qur'an and the Hadiths contain narratives that concern the events leading to and about the birth, the mission and the final end of Jesus as the *Messiah* and the "Son of Mary". Hence, an "Islamic Christology" will concern itself with discourses that relate to the mission and to the final end of Jesus the "Prophet" and the "Messenger of Allah". In this way, this chapter draws from a theological reading of some Qur'anic texts, Hadiths and the views of classical Islamic commentators on the life, the mission, and the final end of "Jesus, the *Messiah*, the "Son of Mary". It also clarifies Theologica-doctrinal issues such as the *Tawhid, original sin, prophetic guidance,* and *Jesus' relationship with the Holy spirit.*

Having understood the Christian and the Islamic perspectives on Christology and the traditions that inspire these different perspectives, Chapter Six then focuses on Christology as an exercise in learning. It provides a deeper analysis of some Christological titles and themes which emerged in Chapter Four and Five. Some of these Christological themes and titles include: *Messiah, Word of/from God, Spirit of/from God, the Son of God, the Trinity, the death and the resurrection, the virginal conception, the ascension* and *the second coming of Jesus* among others. Through the method of critical correlation, one discovers that Christology is both a *bridge* and a *barrier* to Christian-Muslim dialogue. In this way, the analyses under this chapter contributes to disclosing the similarities and the differences between these two perspectives on Christology, and thus, highlights the significant place Jesus occupies in both religious traditions.

Chapter Seven focuses on Christian-Muslim dialogue for the promotion of common values. It provides further reflections on the "Jesus-significance" in Islam and in Christianity and how these point to values which are at the heart of each religious tradition. It is this context of Jesus-*significance* which paves the way for the teasing out or the discovery of common values such as "prayer and submission to God", "peace and peaceful co-existence" and "Solidarity with the poor and the marginalized". These values are considered *common* to Islam and Christianity because they are also espoused by the Qur'anic Jesus and the Jesus of the Gospels.

Finally, Chapter Eight focuses on the conclusion and the evaluation of the preceding chapters in the light of the book's objectives. As a conclusion, this chapter provides a bird's eye-view of the Christological issues anticipated and fulfilled from the start of this "dialogical journey" – a journey that is not embarked upon for its own sake, but in response to God who invites both Muslims and Christians to commitment to His will. For Islam, the will of God is constituted by the obligation to the *Tawhid,* the *Covenant of Alast and the Trust* (the commitment to viceregency). In Christianity, the will of God is constituted by the "love of God" and the "love of a neighbour". Consequently, this "dialogical journey" is characterized by a Christian-Muslim conversation on how each understands Jesus Christ and how this understanding facilitates their fundamental call to submit to the *will of God* and to promote issues of *human flourishing.* As an evaluation, it provides an appraisal of how each chapter responded to the book's stated purpose.

CHAPTER ONE
INTERRELIGIOUS DIALOGUE AND LEARNING

1.1 The Introduction

This chapter tangentially acknowledges the differences that exist in Christian-Muslim conceptions of Jesus, and yet, advocates for dialogue between them on Christology. It reviews various definitions of the concept *interreligious dialogue* and proposes one that circumscribes and characterises the whole approach to interreligious dialogue in the book. Hans Küng once indicated that the central issue in any interreligious dialogue undertaking lies in the response to the question: "Is there a theologically justifiable way that allows Christians to accept the truths of other religions without relinquishing the truth of their own religion and their own identity?"[41] While Küng identifies that it is theology that must provide an adequate response to the tensive relationship between *commitment* and *openness* in interreligious dialogue,[42] this chapter reviews the tripartite traditional models of dialogue (*exclusivism*, *inclusivism* and *pluralism*) to see the extent to which they provide an adequate response to Küng's relevant challenge.

In the various subsections in this chapter, the study demonstrates that the models of *exclusivism, inclusivism,* and *pluralism* fail to effectively negotiate the tension between *openness* and *commitment* in interreligious dialogue, especially, Christian-Muslim dialogue on Christology. It thus presents "dialogue as an exercise

---

41 Hans Küng. "Dialog ability and Steadfastness: On Two Complementary Virtues". 1991, p.242.

42 See, Marianne Moyaert. *Fragile Identities*. 2011, p.3.

in learning"[43] as the *new turn* to engaging Christians and Muslims in dialogue – one which provides adequate response to Küng's question. Within the context of Christian-Muslim dialogue on Christology, dialogue as an exercise in learning involves conversations within which one seeks to help the other to understand the reality, the identity and the mission of Jesus Christ as it pertains to their tradition-specific contexts. It involves the sharing of mutual testimonies of belief – a sharing that is defined by the interest to listen to, to learn from and to understand the other's viewpoint about the identity and the mission of Jesus Christ. In this way, we shall demonstrate how dialogue as an exercise in learning offers a unique kind of encounter between the *self* and the *other* – an encounter that is far removed from the contentions and argumentations that often characterize the dialogues between Christians and Muslims on Christology.

It must be reiterated that the motivation for approaching Christian-Muslim dialogue from this perspective is informed by the growing dissatisfaction in the three traditional paradigms of dialogue, especially in their failure to preserve the integrity of the identity and belief-systems of the religious other.[44] Today, there is a growing awareness and acceptance of the reality of religious plurality and the context of *otherness*, stimulated by the repeated calls for the preservation of the identity and the integrity of both the *self* and the *other* in dialogue. The three traditional paradigms seem to fall short in this respect. Thus, the lack of adequate paradigms which engage the *self* and the *other* in fruitful dialogues prompted the need for a new approach. As we shall see, dialogue as an exercise in learning focuses primarily on learning from and about the other. The goal of such learning is:

---

43 Paul Ricoeur's hermeneutic concept of *attestation* which involves commitment to and openness to the other in the sharing of their respective testimonies of beliefs will guide the approach to dialogue as an exercise in learning (see, Paul Ricoeur. *Oneself as Another.* 1995, p.)

44 Michael Barnes. *Theology and the Dialogue of Religions.* 2002.

the profound knowledge of oneself; the authentic knowledge of the other; and the mutual relationship this espouses. As Moyaert put it, a dialogue that can "lead to being more strongly rooted in one's tradition"[45] is in itself a viable one. Let us now briefly review some definitions of interreligious dialogue as a means of providing clarity to the definition of interreligious dialogue which guides this current study.

1.2 The Meaning of Interreligious Dialogue

In the face of religious diversity and ideological conflicts among the religions today, many have proposed the need for more interreligious dialogues and cooperation among the religions. This necessity for dialogue today is aptly captured by Hans Küng's famous statement that there will be: "no peace among the nations without peace among the religions. No peace among the religions without dialogue between the religions. No dialogue between the religions without investigations of the foundations of the religions."[46] Not only does dialogue provide the space for the various religions to converse together and to get to know one another in an atmosphere of openness and mutual sharing but it also has the potential to ameliorate the tensions that exist among the religions.

To achieve these laudable goals, there is the growing need for clarity on what interreligious dialogue is all about, its concerns and its goals and the processes it must pursue to achieve these goals. Thus, the discourse below is a brief consideration of the views of some scholars on the definition and the goals of interreligious dialogue. The interest here is to find the appropriate

---

45 Marianne Moyaert. Absorption or Hospitality". 2010, p.67.
46 Hans Küng. *Global Responsibility: In Search of a New World Ethic.* 1991, p.171; Küng, Hans. *Islam: Past, Present & Future.* 2007, p. xxiii.

gateway into the hermeneutic issues that characterise the concept and to clearly define the *form* and the *goal* of the sort of dialogue this study proposes for Christian–Muslim conversations on Christology. It must be stated rather prematurely here that for interreligious dialogue to be successful, it must be characterised by one's *commitment* to the home tradition and *respect for* and *openness to* the traditions of a religious other – one within which the interlocutors accept each other as *equal-partners* in dialogue. However, before this assertion can be substantiated, let us briefly consider some of the definitions of *interreligious dialogue* as proposed by some scholars.

John V. Taylor[47] defined interreligious dialogue as the, "sustained conversation between parties who are not saying the same thing and who recognize and respect contradictions and mutual exclusions between their various ways of thinking."[48] For Taylor, the object of this form of dialogue, "is understanding and appreciation, leading to further reflection upon the implication for one's own position on the convictions and sensitivities of the other traditions."[49] Taylor's view that the goal of this "sustained conversation" is "understanding and appreciation" of the religious *other* and how this leads to further reflection on one's own religious views is very significant for interreligious learning. If interreligious dialogue leads the dialogical partners to respect and appreciate each other's religious traditions, then we could say that dialogue is all the more worth pursuing. For Jason Barker, interreligious dialogue is, "a formal process in which authoritative members of at least two religious communities come together for an extended and serious discussion on the beliefs and

---

47 The Right Reverend Dr John V. Taylor was a theologian and Bishop of Winchester, England (1974–1984).

48 J.V. Taylor. "The Theological Basis of Interfaith Dialogue". 1979, p.373.

49 J.V. Taylor. "The Theological Basis of Interfaith Dialogue" in the *International Review of Mission* 1979, p.373.

practices that separate the communities."[50] Though we know that dialogue is both formal and informal, Barker's definition seems to limit dialogue to its formal aspect which only engages scholars and religious authorities. However, dialogue equally takes place among grassroots and can be informal. So, it has both a formal and an informal dimension.

For Leonard Swidler, interreligious dialogue is, "a conversation between two or more persons with differing views, the primary purpose of which is for the participants to learn from each other so that both can change and grow."[51] For Swidler, "the very fact that I learn that my dialogue partner believes 'this' rather than 'that' changes my attitude toward that person; and a change in my attitude is a significant change and growth in me."[52] In other words, we enter into dialogue with the *other* so that we can learn, change and grow. This transformative dimension of dialogue is not forced on the *other* but emerges as a result of the event of dialogue. Thus, it could be said that Swidler's attention to the goal of dialogue as "learning, changing and growing" is a significant contribution to the understanding of the hermeneutics of interreligious dialogue. On the question of the goals of dialogue, Swidler suggests three goals for interreligious dialogue: (1) "to know oneself ever more profoundly", (2) "to know the other ever more authentically", and (3) "to live ever more accordingly".[53] Here, one finds that dialogue is oriented not just towards learning about but also towards learning from the other which leads to a better understanding of oneself. However, the success of this form of dialogue presupposes some degree of respect and openness to the other.

The Pontifical Council for Interreligious Dialogue also identified three ways of understanding dialogue: (1) At the purely human

50 Jason Barker. *Christians and Interreligious Dialogue*. The Watchman Expositor, Vol. 5 No. 4 1998.

51 Leonard Swidler. *Towards a Universal Theology of Religions*. 1988, p.6.

52 Leonard Swidler. *Towards a Universal Theology of Religions*. 1988, p.6.

53 Leonard Swidler. *Towards a Universal Theology of Religions* 1988, p.26.

level, it identifies dialogue as reciprocal communication which eventually leads to common goals or interpersonal communion at a deeper level; (2) dialogue is also seen "as an attitude of respect and friendship, which permeates or should permeate all those activities constituting the evangelizing mission of the Church."

This dimension of dialogue is identified as *the spirit of dialogue*; and (3) within the context of religious plurality, the council defines interreligious dialogue as, "'all positive and constructive interreligious relations with individuals and communities of other faiths which are directed at mutual understanding and enrichment, in obedience to truth and respect for freedom.'"[54] It is this third meaning to the concept that the council applies within the overall context of dialogue among the religions. One finds significant traits to a well-constructed mode of conceptualising interreligious in the three definitions of dialogue put up by the council. That is, when dialogue is perceived and entered into as a "reciprocal communication" on issues of religious significance, guided by the "attitude of respect" for the beliefs of "individuals and communities of other faiths", and "directed at mutual understanding and enrichment." Such a dialogue is bound to be constructive, positive, and transformative.

Consequently, from the review of the definitions of interreligious dialogue above, one finds some hermeneutic issues that speak to the heart of the interreligious dialogue project. These issues include the understanding of dialogue as: *a conversation, a form of learning*, directed towards *mutual understanding, growth and enrichment*. If we understand a conversation as a form of interaction between people or groups of people on a shared subject matter (whether formal or informal), then we could say that dialogical conversations need to be non-confrontational and acrimonious.

---

54 The Pontifical Council for Interreligious Dialogue: Dialogue and Proclamation # 9: http://www.vatican.va/roman_ curia/pontifical_councils/interelg/documents/rc_pc_interelg_doc_ 19051991_dialogue-and-proclamatio_en.html (30/04/20).

This is because dialogical conversations are always guided by the dialectics of questions and answers. As Gadamer intimates, "it belongs to every true conversation that each opens up himself to the other, truly accepts his point of view as valid ..." What is to be grasped is the substantive rightness of his opinion, so that we can be at one with each other on a subject.[55] Within this context, Gadamer indicates that a person who wants to understand must question what lies behind what is said.

This questioning always bring out the undetermined possibilities of a thing.[56] Here, confrontations and debates are limited because the dialectic of questions and answers is not an art of arguing which can make a strong case out of a weak one but an art of thinking which can strengthen objections by referring to the subject matter. Due to this art of strengthening, what is said is continually being transformed into the uttermost possibilities of its rightness and its truth.[57] At the heart of this model of dialogical conversation is what Gadamer calls "the good-will to dialogue" – that is, the good-will or the *openness* to learn from and about the other.

Having considered the above views on the subject, we therefore define interreligious dialogue as *the constructive and the positive conversation between people of different religious traditions, on issues of religious significance, for the purpose of mutual learning and enrichment.*[58] This definition reveals three key definitive concepts that guide our discourse on interreligious dialogue. That is: (1) the *process* of dialogue as a "constructive and positive conversation"; (2) the *subject* of dialogue as "issues of religious significance"; and (3) the *goal* of dialogue as "mutual learning and enrichment".

---

55 Hans Georg Gadamer, *Truth and Method (hereafter TM)*, 1989, p. 385.

56 Gadamer. T.M., 1989, p.375.

57 Gadamer. T.M., 1989, p.367.

58 This definition of interreligious dialogue is guided by the review of several definitions of the concept and the interest it serves in helping to achieve the goal of this current study – that is, Christian-Muslim dialogue on Christology.

While we conceive *mutual learning* and *enrichment* as the intended goals of the dialogical process, the process itself raises multifarious questions and challenges especially when it comes to understanding across different religious traditions like Christianity and Islam. Catherine Cornille notes that some of these questions relate to the following: the *im*-possibility of crossing religious boundaries to learn and to understand the meanings of particular teachings and practices in their original religious context, the allowance for such a crossing and the dynamics and the ethics that this entails.[59]

Similar to Catherine Cornille's point about the need to preserve the alterity of the other in interreligious dialogue, Raimon Panikkar also notes that, "to cross the boundaries of one's culture without realizing that the other may have a radically different approach to reality is today no longer admissible. If still consciously done, it would be philosophically naïve, politically outrageous and religiously sinful."[60] It is therefore in the light of the above concerns for the protection of the identity and the integrity of the religious other that we find the three traditional paradigms of dialogue (that is, *exclusivism, inclusivism* and *pluralism*) inadequate in responding to the question of *otherness*[61] in

---

59 There are epistemological, ethical and theological challenges to this: epistemologically, interreligious dialogue confronts one with the problem of understanding the other's religious traditions, its teachings and practices within its own context; ethically, the challenge lies on the allowance for such understanding and the hermeneutical lens within which one uses in exploring the other's tradition; and theologically, the challenge focuses on the level of commitment to one's religious tradition, and openness to the other's tradition in order to understand it (See, C. Cornille. & C. Conway. *Interreligious Hermeneutics.* 2010, p.ix).

60 Raimon Panikkar. *Myth, Faith and Hermeneutics.* 1979, p.9.

61 *Otherness* often concerns that discursive process by which 'a dominant in-group (us or the self) constructs one or many dominated out-groups (them or the other) by stigmatizing a difference- real or imagined – presented as a negation of identity and thus a motive for discrimination' (see, Min, Anselm, K. *The Solidarity of Others in a Divided World.* 2004, p.8).

interreligious dialogue. Their inadequacies are not only evident in terms of their failure to understand and appreciate the alterity of the religious traditions of the other, but also each in a way, loses touch with the home tradition.[62] Let us undertake a succinct overview of these three traditional paradigms of interreligious dialogue by bringing out their meanings and their respective inadequacies as intimated.

1.2.1 Exclusivism as a Paradigm of Dialogue

According to Pratt, *religious exclusivism* "amounts to the material identification of a particular religion with the essence and substance of true universal religion, thereby excluding all other possibilities to the claim."[63] Soteriologically, exclusivists hold that believers of other religions can only be saved when they convert to the home religion. Whereas this evaluation of other religions is said to be very common with the Abrahamic religions (that is, Judaism, Christianity and Islam), its Christian context was more defined by the axiom; *extra ecclesiam nulla salus* (that is, outside the church, there is no salvation).[64] Theologically, the basis of this axiom suggests that Jesus Christ is the only efficacious source of

---

62 James Fredericks. *Faith Among Faiths: Christian Theology and Non-Christian Religions.* 1999, p.1–8.

63 Douglas Pratt. *Faith to Faith: Issues in Interreligious Engagement.* 2008, p.69-70.

64 Within the Catholic perspective, Exclusivism was very much defined by the axiom that; '*extra ecclesiam, nulla salus,*' linked to the writings of Origen (185-254), Cyprian (210-258), Augustine (354-430) and Fulgentius of Ruspe (468-533). It is acknowledged that this axiom did not originally refer to members of other religions, but for the members of a Christian church who thought of leaving the church at the time. Within the protestant settings, exclusivism is traced to Karl Barth's *Church Dogmatics* (1956 ½:295-300).

salvation, and that, he established the Christian Church as the only means by which salvation is made possible for all.

While this exclusivist mentality was the rationale for evangelisation in the Catholic Church, especially from the third century onwards, perspectives changed along the paths that led to the Second Vatican Council in 1964. The Church took on an inclusivist position at this Council where it admitted that there are some *salvific elements* in non-Christian religions (that is, the presence of *seeds of the word* in the religions).[65] Various references are made to this effect in the *Vatican II* document about this inclusivists views of the Church: *Nostra Aetate* speaks of the presence in these religious traditions of "a ray of that Truth which enlightens all men" (NA #2). *Ad Gentes* recognizes the presence of "seeds of the word", and points to "the riches which a generous God has distributed among the nations" (AG #11). Again, *Lumen Gentium* refers to the good which is "found sown" not only "in minds and hearts", but also "in the rites and customs of people" (LG #17).[66] Although exclusivism is still very common with some evangelical Pentecostal churches, one also finds it in Islam and Judaism. In Judaism the interpretation of the concept of Israel as the "chosen people of God" eliminates all who do not accept or form part of Jewish monotheism.[67] In Islam, Christians are accused of wrongdoing because of their *Trinitarian* beliefs (Surah 4: 171). Thus, there are still religions which hold the view that salvation is only made possible within the confines of their religious traditions.

---

65 Vatican II: *Nostra Aetate #2; and for Muslims, #3.*

66 See also, "The Pontifical Council for Interreligious Dialogue: Dialogue and Proclamation" #16: "The Effects of Divine Grace". http://www.vatican.va/roman_curia/pontifical_councils/interelg/documents/rc_pc_interelg_doc_19051991_dialogue-and-proclamatio_en.html (30/04/20).

67 Jeremiah 16: 20 and Micah 4: 5 for elements of the concept of the "chosen people."

However, could this level of exclusivism be the measure of the sort of *commitment* needed for interreligious dialogue to occur? If *commitment* defines the quality of being dedicated to a cause, an activity or to a way of life, does not religious *commitment* demand one's exclusive dedication to one's object of worship? From a postliberal theological point of view, this sense of exclusivity points to the understanding that one's religious tradition has the capacity to provide all the answers to one's spiritual quest for God and the obligations that this brings. While this might be the case, within the context of dialogue, the absence of *openness* to one's dialogical partner betrays the exclusivist position as inimical to dialogue.

For the exclusivist, there is no need to dialogue with the religious other because there is nothing worthwhile to learn from them. Truth can only be found in the home tradition. So, whether in its *open, close* or *extreme* forms,[68] exclusivism creates little room for dialogue with the *other*. The *other* can only be real when it becomes the *self*. As Moyaert intimated, when such exclusive claims are made at the expense of openness, "God becomes a tribal god".[69] This explains why exclusivism as a paradigm of interreligious dialogue falters at the mere sight of the other who seeks to be heard and understood in their alterity.

1.2.2 Inclusivism as a Paradigm of Dialogue

Inclusivism is structured on the claim that whereas one's religious beliefs are absolutely true; the other's beliefs are only partially true and find their fulfilment in one's beliefs. According to Pratt, inclusivism is, "the effective identification of a particular

---

68 Douglas Pratt. *Faith to Faith: Issues in Interreligious Engagement.* 2008, p.69-72.

69 Marianne Moyaert. "Absorption or Hospitality". 2010, p.62.

religion as the universal, with some allowance made for others."[70] In contrast to exclusivism, inclusivism does not deny in advance the truth or the soteriological value of other religious traditions. It rather claims that while one's religious traditions hold absolutely apodictic truth; other religions are only true if they contain religious features that are common to the truth claims of the home religion.

In a particularly Christian context (Roman Catholic), inclusivism asserts that salvation is possible in other religions, but these find their fulfilment in Christianity because Jesus Christ is the one, absolute, and universal "Saviour of the World". For instance, Karl Rahner's "Anonymous Christianity"[71] purports that God's salvific plan and universal self-communication, established in the covenant with Noah, was not just for some people but for all humanity (Genesis 9: 16).

According to Rahner, God's salvific will is for all to be saved as the text of 1 Timothy 2: 4 supports – "God wants all to be saved and reach full knowledge of the truth." It follows then that; if Christ is the ultimate fulfilment of the salvific plan of God, then Christ came for all to save all.[72] In this way, salvation is not only limited to an *explicit knowledge* and *profession of faith in Christ,* but includes all who live in the state of *Christ's grace* through faith, hope, and love, even though they may have no explicit knowledge that their lives are oriented in grace-given salvation to Jesus Christ.[73] Thus, Rahner indicates that the grace of Christ is also

---

70 Douglas Pratt. *Faith to Faith.* 2008, p.72.
71 Karl Rahner's "Anonymous Christianity" lays the claim that: God who desires all to be saved cannot possibly consign non-Christians to hell. If Jesus Christ is the only means of God's salvation, then it means that non-Christians who end up in heaven must have received the *grace of Christ* without realizing it (Karl Rahner. *Theological Investigations 1.* Darton; London. 1964, p.75-76).
72 Karl Rahner. *Theological Investigations 1.* 1964, p.391.
73 Karl Rahner. *Theological Investigations 1.* 1964, p.283.

active in the lives of those who have never heard the Gospel message of Christ. It is always active, "seeking the fulfilment of its nature to become Christian in all its dimension even though the preaching of the message may not be present explicitly."[74] In this way, Rahner established the uniqueness and the universality of the Christian dispensation of salvation in Jesus Christ as the concrete manifestation of the Ultimate divine. The question many however ask in respect of Rahner's "Anonymous Christian" designation is whether non-Christians are saved *despite* their religious beliefs and practices or are they saved *through* them?[75]

In response, Rahner indicates that, while the universal and the supernatural salvific will of God is operative in the world, the event of salvation has a historical and cultural character. In other words, it is precisely because God's salvation is experienced through cultural and historical processes that enables Christians to talk about this form of God's salvific action in the world.[76] The incarnation is that concrete manifestation of God through human history and culture. In this way, Rahner asserted that divine grace is made possible not apart from one's religious beliefs and practices but through them. Thus, he affirmed that God's salvation is made possible through the religious beliefs and the practices of the religious other. The Second Vatican Council also affirms this intrinsic element of the universal gift of God's salvation in the other religions in *Nostra Aetate* (No. 2) when it exhorts Christians to, "recognise, preserve and promote the good things, spiritual and moral as well as the socio-cultural values found among these people (the other believers)". In *Lumen Gentium* too, the Council also recognised the possibility of salvation for non-Christians when it indicated that, "those who through no fault of their own do not

---

74 Karl Rahner. *Theological Investigations 14,* p.307; cited in John Pasquini. *Atheism and Salvation.* 2006, p.20.

75 See Michael Barnes. *Interreligious Learning.* 2012, p.15.

76 Karl Rahner. *Foundations of Christian Faith.* 1978, p.313. (See also Michael Barnes. *Interreligious Learning.* 2012, p.15).

know the Gospel of Christ or His Church but who nevertheless seek God with a sincere heart and are moved by grace, try in their actions to do His will as they know it through the dictates of their conscience – those too may attain eternal salvation."[77]

However, in more explicit terms, Christian theological inclusivism reflects Walter Kasper's view that, "the one God has once only, yet wholly, definitively and unreservedly communicated himself historically in Jesus Christ."[78] If God communicated himself in this way, then it follows that, "Christ is both *id quo maius cogitari nequit* (that than which nothing greater can be thought) and *id quo Deus maius operari nequit* (that than which God can do no greater)."[79] This implies that no other religion or culture can add to or surpass that which God has manifested in Christ. Consequently, Kasper affirmed that, "everything true and good that the other religions contain is a participation in what appeared in its fullness in Jesus Christ."[80] In this way, inclusivism within a particularly Christian context, perceives the other religions as possibly possessing *"seeds of the word"*[81] or the *"ray of that truth which enlightens all men"*.[82] As a result, the inclusivist goal of dialogue with the other entails the interest to identify these "seeds of the Word" in the other's religious tradition which find their fulfilment in the Christian dispensation of salvation. Thus, Christian missionary activities serve to purify and perfect the good in the religions. As the Vatican Council indicated clearly: "Whatever truth and grace are to be found among the nations, as a sort of the secret presence

---

77 "Dogmatic Constitution on the Church – *Lumen Gentium* #16 (Vatican Council II).

78 Walter Kasper. "The Uniqueness and Universality of Jesus Christ." 2004, p.16.

79 Walter Kasper. "The Uniqueness and Universality of Jesus Christ." 2004, p.16.

80 Walter Kasper. "The Uniqueness and Universality of Jesus Christ." 2004, p.16.

81 Vatican II: *Ad Gentes* # 11, p.15.

82 Vatican II: *Nostra Aetate* # 2.

of God, missionary activity frees from all taint of evil and restores to Christ its Maker ... And so, whatever good is found to be sown in the hearts and in the minds of men, or in the rites and cultures peculiar to various people, is not lost. More than that, it is healed, ennobled, and perfected for the glory of God" (Ad Gentes # 9)[83] through Christian missionary encounter with the religions and the cultures of the world.

Today, inclusivism seems to be popular among Christian scholars such as Kenneth Craig, Hans Küng, Jacques Dupuis,[84] Gavin D'Costa and Mark Heim[85] among others. While many agree that inclusivism is more open to interreligious dialogue in contrast to exclusivism, it is nonetheless criticised in the way inclusivists restrict their *openness* to only what is common between the *self* and the *other*. In John Hick's view, inclusivism rests upon the claim that, "non-Christians can be saved because unknown to them Christ is secretly 'in a way' united with them."[86] Here, the affirmation of the unity and the universality of the Christian dispensation of salvation is often viewed by some scholars as, "an imperialism that swallows up, co-opts or oppresses the religious other."[87] As Barnes put it, "the question of the other is not to be

83 See also, "The Pontifical Council for Interreligious Dialogue: Dialogue and Proclamation" # 18: "The Role of the Church's Activities": http://www.vatican.va/roman_curia/pontifical_councils/interelg/documents/rc_pc_interelg_doc_19051991_dialogue-and-proclamatio_en.html (30/04/20).

84 Jacque Dupuis. *Towards a Christian Theology of Religious Pluralism*. 2001.

85 Mark Heim. *Salvation, Truth and Difference in Religion*. 1995.

86 John Hick. *Disputed Questions in Theology and the Philosophy of Religion*. 1993, p.84.

87 Walter Kasper debunks this in his work on "Uniqueness and Universality of Jesus Christ". For Kasper, the unity and the universality of the Christians dispensation of salvation rather defends and guarantees the inalienable rights of every religion because it not only lays the foundation for tolerance and respect for them, but it also establishes the possibility of a dialogical and a diaconal relationship with them (See, Walter Kasper. "The Uniqueness and Universality of Jesus Christ". 2005, p.17).

answered by self-referential schemes. Difference cannot be side-lined without doing serious violence to the fragile fabric of human religiosity."[88] Respecting the *alterity* of the other is essentially part of the relevant content of interreligious dialogue today.

In his work on intrareligious dialogue, Panikkar emphasizes that genuine interreligious dialogue needs to be based on the assumption that the other is an original source of understanding, one who is capable of communicating their unique experience of God. He indicates that genuine interreligious dialogue must begin on the basis of a certain trust in the "other *qua* other", whereby the *other* is viewed as an equal source of self-understanding and interpretation.[89] At the heart of genuine interreligious dialogue is the deliberate effort to engage openly and respectfully with the other as an equal partner in dialogue; a willingness to listen and to understand what the other has to say about themselves; a readiness to learn and be challenged by the perspectives of the other about their otherness. Genuine and honest dialogue demands that while the non-negotiable elements of one's religious tradition are affirmed, the integrity of those of the religious other are also respected. As George Dardess and Krier Mich put it, genuine interreligious dialogue means "attentiveness to the other's views. Listening to those views patiently rather than jumping to conclusions about them or about those who hold them; it means resisting stereotypes of the other."[90]

88 Michael Barnes. *Interreligious Learning*. 2012, p.21.
89 Raimon Panikkar. *The Intra-Religious Dialogue*. 1999, p.30.
90 George Dardess and Marvin Krier Mich. *St Francis and the Sultan*. 2011, p.11.

1.2.3 Pluralism as a Paradigm of Dialogue

Unlike *exclusivism* and *inclusivism*, *religious pluralism* posits all religions as different expressions of one divine reality.[91] In other words, pluralism perceives all the religions as different streams leading to the same ocean. This pluralist's approach to the religions seek to achieve the following goals: (i) a phenomenology of commonality; (ii) the de-absolutisation of religious truths; (iii) a symmetrical reciprocity between the religions; and (iv) a dynamic relational understanding of identity.[92] That is, while the various religious traditions may be conspicuously different, they are interconnected. Their commonality lies in the fact that they are diverse expressions of the same divine reality. This explains why religious pluralism, "considers the religious traditions to be mere variations of the *same* common ground, variations of the *same* soteriological theme."[93] Along these lines, religious pluralism purports to recognise the equality of all the religions; in that, it considers their respective expressions of truth are but partial expressions of the ineffable and mysterious Ultimate Real who transcends the symbols and doctrines of a particular religion.

As a consequence, the pluralists consider the beliefs of other religious traditions as the supplementations of one's own belief-systems since they contribute to providing a better view of the Ultimate Real.[94] Here, one's religious identity is just like one's tradition – dynamic and always subject to growth, change and enrichment. As a proponent of the liberal pluralist understanding of the religions, John Hick for instance, perceives all the religions as historically and culturally determined interpretations of the

---

91 Douglas Pratt. *Faith to Faith: Issues in Interreligious Engagement.* 2008, p.79.

92 Marianne Moyaert. *Fragile Identity.* 2011, p.67.

93 Moyaert, Marianne. "Scriptural Reasoning as Interreligious Dialogue." 2013, p.66.

94 Marianne Moyaert. *Fragile Identity.* 2011, p.69.

ineffable Real. In other words, the conceptions, belief systems, and practices that define the various religious traditions are only partial expressions of the Ultimate Reality.[95] For Hick, the different religious traditions are comparable to different paths that lead to the same mountain top; or they represent the different colours of the rainbow. As a consequence, Hick argues for a shift away from Christian Christocentricism to a theocentric approach to religion.[96] Put in his own words, Hick describes this shift as the "Copernican revolution" which necessitates a movement "away from the dogma that Christianity is at the centre, to the realization that it is God who is at the centre and all religions including our own serves and revolves around him."[97] While it is no longer acceptable to disregard the alterity of the religious other within the context of dialogue, Hick's attempt to reduce the alterity of religions as different versions of the same Ultimate Reality, caricatures these religions against their own self-understanding. As Barnes put it, "what we have is a 'view from nowhere', a theory that, precisely seeks to stand apart from and above the living reality of the religious traditions, has nothing to say to that reality".[98]

   In his pluralist theocentric approach to the religions, Paul Knitter also considered that the Christian belief in the uniqueness of Christ as normative and constitutive for any true encounter with God is an obstacle and an unnecessary barrier that stands in the way of authentic dialogue. For him, Jesus most likely experienced himself as a prophet anointed specially by God's Spirit

95 John Hick. *An Interpretation of Religion: Human Response to the Transcendent*. 1989, p. 235-36.

96 John Hick. *God and the Universe of Faith: Essays in the philosophy of religion*. 1988.

97 For Hick, if God wishes that everyone should be saved, then it is inconceivable that God will reveal himself in such a way that only a small part of humanity can be saved (See Hick, John. *God and the Universe of Faith*. 1922 and Hick in Alistair McGrath. *Christian Theology: An Introduction*. 1997, p.537).

98 Michael Barnes. *Interreligious Learning*. 2012, p.16.

to complete the mission of the earlier prophets by announcing and ratifying the good news of the reign of God.[99] In his move for a soteriocentric and correlational model of dialogue, Knitter asserts that the dialogical task today should not be centred on "right beliefs" in Christian uniqueness but "right practice" with other faith traditions in the promotion of the reign of God's saving mission. In this way, the uniqueness of Jesus should be construed adverbially in correlation to other salvific mediators. In other words, Christians can affirm that, "Jesus is *truly* divine and saviour, but they no longer need to announce that he is *solely* divine and saviour"[100] because of the presence of other saviour figures in the religions. While Knitter's position has been severely criticised for its heavy-handedness against the Christian faith and its "evangelical responsibility towards the other",[101] the obvious in Knitter's position is a reductionist Christology that blunts the sharpened edge of the Christian perception of the identity and the significance of Christ. For Christian faith, Jesus is the universal, definitive, and unreserved self-communication of God to humanity. While this understanding has salvific and evangelical implications, its place at the heart of the Christian faith and proclamation must not be jettisoned for reasons of dialogue.

When one considers the pluralists approach to dialogue, it appears to be conducive for interreligious dialogue in the way it offers equal opportunity to all the religions through its "common ground approach to the religions".[102] However, as Moyaert put it, the pluralists' are "so eager to promote dialogue that they tend to forget the irreducible differences that exist between the

---

99 Paul Knitter. *One Earth Many Religions*. 1996, p.27.
100 Paul Knitter. *One Earth Many Religions*. 1996, p.35.
101 See, Michael Barnes. *Theology and the Dialogue of Religions*. 2002, p.17.
102 Here, while Gilkey (1987: 37) views all the religions as more or less equal contexts of salvation, and thus enjoying a "rough parity," Cobb (1990: 604) views them as sharing similar experiences which establish "common grounds in a deeper way."

religions."[103] For instance, it is doubtful whether committed believers in Christianity, Judaism or Islam will succumb to John Hick's relativizing understanding that their religious beliefs and practices are partial expressions of the Ultimate Real. This explains why Gavin D'Costa asserted that the fundamental problem of pluralism lies in its, "desire to flee from the particularity of any religious claim; be it Christian or non-Christian."[104] By so doing, the pluralist approach to the religions end up constructing an image of God (the Ultimate Real) that is neither known or shared by the religions.

From the above analysis of the three paradigms, it could be said that while *exclusivism* closes all doors to dialogue with the *other*, it is the *self* that determines the degree of openness to the religious *other* in *inclusivism*. However, by declaring a limitless playfield of openness for all religions, *pluralism* only ends up caricaturing the real identities of both the *self* and the *other*.[105] Hence, not only do these paradigms fail to adequately preserve the integrity of the identity of the *other* in the light of the specificity of their traditions, they also fail to maintain the *self's* commitment to the home tradition in the case of religious inclusivism and pluralism. Pluralism "fails to take seriously the variety of religions and the differences between them."[106] To put it more precisely, Michael

---

103 Marianne Moyaert. "On Vulnerability: Tracing the Ethical Dimension of Comparative Theology," in *Religions III.* (2012), p.1148.

104 Gavin D'Costa. *The Meeting of Religions and the Trinity.* 2000, p.28.

105 Michael Barnes rightly points out that exclusivism and inclusivism take their rise from a question that is derived from a Christian soteriology: can the non-Christian be saved? Here, the religious other is deliberately placed outside the boundaries of a Christian world (exclusivism) or they are given a secondary place within (inclusivism). For the pluralists however, all religions are descriptions of a common experience. Barnes sees these three typologies as three stages of development in the changing perceptions of the religious other (see Michael Barnes. *Interreligious Learning.* 2012, p.10).

106 Michael Barnes. *Interreligious Learning.* 2012, p.17.

Barnes indicates that while, "exclusivism privileges one's tradition against all others; inclusivism patronises other traditions as less or a partial versions of what is realized in only one; and pluralism argues for the relativizing of all others including one's own."[107] Barnes therefore views these three approaches to the religions as an, "illegitimate simplification of highly complex issues 'forcing diverse materials into easily controlled locations.'"[108]

In his assessment of the three traditional paradigms of dialogue, Douglas Pratt also indicates that inclusivism and pluralism seem to assume that there is a link between the religions. Yet "there is no reasonable ground to assume a link across religions; their individual or their particular identities militate against any such linkage."[109] From a Christocentric point of view, Joseph DiNoia asserts that these paradigms obscure basic issues posed by the current situations relating to religious engagements, especially on how to affirm the universality of the Christian dispensation without sacrificing its particularity.[110] The apparent inadequacies in the three traditional paradigms of dialogue call for new and better ways of engaging the other in genuine dialogue. As Anselm Min intimated, "we are living in a new *kairos* that demands a new paradigm of its own,"[111] one which needs to *turn* away from the threefold traditional paradigms of dialogue to models that engage the religions in meaningful and beneficial ways. One of such models is the experience of dialogue as an exercise in learning.

---

107 Michael Barnes. *Theology and the Dialogue of Religions.* 2002, p.8.

108 Michael Barnes. *Theology and the Dialogue of Religions.* 2002, p.8.

109 Douglas Pratt. "Contextual Paradigms for Interfaith Relations." in *Current Dialogue 42* (2003), p.8.

110 Joseph DiNoia. *The Diversity of Religions: A Christian Perspective.* 1992, p.180.

111 Anselm Min. *The Solidarity of Others in a Divided World.* 2004, p.3.

1.3 Dialogue as An Exercise in Learning

The Pontifical Council for Interreligious Dialogue has clearly identified four forms of interreligious dialogue: that is, *the dialogue of life, the dialogue of common action, the dialogue of theological exchange* and *the dialogue of religious experience*.[112] While the "dialogue of life" concerns those engagements where interlocutors strive to live in open and neighbourly spirit, sharing their joys and their sorrows, their human problems and preoccupations, the "dialogue of common action" concerns the collaborations between people of different religious beliefs for the integral development and liberation of others. However, the dialogue of theological exchanges involves experts from different religious traditions who seek to deepen their understanding of the other's religious traditions as a means of appreciating their spiritual values and their significance. When dialogue involves the sharing of spiritual riches like forms of prayer, contemplation, faith, ways of searching for God, it is termed the "dialogue of religious experience".[113]

112 "The Pontifical Council for Interreligious Dialogue: Dialogue and Proclamation". http://www.vatican.va/roman_curia/pontifical_councils/interelg/documents/rc_pc_interelg_doc_19051991_dialogue-and-proclamatio_en.html (29/02/202).

113 "The Pontifical Council for Interreligious Dialogue: Dialogue and Proclamation". http://www.vatican.va/roman_curia/pontifical_councils/interelg/documents/rc_pc_interelg_doc_19051991_dialogue-and-proclamatio_en.html (29/02/202).

While the Council affirms that these different forms of dialogue are interconnected,[114] Barnes indicates that, "the one thing all forms of dialogue share is the experience of learning"[115] – a learning which is not just about the other, but also about oneself. It is within this context of learning that this study on Christian-Muslim dialogue on Christology takes its rise. The study focuses on "dialogue as an exercise in learning".[116]

To "learn from and about the other" implies the desire to acquire knowledge about the other. It is letting the other communicate to oneself who they are and the things that matter to them. In respect of Christian-Muslim dialogue on Christology, "to learn from and about the other" therefore defines a certain interest in knowing the Islamic or the Christian tradition-specific understanding of Christology. By "tradition-specific understanding", we mean the Christian or the Islamic orthodox understanding of Christology which answers the question: who is Jesus Christ in Islam or in Christianity? Any response to this very

---

114 The Council identifies the interdependence of the four forms of dialogue in the sense that contacts in daily life (*dialogue of life*) and common commitment to action (*dialogue of common action*) can open the door for cooperation in promoting human and spiritual values; they could also "eventually lead to the *dialogue of religious experience* in response to the great questions which the circumstances of life do not fail to arouse in the minds of people" (see, "The Pontifical Council for Interreligious Dialogue: Dialogue and Proclamation". http://www.vatican.va/roman_curia/pontifical_councils/interelg/documents/rc_pc_interelg_doc_19051991_dialogue-and-proclamatio_en.html).

115 Michael Barnes. *Interreligious Learning*. 2012, p. x.

116 Catherine Cornille explains that "dialogue as an exercise in learning" goes beyond the accumulation of facts about the other. It "consists of an open and constructive exchange between individuals belonging to different religious oriented to the possibility of change and growth". In this way, it is not just a verbal exchange but also involves serious engagement with texts, the teachings and the practise of the religious other (Catherin Cornille. *The Impossibility of Interreligious Dialogue*. 2008, p.3).

pertinent question should lead Christians and Muslims to clearly articulate and communicate their religious stance on the identity and the mission of Jesus Christ. If knowledge of the other is to be shared, then it demands that the other truly knows who Jesus is within their tradition-specific context and should be committed to authentically communicating this body of knowledge to the understanding of the self. Knowledge of one's tradition and a *commitment* to it is viewed here as a *sine qua non* for the success of dialogue as an exercise in learning.

To learn from and about the other goes beyond the mere acquisition of knowledge about the other's belief-systems on Christology. To the minimum, it embraces letting the authentic belief-systems of the other transform one's perceptions and one's relationship with the other. It involves the readiness to meaningfully integrate this knowledge into one's way of life and relationship in a creative and enriching manner. It is this sense of transformation and enrichment which contributes to eradicating prejudices, stereotypes and the false perceptions one may harbour about the other. Learning from the other could also lead to a sharpened awareness of the particularity of one's own religious beliefs and the significant place they occupy in one's response to God and to the world of the other. Unbeknown to the self and the other, dialogue as an exercise in learning could also lead to the discovery of similarities in their belief-systems which they hitherto did not know. In whichever way this occurs, the experience of learning would have been fruitful. In this "experience of learning" as understood by Michael Barnes, such learning "is not just that one learns about the other, one also learns more about the self."[117]

Leonard Swidler identified these forms of learning in what he called the *three goals of interreligious dialogue*: (1) "to know oneself ever more profoundly and enrich and round out one's appreciation of one's own faith tradition"; (2) "to know the other ever more authentically and gain a friendly understanding of others as they

---

117 Michael Barnes. *Interreligious Learning.* 2012, p. x.

are and not in caricature"; (3) "to live ever more fully accordingly and to establish a more solid foundation for community of life and action among persons of various traditions."[118] What these three goals of interreligious dialogue presuppose is the exercise of learning. This is because, the ascent to knowledge (to know) occurs at the backdrop of the exercise of learning. It is mostly through learning that one's acquisition of knowledge occurs, and learning occurs through the encounter between the learner and what is learnt. In the same way, the encounter with the other is always a propitious occasion to learn from and about them. This encounter generates new insights with the possibility of becoming a source of enrichment for both.[119] Hence, for dialogue as an "exercise in learning" to achieve the aforementioned tripartite goals of interreligious dialogue, the interlocutors need to develop certain dispositions or what is commonly called *dialogical attitude*. The *dialogical attitude* connotes what Gadamer in another context identified as the "will to dialogue" – which implies the willingness of the self and the other to engage together in commitment to the truths of their religious traditions and the readiness to allow themselves to be transformed by the profundity of their dialogical encounter. [120]

In style and method, dialogue as an exercise in learning is in many ways similar to what is today referred to as *interreligious learning*.[121] As an emerging interdisciplinary field, Kujawa-Holbrook

---

118 Leonard Swidler. *Towards a Universal Theology of Religions*. 1988, p.26.

119 Catherine Cornille. *Interreligious Hermeneutics*. 2010, p. xv.

120 The Pontifical Council for Interreligious dialogue indicated that the "dialogical attitude" very often implies developing a balanced attitude towards the one with whom one is dialoguing. http://www.vatican.va/roman_curia/pontifical_councils/interelg/documents/rc_pc_interelg_doc_19051991_dialogue-and-proclamatio_en.html.

121 See, Sterkens, Carl. *Interreligious Learning: The Problem of Interreligious Dialogue in Primary Schools*. 2001, p.235; Barnes, Michael. *Interreligious Learning: Dialogue, Spirituality and the Christian Imagination*. 2012, p.261-266; Kujawa-Holbrook, Sheryl, A. *God Beyond Borders: Interreligious Learning Among Faith Communities*. 2014, p.2.

indicates that interreligious learning aims to help people from diverse religious traditions to acquire the knowledge, the attitude, and the skills needed to interact, to understand and to communicate their religious beliefs and practices. The purpose is to learn from and about the other's religious beliefs and practices, which leads to the discernment of shared religious values. Interreligious learning, the kind conceptualized by Kujawa-Holbrook, draws its content, its conceptual framework and its processes from different disciplines such as hermeneutics, theology, religious studies, religious education, phenomenology and sociology, to facilitate the learning process.[122] While understanding the theology and the religious beliefs and the practices of the religious other is at the heart of interreligious learning, it values cultural or religious differences and emphasizes on one's commitment to one's faith tradition and openness to learn and to understand the beliefs of the other. As Kujawa-Holbrook indicated, "learners and their life histories and experiences are at the centre of interreligious learning."[123]

While the authentic communication of one's belief-systems or theology is a requirement, learning occurs through questioning, critical thinking, and addressing the challenge of difference in the belief-systems of the self and the other.[124] Consequently, while concepts like *commitment*, *openness* and *difference* are central to the interreligious learning encounter, these concepts carry hermeneutic overtones which need to be carefully articulated

---

122 See, Kujawa-Holbrook, Sheryl, A. *God Beyond Borders: Interreligious Learning Among Faith Communities*. 2014, p.2.

123 According to Kujawa-Holbrook, "interreligious learning begins with stories and identifying shared values. As a process, it should be grounded on the spiritual journey of individuals and groups connected to a vision for humankind to love one another as neighbours" (See, Kujawa-Holbrook, Sheryl, A. *God Beyond Borders: Interreligious Learning Among Faith Communities*. 2014, p.2).

124 Kujawa-Holbrook, Sheryl, A. *God Beyond Borders: Interreligious Learning Among Faith Communities*. 2014, p.3.

if dialogue as an exercise in learning from and about the other is to be achieved. In the encounter between the *self* and the *other*, *openness*, *commitment*, *difference and transformation* raise certain hermeneutic questions. As we shall later see in Chapter Two, these hermeneutic issues raise questions such as: What is openness and commitment? To what extent is the dialogical call to openness related to commitment? Are there limits to openness? What is religious identity? Is not openness to the religious other a threat to one's identity? If interreligious learning demands that the interlocutors unite the attitude of *commitment* to one's tradition and *openness* to the other, how can this occur without the loss of alterity? Is the religious other a threat or an enrichment? If the latter holds true, what is the nature of that enrichment?[125] Effectively responding to these questions is considered relevant because religious traditions are very often distinct and different. They contain the stories, the belief–systems, the practices and the experiences that have formed and shaped the lenses through which adherents perceive Ultimate Reality. Thus, commitment to a religious tradition implies, "the deliberate identification with the teachings and the practices of a particular tradition."[126]

While there is a tension between commitment on the one hand and openness on the other hand, some scholars indicate that, "the attitude that makes dialogue possible consists precisely in balancing this tension."[127] But there is a lack of clarity on precisely how one must negotiate this tension to allow dialogue as an exercise in learning to occur. The above questions therefore relate to the nature of the epistemology and the ethicality in

---

125 Marianne Moyaert raised these significant questions in respect of the lack of clarity on the tension between commitment and openness and selfhood and otherness (see, Marianne Moyaert. *Fragile Identities.* 2010, p.1-2).

126 Catherine Cornille. *The Impossibility of interreligious Dialogue.* 2008, p.66.

127 Marianne Moyaert. *Fragile Identities.* 2010, p.1.

the relationship between the self and the other in dialogue. The discourse in Chapter Two therefore provides clarity in respect of the relationship between *selfhood* and *otherness*, and how this opens the space for understanding the relationship between *commitment* and *openness* within the context of dialogue as an exercise in learning. That is, it provides an account of identity which is not trapped by the polarity between selfhood and otherness, sameness and difference, insider and outsider perspectives.[128] This is achieved through recourse to Paul Ricoeur's hermeneutics on selfhood and otherness.[129]

Paul Ricoeur is often labelled as a philosopher of mediation who never gives up on the "space-between".[130] Within the contexts where the relationship between the self and the other are considered estranged, Ricoeur looks for the possibility of tearing down the walls that separate them to allow for some degree of intersubjectivity. In her reading of Ricoeur, Moyaert indicates that Ricoeur's question within the context of religious pluralism is: "how can we bring people who belong to different religious traditions together? ... How can we overcome the threat of incommensurability?"[131] As a basis for establishing intersubjectivity, Ricoeur asserts that *selfhood* implies *otherness* to such an extent that selfhood and otherness cannot be separated.[132] Ricoeur substantiates the above claim through his hermeneutics on personal identity. As we shall see in Chapter Two, Ricoeur indicates that *personal identity* is constituted by two modes of identity: *idem* (sameness) and *ipse* (selfhood) identities. While *sameness* refers to the *things,* we hold onto which are *permanent in time* – the

---

128 Marianne Moyaert. "Absorption or Hospitality". 2010, p.74.
129 Paul Ricoeur. *Oneself as Another.* 1992; *Time and Narrative I.* 1984; *Time and Narrative III.* 1988; "Narrative Identity" in *Philosophy Today* 35: 1 (1991), p.73-81; *On Translation.* 2006.
130 Marianne Moyaert. "Absorption or Hospitality". 2010, p.75.
131 Marianne Moyaert. "Absorption or Hospitality". 2010, p.75.
132 Paul Ricoeur. *Oneself as Another.* 1992, p.3.

essential unchanging core, human beings are also thinking beings – critical, reflective, creative and always changing. Ricoeur refers to this mode of identity as *selfhood*.[133] He asserts that *selfhood* is not *sameness*.[134]

While *idem* and *ipse* modes of identities both constitute a personal identity, Ricoeur emphasizes that it is through narratology that the intersubjective relationship between the self and the other are established. This is because, "in narrating the stories of our lives, we soon realise that others contribute to our narratives and we to theirs."[135] As we shall see in the chapters following, this intersubjectivity of narratives will open up the space for dialogue between the self and the other. Ricoeur's effort to re-engage the self and the other in contexts where they are considered estrange sets the context for Christian–Muslim dialogue on Christology as an exercise in learning.

---

133 Marianne Moyaert. "Absorption or Hospitality". 2010, p.77.
134 Paul Ricoeur. *Oneself as Another.* 1992, p.116.
135 Paul Ricoeur. "Pastoral praxeology: Hermeneutics and Identity". 1995, p.309.

CHAPTER TWO
RICOEUR AND THE HERMENEUTICS
OF THE SELF AND OTHER

2.1 The Meaning and the Development of Hermeneutics

Over the past hundred and fifty (150) years or more, the concept "Hermeneutics" has been approached from diverse perspectives by many scholars as a consequence of its far-reaching developmental processes and subsequent embracement of variegated subjects in the Sciences and Humanities. However, any understanding or meaning associated with the concept irrespective of the particular area of concern or approach never eludes the general understanding that hermeneutics is, "the theory or the philosophy of the interpretation of meaning."[136] The driving force for such an understanding may be the consequence of the etymology of the concept itself. It comes from the Greek verb *hermeneuein* (transliterated) meaning "to translate" or "to interpret" and its noun *hermeneias* meaning "translation" or "interpretation".

The history of hermeneutics goes back to the name *Hermes*,[137] the mythological Greek deity who was known to be a messenger

---

136 Josef Bleicher. *Contemporary Hermeneutics: Hermeneutics as methods, philosophy and critique*. Routledge and Kegan Paul, London, Boston and Henley. 1980, p.1.

137 In his article "The Relevance of Gadamer's Philosophical Hermeneutics to Thirty-six Fields of Human Activity", Richard E. Palmer asserts that, as a messenger of the gods, Hermes carried messages from Zeus to everybody else. In doing so, he had to bridge the ontological gap between the thinking of the gods and that of the humans. He equally bridged the difference between the following: the invisible and the visible; the unconscious and the conscious. http:/www.mac.edu/richardpalmer/relevance.html (29/10/11).

of the gods to humanity. As a messenger, Hermes did not only announce the message of the gods to humanity, but he also acted as an "interpreter" by rendering this message in the most intelligible and meaningful way to his subjects. His role was therefore the transmutation or the rendition of what was an unfamiliar, alien, and transcended human understanding to the limits of the familiar and human intelligibility. From this etymological perspective then, we could say that the origin of the modern words "hermeneutics" and "hermeneutical" suggests the process of "bringing to understanding" that which transcends human comprehension.[138]

As an interpretive process, Richard E. Palmer intimates that the ancient Greek usage of the verb *Hermeneuein* in the light of the distinctive role played by Hermes points to three basic directions of meaning; namely: (1) *hermeneuein* as, "to express aloud in words"; (2) *hermeneuein* as, "to explain a situation"; and (3) *hermeneuein* as, "to translate".[139] Although these three dimensions find their singular expression in the verb; "to interpret", they nonetheless point to three nuanced but significant subjects in the very art of interpretation and understanding in the "Hermes process".[140] These significant subjects are interpretation as oral recitation, interpretation as rational explanation, and interpretation as the translation of a foreign language.[141] These three dimensions of the "Hermes process" in the light of the ancient Greek usage set the direction for the unfolding development of the concept

---

138 Richard Palmer. *Hermeneutics: Interpretation Theory in Schleiermacher, Dilthey, Heidegger, and Gadamer.* 1969, p.13.

139 Richard Palmer. *Hermeneutics.* 1969, p.12-32

140 In the light of Hermes' role as a mediator, Palmer conceives the "Hermes process" as the rendition of something strange, unfamiliar and separated from time, space and experience to the horizons of the familiar, present and comprehensible (see, Richard Palmer. E. *Hermeneutics. 1969, p.14).*

141 Richard Palmer. *Hermeneutics.* 1969, p.12-32

as they occupied the attention of various interlocutors from ancient Greek philosophy if not earlier, to our contemporary time.

Whereas we acknowledge that within the context of ancient Greek philosophy, we find some hermeneutical underpinnings in the Socratic and particularly Platonic dialogues in which a contrast is made between hermeneutic knowledge and *Sophia*,[142] Aristotle also gave the term a further push in his work on the relationship between logic and semantics in *Peri Hermeneias*,[143] laying the foundation for further theorizing on interpretation and semantics. In the middle ages, the Platonic reflection on hermeneutics as religious knowledge emerged more significantly as an important aspect of Biblical studies, later encompassing studies like ancient and classical culture.[144]

The focus of hermeneutics in this period was more on legal and theological methodology ensuring the rightful application of civil law, canon law and Biblical interpretation. From this period, hermeneutics sporadically emerged and advanced in its development as the theory of interpretation of authoritative literature under conditions in which the original meaning of a text was either disputed or remained hidden due to temporal distance and linguistic differences. In such fashion, the need for interpretative explications to render the text more transparent became

---

142 Plato identifies hermeneutic knowledge as religious knowledge and *Sophia* as knowledge of the truth-value of utterances. The question is: could Plato's association of hermeneutic knowledge to religious truths not be influence by the concept's etymological underpinnings as we demonstrated above?

143 In *Peri Hermeneias*, Aristotle narrowed the meaning of hermeneutics to the determination of the truths and falsities of assertions. But Richard Palmer affirms that *hermeneuein, hermeneias* and their cognates were widely used in ancient Greek to mean interpretation in several senses such as: (1) oral interpretation of Homer and the classic texts; (2) the translation of one language to another; and (3) the exegesis of text.

144 Stanford Encyclopedia of Philosophy. *Hermeneutics.* (29/10/11).

relevant.[145] Understood in this sense, Josef Bleicher intimates that the concept was employed in three capacities: "one, to assist discussions about the language of a text giving rise to philology; two, to facilitate exegesis of Biblical literature; three, to guide jurisdiction."[146]

As it is not our intention to present a thesis on the historical development and meaning of hermeneutics in this introductory section, we nonetheless want to assert that the whole process of "the art of understanding and interpretation" as hermeneutics went through a period of gradual, continuous, unfolding and grasping of a deeper meaning of the concept forming different strands of hermeneutic systems which range from the simple to the complex, from particular to universal, from the ancient to the contemporary, without each necessarily repudiating the other. For in Ast and Wolf, we find that hermeneutics turned into the philological rules of interpretation of a particular text.[147] Schleiermacher crystallized these rules to form a universal hermeneutic for the interpretation of any text. Dilthey builds on this universal character

---

145 Josef Bleicher. *Contemporary Hermeneutics: Hermeneutics as methods, philosophy and critique.* 1980, p.11.

146 Bleicher, Josef. *Contemporary Hermeneutics.* 1980, p.11: For a more comprehensive treatment of hermeneutics considered as philology, exegesis and a guide to civil law, confer p.12-13 of the above book by Josef Bleicher.

147 Ast and Wolf's philological rules gave rise to what we call regional hermeneutics in which the methodology for textual interpretation was determined by the type of text to be interpreted. Thus, literary text gave rise to philological hermeneutics, legal text to juridical hermeneutics, sacred text to biblical hermeneutics (see, Ormiston, Gayle, L. & Schrift, Alan, D. (editors). *Hermeneutic Tradition: From Ast to Ricoeur.* 1990, p.11). Josef Bleicher. *Contemporary Hermeneutics.* 1980, p.14.

of hermeneutics to produce his *Geisteswissenschaften*.[148] Here, Dilthey's aim was to develop an objectively valid interpretation of "expressions of inner life" with concrete, historical, and lived experiences as the starting points, over against speculative expressions[149] through his typology of *experience-expression-explanation*. While Dilthey saw his hermeneutics as finding an historically oriented methodology for the *Geisteswissenschaften*, Heidegger sought to study hermeneutics within the larger context of ontology, the hermeneutics of *Dasein*[150] — an agenda whose primary aim was to go beyond the roots of western conception of *being* and to make visible the presuppositions that they shared. In Heidegger, hermeneutics turned phenomenological.

---

148 Geisteswissenschaften was traditionally a division of the faculty in German Universities that covered subjects such as Philosophy, Philology, Social Science, History, Theology and Jurisprudence; what is today called the humanities. However, in the medieval period, Philosophy encompassed these subjects including the natural sciences and Mathematics under the category of *Naturwissenschaften*. Dilthey argued for a separation between Philosophy and the Historical sciences (the human sciences) from that of the Natural Science and Mathematics (*Naturwissenschaften*). He placed the human sciences under the category of *Geisteswissenschaften* with their unique methodology (see, R. Palmer, *Hermeneutics. 1969*, p.98-99).

149 Dilthey's reason for such a starting and ending point is his argument that, "Behind life itself, our thinking cannot go". Our thinking and questioning are all done within the context of our existential experiences. This should not be bypassed in preference to the realm of ideas (see, R. Palmer, *Hermeneutics. 1969*, p.98-99).

150 *Dasein* is a concept that Heidegger used to conceive of existence. It stands for "Being-in-the-world". In his hermeneutical phenomenology, he sees existence as taking place in a world that is already given, which we take for granted. Many of the elements that shape *Dasein* are hidden and require interpretation for existence to be understood. His whole project was therefore to uncover these hidden phenomena of *Dasein*. (see, Martin Heidegger. *Being and Time*, (trans. Macquarrie, J. & Robinson, E) p.183-194).

With Heideggerian hindsight, Gadamer asserted that any understanding we have of ourselves or of the world is based on a prior understanding. In opposition to Schleiermacher and Dilthey, Gadamer asserted that hermeneutics is not a method of understanding, but the attempt to clarify the conditions that make understanding possible. Among these conditions are prejudice and the fore conceptions in the mind of the interpreter.[151] Gadamer defined hermeneutics as the dialogical encounter between the reader and the text, often personified as the *thou* of the encounter. In this way, he identifies dialogical conversations as the dialectics of question and answer which eventually leads to the fusion of horizons between the text and the reader. As a consequence, Gadamer "represents a radical reworking of the idea of hermeneutics that constitutes a break with the preceding hermeneutical tradition, and yet also reflects back on that tradition."[152] In Gadamer, hermeneutic turned philosophical.

The Gadamerian philosophical hermeneutics on prejudice and the fusion of horizons met some opposition from Critical hermeneutics. This hermeneutic system emerged from a renewed fidelity to the Cartesian certainty and the influential theories of Karl Marx, Wilhelm Nietzsche and Sigmund Freud[153] giving rise to the growth of critical theorists such as Jürgen Habermas, Emilio Betti, Eric D. Hirsch, Karl-Otto Apel and Jacque Derrida. At this point, we may find a tension between philosophical hermeneutics and critical hermeneutics on the one hand, and the challenge of

---

151 Gadamer. *Truth and Method* (second edition). 1989, p.307.

152 Stanford Encyclopedia of Philosophy; *Hans-Georg Gadamer*. http://plato.stanford.edu/entries/gadamer/ (18/02/2012).

153 These three masters indicated that textuality can be infiltrated by powers and forces that are extraneous to it. For Marx, it can be warped by capitalist and class-based ideologies; Nietzsche, by cultural norms; and Freud, the unconscious. These extraneous powers and forces according to them, are capable of penetrating deep into the text by weaving into its linguistic fabric.

deconstruction on the other. The tension lies in whether or not it is enough to espouse hermeneutics as a methodological search for objective knowledge or if it transcends methods to embrace the conditions that make understanding possible? The other side of the quandary is whether from the deconstructive perspective, it is even possible to talk at all about critical hermeneutics and philosophical hermeneutics.

It is in response to the above tension that we properly locate Paul Ricoeur's contributions to hermeneutics meaning and development. While affirming the Gadamerian model of conversation in hermeneutics, Ricoeur also argues for the introduction of relevant explanatory methods which can challenge or even correct one's initial understanding of the other, "by showing how certain structures and other linguistic, cultural, social, economic, religious, historical networks embedded in texts can be decoded through the use of the relevant methods."[154] The purpose was not to replace Gadamer's model, but to enrich it. For Ricoeur, while dialogical conversation is at the beginning and at the end of hermeneutics, the explanation serves to interrupt the process to uncover the meaning "behind texts" to facilitate understanding. This temporary interruption is what Ricoeur calls the hermeneutics of suspicion which is allied to critical theory. While the Ricoeurean hermeneutics of suspicion relies on methods such as the structuralist, historical-critical, semantic, formal and aesthetic methods, the purpose is to help spot and to heal the problem disrupting the conversation between reader and text to facilitate understanding.[155]

In this way, Ricoeur develops a unique form of hermeneutics. With a Hegelian influence, he employs a methodology he calls "refined dialectics", in which "he weaves together heterogeneous

---

154 David Tracy. "Western Hermeneutics and Interreligious Dialogue". 2010, p.11.

155 David Tracy. "Western Hermeneutics and Interreligious Dialogue". 2010, p.12.

concepts and discourses to form a composite discourse in which new meanings are created without diminishing the specificity and difference of the constitutive terms."[156] Like Hegel, this dialectic involves identifying key oppositional terms in a debate, and then proceeding to articulate their synthesis into a new and more developed concept. Unlike Hegel, the Ricoeurean synthesis does not have the uniformity of a Hegelian synthesis but demonstrates how the meanings of two seemingly opposed terms are implicitly informed by each other. Here, the terms maintain their differences at the same time that a "common ground" is formed: teasing out a unity of continuity in discontinuity, convergence in divergence, and a similarity in difference.[157] It is along these lines that the concept of the "hermeneutic process" in this study is built. In this way, we conceptualize *hermeneutics* as that *method*, *theory* and *praxis* of interpretation which seeks to comprehend the meaning of a *text* that is obscured by temporal or cultural distance. A "text" here can either be spoken or written words. It is a *theory* because it deals with the epistemological validity and the possibility of understanding and interpretation; a *method* because it demonstrates how the project of understanding and interpretation is made possible; and *praxis* because it engages in the actual process of interpretation and understanding of "text". Yet, all these layers in the meaning of the concept remain unachievable without particular concern for the conditions that make understanding possible.

In consequence, the hermeneutic issues we shall raise in this study will be particularly Ricoeurean. First of all, the hermeneutic discourse on *selfhood* and *otherness* in this chapter is guided by how Ricoeur presents the *attestation* of the self as a bridge between the self and the other. The interest here is not only to

---

156 Atkins Kim. Stanford Encyclopedia of Philosophy: "Paul Ricoeur". (02/02/2012).

157 Atkins, Kim. Stanford Encyclopedia of Philosophy: "Paul Ricoeur". (02/02/2012).

demonstrate how Ricoeur's notion of *attestation* creatively mediates the epistemological gap created by the impasse between Descartes' cogito and Nietzsche's demolition of it, but more so, to show how *attestation* serves to remove dialogue from an argumentative and confrontational context into the mutual sharing between the self and the other. The purpose is to facilitate learning and understanding of the self and the other. As we indicated before, the results of this exercise in learning could lead to the eradication of prejudices and stereotypes one has about the other; it could also lead to a sharpened awareness of the fastidiousness of one's own religious beliefs and their significance; or it could also lead to the discovery of common values. In this way, the study asserts that Christian-Muslim attestations to their faith convictions about the identity and the mission of Jesus Christ traverses the problem of parallel monologues and creates the space for mutual understanding and learning.

Secondly, through *idem, ipse* and *narrative identities,* Ricoeur also demonstrates the essential constitution of our identities, how they are formed and how others contribute to the enrichment of our identities and we theirs. For Ricoeur, literary narratives and life histories are not exclusive from each other because narratives are always part of us before they are exiled from life into writing and return to life along the multiple paths of appropriation.[158] For Ricoeur, in narrating our history, we find that, "whole sections of our lives are part of the life history of others – that is, of my parents, my friends, my companions in work and in leisure."[159] Hence, in narrating the story of one's life, one finds others who are co-authors to one's narrative identity. "Learning to narrate oneself is also learning how to narrate oneself in other ways."[160] Situating these aspects of personal identity within the context of dialogue as an exercise in learning, we shall demonstrate

---

158 Paul Ricoeur. *Oneself As Another.* 1992, p.163.
159 Paul Ricoeur. *Oneself As Another.* 1992, p.161.
160 Paul Ricoeur. *The Course of Recognition.* 2005, p.101.

how they apply to the identities of the Christian and the Muslim and how they set the context for Christian–Muslim dialogue on Christology.

2.2 Attestation as Mediation in the Crisis of the Cogito

Reflexivity "refers to the capacity to reflect on oneself, to take responsibility for oneself and to act upon oneself. These reflexive acts of the self are basic features of selfhood."[161] However, as we shall see, the concept of the self together with the possibilities and the limits of reflexivity are highly contested in both philosophical and theological discourses. In other words, while the modern emphasis on reflexivity laid the foundations for "a self-transparent, self-grounding knowing subject who is also an autonomous lawgiver and sufficient moral agent",[162] others think that this emphasis on reflexivity has severely distorted our understanding of human existence, deepening our egocentricity and nurturing the illusions of the self. In *Oneself as Another*, whereas Ricoeur views Descartes, Kant and Husserl among others as espousing the philosophies of the exalted subject,[163] he presents Nietzsche as Descartes' a "privileged adversary" whose critique of the self, shatters and humiliates the philosophies of the "exalted cogito". In Ricoeur's view, the aftermath of Nietzsche's assault on the "exalted cogito" left it in a critical condition. For Ricoeur, the philosophies of the "exalted cogito" overlook the distortions that may be inherent in self-interpretation. While

161 Brian Gregor. *A Philosophical Anthropology of the Cross: The Cruciform Self.* 2013, p.23.

162 Brian Gregor. *A Philosophical anthropology of the Cross: The Cruciform Self.* 2013, p.23.

163 Paul Ricoeur. *Oneself As Another.* 1992, p.4.

being a reminder of the possibility of self-deception, Nietzsche's "shattered cogito" only leads to the all-consuming abyss of suspicion. With this impasse, Ricoeur introduces *attestation* as a new form of the certainty of the self. The attestation of the self, "is a matter of identifying oneself, of recognizing who one is and of taking responsibility for oneself."[164]

In the *Meditations on First Philosophy,* Descartes constructs a hypothesis of an all-encompassing metaphysical doubt to indicate the disproportions within a particular area of certainty.[165] To dramatize the doubt he creates the hypothesis of the great deceiver or an evil genius as the one behind every conceivable thought in me. He then concludes that there must be a "cogito" for the evil genius to deceive, otherwise it would be an empty enterprise. Hence, "if the cogito can arise out of this extreme condition of doubt, it is because someone is doing the doubting."[166] This led to the philosophy of the Cartesian certainty – "cogito ergo sunt" (the philosophies of the exalted cogito). It is this kind of philosophy that Kant and Husserl among others would later develop. For instance, Husserl asserted that consciousness is determined by intentionality. To be conscious is to be conscious that *I am* a 'true' being – definitively decided or a definitively decidable being. So, if *I* abstain from believing or accepting the already established philosophical foundations and my experience of the world around me, "I do so now as the ego that philosophizes and exercises the aforesaid abstention."[167] In a Kantian sense, Husserl also reckons that, "all reality is pure phenomena"[168] – the only data from which we can begin. They appear in the mind and in the form of unchanging and invariable

164 Brian Gregor. *A Philosophical Anthropology of the Cross.* 2013, p.25.
165 Paul Ricoeur. *Oneself as Another.* 1992, p.5.
166 Paul Ricoeur. *Oneself as Another.* 1992, p.5.
167 Edmund Husserl. *Cartesian Meditations.*1999, p.19.
168 Edmund Husserl. *Cartesian Meditations* 1999, p20.

types and essences.[169] Through *epoché*,[170] intentional consciousness effects an eidetic intuition which makes objects present to
the subject. Thus, epoché is, "the radical and the universal method by which I apprehend myself purely: as ego and with my own
conscious life, in and by which the entire objective world exists
for me and is precisely as it is for me."[171]

Consequently, Husserl asserted that this state of being reveals
a *transcendental ego* whose intentional act is the source of objective knowledge of the world. In this way, "anything belonging
to the world, any spatiotemporal being, exists for me – that is to
say, is accepted by me – in that I experience it, perceive it, remember it, think of it somehow, judge it, value it, desire it or the
like."[172] Thus, the *other* is for me absolutely nothing other than
the way I conceive it to be in my conscious *cogito*. This emphasis
on the cogito led to Michael Barnes' assertion that the Husserlian
Egology implies that, "the world is ordered round me as the centre. Temporally and spatially, I am at the centre with everything
and everyone, near and far, dependent on me insofar as they appear to me."[173] Here, the cogito is posited as the exclusive claimant of truth, the archetypal of religious exclusivism. It is the self
who gives meaning to the other without reference to the other's
self-understanding.

Opposed to this Husserlian *Egology* is the Levinasian emphasis on the infinity and the ethical transcendent of the other. For
Levinas "infinity remains ever exterior to thought and overflows
the thoughts that think it."[174] The self's relation with the other is a "relation without relation". This is because the other who

---

169   Michael Barnes. *Theology and the Dialogue of Religions*. 2002, p.74.
170   Edmund Husserl. *Cartesian Meditations*.1999, p.20-21.
171   Edmund Husserl. *Cartesian Meditations*.1999, p.20-21.
172   Edmund Husserl. *Cartesian Meditations* 1999, p.20-21.
173   Michael Barnes. *Theology and the Dialogue of Religions*. 2002, p.74.
174   Emmanuel Levinas. *Totality and Infinity: An Essay on Exteriority*. 1969,
      p.195.

is, first of all, not reducible to the same, remains unknowable, is outside the totality of the same and calls Egology to question. Secondly, when the "I" encounters the other, the "I" is called back to the meaning of its freedom – a freedom which is founded by the other. Here, the genuine freedom of the "I" is based on its responsibility and its obligation towards the other.[175] In other words, the ethical responsibility of the "I" is to guard the infinite other against any systematic determination of moral principles. These set of *priori* principles are considered as violations to the alterity of the *other*.

While Levinas' conception of the infinite other more or less dethrones the Husserlian cogito, Ricoeur presents a Nietzschean position[176] in *Oneself as Another* which shatters the exalted Cogito's hyper-certainty as mere illusions. Nietzsche's attack against the above foundational claim to philosophy is based on his critique of language in which philosophy expresses itself. For Nietzsche, language is figurative and is thus reputed to be deceitful. It is a paradox in a double sense: "first, in that, from the opening lines, life, apparently taken in a referential and nonfigural sense, is taken as the source of the fable by which it sustains itself.[177] Secondly, language is paradoxical in that, "Nietzsche's own discourse on truth as a lie ought to be drawn into the abyss of the paradox of the liar. But Nietzsche is precisely the thinker who assumes this paradox to the end."[178] Thus for Nietzsche, this *turn* is, "missed

---

175 Emmanuel Levinas. *Totality and Infinity: An Essay on Exteriority*. 1969, p.79.

176 Ricoeur presents the views of Nietzsche, Freud and Marx as representing what he calls the "hermeneutic of suspicion" because of the way they attempt to expose false consciousness. Even though he refers to them collectively as the masters of suspicion; in *Oneself as Another* (1992), Ricoeur presents Nietzsche alone as Descartes "privileged Adversary". (See, Brian Gregor. *A Philosophical anthropology of the Cross: The Cruciform Self*. 2013, p.24).

177 Paul Ricoeur. *Oneself as Another*. 1992, p.12.

178 Paul Ricoeur. *Oneself as Another*. 1992, p.12.

by the commentators who take the apology of life, of the will to power, to be the revelation of a new immediacy, substituted in the very place and with the same foundational claims of the cogito."[179]

In consequence, Nietzsche asserted that the Cartesian certainty is an illusion because in Descartes' effort to establish an Archimedean point from which he can freely inspect the world, certain forces, certain will to power, already conditions the way Descartes regards the data.[180] The cogito therefore, "flatters itself that it can gain a transparent view of itself, that it can set itself on display and the reflection but this self-consciousness is actually self-deception."[181] For Nietzsche, the human being is an animal who has cultivated the illusions of culture and civilization but the bestial nature remains and this is what underlines the cogito.[182] Thus, truth is not the correspondence between signs and reality as the cogito implies. "Reality is just a matter of conventions that we fit to our preferences",[183] and so truth is the obligation to lie according to these conventions. There is no factual reality beyond these conventions. All we have are interpretations.[184]

From the discourses above, one finds a dialectic tension between Descartes' "exalted cogito" and Nietzsche's "shattered cogito".[185] Even though Ricoeur agrees with Nietzsche's criticism of the Cartesian tradition (the hermeneutics of suspicion), he does not give in to the Nietzscheans total dissolution of the cogito.

---

179 Paul Ricoeur. *Oneself as Another*. 1992, p.12.
180 Friedrich Nietzsche. *On the Genealogy of morals and Ecce Homo*. 1968, p.119-130.
181 Brian Gregor. *A Philosophical Anthropology of the Cross: The Cruciform Self*. 2013, p.24.
182 Brian Gregor. *A Philosophical Anthropology of the Cross: The Cruciform Self*. 2013, p.24.
183 Brian. Gregor. *A Philosophical Anthropology of the Cross: The Cruciform Self*. 2013, p.24.
184 Brian. Gregor. *A Philosophical Anthropology of the Cross: The Cruciform Self*. 2013, p.24.
185 Paul Ricoeur. *Oneself as Another*. 1992, p.16.

According to Ricoeur, one may not be able to attain an absolute certainty about the cogito but one can reach some degree of certainty about it through *attestation*.[186] He defines *attestation* as a kind of *belief*, "but not a doxic belief in the sense in which *doxa* (belief) has less standing than *episteme*."[187] Whereas, "a doxic belief is implied in the grammar of 'I believe that', attestation belongs to the grammar of 'I believe in'."[188] It connotes the sense of *credence*, a belief-in and trust. It is linked with *testimony*, "inasmuch as it is in the speech of the one giving testimony that one believes."[189] In other words, "when I attest to something, I not only believe that, but I believe in something. It is more a statement of confidence and conviction than knowledge and certainty."[190] Here, Ricoeur places *attestation* at an equal distance between the "exalted cogito" and the "shattered cogito". This however does not suggest that it is placed in an exact midpoint between the two. Rather, it implies that *attestation* occupies an epistemic and ontological position beyond the alternatives provided by the exalted cogito and its demolition.[191] To express it symbolically, Greisch asserts that Ricoeur's idea of *attestation* implies that the cogito of attestation is neither a triumphant cogito as with the Cartesians or a crushed cogito as per Nietzsche but a *wounded cogito* that is capable of believing in itself.[192]

This concept of attestation serves as the basis for Ricoeur's

---

186 For Ricoeur, "*attestation* defines the sort of certainty that hermeneutics claim, not only with respective to the epistemic exaltation of the cogito in Descartes, but also with respect to its humiliation in Nietzsche and his successors". (See Paul Ricoeur. *Oneself as Another.* 1992, p.21).

187 Paul Ricoeur. *Oneself as Another.* 1992, p.21.

188 Paul Ricoeur. *Oneself as Another.* 1992, p.21.

189 Paul Ricoeur. *Oneself as Another.* 1992, p.21.

190 David Kaplan. *Ricoeur's Critical Theory.* 2003, p.92.

191 Jean Greisch. "Testimony and Attestation" in *Paul Ricoeur: The Hermeneutics of Action.* 1996, p.84-85.

192 Paul Ricoeur. *Oneself as Another.* 1992, p.86.

development of the hermeneutics of the self. For Ricoeur, "*attestation* is fundamentally the attestation of the self."[193] It is a "trust in the power to say, in the power to do, in the power to recognize oneself as a character in a narrative, in the power, and finally, to respond to an accusation in the form of the accusative."[194] Attestation is "*assurance of being oneself acting and suffering.*"[195] This *assurance* remains the ultimate recourse against all suspicion. It provides the epistemological response to the question: "What knowledge does the self have about itself?" In response, the self is seen as the being that is both an agent and a patient. Ontologically, if it is asked: "who is the self?" For Ricoeur, the self is "the assurance — the credence and the trust — of existing in the mode of selfhood."[196] According to Ricoeur, this *assurance or confidence* is the ultimate recourse against all suspicion; even if it is always in some sense received from another, it is always self-attestation. "It is a self-attestation that every — linguistic, praxis, narrative and prescriptive — will preserve the question 'who?' from being replaced by the question 'what?' or 'why?'"[197] Attestation is credence without any guarantee but also a trust greater than any suspicion. The certainty of attestation is not a scientific one but a trust, a confidence, an assurance that cannot be demolished completely by suspicion.

Within the context of Christian-Muslim dialogue, Christology is one of the most contentious theological subjects which divides the two religions irreconcilably. This is because whereas Christians believe that Jesus Christ is the "Son of God" (human and divine), Muslims believe that this very Jesus is only a "Prophet" of Allah bereft of divine connotations. The Islamic doctrine of the *Tawhid* (the oneness of God) serves as the basis

---

193 Paul Ricoeur. *Oneself as Another.* 1992, p.22.
194 Paul Ricoeur. *Oneself as Another.* 1992, p.22.
195 Paul Ricoeur. *Oneself as Another.* 1992, p.22.
196 Paul Ricoeur. *Oneself as Another.* 1992, p.302.
197 Paul Ricoeur. *Oneself as Another.*1992, p.23.

from which God is understood as absolutely transcendent. Since there is only one God (Surah 5: 73) in Islam, Jesus only functions as the "Messenger" or as a "Prophet" of Allah within the context of the *Tawhid*. This underscores the Islamic truth claims on Christology. In contrast, the Christian experience of God as the *Holy Trinity* also serves as the formidable grounds on which Jesus Christ is understood as the "Son of God" (the second person of the Holy Trinity).

Consequently, when one focuses on the right claim to Christological truths between Christianity and Islam, one only creates the hotbed for theological confrontations. As Pratt put it, "not only have internal theological debates and discussions been hotbeds of high emotions and deep dissent but such engagement between the religions ... have been equally, if not more so, contentious and fraught"[198]in the history of Christian-Muslim relations. As religions of belief, the theologies of Islam and Christianity constitute self-enclosed systems of meaning and doctrine which can only be measured by their internal logic and coherence.[199] Here, the truth claims that one religious tradition cannot be used as the standard of measurement for the truthfulness of another. The attempts to engage the two traditions in such forms of dialogue only leads to a parallel monologue or the context of claim and counterclaim, and in the end, the mutual dismissal of the other's viewpoint.[200]

In this way, what is required today is the kind of Christian-Muslim dialogue on Christology which allows the self and the other to tell their stories about the life and the mission of Jesus Christ in a mutual atmosphere of give and take – a conversation

---

198 Douglas Pratt. *The Challenge of Islam*. 2005, p.203.
199 Catherin Cornille. "Meaning and Truth in Dialogue between Religions" in Depoortere, F &Lambkin, M. (Eds.). *The Question of Theological Truth. Philosophical and Interreligious Perspectives*. 2012, p.137-139.
200 Catherine Cornille. "Meaning and Truth in Dialogue between Religions". 2012, p.138.

which is neither defined by the Cartesian style of the "exalted cogito" nor shaped by the Nietzschean sense of it. Instead, what is needed is the Ricoeurean sense of *attestation* whereby Christians and Muslims *attest* to their respective truth claims on Christology within the overall process of dialogue as an exercise in learning from and about the other. Here, the question is not who is right about Christology but what can be learnt from the stories and testimonies of belief that the other tells about the identity and the mission of Jesus Christ in their tradition-specific context. In other words, *attestation* in Christian–Muslim dialogue on Christology focuses on the mutual sharing of testimonies of one's beliefs about Jesus, while maintaining some degree of openness to learn from the other's testimonies of faith in Jesus. The purpose is to learn from and about the other and to grow as a consequence of this learning. This process of religious learning and growth is at the heart of the discipline of interreligious learning. As an exercise in learning from and about the other, dialogue guided by the Ricoeurean notion of *attestation* is far more likely to succeed than the often argumentative and confrontational forms of dialogue based on truth-claims. A dialogue between two competing "exalted cogitos" lead to dialogical aporias.

While we argue for the case of *attestation* as the appropriate context for Christian–Muslim dialogue as an exercise in learning from and about the other, this form of dialogue also raises epistemological and ethical questions in respect of the relationship between the self and the other. In other words, if learning about the other leads to learning about oneself, then the question is: how can the other's self-enclosed systems of belief that become the context for reflection about one's beliefs? As Barnes put it, "how precisely is faith deepened – and what is learnt?"[201] Furthermore, what becomes of the identity of the other after this learning? Does it remain the *same* or is it a matter of becoming

---

201 Michael Barnes. *Interreligious Learning.* 2012, p. x.

and growing – and thus of change and transformation?[202] If the latter pertains, how does it occur without the self, losing itself?

We shall respond to these questions with the aid of Ricoeur's hermeneutics of the self, expressed in *idem, ipse* and *narrative identities*. By engaging these three aspects of personal identity, we shall argue that they disclose the possibilities of the intertwinement of personal narratives in contexts where they are considered exclusive of each other. By engaging in this form of dialogue as an exercise in learning, one might be surprised, to borrow Leirvik's words, at how "dialogical overtones in Bakhtin's sense may strike a note anywhere in the scale between parody, polemics and affirmations."[203] We shall first of all, argue that such a *disclosure* is in itself an exercise in learning about a subject which has remained contentious in Christian–Muslim relations (Christology). Secondly, while being committed to their traditions and open to learn from the traditions of the other, when the content of these disclosures lead to the common cognition of common values which require collective actions in response to them, then dialogue as an exercise in learning is all the more successful on the basis of its goal. Here, the other's tradition-specific understanding of Christology does not change *per se*. What may change as a consequence of the dialogue is their mutual interrelationship – which is transformed from disparate actions to collective action. As a starting point, let us first of all, see how Ricoeur's views on *idem, ipse* and *narrative identities* prepare the grounds for the possibility of Christian–Muslim conversations on Christology.

---

202 Marianne Moyaert. *Fragile Identities*. 2011, p.2.

203 See, Oddbjørn Leirvik. *The Images of Jesus Christ in Islam*. 2011, p.16; Bakhtin, Mikhail. *Speech Genres and Other Late Essays*. 1986, 92, p.93-107.

2.3 The Two Poles of Personal Identity

In *Oneself as Another*, Ricoeur identifies two modes of personal identity: *idem*-identity and *ipse*-identity. While *idem*-identity is characterized by *sameness* or the permanent features of things, *ipse*-identity concerns the self-constancy needed for keeping one's word. For Ricoeur, these two modes of identity define two modes of *permanence in time*.[204] Ricoeur presents *character* as conveying the equivocalness or double valence of the mode of identity as *sameness* and *selfhood*. Hence, the self is the embodiment of *idem*-identity and *ipse*-identity; and *narrative identity* holds together the dialectics of *idem*-identity and *ipse*-identity in the person. Let us begin this hermeneutic journey by examining Ricoeur's notion of *idem, ipse* and *narrative identities*.

2.3.1 The Mode of the Self as an Idem-identity

In real life experience we normally distinguish one person from another by their appearances. For Ricoeur, their body and their character which differentiates them from one another, gives them a specific identity. Ricoeur identifies this form of identity as *sameness* or *idem*-identity. Identity here is viewed as either a state of being the same or a state of being oneself or one thing and not another. According to Ricoeur, *idem–identity* is a constituent of personal identity, which is stable and sedimented in the person. Ricoeur presents four criteria by which *sameness* can be understood: *numerical identity, qualitative identity, uninterrupted continuity*, and *permanence in time*.[205]

Numerical identity connotes the sense of oneness or unity as opposed to plurality. In other words, "we say that two occurrences

---

204 Paul Ricoeur. *Oneself as Another.* 1992, p.116.
205 Paul Ricoeur. *Oneself as Another.* 1992, p.116-118.

of a thing, designated by an invariable noun in ordinary language, that they do not form two different things but 'one and the same' thing."[206] For Ricoeur, the first component of this notion of identity corresponds to the notion of *identification* whereby the same thing can be reidentified twice, thus making cognition recognition: that is, identifying the same thing twice, *n* times.[207] *Qualitative identity* however relates to similarity over difference. According to Ricoeur, qualitative identity relates to the category of extreme resemblance where for instance, "we say that *x* and *y* are wearing the same suits – clothes that are so similar that they are interchangeable with no noticeable difference".[208] These two components of identity apply when we speak of the physical identity of a person. "We have no trouble recognizing someone who simply enters and leaves, appears, disappears and reappears."[209] Hence, *qualitative identity* helps us to resolve problems where numerical identity fails. For instance, in a case where one is unsure about whether or not two appearances correspond to "one and the same thing" as indicated earlier, one can resort to the criterion of qualitative identity to ascertain their resemblance.[210]

However, Ricoeur asks the question; "how do we know that the person standing here in court is the author of a crime committed ten years ago?" For Ricoeur, this question exposes the weakness in *qualitative identity* because changes may have occurred in the appearance of the person after ten years. Thus, temporal distance and the changes that occur within it weakens the idea of qualitative identity due to its reliance on the criterion of similitude. This suggests the need for another criterion of identity, one which belongs to the third component of the notion of

206 Paul Ricoeur. *Oneself as Another*. 1992, p.116.
207 Paul Ricoeur. *Oneself as Another*. 1992, p.116.
208 Paul Ricoeur. *Oneself as Another*. 1992, p.16.
209 Paul Ricoeur. *Oneself as Another*. 1992, p.116-117.
210 Paul Ricoeur. "Narrative Identity" *in Philosophy Today* 35: 1 (1991), p.74.

identity, namely *uninterrupted continuity.*[211] For Ricoeur, it is *uninterrupted continuity* which helps us to identify persons or things in spite of change over time. This explains why we can say that an oak tree is the same from the acorn to the fully developed tree. This form of continuity, "rests upon the ordered series of small changes, which, taken one by one, threaten resemblance without destroying it."[212] In this way, Ricoeur sees *time* within the context of *uninterrupted continuity* as, "a factor of dissemblance, of diversity and of difference. The threat of time "represents identity that is not entirely dissipated unless we can posit at the basis of similitude and uninterrupted continuity, a principle of *permanence in time.*"[213]

The principle of permanence in time could be seen in a tool which maintains its structure despite the replacement of all its parts, or in the genetic code of a biological individual. What remains permanent in these two subjects is their structure, and their "structure" for Ricoeur, reflects the sense of *permanence in time.*[214] *Permanence in time* is viewed by Ricoeur as the most complete criterion of identity as *sameness.* While *numerical* and *qualitative identity* do not properly appropriate the problem of the passage of *time, uninterrupted continuity* takes into consideration the *time* problematic but leaves identity as *sameness* with the difficulty of following the trajectory of a thing through time. However, the criterion of *permanence in time* resolves the time problematic in that it focuses on the structure of a thing, which remains the same through time.

Having considered the four criteria that determine *idem*-identity as sameness, Ricoeur then seeks to find out whether there is a form of *permanence in time* which is not simply the schema of the category of substance. In other words, "is there a form of

211 Paul Ricoeur. *Oneself as Another.* 1992, p.117.
212 Paul Ricoeur. *Oneself as Another.* 1992, p.117.
213 Paul Ricoeur. *Oneself as Another.* 1992, p.117.
214 Paul Ricoeur. *Oneself as Another.* 1992, p.117.

permanence in time which can be connected to the question *who?* inasmuch as it is irreducible to the question *what?* Is there a form of permanence in time that is a response to the question 'whom am I?'"[215] For Ricoeur, while the response to the question (who?), directs us to *person*, the question (what?) focuses on *things*. In this way, Ricoeur indicates that when we speak of ourselves, we in fact have two models of permanence in the time available to us. These are: "character" and "keeping one's word". The polarity between these two models of permanence in time with respect to persons results from the fact that, "the permanence of *character* expresses the mutual overlapping of the problematic of *idem* and *ipse,* while "faithfulness in keeping one's word" marks the extreme gap between the permanence of the *self* and that of the *same*.[216] As we shall later discover, Ricoeur will present *narrative identity* as the mediation between the poles of character where *idem* and *ipse* tend to coincide. However, he indicates that it is in *self-maintenance* that *selfhood* frees itself from *sameness*.

According to Ricoeur, *character* expresses another kind of *sameness* which constitutes an aspect of personal identity. He defines *character* as, "the set of distinctive marks which permit the reidentification of a human individual as being the same"[217] or "the set of lasting dispositions by which a person is recognised."[218] As a set of permanent dispositions, whereas character gives to personal identity the stability which is proper to identity as *sameness,* also expresses a dimension of ipseity through the permanent dispositions in the person who answers the question "who am I"? In this way, character demonstrates an overlap between *idem*-identity and *ipse*-identity. If we understand *character* as the set of permanent dispositions in a person, then character reflects the sense of *numerical identity* in that it can be identified and re-identified as

215 Paul Ricoeur. *Oneself as Another*. 1992, p.118.
216 Paul Ricoeur. *Oneself as Another*. 1992, p.118.
217 Paul Ricoeur. *Oneself as Another*. 1992, p.119.
218 Paul Ricoeur. *Oneself as Another*. 1992, p.121.

"one and the same thing" in a person. It also expresses *qualitative identity* because it defines the features in the individual which allows for easy comparison of one character with another. For example, one could say to his long-time friend: "you really haven't changed after all these years." *Uninterrupted continuity* also helps us to see the same person we knew some years ago despite some changes in them (physical or psychological). The *permanence in time* of character is situated within "the set of distinctive marks" that remain constant in the person.

Ricoeur identifies character as constituted by two main factors: *habits* and *acquired identifications*.[219] *Habits* are the sedimentations of practices in a person. These sedimented practices somewhat form a "second nature" in the person. According to Ricoeur, what we do and learn by doing affect our *habits* and our *habits* define to some extent, who we are and guide our orientations. They are formed without the conscious attention to the question; "who to be?" *Habits* have a twofold valence: those that are formed and habits that are acquired.[220] These two forms of habits give character a history – "a history in which sedimentation tends to cover over the innovation which preceded it, even to the point of abolishing the latter."[221] Character also relates to "the *acquired identifications* by which the other enters into the composition of the same."[222] These acquired identifications denote the values, norms, ideals, models and heroes *in* which a person or a community assumes as proper and recognize itself *by*.[223] These identifications clearly display how one takes on otherness and makes it one's own. In other words, through *acquired identifications,* what was initially alien to a person or the community now becomes part of oneself. In this way, the person or the community

---

219 Paul Ricoeur. *Oneself as Another.* 1992, p.121.
220 Paul Ricoeur. *Oneself as Another.* 1992, p.121.
221 Paul Ricoeur. *Oneself as Another.* 1992, p.121.
222 Paul Ricoeur. *Oneself as Another.* 1992, p.121.
223 Paul Ricoeur. *Oneself as Another.* 1992, p.121.

begins to understand these identifications as necessary for their survival. This sense of necessity elicits an element of loyalty that is incorporated into character and makes it turn towards fidelity and hence, towards maintaining the self. How does this aspect of identity apply in the case of the Christian and the Muslim tradition-specific understandings of Christology?

Raymond Brown indicates that *Christology*, "discusses the evaluation of Jesus Christ in respect of who he was and the role he played in the divine plan."[224] Within this evaluative context, while Christians believe that Jesus is God and the "Son of God", Muslims believe that he is only a "Prophet" or the "Messenger" of Allah. These different theological evaluations of Jesus along with other religious doctrines contribute to defining the horizons which shape the Christian and the Muslim belief and understandings of Christology. If Ricoeur points out that *idem*-identity denotes *sameness* – that is, the set of lasting dispositions which one does not choose but by which one is recognised, then Muslims and Christians equally share this dimension of *sameness* within their respective views on Christology – referred to here as their "tradition-specific understandings of Christology. Here, *sameness* constitutes the religious practices, rites, symbols, customs and traditions which the adherent does not choose but from which his or her religious identity is derived. As Moyaert indicated, Christian identity for instance means the, "identification with particular Christian norms, values, doctrines, Biblical texts, rituals and the like."[225]

Christians believe in the *Holy Trinity* because of their experience of God as the *Father,* the *Son* (Jesus Christ) and the *Holy Spirit.* The doctrine of the *Holy Trinity* is therefore constitutively part of the "deposit of faith" that has been handed on from the Apostles to successive generations of Christians. This deposit of faith which is passed on to every Christian through formal

224 Raymond Brown. *Introduction to New Testament Christology.* 1994, p.3.
225 Marianne Moyaert. "Absorption or Hospitality." 2010, p.79.

education (catechises) contributes to forming and shaping the identity of the Christian. Within this doctrine, Jesus Christ is only understood as the "Son of God" and the "Saviour of the World". Hence, the Bible, the norms and practice of Christian ritual, all give expression to this belief in Jesus Christ as the "Son of God". This defines the *idem aspects* of Christian identity. In Islam too, belief in the Qur'an, the profession of the *Shahada* and observing the *five pillars* of the religion among other religious practices shape the identity of the Muslim. For instance, the obligation to the *Tawhid* forms the root of Islamic monotheism. The confession that "there is no god but One God" (Surah 5: 73) is a fundamental statement of Islamic belief and all Muslims are identified by that confession. Hence, the *Shahada* and the *Tawhid* which inform many Islamic faith practices define the *idem*-dimension of the Muslim's identity. They are the same for all Muslims within their tradition-specific contexts. As Moyaert observes, "*idem* is not added to the faith commitment but is constitutive of it."[226]

In this way, "by reading certain texts, adhering to certain rules, agreeing with specific doctrines and by performing certain religious practices which rather remain stable, the believer (Christian or Muslim) submits his or her life to God."[227] Although sedimented in the believer, this *idem* dimension of religious identity is delicate in the sense that it is the immediate aspect of every religion which could be in danger of being lost in the face of religious plurality and interreligious dialogue. As a consequence, Ricoeur notes in a different context that some religions tend towards a "protective withdrawal" from the religious other because of the fear of losing this aspect of their identity.[228] Within the context of dialogue as an exercise in learning, we agree with Moyaert that, "there is thus no single reason to formulate a negative judgement

---

226 Marianne Moyaert. "Absorption or Hospitality." 2010, p.79.
227 Marianne Moyaert. "*Fragile Identities.*" 2011, p.254.
228 Paul Ricoeur. "Reflections on a New Ethos for Europe." 1996, p.4.

about the *idem* dimension of religious identity."[229] Whereas for Moyaert, the reason is that, "the *idem* aspect is not added to faith commitment but is constituted of it", for us, another compelling reason also lies in the fact that religious truths are self-enclosed systems of meaning (*Trinity* vis-a-vis *Tawhid*) which can only be measured by their internal coherence. Hence, no particular system (whether Islam or Christianity) can be used as a standard of measurement for the truthfulness of the other. The *idem*-identity of the Christian or the Muslim very often forms their second nature – the sedimented part of their identity which the faithful believer protects at all cost. It is for this reason that interreligious learning emphasizes caution and respect for the religious beliefs of the other. If *idem aspect* of religious identity refers to the *unchanging* aspects of the religions, what defines their *ipseity*?

2.3.2 The Mode of the Self as an Ipse Identity

According to Ricoeur, when the question "who are you?" is asked, people may respond to this by appealing to the "*what?*" of themselves. For instance, when asked, "who are you as a Muslim?" the response is likely to be, "I believe in the one God and in Muhammad as his Messenger." Of course, this response reflects the Muslim confession of the *Shahada* which is at the heart of Islamic faith. However, while every Muslim confesses the *Shahada*, not all Muslims live out the *Shahada* in the same way. In other words, there are varying degrees in their submission to the will of Allah. The same applies to Christians in their confession of faith in God as the *Holy Trinity*. One always finds variations in the living out of what is confessed as faith in Christianity. Thus, we could say that it is not just the mere confession of faith in God that matters for the believer but also the living out of what is confessed – this makes one truly Christian or Muslim.

---

229 Marianne Moyaert. "*Fragile Identities.*" 2011, p.255.

In this way, even though we often answer to the "who?" of ourselves by appealing to the "what", the *"what?"* *dimension* of ourselves (*idem*) does not fully express *who we are* as Muslims or Christians. There is more to the Christian or to the Muslim way of life than just the mere confession of religious beliefs and following religious practices. This suggests that there is another aspect of identity which reflects, for instance, the Muslim's degree of *commitment* to the confession of the *Shahada*. This concept of *commitment* is directly linked to the Muslim's promise to keep and to live the *Shahada* in every circumstance. Here, when I promise to observe the *Shahada*, I affirm that in times of changes, disappointments and motivations that lead me to contrary alternatives in respect of my belief in the one God and in Muhammad as his Messenger, I will still hold firm to this *belief.* Ricoeur identifies this dimension of the self-maintenance of the believer as *ipseity* or *ipse*-identity.

According to Ricoeur, *ipse*-identity is another mode of personal identity which conforms to the criteria of *permanence in time*. It is defined by the self-constancy necessary for *keeping one's promise* or *faithfulness to one's word.*[230] For Ricoeur, a person's commitment to what he or she promises, even in the face of danger, disappointments, uncertainties, and new opportunities, demonstrates that the person is reliable and can be counted on.[231] In Marianne Moyaert's view, Ricoeur believes that this reliability and self-constancy is the condition for lasting relationships because, "people are not characters; they are relational beings. A human being becomes a person only when others can count on him or her."[232] While with *character* the identity of the self is supported by *habits and acquired identifications*, in *keeping one's promise,* the self is affirmed without the need for the permanence entailed in character. Keeping one's promise, "does not appear as

230 Paul Ricoeur. *Oneself as Another.* 1992, p.119.
231 Paul Ricoeur. *Oneself as Another.* 1992, p.124.
232 Marianne Moyaert. "Absorption or Hospitality." 2010, p.78.

a challenge to time, a denial of change: even if my desires were to change, even if I were to change my opinion or my inclination, 'I will hold firm.'"[233] Here, it is not necessary for *promise* to be placed in the context of being-towards-death, but its ethical justification suffices for itself – "a justification which can be derived from the obligation to ... respond to the trust that the other places in my faithfulness."[234]

In consequence, while *sameness* refers to the *sedimentations* of the self, that is habits and attitudes that are part of us, *promise-keeping* sometimes breaks with the past and affirms an identity that is grounded on the *innovations* of the present. For instance, my promise to start praying regularly and going to Church every Sunday after fifty years of not doing so, demonstrates a break with my way of life in the past and a commitment to a new beginning which presents a future challenge. This challenge is that despite the disruptions in the history of my *sameness* (that is, my cultivated habits of not praying regularly and not going to Church every Sunday), because of my promise to be faithful, I will hold firm to the promise made. Here, the break between *idem and ipse* identities lies in the fact that the *sameness* of one's life now gives way to a new way of life defined by the *promise* to be faithful to God through regular prayers and attending Sunday services. How then is *ipse identity* related to the question of religious identity?

Even though we mentioned that to be a Christian or a Muslim, is to adhere to the doctrines, rites, customs and practices of Christianity or Islam (*idem-identity*), these *idem* aspects of the religions do not define the totality of the identity of the Christian or the Muslim. Mere conformity to the *idem*-dimension of the religion is not enough. It demands a certain sense of *commitment* which goes deeper than mere conformity to rituals. As Moyaert implied, religious identity also implies a relationship with God – a commitment to God which is expressed through the practice

---

233 Paul Ricoeur. *Oneself as Another*. 1992, p.124.
234 Paul Ricoeur. *Oneself as Another*. 1992, p.124.

of faith.[235] This *commitment* establishes a living relationship between the believer and God such that one continuously chooses to be in that relationship amidst changes, disappointments or contrary motivations. This is what Ricoeur calls, "the self-constancy necessary for *keeping one's promise*."[236] Here, Moyaert explains that through this commitment, the believer binds his or her life to God, as it were and says, "'whatever happens, I promise to remain faithful to you.'"[237]

Consequently, *ipse*-identity grows from the creative involvement of the adherent in co-fashioning his or her identity within in the community of faith on the one hand and on the other, his or her experience of life and their encounter with *others*. In this way, faithfulness to God is not merely limited to *idem*-identity but it goes beyond just the traditions to seek God where God can be found. In other words, to be a Christian for instance, implies as Moyaert put it, "encountering God in reading the Bible, in performing daily rituals and maintaining the tradition on the one hand and on the other hand, letting God break open the tradition so that God's transcendence does not become fastened down to it."[238] It is being open to where God calls and sends; for God's transcendence means God speaks where God wills, and this could be both within and without one's religious traditions. It is this inspiration which sometimes stimulates the self to want to know and learn from what God is saying in the traditions of the religious other. Since these two poles of identity are operative in the same person, Ricoeur asserts that *narrative identity* keeps the two poles dialectically creative in the fashioning of one's identity. What then is *narrative identity*?

---

235 Marianne Moyaert. *"Fragile Identities."* 2011, p.255.
236 Paul Ricoeur. *Oneself as Another.* 1992, p.119.
237 Marianne Moyaert. "Absorption or Hospitality." 2010, p.80.
238 Marianne Moyaert. "Absorption or Hospitality". 2010, p.80.

2.4 Narrative Identity in the Formation of Personal Identity

According to Ricoeur, personal identity is constituted by the two poles of identity we have discussed above. The *self* is the embodiment of these two poles and *narrative identity* holds them together in the self. Ricoeur believes that there is a relationship between narrative and life. According to him, human life becomes more readable when interpreted in the context of the stories people tell about themselves.[239] Hence, life can be understood narratively. In *Time and Narrative*, Ricoeur demonstrates how narrative identity evolves through his theory of the "threefold mimesis".[240] Although he takes up the same project in *Oneself as Another*, we shall follow closely how this theory serves to elucidate his concept of narrative identity as a mediating principle. The clarity that *Oneself as Another* brings to this context also remains significant to the discourse since Ricoeur reckons that his work in *Oneself as Another* somewhat serves to clarify some of the issues raised in *time and narrative*.[241]

According to Ricoeur, the life of a person or a community is understood through the narratives that they tell about themselves. Narratives are essentially temporal because they can only be mediated through temporal experience.[242] In his analysis of Aristotle's *Poetics* that extends beyond tragedy, Ricoeur focused his attention on *emplotment* and *mimetic activity* to demonstrate the relationship between time and narrative and how human actions are *prefigured, configured*

---

239 Paul Ricoeur. "Narrative Identity" in *Philosophy Today*. 35: 1 (1991), p.73.

240 What is significant in Ricoeur's "theory of mimesis" is that Ricoeur shows the essential relationship between time and narrative. For him, time becomes human to the extent that it is articulated through a narrative, and a narrative attains its full meaning when it becomes the condition of temporal existence (Paul Ricoeur. *Time and Narrative Volume I*. 1984, p.3, 52).

241 Paul Ricoeur. *Oneself as Another*. 1992, p.140.

242 Paul Ricoeur. *Time and Narrative Volume I*. 1984, p.3.

and refigured narratively.[243] For Ricoeur, "imitating or representing is a mimetic activity inasmuch as it produces something, namely, the organization of events by emplotment."[244] The plot is the model of concordance which is characterized by completeness, wholeness and an appropriate magnitude.[245] Concordance also includes discordance in the sense of the phenomenon of a tragic action which Aristotle calls *reversal*. In tragedy, reversal turns good fortunes into bad ones, yet this direction can also be reversed. Hence, the art of composition consists in turning discordance into concordance.[246] Ricoeur demonstrates this through the theory of the threefold mimesis – *mimesis1* refers to *prefiguration*, *mimesis2* refers to *configuration and mimesis3* relates to *refrigeration* or the reader's reception of the narrative composition.

Without the intention to go into the details of these *mimetic activities*,[247] what is significant to note in *mimesis1* is that many events and incidences occur in our lives (prefiguration of narratives). So, to compose a plot of our lives, it is first necessary to take into consideration its semantic, symbolic and temporal structure. In *mimesis2*, Ricoeur shows that the events and the incidents which occur in our lives only make meaning when they are composed into narratives (narrative configuration). In other words, *mimesis2* constitutes the configuration of actions that are accomplished through "emplotment."[248] Understood as "a well-constructed history", *em-*

---

243 Paul Ricoeur. *Oneself as Another.* 1992, p.140-160.

244 Paul Ricoeur. *Time and Narrative Volume I.* 1984, p.34.

245 Paul Ricoeur. *Time and Narrative Volume I.* 1984, p.38.

246 Paul Ricoeur. *Time and Narrative Volume I.* 1984, p.43.

247 For more information on Ricoeur's presentation on the *mimetic activities* as described, read Paul Ricoeur's *Time and Narrative Volume I.* 1984, p.34-43).

248 "Emplotment" is a borrowed term from Aristotle's concept of "composition" which has a double meaning. On the one hand, it could mean a "fable," yet on the other, it also means a "plot" in the sense of a "well-constructed history." Ricoeur borrows the second meaning. (see, Paul Ricoeur. "Life: A Story in Search of a Narrator" in *Facts and Values*. 1986, p.122 & *Oneself as Another*. 1992, p.141-143).

plotment connotes the synthesis of heterogeneous elements like the agent, the action, accidental or anticipated configurations, interactions, means, and the outcomes that are found in a story. Thus, *configuration* as emplotment refers to the art of composition which mediates between concordance and discordance through the, "synthesis of the heterogeneous which accounts for the diverse mediations performed by the plot."[249] Here, the world of action configured by emplotment has an ontological status of "being-as",[250] and "being-as" implies that the world of the narrative is the real world as it is given. But this world can only be reached when the text is received by the reader (*mimesis3*).

Hence, *mimesis3* refers to the reception of the narrative by the reader. It concerns the moment when the narrative is received through dialogue. According to Ricoeur, narratives achieve their full development only in the intersection between the world of the text and the world of the reader – that which Gadamer in a different context calls the *fusion of horizons*.[251] Here, the world of the text unfolds itself through the mediation of the world of the reader. The reader *fulfils* the meaning of the text by *dwelling* in the text's world.[252] As Ricoeur puts it, what is interpreted in the text, "is the proposing of a world that I might inhabit and into which I might project my own most powers."[253] In other words, by reading the narrative, the reader is enriched by the text's world of possibilities. This triggers a mutual dialogue between the world of the text and the world of the reader, which leads to the "fusion of horizons" of the reader and the text. The continual interaction between narrative and reader (implied in

249 Paul Ricoeur. *Oneself as Another*. 1992, p.141.
250 Paul Ricoeur. *Oneself as Another*. 1992, p.80.
251 Hans-Georg Gadamer. *Truth and Methods*. 1990, p.306-307, p.374-375.
252 Paul Ricoeur. "Life: A Story in Search of a Narrator" in *Facts and Values*. 1986, p.126.
253 Paul Ricoeur. *Time and Narrative Volume I*. 1984, p.81.

the interaction within *mimesis1, mimesis2* and *mimesis3*) gives rise to what one might call the *circular mimetic movement* (the hermeneutic circle) in which the prefigured experience of *mimesis1* is configured in *mimesis2* and re-figured in *mimesis3* in a circular or more accurately, in a spiral form.[254] In other words, the experience which comes from the world of action (already mediated by narrative) is configured in narration which in turn re-figures the world of experience. This leads to a continuous enrichment of the world of action.

Ricoeur's notion of *narrative identity* presupposes this mimetic activity — a narrated experience that is mediated by emplotment and re-figured through the reception of narratives. In other words, "to state the identity of an individual or a community is to answer the question, 'who did this?' 'Who is the agent or the author?'"[255] For Ricoeur, the answer to this question resides in narratives. To answer the question *who*? means to tell the story of a life. The story told tells about the action of the *who* and the identity of this *who* is a narrative identity.[256] As a transition from narrative to character, Ricoeur asserts that emplotment is not only applicable to a narrative but also to a character, and personal identity is comparable to the "emplotment of characters".[257] The emplotment of characters consists in the different elements which are commonly present in the story of one's life: a person's interaction with others, the actions that a person performs

254 Paul Ricoeur talks of a "hermeneutic arc" that recognizes the need for a starting point in the hermeneutic process. (See, Paul Ricoeur. *Time and Narrative Volume I.* 1984, p.72; Kevin Vanhoozer. (editor). *Postmodern Theology.* 2003, p.81–82).

255 Paul Ricoeur. *Time and Narrative III.* 1988, p.246.

256 Paul Ricoeur. *Time and Narrative Volume I.* 1984, p.246.

257 Ricoeur sees narrative identity, not just as the "emplotment of action," but also as the "emplotment of characters" where "an emplotted character is someone seeking his or her identity." (Paul Ricoeur. "Pastoral Praxeology, Hermeneutics, and Identity" in *Figuring the Sacred: Religion, Narrative and Imagination.* 1995, p.309).

and his or her physical and psychological features which together constitute the identity of the person.

Hence, *narrative identity* is understood as the formation of one's identity by the integration of one's life experiences into an internalized evolving story of the self which provides the individual with a sense of unity and purpose. It is not a stable or a seamless identity but a continuous effort whereby a *self*-reinterpreting identity is repeated in response to different encounters with different *others*. Ricoeur emphasized here that, "the art of storytelling is the art of exchanging experience."[258] As a result, by narrating the stories of our lives, we soon realize that we are subjects in others' stories and others are subjects in our stories.[259] We discover that our narratives are essentially interwoven with other narratives such that we find ourselves as characters in others' narratives and histories – we are our parents' child, our partner's partner, our friends' friend – and they are characters in our narratives.[260] So, through our encounter with others, we facilitate the articulation and the direction of their narratives and they ours. In this way, identity is continually being formed and the self is involved in this formation in a productive way. It is this productive dimension of the formation of the self which leads to the enrichment of the self. As Moyaert put it, "every believer is called upon to give account to his or her commitments. In and through narration, the believer expresses his or her steadfast fidelity to his or her faith; his or her religious belonging is a continuous choice."[261] Here, narrating the story of one's life is a form of attestation to one's faithfulness.[262]

---

258 Paul Ricoeur. *Oneself as Another*. 1992, p.164.
259 Paul Ricoeur. *Oneself as Another*. 1992, p.141.
260 Paul Ricoeur. "Pastoral Praxeology, Hermeneutics, and Identity" in *Figuring the Sacred: Religion, Narrative and Imagination*. 1995, p.310.
261 Marianne Moyaert. "Absorption or Hospitality". 2010, p.82.
262 Marianne Moyaert. "Absorption or Hospitality". 2010, p.82.

How does the above sense of narrativity apply in the case of Christian–Muslim dialogue on Christology as an exercise in learning? We indicated earlier that dialogue as *an exercise in learning from and about the other* is facilitated by the method of *attestation* whereby Christians and Muslims share their mutual testimonies of faith about the life and mission of Jesus Christ. The purpose here is for the interlocutors to learn and understand the other's narratives about Jesus and be enriched by this learning. It is a form of dialogue where Christians for instance, "are called not just to speak of the God who is revealed in Christ but to listen critically yet with generosity to what is spoken about God by the other."[263] Islam and Christianity have uniquely different narratives about the identity and the mission of Jesus Christ. These narratives are constituted by the *idem* and the *ipse* aspects of the religious identities of their respective believers. So, in sharing the story of one's life with the other, Christians or Muslims are called upon to know and to be committed to the traditions that define their respective understandings of Jesus Christ while being open to listen to the other's narratives about Jesus. Thus, dialogue as an exercise in learning concerns Christian–Muslim mutual exchange of narratives as a means of learning from and about the other's viewpoints. As Ricoeur indicated, by narrating the stories of our lives this way, we discover that our narratives are essentially interwoven with other narratives.

Whereas the intertwinements of Christian and Muslim narratives about Jesus Christ are not the compelling outcome to this form of dialogue, its occurrence is nonetheless celebrated as part of the success of the dialogue. For instance, if dialogue leads to the disclosure of *similarities* or *differences* between the Christologies of the two faith traditions, then dialogue as an exercise in learning is considered successful on the basis of its goal. Furthermore, if dialogue also leads to the discovery of common values, then dialogue is all the more worth pursuing. As its primary goal, dialogue

---

263 Michael Barnes. *Theology and the Dialogue of Religions.* 2002, p.23.

as an exercise in learning focuses on knowing oneself profoundly, knowing the other authentically and living together more creatively.[264] If learning from the other's tradition is supposed to lead
to an enrichment of the self, what becomes the identity of the self
after such learning? In other words, what becomes of the identity of the self who crosses over to a different religious tradition to
learn from them and be enriched by this learning? Does not the
self or the other expose themselves to the danger of losing their
identity through this form of learning? How does Ricoeur resolve
this danger of identity fragmentation in order to give the self a
stable and a definitive identity in its encounter with the other?[265]
Ricoeur resolves this quandary through the attestation of the self.

2.5 Attestation in the Context
   of the Fragility of the Self

From the discourse above on *narrative identity,* Ricoeur indicates
that the formation of personal identity is not stable or seamless
but is a continuous effort whereby a self-reinterpreting identity is repeated in response to different encounters with different
others. This means that I can tell many stories about myself and
read many interpretations into these stories. I can even read the
narratives of my life from different perspectives and evaluate the
stories others tell about me in different ways. So, in these different narratives I make for myself Ricoeur would ask the question;
who am I?[266] For Ricoeur, the variations of the narratives of my

264 Leonard Swidler. *Towards a Universal Theology of Religion.* 1987, p.26.

265 See, Marianne Moyaert for a comprehensive interrogation of these
     issues in her work on *Fragile Identities: Towards a Theology of Interreli-
     gious Hospitality* (2011).

266 See, Paul Ricoeur. "Pastoral Praxeology: Hermeneutics and Identi-
     ty." 1995, p.310.

life make me feel that I have no definitive or stable identity. I am just a bundle of influences that cannot be categorized under a single unit as my identity. If the self or the other has to live with these imaginative variations of itself, then it could be assimilated or absorbed as a consequence of its encounter with the other. How does Ricoeur resolve this problem of the fragmented self?

For Ricoeur, the capacity of the self to promise and to believe that it is the self that is acting and suffering through *attestation and* resolves its fragility to some extent. Through *attestation* the self can choose one narrative over another through its confidence that the chosen narrative better expresses who the self is. The capacity for the self to make such choices is informed by its embodiment as both *idem* and *ipse*. Since *idem* defines the sedimented part of the self, the self is capable of knowing that which conforms to its *idem*-identity and that which is alien to it. Since *ipse*-identity defines the self-maintenance achieved through promise-keeping, then through attestation, the self is capable of attesting to its definitive identity against the variant possibilities of its identity construction. In this way, *narrative identity* is made complete through *attestation*. It is an *attested to* identity – an identity constructed on the credence of the self in a particular narrative configuration as expressive of who the self is. So, in my encounter with the other which exposes me to many possibilities of identity construction; attestation as belief in, a commitment to and credence in, helps me to make informed choices as to which narrative variations conform to my true self identity.

Consequently, the *attested to self* gives the self a foundation from which it encounters the other who equally has an attested to self, a foundation or a tradition of their own. So, by narrating or sharing the story of one's life through dialogue, one witnesses to one's identity as it pertains to their religious tradition constituted by the dialectic interplay of *idem* and *ipse identities*. As indicated earlier, the significance of this sharing of mutual testimonies of faith between the self and the other lies in how this could lead to the discovery of the intersubjective or interconnected character of their narratives or the sharpening of their awareness of how different their respective narratives are to each other. In whichever way this might occur, dialogue as an exercise in learning from and about the other would have been considered successful.

In conclusion, it must be reiterated that Ricoeur never applied *idem, ipse* and *narrative identities* to the specific contexts of Christian-Muslim dialogue on Christology as we have done. As Moyaert indicated, Ricoeur was aware of the problems of interreligious violence and conflicts among the religions. But he never applied his hermeneutics on personal identity to this particular area of interreligious dialogue.[267] Consequently, by applying these aspects of personal identity to issues of interreligious dialogue, the interest is to see how they offer the framework for reflecting on the challenges presented by dialogue as an exercise in learning. Narrating the stories of one's life through dialogue as an exercise in learning helps another to understand and to learn from this story. As a result, learning through the other's narratives contributes to one's understanding of who the other really is, and what informs their worldviews and perceptions of reality. This form of learning inevitably contributes to changing one's perceptions of the other and facilitates a relationship of openness and trust between the self and the other. Within the context of the practice of dialogue, the overarching question is: "what can Christians and Muslims learn from each other from their respective tradition-specific understandings of Christology?"

The form of Christian-Muslim dialogue proposed here is one of Scriptural dialogues on Christology – an engagement between the Qur'an and the Gospels on the identity and the mission of Jesus Christ. Scriptural dialogue in the form proposed here brings with it the challenge of understanding religious texts, doctrines and practices of another religion in the light of the differences that exist between them. Tim Winter indicates that in the settings of the dialogue of scripture, there is, "the challenge of accepting the semiotic reality of the other's universe of meaning

---

267 See, Marianne Moyaert. "Absorption or Hospitality". 2010, p.75.

and relating that to the way our own community discerns the language of God."[268] So, crossing over from one's scriptural tradition to read and understand text in another always brings with it certain challenges. For George Lindbeck and the postliberal school, the *intratextual* nature of religious texts and doctrines do not permit the possibility of crossing over to another's tradition to understand texts without distorting them. If *intratextuality* implies that religious texts are context-driven, does this mean that meaningfulness is absolutely determined intratextually and that one cannot cross over to another tradition to learn texts and doctrines in their original religious context? Let us see how Ricoeur's hermeneutics helps us to traverse the problem of intratextuality to facilitate the understanding of texts across traditions.

2.6 Interreligious Learning and the Problem of Intratextuality

Understanding Christian–Muslim dialogue as an exercise in learning, "takes seriously diversity and tradition, openness and truth, allowing neither to decide the meaning of our religious situation without recourse to the other."[269] It involves the crossing over to another religious tradition to critically understand the rituals, belief-systems, texts, norms and practices of another tradition by critically correlating them with one's own tradition. However, how does interreligious learning pursue this project in the light of the assertion that religious *texts* are *intratextually* determined? By *text,* we mean the written or the spoken discourses which define the identities of the religions. For instance, Islam and Christianity

---

268 Tim Winter. "Scripture in Dialogue I". In: Michael Ipgrave (ed.). *Scriptures in Dialogue: Christians and Muslims Studying the Bible and the Qur'an Together.* 2004, p.43.
269 Francis Clooney. *Comparative Theology.* 2010, p.8.

possess different *classic text* which informs and defines their respective theological understandings of Jesus Christ. As the *Word of God* or the *Word of Allah*, the Bible and the Qur'an enjoy the authority to guide Christians and Muslims respectively in terms of what God demands of them and how they are to order their lives in response to this demand. Even though for both Christians and Muslims, the Bible and the Qur'an are the Word(s) of God, each *text* contains different revelatory experiences, written by different authors, in different linguistic settings and in completely different cultural metric – giving rise to differences in narrative histories and ways of theologizing about God. Into this context of *difference* is Jesus Christ situated; common to both traditions as a historical person, yet different in the way he is construed.

On the one hand, the *differences* in *texts, history and tradition* of both religions signal the fact that the two traditions possess strong elements of *intratextuality*. Hence, it will be an act of immerse naiveté to simply assume that both *sacred texts* mean one and the same thing when engaging in scriptural dialogue on the identity and the mission of Jesus Christ. Yet, on the other hand, the common cognition that Jesus is not only a historical person but one who also uniquely played distinctive roles in both religions as the proclaimer of a unique message of God also draws in some elements of *similarities*.[270] Thus, the question is: should the *similarities* in textual testimonies be compromised for reasons of *difference*? If dialogue as an exercise in learning emphasizes on *commitment* to the home tradition and *openness* to the tradition of the other, then learning across religious traditions is possible because such learning is made possible through the scriptural attestations of the other in respect of the identity and the mission of Jesus Christ. Thus, dialogue as an exercise in learning and defends the *irreducibility* of the identity of the other and asserts the possibility of understanding texts across religious traditions.

---

270 Some similarities in narratives concerning Jesus include: the virginal conception, the miracles Jesus performed and the second coming.

Hence, by engaging George Lindbeck (intratextuality) and Paul Ricoeur (translation) in conversation, we hope to demonstrate how dialogue as an exercise in learning responds to the challenge of *intratextuality*. Whereas we shall acknowledge Lindbeck's view that *religious texts* are *intratextual* to some extent, we shall also argue that one can reach a certain understanding of *texts* through *translation*.[271] For Ricoeur, the power of *translation* makes communicability possible. In other words, translation always presupposes interpretation and t*exts* can be interpreted and understood to some extent. We shall argue that while Lindbeck's intratextual stance serves to remind every theologian about the need to be sensitive to the unique meanings and functions texts play within particular religions, Ricoeur views on *translation* re-engage religious texts in dialogue, aware that there can never be perfect translations.

Intratextuality defines that aspect of hermeneutics which asserts that religious *text* and the meanings are *untranslatable*.[272] *Untranslatability* refers to the understanding that religious meaning is located within a semiotic system. As Moyaert put it, "religious words, practices and experiences derive their meaning from the religious language game from which they function. They can only be understood within their own religious context."[273] Thus, George Lindbeck's *cultural linguistic* theory of religion emphasizes that religions are all-encompassing schemas on the basis of which all reality is given significance: that is a religion is, "a

---

271 By *translation,* we mean the communication of the meaning of texts from its source-language or tradition, to another language or tradition (from the self to the other) for easy comprehension by those outside of the original tradition.

272 Untranslatability refers to the understanding that, text, utterance and language have no equivalent meaning or understanding outside of their contexts. As a consequence, their meaning is only context driven.

273 Moyaert, Marianne. "Absorption or Hospitality." 2010, p.66.

comprehensive interpretive scheme embodied in myths or narratives and are heavily ritualized."[274] Thus, only those who belong to this scheme and share its worldview can experience reality within it.[275] For Lindbeck, the vocabulary of a religion includes symbols, concepts, rites, commandments and stories which only find their rightful meaning within the religion itself as a system.[276] So, the Bible for instance, functions as an authoritative narrative text that creates and imagines its own world and invites people to live in and through this world. Hence, people who *live outside the world of the Bible* cannot properly interpret or understand this world. Here, *meaning* is inseparably connected to *context* which is *intratextually* determined.[277]

In this way, Lindbeck asserted that if Christian language ultimately refers to Christ, then it is only Christians who can understand what it means to love God through Christ.[278] Saving faith is an explicit response to the Gospel of Christ. Thus, the essential task of theology today does not lie in the working out of connections between the Christian *text* and other religious *text,* "but in understanding and describing the internal grammar of Biblical, Christian life, speech and action."[279] As a matter of critique, one could say that Lindbeck's stand on *intratextuality* underscores the need to *respect* the boundaries that separate the religions. Religions possess unique texts, traditions and horizons of interpretation and an understanding of reality. Thus, one

---

274 George Lindbeck. *The Nature of Doctrine: Religion and Theology in a Postliberal Age.* 1984, p.32.

275 It must be emphasized here that, Lindbeck's thesis on *untranslatability* has nothing to do with natural language or the translation of the Bible from Greek to English. His emphasis is on *religious language,* which for him materially constitutes the substitutable memories and the narratives which shape the identity of a religious community (Ibid, p.423).

276 Moyaert, Marianne. *Fragile Identities.* 2011, p.133.

277 George Lindbeck. "The Gospel's Uniqueness." 1997, p.424–426.

278 George Lindbeck. *The Nature of Doctrine.* 1984, p.59.

279 Moyaert, Marianne. "Absorption or Hospitality." 2010, p.67.

could see Lindbeck's position as emphasizing the need to avoid the tendency to homogenise the differences between the religions into neat schemas of commonality. In this way, one would agree with Lindbeck that hermeneutical openness consists in recognising the *distance between the religions* and respecting that distance.[280] However, Lindbeck's radical separation of the religions from each other lives is much to be desired. It only succeeds in inflating the "space-between" the self and the other, disallowing the possibility of dialogue between them. To borrow the words of Moyaert, what is left with Lindbeck's position is, "a broken middle with no hope of reconciliation."[281]

In this way, *intratextuality* poses a difficult challenge to interreligious dialogue as an exercise in learning, in that, it creates a gulf that makes it impossible to cross over to another tradition to learn texts and religious doctrines. Thus, how does the hermeneutics of dialogue as an exercise in learning negotiate this "space-between" to allow the possibility of dialogue between the self and the other? It is in response to these questions that we turn to Ricoeur's view on *translation*. The concept *translation* is commonly understood as the communication of the meaning of *texts* from one language to another. Understood interreligiously, Moyaert asserts that *translation* involves, "explaining, clarifying and elucidating particular religious meanings by searching for correlations and possible analogies between the strange and the familiar language."[282] Thus, the process of translation demands that one does not, "simply remove and abstract words, actions, practices and doctrines out of their original context but reflects precisely on the way they ... are embedded in the broader field of religious meaning."[283] Since translation always involves the explanation of one's own religious texts to another, it constantly

---

280 Marianne Moyaert. "Absorption or Hospitality." 2010.
281 Marianne Moyaert. *Fragile Identities.* 2011, p.68.
282 Marianne Moyaert. *Fragile Identities.* 2013, p.220.
283 Marianne Moyaert. *Fragile Identities.* 2013, p.221.

mediates between the *familiar* and the *strange* in order to make the transfer of meaning possible.[284] If the communication of *meaning* is the goal of translation, then one can say that *translation* applies directly to both the "insider" and the "outsider", since both constantly seek meaning as an exercise in understanding *texts*.

In "Reflections on a New Ethos for Europe",[285] Ricoeur asserts that the *translation* of one language to another, "displays an irreducible pluralism which is infinitely desirable to protect."[286] Europe is neither interested in giving a chance to another Esperanto which threatens it nor giving in to a single cultural language as the only means of communication. Unlike Lindbeck, Ricoeur asserts that the threat to Europe today lies in giving in to, "the danger of incommunicability through a protective withdrawal of each culture into its own linguistic traditions."[287] Since Europe remains ineluctably polyglot, it is *translation* which makes communication possible within its linguistic diversity. A person's mother tongue does not lock him or her in an exclusive ethnic belonging but potentially opens him or her to the whole of humanity. Through our mother tongue, we learn other languages and become acquainted with other cultures.[288] Hence, language is not a closed system but is always in a way, open to what is outside. Language makes dialogue possible and the possibility of dialogue makes mutual understanding and learning possible.

In *On Translation*,[289] Ricoeur takes up the problem of *translatability* and *untranslatability* and seeks to work out the dialectics of the *gain* and the *loss* in meaning in *translation*. He first poses the question: "how is it possible to mediate between two separate languages with different semantic resonances, incompatible

---

284 Marianne Moyaert. *Fragile Identities*. 2013, p.220.
285 Paul Ricoeur. "Reflections on a New Ethos for Europe." 1996, p.3-13.
286 Paul Ricoeur. *Oneself as Another*. 1992, p.4.
287 Paul Ricoeur. *Oneself as Another*. 1992, p.4.
288 Paul Ricoeur. *Freedom and Nature: The Fallible Man*. 1986, p.19.
289 Paul Ricoeur. *On Translation*. 2006.

syntactical structures and different lexical systems?" These differences are so pronounced that they seem to make translation impossible. So, how is the transfer of meaning from one particular language to another possible? For Ricoeur, since a translator is a *go-between* — always mediating between the familiar and the strange, the discourses on *untranslatability* highlights the inevitable problems that translators face in their exercise of translation. The problems lie in the fact that the *strangeness* of the text always presents itself as, a "lifeless block of resistance to translation."[290] This makes the desire for a perfect translation an illusion. But the absence of a perfect translation does not also annul the possibility of translation.[291] In the work of the translator, there is always a tension between what is translatable and what is not — a tension which, "corresponds to the somewhat uncomfortable situation of the translator who serves two masters: the foreign and the familiar."[292] The translator takes a vow of faithfulness to the text and lives constantly with the risk of betrayal. The risk lies in the promise and the commitment of the translator to transfer the actual meaning of the text. Yet the translator is also aware that this exercise of translation involves an inevitable loss of meaning.

Consequently, in the exercise of translation, the translator must be conscious of the dynamic interplay between what is translatable and that which is not. This awareness enables the translator to know that there is never a perfect translation. Yet he or she is called upon to do justice to the text's translation. The constant dialectic interplay between *faithfulness* and *betrayal* in the exercise of translation leads to better translation. This is because while committed to the exercise of translation, the translator's consciousness of the risk of betrayal provides the hermeneutic vigilance needed to render the appropriate transfer of meaning of the text to the other. Within this exchange, Ricoeur asserts that

---

290 Paul Ricoeur. *Oneself as Another*. 1992, p.5.
291 Paul Ricoeur. *Oneself as Another*. 1992, p.14.
292 Marianne Moyaert. *Fragile Identities*. 2011, p.229.

what is demanded is a sense of *active receptivity* where, "the pleasure of dwelling in the other's language is balanced by the pleasure of receiving the foreign word at home, in one's own welcoming home."[293] Here, *translation* is seen as a way of, "living with the *other* in order to take the *other* to one's home as a guest."[294] It entails making room for the strange other in one's space or receiving the other in a way that does justice to their *alterity*. It is against this background of Ricoeur's hermeneutics of hospitality that we consider religious texts to be translatable, interpretable and rendered meaningful to the other.

In this way, since *translation* makes the communication of the meaning of texts to another possible, one can learn from Qur'anic or Biblical texts on the *identity* and the *mission* of Jesus Christ through translation which is made possible by experts and adherents of the religious tradition to which they belong. Often, this is made possible through the interpretation of meaning brought to them by Islamic commentators and Christian scriptural scholars and theologians. Whereas these scholars provide the *insiders'* point of view on the tradition-specific meanings of the texts concerned, it is through dialogue as an exercise in learning that the other is enabled to know the meanings of texts that are considered intratextually defined. For Ricoeur, to understand is to translate because translation makes meaning possible.[295]

The understanding of meaning made possible through translation, also enables the dialogical interlocutors to discern differences or similarities in the meanings of their scriptural texts on the identity and the mission of Jesus Christ. It is this acquisition of meaning through dialogue as an exercise in learning which leads to the enrichment or to the transformation of the dialogical parties. As Moyaert put it, "the gain of translation is the

---

293 Paul Ricoeur. *On Translation*. 2006, p.10.

294 Paul Ricoeur. "Reflections on a New Ethos for Europe." 1996, p.5.

295 Paul Ricoeur. *On Translation*. 2006, p.11; see also, Marianne Moyaert. *Fragile Identities*. 2011, p.232.

nourishment of the familiar with the unknown and hence keeping the familiar alive." Translation, "has the potentiality of opening people to new horizons of meaning."[296] What is necessary is the interlocutors' openness to receive the wealth of meaning offered by the text. In respect of the intersubjectivity in textual meanings, Scott Holland indicates that, "the critical and the analogical reading of texts discloses numerous points of intersection with other texts."[297]

2.7 Conclusion

From discourses in Chapter One, we did acknowledge along with other scholars (namely Anselm Min, Gavin D'Costa and Michael Barnes) that the three traditional paradigms of interreligious dialogue are inadequate in meeting the needs of our current context of interreligious dialogue. Today, not only are we called to be respectful to the voice of the other about their religious beliefs, but dialogue also demands that we learn from what the other has to say about their beliefs. This explained why dialogue as an exercise in learning was deemed the appropriate method of interfaith engagement today. While it involves the crossing over to another's religious tradition to learn and understand texts, doctrines and practices as they pertain to their original tradition-specific contexts, it also affirms the significance of the commitment of the adherent to religious beliefs and practices of the home tradition. By way of reiteration, we indicated that the goal of this form of dialogue is: (1) to reach knowledge of one's tradition, (2) to reach an authentic knowledge of the other's tradition and, (3) to live together with the other in more meaningful and creative ways.

---

296 Marianne Moyaert. *Fragile Identities*. 2011, p.231.
297 Scott Holland. *How Do Stories Save Us?* 2006, p.90.

In this current chapter, we demonstrated how Ricoeur's hermeneutics on personal identity provided the framework for addressing the challenges presented by dialogue as an exercise in learning. It showed how the narrative self is in one way or another, connected to the narratives of others, such that in narrating the stories of our lives, we find that others contribute to our narratives and we to theirs. This understanding of narrative identity demonstrated how Jesus Christ is at once common to Christianity and Islam as a historical person, and yet, is understood differently between them. While *attestation* is the "password" to Ricoeur's hermeneutics of the self, it opens up a new form of Christian-Muslim dialogue where dialogue is viewed as the sharing of mutual testimonies. Here, the dialogical context is more of a statement of confidence and conviction in what one believes while being open to listen to and learn from the faith testimonies of the other. As Kaplan put it, Ricoeur's dialogue, "presupposes the ability to take the perspective of the other, learn from one another, communicate and convince each other and reach an understanding over generalizable interests."[298] While this remains the case, understanding and accepting difference also forms part of the Ricoeurean hermeneutic motif. So, we asserted that when Christian-Muslim dialogue on Christology is defined by attestation, it is more likely to be constructive and beneficial.

Ricoeur further explains how *self-esteem* or *self-respect* transforms into *solicitude* or *esteem* or *respect* for others at the interpersonal levels and at the level of institutions under what he called the *ethical intention*. What follows in Chapter Three is a demonstration of how Ricoeur developed these themes and how they provide the appropriate context for reflecting on the possible challenges posed by engaging Christians and Muslims in dialogue on Christology as an exercise in learning. By so doing, Chapter Three also demonstrates how these themes provide clarity on the sort of dialogical attitudes needed for Christian-Muslim dialogue

---

298 Kaplan, David, M. *Ricoeur's Critical Theory*. 2003, p.99.

on Christology as an exercise in learning from and about the other. In concert, while Chapter Two provided the epistemological grounds which support the engagement between the self and the other in contexts where they are considered estranged, Chapter Three provides the ethical validity for this engagement.

CHAPTER THREE
ETHICAL AND MORAL IMPLICATIONS
OF NARRATIVE IDENTITY

3.1 Introduction

From the discourse in Chapter Two, it was asserted that despite the contentious nature of Christology in Christian-Muslim relations both in the past and the present, dialogue as an exercise in learning negotiates these contentions to facilitate effective Christian-Muslim conversations on the subject. Though Islam and Christianity construe the identity and the mission of Jesus Christ differently, Jesus still remains a common historical person who plays distinctive roles in both religious traditions. For instance, not only do Muslims view him as the "Word of Allah" in the Qur'an (Surah 3: 45), he is also perceived as the precursor and the guarantor of the coming of the Prophet Muhammad (Surah 62: 6). For Christians, Jesus does not only proclaim the "Word of God", but he is the "proclaimed Word" itself and the "Saviour of the World". Thus, between Christianity and Islam, one finds some similarities and differences in their Christological understandings. Hence, dialogue as an exercise in learning offers the best opportunity to explore the deeper meanings and significance of both the Qur'anic portrayals of Jesus and the Biblical accounts of the historical Jesus who is shared by both religious traditions but divided between them.

Ricoeur's hermeneutics on personal identity provided the under structure for negotiating the observed estranged relationship between the self and the other. This estranged relationship is highlighted by the contradistinctions between the Christian and the Muslim views on Christology. Even though Ricoeur did not directly address issues relating to Christian-Muslim dialogue on Christology, he nonetheless offers the hermeneutic framework which supports reflections on the challenges presented by the encounter between the self and the other. Here, Ricoeur emphasised that selfhood implies otherness such that selfhood and otherness cannot be separated. While this *intertwinement* between the self and the other points to the possibility of the interrelationship between them, fundamental to this relationship are the ethical and the moral underpinnings to it. In what is considered his "little ethics" which he articulates in what he calls the *ethical intention*, Ricoeur discusses the ethical and the moral implications in the encounter between the self and the other. He defines the "ethical intention" as "aiming at the good life with and for others in just institutions."[299]

Ricoeur divides his "ethical intention" into three components: (1) *the good life*; (2) *with and for others*; and (3) *just institutions*. These three components correspond to self-esteem, to self-respect, to solicitude, respect for others and equality. In a context where Christology continues to pose difficult theological and doctrinal challenges which seem to impede the possibility of dialogue between Christians and Muslims, Ricoeur's "little ethics" offers the framework for reflecting on the appropriate dialogical attitudes that are necessary for engaging Christians and Muslims in dialogue on Christology as an exercise in learning. Through these reflections, not only does Ricoeur's *ethical intention* bring clarity to the challenges posed by the encounter between the self and the other, it also offers the way forward in terms of the ethical and the moral issues which support the constructive engagements between them. It must be reiterated that Ricoeur's hermeneutic views do not provide direct answers to the challenges posed by Christian-Muslim dialogue on Christology as an exercise in learning. They only provide the framework for reflecting on these challenges in the quest to find better ways of engaging the two traditions in positive and constructive dialogues. Consequently, whereas Chapter Two focused on the epistemological validity for engaging Christians and Muslims on dialogue

---

299 Paul Ricoeur. *Oneself as Another.* 1992, p.172.

on Christology, Chapter Three focuses on the ethical and the moral implications to this engagement.

Douglas Pratt reports that from the fifteenth to the eighteenth century and beyond, "the attitude between Christianity and Islam [towards each other] oscillated between indifference and hostility."[300] Jean-Marie Gaudeul explains that both Islam and Christianity at this time, "shared the same planet but mentally they lived in different worlds and as time went on, the mental universe of each society grew impervious to the thinking, the values and the motivations and indeed the whole mental universe of the other."[301] Here, while Christians viewed Islam as another form of heresy which has to be eradicated, if need be; Muslims perceived Christianity as a distorted religion which has lost its sense of God through its alignment with western powers.[302] Although today, there are more efforts at engaging the two religions in dialogue, sufficient attention has not been directed to the problem of "dialogical attitudes" – that is, the sort of *balanced attitude* defined by commitment to the religious beliefs in one's tradition and openness to learning from those of the other. As the Pontifical Council for Interreligious dialogue indicated, this form of commitment and openness, "includes both witness and the exploration of respective religious convictions."[303]

However, the attitude that often characterizes Christian-Muslim dialogue on Christology both past and present is one of "claim and counterclaim" and in the end, the mutual dismissal of the

---

300 Douglas Pratt. *The Challenge of Islam.* 2005, p.113.

301 Gaudeul, Jean-Marie. *Encounters and Clashes: Islam and Christianity in History.* 1990, p.191.

302 Pratt reports that between Christianity and Islam at the time, one finds "evidence aplenty of enmity, of dismissive, derogatory prejudice that makes of the religious other an enemy to be fought and vanquished." (Douglas Pratt. *The Challenge of Islam.* 2005, p.117).

303 Pontifical Council for Interreligious Dialogue and Proclamation: *Numbers 9 and 47* https://astro.temple.edu/~swidler/swidlerbooks/ universal_theology.htm (29/02/2020).

other's claims on the subject. Thus, in proposing the contexts for dialogue between them, some scholars suggest a form of dialogue on the ethics of Jesus as a means of avoiding the Christological contentions. As Beaumont put it, "since belief in the status of Jesus Christ causes disputes between Christians and Muslims, it might seem simpler to avoid dialogue on his status and discuss his teachings instead."[304] But does not the status of Jesus serve as the basis from which his teachings derive their authority and their authenticity? Dialogue on the teachings of Jesus cannot possibly avoid his status since the status of Jesus, for instance, grants him the authority to instruct Christians about the will of God and the human response to it. Thus, Christian-Muslim dialogue on Christology must first begin from the status of Jesus and proceed to his teachings. This procession from the status of Jesus to the ethics he espouses is made possible through the cultivation of certain "dialogical attitudes". It is here that Ricoeur's "little ethics" provides the appropriate framework for reflecting on what is considered in this study as *the appropriate dialogical attitudes* to interreligious dialogue as an exercise in learning – namely, *commitment* to one's tradition, *openness to* and *respect for the traditions of the other* and viewing the other as an *equal-partner-in-dialogue*.

3.2 The Ethical and the Moral Dimension of Narrative Identity

We indicated that Ricoeur's hermeneutics of personal identity (whether at the level of the individual or the community) is constituted by two modes of identity: *idem and ipse* identities.[305] While the *idem* is a sedimented form of permanence in time and does not change, the *ipse* aspect of personal identity is a form of

---

304 Mark Beaumont. *Christology in Dialogue with Muslims*. 2005, p.211.
305 See also Marianne Moyaert. "Absorption or Hospitality". 2010, p.77.

permanence in time that is innovative and thus subject to renewal, transformation and enrichment. From the perspective of the dialectics of *idem* and *ipse* identities, Ricoeur identifies the ethical dimension of *idem*-identity as symbolised by the phenomenon of *character* by which a person is identified and reidentified. *Ipse*-identity is however represented by the ethical notion of *self-constancy* – that manner of conducting *myself* so that others can *count on me*. "Because someone is counting on me, I am *accountable for* my actions before another."[306] Hence, between "counting on" and "being accountable for", Ricoeur discerns the idea of *responsibility* which unites both terms such that in the question; "where are you?" which is posed by the other who needs me, the response, "here I am" becomes a statement of self–constancy.[307]

However, to the question: how can we bridge the gap between the *narrative identity* question: "who am I?" and the moral identity response "here I am!" for the benefit of their living dialectics, Ricoeur's response is: the answer "here I am!" implies that I recognize myself as a subject of *imputation*. So, between "the imagination that says, 'I can try anything' and the voice that says everything is possible, but not everything is beneficial, a muted discord is sounded. It is this discord that the act of promising transforms into a fragile concordance: 'I can try anything,' to be sure, but 'here is where I stand!'"[308] This affirmative sense of the self, underscores the self–constancy implied in the *ipse* identity and hence the *attested to self*.

We indicated in Chapter Two that *attestation* changes dialogue from debates, argumentations, and confrontations to the *mutual sharing of testimonies*. As an exercise in learning, we indicated that interreligious dialogue involves crossing–over to another's religious tradition to learn and to understand texts, doctrines and practices. As the *Pontifical Council for Interreligious Dialogue and Proclamation*

---

306 Paul Ricoeur. *Oneself as Another*. 1992, p.165.
307 Paul Ricoeur. *Oneself as Another*. 1992, p.165.
308 Paul Ricoeur. *Oneself as Another*. 1992, p.167-168.

indicated, this form of dialogue involves, "'all positive and constructive interreligious relations with individuals and communities of other faiths which are directed at mutual understanding and enrichment', in obedience to truth and respect for freedom."[309] Thus, dialogue always involves the crossing over to another religious tradition to learn from and about them. This act of *crossing* usually raises some ethical and moral questions on the im/possibility of crossing religious boundaries to understand texts, doctrines and practices as they pertain to their original religious contexts, the religious allowance for such crossing and one's response to *difference*. In other words, what ethical and moral principles best serve the interest of dialogue as an exercise in learning when confronted by the reality of *difference* in the religions?

In response, Richard Kearney indicates that, "if ethics rightly requires me to respect the singularity of the other person, it equally requires me to recognize the *other* as another self ... capable of recognizing me in turn as a *self*, capable of respect and esteem."[310] While Kearney's view may hold true, Ricoeur demonstrates in his "little ethics" the kind of attitudes the *self* and the *other* must cultivate towards each other in the accomplishment of the *ethical intention*. For Ricoeur, *self-esteem, self-respect, respect for others* and *equality* are significant factors for living out the "good life."[311] Whereas Ricoeur's "ethical intention" will be used as the context for reflecting on the meaning and the significance of dialogical attitudes such as *commitment, openness, respect* and *equality* in dialogue as an exercise in learning. It must be said again that

---

309 Pontifical Council for Interreligious Dialogue and Proclamation: *Numbers 9* https://astro.temple.edu/~swidler/swidlerbooks/universal_theology.htm (29/02/2020).

310 Richard Kearney. *Strangers, Gods and Monsters.* 2003, p.80.

311 Paul Ricoeur's notion of the "good life" captures Aristotle's notion of *"eudaemonia"* which connotes "happiness," "living well" or "human flourishing." In Book One of the *Nichomachean Ethics,* Aristotle views every action or decision as directed towards achieving something good.

his ethical intention does not provide direct answers to the challenges posed by the dialogical encounter between Christians and Muslims on Christology. They only offer the framework for reflecting on these challenges.

In his ethics of the self, Ricoeur attempts to justify the primacy of the Aristotelian teleological aim (the ethical aim) over the Kantian deontological moment (the moral norm). On the one hand, Aristotle's teleological aim derives moral duty or obligation from whatever is good and desirable as an end to be achieved. Also referred to as the *consequentialist ethics*, it emphasizes actions that should be judged right or wrong on the basis of their outcome.[312] On the other hand, Kant's deontological ethics holds that the basic characteristics of morally right actions go beyond what is merely good or desirable or otherwise. Here, an action is considered good on the basis of the action itself and not on the basis of its consequence.[313] Between these two forms of ethics, Ricoeur develops "practical wisdom" (*phronesis*) as the non-synthetic third term which helps in rendering appropriate and just judgement in the living out of the "good life" especially in morally aporetic situations. As Kaplan put it, Ricoeur designed his "little ethics" in two axes: "the horizontal axis of moral philosophy refers to the dialogical constitution of the self in relation to others socially and politically, as friends and as citizens; the vertical axis refers to the predicates we attribute to agents and acts such as 'good' or 'obligation'."[314]

In following Ricoeur's "little ethics", the interest is not to re-*present* Ricoeur's work on how Aristotelian teleology (ethics) mediates Kantian deontology (morality), but to show how in the course of doing this, Ricoeur provides a hermeneutic framework

312 See, The Editor of the Encyclopaedia Britannica: https://www.britannica.com/topic/teleological-ethics (15/03/2020).

313 See, The Editor of the Encyclopaedia Britannica: https://www.britannica.com/topic/deontological-ethics (15/03/2020).

314 David Kaplan. *Ricoeur's Critical Theory*. 2003, p.101.

for reflecting on the meanings and the significance of *commitment, openness, reciprocity of respect* and *equality* as constructive "dialogical attitudes"[315] best suited for dialogue as an exercise in learning. In a world where there is increasing acceptance of the plurality of religions and the awareness of the potential blessings the religions could bring to human society, the goal of dialogue as a desire to live the "good life" with and for the others in just institutions cannot be understated. Let us see how Ricoeur achieves this form of ethical self in the encounter with the other.

3.3. Ricoeur and the Concepts of Ethics and Morality

Unlike common practices where people use "ethics" and "morality" interchangeably, Ricoeur draws clear distinctions between the two terms. For him whereas "ethics" defines that which *is considered to be good,* "morality" concerns that which *imposes itself as obligation.* While ethics attempts to answer the question *how should I live?* morality responds to the question *what must I do?* In this way, ethics focuses on the "aim of an accomplished life", while morality focuses on "the articulation of this aim into norms."[316] The former is predicated on "good" or the question of "what is?" while the latter is based on "obligation" or the question of "what ought to be?"[317] In terms of the relationship between the two, Ricoeur emphasizes on the primacy of the Aristotelian *teleological* perspective (ethics) over the Kantian *deontological* point of view (morality). So, between ethics and morality, Ricoeur asserts "(1) the primacy of ethics over morality, (2) the necessity for the ethical aim to pass through the sieve of the norm, and (3) the

---

315 By "constructive dialogical attitudes", we mean the necessary conditions which make dialogue as an exercise in learning possible.

316 Paul Ricoeur. *Oneself as Another.* 1992, p.170.

317 Paul Ricoeur. *Oneself as Another.* 1992, p.170.

legitimacy of recourse by the norm to the ethical aim whenever the norm leads to impasses in practice."[318] Morality is perceived here as a limited form of ethics since ethics encompasses morality. While being subordinate to ethics, morality is necessary for the actualization of ethics. This final recourse of morality to ethics occurs through what Ricoeur calls *Phronesis* – a form of practical wisdom geared towards the appropriate application of universal norms in particular situations. But how is the discourse on ethics and morality linked to Ricoeur's examination of selfhood?

Ricoeur demonstrates the link between ethics, morality and selfhood by situating the teleological aim and the deontological moment within the predicates of "good" and "obligation" respectively. He sees the teleological aim to correspond to "self-esteem" while the deontological moment corresponds to "self-respect". Following the same pattern which defines the relationship between ethics and morality, Ricoeur asserted the following: "(1) that self-esteem is more fundamental to the development of selfhood than self-respect; (2) self-respect is the aspect under which self-esteem appears in the domain of norms; and (3) in the aporias of duty where no norm provides guidance for the exercise *hic et nunc* of respect, self-esteem becomes not only the source but a recourse for self-respect."[319] In this way, self-esteem and self-respect together represent the most advanced stages of the growth of selfhood, and it is impossible to conceive a moral self without reference to the other. To demonstrate how this ethical or moral self is connected to the other, Ricoeur traces the notion of the self with respect to itself, to others, and even to the anonymous third parties both on the ethical and on the moral planes. He then demonstrates how the *autonomy of the self* is, "tightly bound up with *solicitude* for one's neighbour and with *justice* for each individual."[320] Let us, at this point, attend to these hermeneutic issues

---

318 Paul Ricoeur. *Oneself as Another.* 1992, p.170.
319 Paul Ricoeur. *Oneself as Another.* 1992, p.171.
320 Paul Ricoeur. *Oneself as Another.*1992, p.18.

following Ricoeur's lead. Here, the focus is on the three components of the *ethical intention* as expounded below.

3.3.1 The Hermeneutics of the Self and the Ethical Aim

Ricoeur defines the "ethical intention" as: *aiming at the "good life" with and for others, in just institutions*. He finds in this definition, three essential components of the ethical intention: (1) aiming at a "good life"; (2) "with and for others"; and (3) "in just institutions." As we shall see, whereas the "good life" on its own does not directly refer to selfhood in relation to otherness, the "good life" lived "with and for others" finds itself within a dialogic structure where the *self* and the *other* meet at the interpersonal level (solicitude). However, at the level of institutions (the plurality of society) where relationships are not necessarily interpersonal, the *principle of justice and equality* goes beyond the limitations of solicitude to ensure *justice* and *equality* for all in social life. It is here that we find *self-esteem, solicitude and equality* as providing the hermeneutic framework for reflecting on *commitment, openness, respect* and the virtue of *equal-part-ners-in-dialogue* as necessary conditions for dialogue as an exercise in learning. What follows below is a brief consideration of these ethical components.

3.3.1.1 Aiming at the "Good Life"

As we indicated earlier, Ricoeur's notion of the "good life" also refers to what Aristotle called "living well." For him, every action and decision are always directed towards the good; that which MacIntyre understood as internally good in-itself. A good life is that which everyone seeks to achieve because of its *internal goodness* in other words those actions which are "good–in–themselves".[321] Hence, to say that a person is *good* is to think of the person in terms of virtue, and a *virtue* is the quality a person acquires which enables him or her to achieve the internal good to practice. Here, the notion of *good* is understood as *internal good* immanent to practice, gives "support for the reflexive moment of self-esteem, to the extent that it is in appraising our actions that we appraise ourselves as being their author."[322] On the question of *life*, Ricoeur considers *life* as denoting, "the biologic rootedness of life and the unity of the person as a whole, as the person casts upon himself or herself the gaze of appraisal."[323] Put together, Ricoeur sees the "good life" as "the nebulous of ideals and dreams of achievements with regard to which a life is held to be more or less fulfilled or unfulfilled."[324] It is the idea of a higher finality which never ceases to be internal to human action. The "good life" is itself an ideal and a standard of excellence which sets a limit to how I should live and how we should live together.[325] It is the standard of excellence which provides the basis for my self-esteem. For Ricoeur, the pursuit of this higher finality (the good life) comes with the practical choices we make for ourselves.

Here, between the aim of the "good life" and the "practical choices" we make, a sort of hermeneutic circle is traced by the back–and–forth motion between the idea of the "good life" and the most important decisions we make for our existence.[326] This back and forth movement is comparable to the interpretations of a text in which the whole and the parts can be understood in terms of the other, in other words the agent who interprets the text of an action is, by so doing, also interpreting himself or

---

321 David Kaplan. *Ricoeur's Critical Theory.* 2003, p.103.
322 Paul Ricoeur. *Oneself as Another.* 1992, p.177.
323 Paul Ricoeur. *Oneself as Another.* 1992, p.178.
324 Paul Ricoeur. *Oneself as Another.* 1992, p.179.
325 David Kaplan. *Ricoeur's Critical Theory.* 2003, p.103.
326 Paul Ricoeur. *Oneself as Another.* 1992, p.179.

herself. This "self-interpretation becomes self-esteem"[327] in the sense that "the interpretations and the choices I make about how I should live my life and attain my ideals involve an understanding of who I am and who I want to become."[328] So, "I am capable of evaluating my actions, assessing my goals and determining if they are good, just as I am capable of evaluating, assessing and determining if I am good."[329] To determine whether I am good or not is not achieved through scientific investigations because living the "good life" is internal to the self. For Ricoeur, the search for the adequation of the interpretation of the character of a person, "involves an exercise of judgement which, at best, can aspire to plausibility in the eyes of the other."[330] In other words, it is the judgement of the other which helps in determining whether I live the "good life". This connection to the other situates "self-esteem" and the "good life" within a dialogic structure which constitutes the second component of Ricoeur's ethical intention. But before we attend to the dialogic structure of self-esteem, let us attempt to situate this Ricoeurean understanding of self-esteem within the context of *commitment* as a necessary condition for dialogue as an exercise in learning.

Many religious traditions have structures which ensure the transmission of religious beliefs, doctrines, customs and practices from one generation to the other. While belief-systems or doctrines define the nature of the "constitutive rules" which one must follow if one is to be considered a member of the religious community, "standards of excellence" point to the outcomes that correspond to the living out the belief-systems of the religion. Thus, to subscribe to a particular religion (Christian or Muslim) is to acknowledge by so doing that, one believes in its doctrines and its practices as capable of providing the necessary guidance

---

327 Paul Ricoeur. *Oneself as Another*. 1992, p.179.
328 David Kaplan. *Ricoeur's Critical Theory*. 2003, p.103.
329 David Kaplan. *Ricoeur's Critical Theory*. 2003, p.103-104.
330 Paul Ricoeur. *Oneself as Another*. 1992, p.180.

to living the "good life", also understood as, "life in submission to God's will". This explains why a considerable knowledge of a religion must precede one's choice to belong to it. Even in the case of "infant baptism" where babies become full members of the Catholic Church through the waters of baptism, this exercise is made possible on the basis of the *informed consent* of the parents who act on behalf of their children. Informed consent presupposes reasonable knowledge of what one is consenting to. Children who are baptised as infants are then taught to know and live the faith as they grow.

Thus, the emphasis on the acquisition of religious knowledge through catechesis or religious instruction is because of the understanding that; knowledge of one's religious tradition is the basis for *commitment* to it. Therefore, the motivation for sticking to one's religious tradition thus emanates from one's esteem for that tradition as capable of providing the necessary guidance for living the "good life" or the life lived according to God's will. So, the sense of esteem for one's religion represents this confidence in its belief-systems. Such a realisation, so to speak, informs and inspires one's *commitment* to both the *idem* and the *ipse*-dimensions of the identity of the religious tradition, aware that in being faithful to God (through this tradition) amidst changes, disappointments and other contrary opinions (the *ipse*), one is following the path to a good life, a life lived in accordance to God's will. In this way, we could say that self-esteem or the esteem for one religious tradition leads to one's *commitment* to it.

While we shall later develop *commitment to the home tradition* as a necessary condition for dialogue, it is essential to mention here that where *religious commitment* is affirmed, the best way to engage in dialogue with the other is through the exercise of learning. Through learning from each other, the interlocutors get to know each other's beliefs-systems and the theological frameworks which support their sense of commitment to the belief-system in their respective religious traditions. As we indicated earlier, *attestation* which is understood as the mutual sharing of testimonies of faith shapes and directs this form of dialogue as an exercise in learning. Even though this response to faith through commitment appears to lie in the choice of the individual believer, the believer is also acutely aware that he or she does not live in isolation, but in a community with other believers who may or may not belong to the same religious tradition. So, how does *commitment to* or the *esteem for* one's religious tradition open up to the esteem for others in the second component of the ethical intention?

3.3.1.2 The Good life "with and for others"

Ricoeur considers *solicitude* as the second component of the "ethical intention". It defines the dialogic structure of self-esteem expressed in the concern for the other or the desire to live the "good life" with others. Here, the self and the other are linked to such an extent that one cannot be reflected upon without reference to the other.[331] As we shall see, when taken in its symmetrical form, *solicitude* emerges as a kind of Aristotelian *friendship* which expresses the mutual and the reciprocal relationship between the self and the other. However, when taken in its asymmetrical form as in the Levinasian sense of the infinite other who summons me to responsibility without reciprocity, *solicitude* emerges as "benevolent spontaneity" or a *sympathy* which is expressed by the desire to understand and to experience the world as the other sees it. But how do we tease out a dialogic structure of self-esteem when we know that the reflexivity of self-esteem carries with it the danger of turning in upon oneself or closing up on openness? In other words, how does the reflexivity of self-esteem connect with solicitude which expresses the reciprocity of openness and concern for the other? In response, Ricoeur asserts that, "solicitude is not something added on to self-esteem from the outside, but it unfolds the dialogic dimension of self-esteem, which up

---

331 Paul Ricoeur. *Oneself as Another*. 1992, p.180.

to now has been passed–over in silence."[332] To justify this claim, Ricoeur turns his attention to Aristotle's analysis of *friendship* in order to demonstrate how the self is dialogically constituted and why we need each other to be able to live the "good life".

According to Ricoeur, Aristotle understands *friendship* as, "a mutual reciprocal relationship that is the highest good towards which life and actions and therefore happiness and pleasure, are oriented."[333] Friendship is based on self–love which is a form of refined *egotism* (*philautia*) because one cares for one's friend for the same reason that one cares for oneself. Two premises are drawn here in the way *egotism* (self–love) is mediated by friendship. The first is that friendship is essentially equivocal and can only be clarified by recourse to its true object i.e. *phil ta* (love).[334] Here, Aristotle says that there are three objects of love: the *good,* the *pleasant and* the *useful*; and that these three objects correspond to three forms of friendship (friendship of *utility,* of *pleasure* and the *good*).[335] The second premise is that, "regardless of the place of *philautia* (self–love) in the genesis of friendship, the latter presents itself from the outset as a *mutual* relationship."[336] Here, *reciprocity* is part of its content because it extends to the commonality of "living together" or in mutual intimacy. This sense of *mutuality* has its own requirements which are different from those eclipsed by the Husserlian notion of the *same* and the Levinasian notion of the infinite *other*. In this form of mutuality, "each loves the other *as being the man he is",*[337] which is different from friend-

---

332 Paul Ricoeur. *Oneself as Another.* 1992, p.180.

333 David Kaplan. *Ricoeur's Critical Theory.* 2003, p.204.

334 Paul Ricoeur. *Oneself as Another.* 1992, p.182.

335 These forms of friendships are: "friendship of utility" (friendship between me and someone who is useful to me in some way), "friendship of pleasure" (friendship between me and someone whose company I enjoy) and "friendship of the good" (friendship based on mutual respect).

336 Paul Ricoeur. *Oneself as Another.* 1992, p.183.

337 Paul Ricoeur. *Oneself as Another.* 1992, p.183.

ship based on *utility* and on *pleasure*. The use of the comparative phrase "*as being*" here expresses the sense of being as the other is. *As being* averts any egoistic leanings by its mutual constitution. In this way, "the reflexivity of oneself is not abolished but is, as it were, split into two by mutuality."[338]

Thus, Ricoeur retains from Aristotle an ethics of reciprocity, sharing and living together whereby friendship adds reciprocity/mutuality to self-esteem. For Ricoeur, "the friend inasmuch as he is the other self of oneself, has the other role of providing what one is incapable of procuring for oneself."[339] So, whereas self-esteem is the primordial reflexive moment of the aim of the good life, friendship makes a contribution to self-esteem without taking anything away. It introduces the idea of *reciprocity* in the exchange between human beings who both esteem each other. In contrast to this Aristotelian concept of friendship is the Levinasian notion of the command of the face of the other who establishes asymmetry with the self. If *solicitude* and *reciprocity* apply to someone who is a friend to me, then what about someone who is not a friend to me; how does solicitude apply in *dissymmetrical* relations? As we saw earlier in Chapter Two, Levinas asserts that the other summons me to responsibility without reciprocity because the other is exterior to me, separate from me and unequal to me. Following Levinas, Ricoeur uses this notion of the *dissymmetrical other* to demonstrate how a new sense of solicitude is established through *benevolent spontaneity*[340] which is intimately connected to self-esteem.

Whereas the Aristotelian sense of friendship is structured on the basis of *giving and receiving;* on the basis of benevolent spontaneity, Ricoeur asserts that *receiving* is placed on an equal footing with the summons to responsibility where the self recognizes the superiority of the other who enjoins him or her to act in

---

338 Paul Ricoeur. *Oneself as Another.* 1992, p.183.
339 Paul Ricoeur. *Oneself as Another.* 1992, p.185.
340 Paul Ricoeur. *Oneself as Another.* 1992, p.188.

accordance with justice.[341] This sense of "equal footing" is not the same as that of friendship in which *giving* and *receiving* are well balanced. Rather, "it compensates for the initial dissymmetry resulting from the primacy of the other in the situation of instruction, through the reverse movement of recognition."[342] Here, the other's inability to reciprocate is viewed as "suffering". *Suffering* here is not the same as experiencing physical or mental pain, but a reduction in the other's *capacity for acting or being-unable-to-act*. The other's incapacity to act is seen as a violation of its integrity because; we are by nature created with the capacity to *give* and to *receive*. With the Levinasian other, the full capacity to act only resides in the self who *gives* his *sympathy* and his compassion by sharing in the pain of the other who lacks the capacity to *give*. Because the Levinasian other is reduced to the condition of only *receiving* without being-able-to *give,* the self is assigned the responsibility of caring for the other by *giving* without expecting.

As a mark of true *sympathy*, "the self whose power of acting is greater than its other, finds itself affected by all that the suffering other offers to it in return. From the suffering other becomes a giving that is no longer drawn from the power of acting and existing, but precisely from weakness itself."[343] Ricoeur indicates that the supreme test of *solicitude* can be located in this act of giving without receiving. For him, it is here that one finds a virtuous friend.[344] He concluded this second component by emphasizing that I cannot have self-esteem unless I esteem others *as myself*. "As myself" means that "you too are capable of starting something in the world, of acting for a reason, of hierarchizing your priorities, of evaluating the ends of your actions and, having done this, holding yourself in esteem as I hold myself in

341 Paul Ricoeur. *Oneself as Another*. 1992, p.190.
342 Paul Ricoeur. *Oneself as Another*. 1992, p.190.
343 Paul Ricoeur. *Oneself as Another*. 1992, p.191.
344 Paul Ricoeur. *Oneself as Another*. 1992, p.191.

esteem."[345] In this way, in the equivalence between the "you too" and the "as myself" lies a trust that is held as an extension of the *attestation* that I can do something and therefore have worth. This equivalence expresses, "the esteem of the *other as oneself* and the esteem of *oneself as an-other.*"[346] How does this dialogical sense of the "self" apply in an interreligious dialogical context?

We indicated earlier that one's esteem for a particular religion is first of all preceded by one's knowledge and conviction in its ability to provide guidance for living the "good life". This knowledge and conviction becomes the basis for the establishment of one's *commitment* to a particular religious tradition. Living the "good life" is not done in isolation but in a community with other believers who also share similar convictions and *commitments* to the religion, albeit the degree. Hence, we can talk of the Christian community or the *Muslim Ummah* (the Islamic community) as constitutive of people who are committed to the belief-systems of their respective religious traditions. Take for instance the *Muslim Ummah* in the light of the individual's relationship to it. Here, the individual Muslim is first related to his immediate family, then his or her relatives and finally to other Muslims in the bond of religious brotherhood understood as the *Muslim Ummah*. To this horizontal axis of relationships is also added the vertical axis which concerns the believer's submission to the will of Allah. It is this vertical axis which gives meaning to the *Muslim Ummah*. In other words, the basis of the Islamic community is not that of a common forefather but that of a common God (Allah), a common Book (the Qur'an) and a common prophet (Muhammad). Consequently, the desire to live the "good life" understood as "life in total submission to the will of Allah" is the reason for the *Ummah*; as the Qur'an says; "Indeed, all the believers are brothers" (Surah 49: 10). In this sense, while the believer is personally responsible for his or

---

345 Paul Ricoeur. *Oneself as Another.* 1992, p.193.
346 Paul Ricoeur. *Oneself as Another.* 1992, p.194.

her level of *commitment* to Allah through the religion of Islam, the believer also knows that he or she needs the support of other Muslims (the community) and vice versa to be able to live the "good life". It is here that the dialogic structure of self-esteem, also understood as religious *commitment*, is expressed as *solicitude*. As Ricoeur indicated, *solicitude* expresses the concern and the interest that one has in another, and the desire to understand and experience the world as the other sees it.

Taken in its interreligious dialogue context, *solicitude* also expresses the concern religious communities give to each other in living their respective notions of the "good life". For instance, in a cosmopolitan context, the *Muslim Ummah* may live in close proximity with other religious communities such as the Christian, Hindu, and Buddhist communities. If these different communities are to be able to live out their respective notions of the "good life", they must show concern for each other through *respect*, friendship and mutual co-existence. This form of *mutuality and friendship* captures the sense of what Ricoeur considered as esteeming the other as I esteem myself. It implies establishing a kind of solicitude with the other, a mutual friendship which is developed out of the understanding that *we must show respect* to the other who desires to live the "good life", a *respect* which is in itself part of living the good life with and for others. In other words, I cannot expect to have my self-esteem honoured by others unless I esteem others *as myself.*[347] Interreligious dialogue as an exercise in learning is defined by this willingness to "give" and to "receive" friendship and respect. While we shall later develop *respect* as a necessary condition for dialogue as an exercise in learning, let us examine how Ricoeur presents the *principle of equality* as the corollary of reciprocity where friendship is placed on the path of justice, and where the life lived together at the interpersonal level, gives way to the life lived together beyond the interpersonal.

---

347 Paul Ricoeur. *Oneself as Another.* 1992, p.193.

3.3.1.3 The Good life with and for others "in just institutions"

According to Ricoeur, aiming at "the good life with and for others" extends beyond interpersonal relationships to include anonymous others in the wider society. So, while solicitude is that which mediates the ethical intention within interpersonal relationships, in the plurality of human society where there are anonymous third parties, the ethical intention is mediated by *just institutions*. *Justice* serves the ethical intention at this level and it produces ethical features like *equality,* which is not contained in *solicitude*. In other words, although there is an interpersonal dimension of a "good life" through solicitude, to achieve a "good life" at the societal level we need *institutions* which would serve our sense of justice through the obligations they impose, and the privileges and the opportunities that they provide to the members of the community.

But what is an *institution*? For Ricoeur, an "institution" connotes the structure of *living together* as a historical community – a people, a nation or even a religion.[348] It defines, as Kaplan put it, "the structures of living together and belonging to a particular community united by the bond of common mores."[349] According to Ricoeur, human society is basically plural, consisting of people who do not necessarily know each other and may not have interpersonal relations. In this *plurality*, one meets the anonymous other – someone I may meet and greet occasionally but whom I do not intimately know. It also includes those whom I may never meet face-to-face. As Ricoeur puts it, "this *plurality* includes third parties who will never be faces."[350] Thus, the plea for this anonymous other is included in the fullest aim of the true life, the "good life". If institutions serve to regulate this state of plurality in human society, then what does it mean to be *just* to these

---

348 Paul Ricoeur. *Oneself as Another.* 1992, p.194.
349 David Kaplan. *Ricoeur's Critical Theory.* 2003, p.105.
350 Paul Ricoeur. *Oneself as Another.* 1992, p.195.

anonymous others in society? And what does it mean to be treated *justly* by them in return?

By virtue of their common mores, *institutions* are rule-governed and they regulate the interactions and the activities of the anonymous others through their own standards of excellence which embody the corporate aspects of the "good life".[351] So, in the idea of "everyone" which is characteristic of social institutions, it is the virtue of *justice* (or fairness) which ensures the "good life" for everyone. Social institutions ensure that this "sense of justice" caters for everyone through the principle of *equality*. *Justice* for Ricoeur is, "the first virtue of social institutions, as truth is of systems of thought."[352] The *sense of Justice* points to two directions: (1) the *good* in respect to the institutional mediation of the desire to live the "good life" together in society; and (2) the *legal* where the judicial system confers upon the law the right of constraint.[353] Here, Ricoeur focuses his attention on the first direction because of his understanding that (1) the idea of *justice* from the onset was not constructed from legal systems but emerged out of the mythical mould of Greek tragedy; and (2) the "sense of justice" is not merely limited to the legal sphere but is at play in human relationships such that; the "sense of injustice" is more poignant and perspicacious than the "sense of justice", because "people have a clearer vision of what is missing in human relations than of the right way to organize it. This is why, even for philosophers, it is injustice that first set thought in motion."[354]

In human society, the "sense of injustice" expressed in forms of inequality is checked by just institutions. Institutions achieve this through the principle of *distributive justice*[355] which "governs the appointment of roles, tasks, advantages and disadvantages

351 David Kaplan. *Ricoeur's Critical Theory.* 2003, p.105.
352 Paul Ricoeur. *Oneself as Another.* 1992, p.197.
353 Paul Ricoeur. *Oneself as Another.* 1992, p.197.
354 Paul Ricoeur. *Oneself as Another.* 1992, p.198.
355 Paul Ricoeur. *Oneself as Another.* 1992, p.199.

between the members of the society"[356]through the principle of *equality* whose direct opposite is *inequality*. Here, the unjust man is considered to be one who takes too much in terms of advantage or not enough in terms of burdens. The intermediate between "taking too much" and "taking less" is *proportional equality* which defines the sense of distributive justice "regulating what is fair to each one as anonymous members of the society."[357] In consequence, Ricoeur asserts that "distributive justice consists in equalizing two relations between, in each case, a person and merit."[358] This *distributive* interpretation of institutions contributes to tearing down the walls that separate the individual from the society, and assures the cohesion between the three components of the ethical aim in other words the *individual*, the *interpersonal* and the *societal*.[359] Thus, while *solicitude* provides to the self, another who is a face in the strong Levinasian sense, *equality* provides to the self another who is the plurality of many *others*. As a result, the sense of justice takes nothing away from solicitude, but presupposes it to the extent that, it adds to solicitude the field of application which extends beyond interpersonal relationships.[360]

From a dialogical perspective, it is well known that Christianity and Islam are two major religious institutions. But Ricoeur's discourse on *just institutions* focuses on the particularity of the institution and its response to issues of justice and equality for the plurality of others who are nonetheless bonded together by common mores. His discourse, therefore, concerns what happens between members of an institution who are tied together by common *mores* and not about the relationships between different institutions. Thus, one might ask: "how can this form of intra-institutional hermeneutic discourse be applied to an inter-institutional

356 Paul Ricoeur. *Oneself as Another.* 1992, p.200.
357 David Kaplan. *Ricoeur's Critical Theory.* 2003, p.106.
358 Paul Ricoeur. *Oneself as Another.* 1992, p.201.
359 Paul Ricoeur. *Oneself as Another.* 1992, p.201.
360 Paul Ricoeur. *Oneself as Another.* 1992, p.202.

context?" In response, what follows below is an attempt to show how Ricoeur's discourse on *just institutions* applies individually to Islam and Christianity as religious institutions on the one hand. It also demonstrates how elements in this discourse provides the framework for reflecting on the *principle of equality* as a necessary condition for dialogue between institutions on the other hand.

As different institutions, Christianity and Islam have different traditions and doctrines which give meaning to the notion of the "good life" and the practice of it. For instance, for Islam: while theology must be informed by the *Five Pillars* of the religion with particular focus on the unicity and transcendence of Allah (*Tawhid*), the daily living out of the "good life" is liturgically expressed in the believers commitment to confessing the *Shahada* and saying the *five daily prayers* (the Salat) amidst other practices. As a result, the confession of the *Shahada* and the *commitment* to the five daily prayers stand as a hub on which the believer's daily living of the "good life" revolves. Unlike Islam, Christian theology revolves around the understanding of God as *Trinity,* where the believer is daily called upon to submit himself or herself to God the Father, through the message of Jesus Christ with the inspiration of the Holy Spirit. This message of Jesus Christ is summarised in the "love of God and the love of a neighbour." Consequently, between Christianity and Islam one finds two religious institutions who at once share similar theological concepts such as *God, Jesus Christ and the Holy Spirit,* but whose theological constructions of these realities differ substantially in the light of the *Tawhid* (in Islam) and the *Holy Trinity* (in Christianity). While these two theological foundations will be taken up and elucidated upon in Chapters Four and Five, it is sufficient to state here that apart from their differences of origin and formation, the different theological concepts such as the *Tawhid* and the *Holy Trinity* systematically differentiates Christianity and Islam, one from the other as religious institutions with different systems of belief.

As different systems of belief, their respective doctrines and practices constitute the *common mores* which bind their respective adherents together. If we understand the essence of institutions as safeguarding the individual and the collective needs of its members, then Islam and Christianity are two separate institutions which fundamentally exist to give guidance to Muslims and Christians in their respective desire to live the "good life". This task of the two institutions first of all, needs to be recognised when engaging in dialogue as an exercise in learning. Secondly, just as institutions also exist to promote the *sense of justice* through the *principle of equality,* one can also apply this *principle of equality* to religious institutions which recognize each other as different institutions with unique traditions and theologies. The realization that each institution is unique and different in its tradition and theology goes to support the claim that one's system of belief cannot be used as the standard of measurement for the truthfulness of the other. If Islam and Christianity are to engage in dialogue on Christology as an exercise in learning, then this dialogue needs to be constructed against the background of what the other has to say about Jesus Christ within their tradition-specific context.

To recognize that the other has something unique to share about Jesus Christ from which one desires to learn, then this *other* cannot be considered as inferior to me but as an *equal partner in dialogue* – one who learns from me and from whom I learn. Since each religion has its unique Christology[361] which is independent of the Christology of the other, *justice* is served when the other is recognized as *an equal partner* – an original source of self-understanding, capable of communicating a unique experience.[362] The above sense of equality opens up the dialogical

---

361 The concept "Christology" is often used to designate a Christian response to the identity and mission of Jesus Christ. As we shall demonstrate in Chapter Five, Islam also has all the resources that enables it to response to the very questions which surround the identity and mission of Jesus Christ within its tradition. It is in this sense that we talk of an "Islamic Christology".

362 Raimon Panikkar. *The Cosmotheandric Experience.* 1993, p.60.

process for the experiences of the other as an equal partner. As Gadamer put it, the *thou* here must be seen truly as a *thou* – "not to overlook his claims, but to let him truly say something to us. Without such openness to one another, there is no genuine human bond."[363] While this *sense of equality* pertains to the plurality of others in particular social institutions, so it also applies to the plurality of religions – with each religious institution emerging as that "anonymous face" whose plea for justice resides in the *respect* and in the *equal recognition* that they deserve.

To sum up Ricoeur's hermeneutics on the ethical intention, it could be said that, if self-esteem expresses itself in the form of the commitment of oneself to one's religious tradition, then solicitude opens up the dialogic structure of self-esteem, inspiring in oneself the desire to want to live the "good life" with and for others at the level of interpersonal relations. However, at the level of inter-institutional relations, what is demanded is the sense of justice expressed as *equal respect* and *recognition* for the other who also possesses authentic, independent and unique theologies about God. It is this uniqueness of theology and faith-experience which becomes the subject of interreligious learning. Having said this, how does Ricoeur relate the above tripartite structure of the ethical intention to the moral norm as its subordination and completion?

3.3.2 Ricoeur's Hermeneutics of the Self and the Moral Norm

At the beginning of the discourse on ethics, Ricoeur asserted the following: (1) the primacy of ethics over morality; (2) the necessity for the ethical aim to be mediated by the moral norm; and (3) the recourse morality must take in ethics to resolve conflicts

---

363 Gadamer. *Truth and Method.* 1989, p.358-383, 361.

and aporias. Under the plane of morality, Ricoeur shows how it is necessary to subject the ethical aim to the test of the norm. Here, our interest is to show how Ricoeur's discourse on morality provides further clarity to our reflections on the values of *commitment, openness, respect for others* and *equality* as necessary conditions for interreligious dialogue as an exercise in learning. Following the same tripartite structure of the ethical aim, Ricoeur first of all, subjects the aim of the "good life" to the test of the norm without recourse to the dialogic structure of the norm. This then leads us to the consideration of the moral norm in the light of *solicitude* which denotes the primordial relation of the self to the other at the ethical level. With *just institutions,* the *sense of justice* (in ethics) is replaced by the *rule of justice* under the category of the moral norm.[364] Here, *self-respect* from the moral plane answers to *self-esteem* from the ethical plane, reaching its full meaning where respect for the norm (in the first stage), blossoms into respect for others and for "oneself as another" (in the second stage). This further extends to respect for everyone with the right to a just share in an equitable distribution (in the third stage).

Ricoeur parallels the tripartite structure of the ethical intention with the moral norm reflected in the three formulations of the Kantian Categorical Imperatives.[365] In this way, the teleological aim towards the good life first of all, "corresponds to the principle of *universality*, in which the agent achieves freedom under

---

364 Ricoeur. *Oneself as Another.* 1992, p.203.
365 Kant presents four formulations of the *categorical imperative*: (1) *The Universal Law of Nature Formula* – "act only on that maxim through which you can at the same time will that it should become a universal law." (2) *The Humanity Formula* – "Act in such a way that you always treat humanity, whether in your own person or in the person of any other, never simply as a means, but always at the same time as an end." (3) *The Autonomy Formula* – "So act that your will can regard itself at the same time as making universal law through its maxims." (4) *The Kingdom of Ends Formula* – "So act as if you were through your maxims a law-making member of a Kingdom of Ends."

self-imposed laws."[366] Secondly, *solicitude* also, "corresponds to the formula of '*end in itself*' in which we are bound to respect others as ends and not as mere means."[367] Thirdly, *living in just institutions*, "corresponds to the obligation to pursue the '*Kingdom of Ends*' in which, we must act in maxims that generate a community of free and equal members, each of whom, will further the aims of others while realising his or her own intentions."[368] So, one notices here that self-respect in the moral plane has the same structure as self-esteem under the reign of ethics. However, the relationship between ethics and morality, according to Ricoeur, is not one of parallelism, but complementarity because the ethical aim has to pass through the sieve of the moral norm in order to find its completion. In other words, whereas the *good* is prior to the *right*, the *good* requires the *right* in order to achieve the full sense of the good life which entails living well, with and for the other, in just institutions.[369] Let us delve into these different aspects of the moral norm.

3.3.2.1 The Autonomy of the Will

Under this first component, Ricoeur examines the self's relation to the norm by isolating the moment of *universality* in which the norm tests the wish to live the good life. Here, the self is examined outside the dialogic moment of the norm. Ricoeur recognizes this turn as pure abstraction because there are no norms which do not take persons into account. However, by embarking on this course of abstraction, he hopes to demonstrate how through the same *universality* the self draws its authority from the reflexive plane. Ricoeur anchors the deontological moment on

---

366 David Kaplan. *Ricoeur's Critical Theory*. 2003, p.106.
367 David Kaplan. *Ricoeur's Critical Theory*. 2003, p.106.
368 David Kaplan. *Ricoeur's Critical Theory*. 2003, p.106.
369 David Kaplan. *Ricoeur's Critical Theory*. 2003, p.106.

the Kantian concept of the "unconditional good will" expressed in his *Groundwork of the Metaphysics of Morals*. Kant asserts that, "it is impossible to conceive anything in the world or even outside of it, which can be taken as good without qualification, except the *good will*."[370] In the Kantian "good-will", that which receives the predicate "good" is the *will*. Here, the *will* takes the place of *desire* which is at the heart of Aristotelian ethics. In other words, while *desire* is recognised through its *aim*, the *will* is recognised through its relation to the *norm* because the *will* responds to the question "what ought I to do?"[371] According to Ricoeur, Kant sees the *will* as self-legislating and acting in response to the duty of obligation. Here, "the morality of obligation is tied to the universality of the will, characterized by the constraint which one imposes on oneself."[372] As Kaplan put it, "a free individual acts under self-imposed laws, according to which each person freely submits to self-discipline."[373] This form of self-legislation or self-discipline is what Ricoeur refers to as *autonomy*. Under autonomy, the self finds support for its moral status without any support from the other. Here, Kant invests in the same subject the power of commanding and obeying.

In Chapter Two under the category of *idem-identity*, we indicated that the *idem* aspects of the identity of the religious other consists of their doctrines, Scriptures, religious practices, rites and customs. These represent that which is *given* to all adherents of the religion. However, the *ipse* aspect of the identity of the believer consists in keeping one's promise. As Ricoeur put it, a person's commitment to what he or she promises even in the face of danger, disappointments, uncertainties and new opportunities

370 Paul Ricoeur. *Oneself as Another.* 1992, p.205.
371 Paul Ricoeur. *Oneself as Another.* 1992, p.206.
372 Paul Ricoeur. *Oneself as Another.* 1992, p.206.
373 David Kaplan. *Ricoeur's Critical Theory.* 2003, p.107.

demonstrates that the person is reliable and can be counted on.[374] Consequently, we asserted that on the level of religious beliefs, though by becoming a member of a religious community, one receives the systems of belief held by the community (*idem identity*); the living out of these belief-systems depends on the adherent's *commitment* expressed in "keeping one's promise" (*ipse identity*). Therefore, *religious commitments* cannot be forced; otherwise they run the risk of being at best superficial and pretentious, and at worst, acts of indoctrination.

Commitment has an "internal" quality which emanates from the personal volition of the individual, measured by the adherent's willingness and readiness to remain faithful to the *idem* aspects of the religion in all circumstances. Even though the object of one's *commitment* is external (dealing with doctrines, customs and practices), the act of *commitment* always finds its roots in the personal decision of the adherent. This defines the *autonomy* of adherents to various religious traditions. Autonomy here points to the free choice and consent that an individual expresses, as interest to belong and be part of the life of a religious institution. Thus, consent always originates from the individual and belongs to him or her. Its autonomy lies in the fact that consent can always be taken back by the individual who gives it.

Consequently, under the category of ethics we indicated that while religious *commitment* is, first of all, preceded by one's knowledge of its beliefs and conviction in its doctrines as providing the necessary guidance for living the "good life", under the plane of morality, *commitment* is sustained by the will to remain faithful to the traditions that give rise to these convictions. However, as abstract as this first component of the triadic structure seems to be, Ricoeur indicates that its significance lies in how it serves as the basis for a progressive movement from the general formulation of the Kantian categorical imperative to its second and third formulations. These formulations provide guidance to the

---

374 Paul Ricoeur, Paul. *Oneself as Another.* 1992, p.124.

understanding of the second and third component of the triadic structure of Ricoeur's ethical intention. What is therefore significant to note here is that just as the *autonomy of the will* is the foundation from which the other two Kantian imperatives are formulated, so also is the notion of *religious commitment* – it serves as the basis from which the virtues of *openness, respect for others* and *equality* are derived. Let us now consider these other components.

3.3.2.2 Solicitude and Respect for others

Ricoeur asserted under the category of ethics that *solicitude* is not something added on to self-esteem, but it unfolds the dialogic structure of self-esteem. So also under the category of the moral norm, the respect owed to persons does not constitute a heterogeneous moral principle in relation to the autonomy of the self, but constitutes its intrinsic dialogic structure on the plane of the obligation of rules.[375] Ricoeur justifies this thesis in two phases: in the *first phase*, he demonstrates how the norm of respect owed to persons is intimately connected to solicitude. He then justifies the claim that the respect owed to persons on the moral plane, relates in the same way to autonomy as *solicitude* relates to the aim of the good life on the ethical plane.[376] In the *second phase*, Ricoeur shows how, "respect owed to persons posited in the second categorical imperative is on the moral plane, in the same relation to autonomy as solicitude was to the aim of the good life in the ethical plane."[377] Let us now consider these two phases following Ricoeur's lead.

Ricoeur in the first phase shows how the norm of respect owed to persons is connected to the dialogic structure of the ethical aim

---

375 Paul Ricoeur. *Oneself as Another.* 1992, p.218.
376 Paul Ricoeur. *Oneself as Another.* 1992, p.218.
377 Paul Ricoeur. *Oneself as Another.* 1992, p.222.

(solicitude). He uses the *Golden Rule*[378] as the appropriate transitional formula between solicitude and the second Kantian imperative: "Act in such a way that you always treat humanity, whether in your own person or in the person of any other, never simply as a means, but always at the same time as an end" (Gr. 66–67/429). According to Ricoeur, interpersonal relationship can sometimes be the occasion of violence which resides in the *power* one exerts over another. Here, he takes pain to differentiate between the expressions: *power-over, power-to-do* and *power-in-common*. While "power-to-do" expresses the capacity possessed by an agent to constitute himself or herself as the author of an action, "power-in-common" defines "the capacity for members of a historical community to exercise in an indivisible manner, their desire to live together."[379] However, "power-over" which relates to what one does to another is held to be the occasion for the evil of violence. For instance, Ricoeur indicates that, "from the domain of physical violence considered as the abusive use of force against others, the figure of evil begins with the simple use of threat, passing through the degrees of constraints and ending in murder."[380] The end result of "power-over" others is sometimes the destruction of their *power-to-do,* and hence, the destruction of their self-esteem and their self-respect.

Consequently, moral norms come as a response to issues of violence. For instance, Ricoeur indicates that the values of *truth, property* and *life* are preserved from violations in the prohibition: "you shall not lie, you shall not steal, you shall not kill, you shall not torture."[381] These prohibitions put constraints on those who would seek to exercise "power-over" others and thus deny them of their "power-to-do" – their self-esteem and their self-respect. So, while solicitude affirms the mutual exchange of self-esteem

---

378 "Treat others as you would want them to treat you (Luke 6: 31)" (see, Paul Ricoeur. 1992, p.219).

379 Paul Ricoeur. *Oneself as Another.* 1992, p.220.

380 Paul Ricoeur. *Oneself as Another.* 1992, p.220.

381 Paul Ricoeur. *Oneself as Another.* 1992, p.221.

at the ethical level, this affirmation is seen as the hidden soul of prohibition on the moral plane where one rejects the indignities inflicted on others through solicitude. The fact that there is a possibility of the spectre of evil in the choices we make suggests that there is always the need to subject the desire to live the good life to the test of the moral norm.

The second phase of Ricoeur's discourse on solicitude and the norm centres on the claim that the respect owed to persons posited in the second formulation of the Kantian imperative, is on the moral plane in the same relation to autonomy as solicitude was to the aim of the "good life" on the ethical plane. For Ricoeur, whereas the link between "solicitude" and the "good life" occurred after a genuine leap on the ethical plane, things are much different with the Kantian imperative because the second formulation of the categorical imperative (that is, *act in such a way that you always treat humanity, whether in your own person or in the person of any other, never simply as a means, but always at the same time as an end*) is here treated as the development of the general form of the imperative. This Kantian imperative reveals two terms which live in dialectic tension: (1) the idea of *humanity,* and (2) the idea of a *person as an end in himself.* The idea of *humanity* as a singular term appears to be an abstract universality which governs the principle of autonomy without the consideration of persons.

The idea of *persons,* "as ends in themselves however demand that one takes into account the plurality of persons, without allowing one to take this idea as far as the conception of otherness."[382] Here, Kant gives priority to the continuity assured by the idea of *humanity* with the principle of autonomy, over the discontinuity which defines the sudden introduction of the notion of *end-in-itself* and the notion of *persons as ends-in-themselves.*[383] So, the idea of *humanity* which is not to be understood as the sum totality of human beings but as the basis from which one is worthy of

382 Paul Ricoeur. *Oneself as Another.* 1992, p.222.
383 Paul Ricoeur. *Oneself as Another.* 1992, p.222.

respect, suggests a sense of universality which is taken from the perspective of the *multiplicity* of persons which Kant called "object or matter."[384] Thus for Kant, *humanity* acts as a screen in the direct confrontation between oneself and another. It is within this context that "the notion of a *person as an end in itself* comes to balance that of *humanity,* to the extent that it introduces in the very formulation of the imperative, the distinction between 'your person' and 'the person of anyone else.'"[385] In this way, the maxim then maintains that never treat humanity *simply as a means.*

But what does it mean to treat humanity in a person as a means? For Ricoeur, it is to exert upon the will of others that power which, full of restraint in the case of influence, is unleashed in all the forms which violence takes roots, culminating in torture.[386] However, persons as rational beings must be considered as ends-in-themselves and "*not merely as means* for the arbitrary use of this or that will."[387] In this way, every man's actions, whether directed to himself or to other rational beings, must always be viewed *at the same time as an end.* The basis for this form of respect lies in the fact that the consciousness of autonomy implies the "fact of reason", and the *fact of reason* implies the existence of morality, and "morality exists because the person himself exists".[388] So, "the *Golden Rule* and the imperative of respect owed to persons do not simply have the same field of exercise, [but] they also have the same aim: to establish reciprocity wherever there is a lack of reciprocity."[389] For Ricoeur, understanding the *Golden Rule* and the imperative this way, "ultimately arms our indignation, that is, our rejection of *indignities* inflicted on others."[390]

---

384 Paul Ricoeur. *Oneself as Another.* 1992, p.223.

385 Paul Ricoeur. *Oneself as Another.* 1992, p.224.

386 Paul Ricoeur. *Oneself as Another.* 1992, p.225.

387 Paul Ricoeur. *Oneself as Another.* 1992, p.225.

388 Paul Ricoeur. *Oneself as Another.* 1992, p.225.

389 Paul Ricoeur. *Oneself as Another.* 1992, p.225.

390 Paul Ricoeur. *Oneself as Another.* 1992, p.221.

From this second component of the moral norm, two things remain significant for Ricoeur and also for our understanding of interreligious dialogue as an exercise in learning from and about the other. While it underscores the dialogic structure, which underlines the autonomy of the self or will (where self-respect leads to the respect for other), it also emphasizes that within this dialogic structure the respect for others must be devoid of any violation of their dignity and their integrity. It must be directed towards a sense of respect for *who they are* and *what they are*. Learning must always begin with a respect for and an appreciation of the subject matter to be learnt and the persons from whom we learn. In other words, this view of respect does not only capture the sense of respect as it pertains to the *Golden Rule*, but it also goes even deeper than that to imply that, even in contexts where one does not treat oneself with respect, the other must still be respected as an end-in-himself or herself. In other words, according the respect that is due to the other must not be measured by how much one respects oneself.

Within the context of interreligious dialogue, respect for the other's religious tradition is a paramount quality to dialoguing with them. It is this understanding which is emphasized by the Pontifical Council for Interreligious Dialogue when it said, these different religious traditions "command our respect because over the centuries, they have borne witness to the efforts to find answers 'to those profound mysteries of the human condition' (Nostra Aetate No. 1), and have given expression to the religious experience, and continues to do so today."[391] As a result, respecting the religious other as an independent source of self-understanding and faith is at the heart of the interreligious dialogue enterprise.

---

391 Pontifical Council for Interreligious Dialogue and Proclamation: *No. 14* https://astro.temple.edu/~swidler/swidlerbooks/universal_theology. htm (29/02/2020).

3.3.2.3 Equality and the Principle of Justice

Still following the same pattern, Ricoeur indicates that just as *solicitude* on the ethical plane corresponds to the Categorical Formula of *ends-in-themselves,* whereby we are bound to respect others not as means but as ends in themselves, so also, the *sense of justice* at the ethical plane corresponds to the *rule of justice* at the moral plane where living in just institutions relates to the obligation of pursuing the *Kingdom of Ends.* Here, one is called to act on a maxim that engenders, "a community of free and equal members, each of whom would further the aims of others while realizing his own intentions."[392] Just as the discourse on the *sense of equality* at the ethical plane, so also at the moral plane, Ricoeur focuses on the *principle of equality* which occurs at the level of the *principle of justice.* On the moral plane, the *principle of justice* ensures the application of *equality* to everyone within the community. This explains why a formal principle of justice is necessary to ensure this application of *equality.* To achieve the above end, Ricoeur turns to John Rawls' conception of procedural justice.

In his *Theory of Justice,* Rawls uses the concept of "fairness" as the key to his notion of justice. This is because Rawls views *fairness* as the basis from which the justice basic to institutions emanates. He attempts to shake off and free his *procedural conception of justice* from the tutelage of the *good* defined by the teleological aim, especially its *utilitarian* version of the notion of justice,[393] whereby the simple pleasure of the individual is sacrificed for the benefit of the greater pleasure of the community. Rawls nonetheless shares Kant's conviction that when the individual's pleasure is sacrificed for the greater good, it means that the individual is being used as a means to an end and not as an end in himself or herself. Thus, his entire work on the *Theory of Justice* is a shift from the question of *foundation* to *mutual consent.* Rawls presents

---

392 Kaplan, David, M. *Ricoeur's Critical Theory.* 2003, p.106.
393 Paul Ricoeur. *Oneself as Another.* 1992, p.230.

his work on justice as a response to three basic questions on the *fairness of deliberation*: (1) what would guarantee the fairness of the situation of deliberation from which an agreement could result concerning the just arrangement of institution? (2) what principle will be chosen in this fictive situation of deliberation? (3) what arguments could convince the deliberating parties to choose the Rawlsian principle of justice rather than utilitarianism?[394]

According to Rawls, we are all self-interested rational beings and therefore we need to stand behind the *veil of ignorance*.[395] By "self-interested rational beings", Rawls means that we are motivated to select in an informed and rational way, that which seems to favour us. So, a self-interest rational person *behind the veil of ignorance* would not want to belong to a social class, a race or a nationality that has been discriminated against. For Rawls, all generations under the *veil of ignorance* are seen to have the same equal rights to resources both now and in the future. What Rawls seeks to preserve here is the equality that each person deserves. Hence, in response to the question: *"what would guarantee the fairness of the situation of deliberation from which an agreement could result concerning the just arrangement of institution?"* Rawls draws up a list of constraints which the individual must know so that the choices they make would depend on a system of distribution of advantages and disadvantages. These constraints are: (1) parties in deliberation must have sufficient knowledge of the general psychology of human nature (its fundamental passions and motivations); (2) the parties must know what every normal human being wishes to possess (the primary social goods which make the exercise of freedom possible); (3) since the choice is between many competing systems of justice, every party must

---

394 Paul Ricoeur. *Oneself as Another*. 1992, p.231.
395 To say that we stand behind "the veil of ignorance" is to assume that we do not know the following sort of things about ourselves: our gender, parents, social class, race, nationality, generation and so on. (See, John Rawls. *The Theory of Justice*. 1971, p.12).

have sufficient knowledge about the competing systems; (4) all the parties must have equal information about the issues concerned; (5) the contract they make must be thereupon stable regardless of the prevailing circumstances.[396] For Rawls, the above constraints would guarantee the fairness of the situation of deliberation from which an agreement could result concerning the just arrangement of institution.[397]

To the second question: *"what principle will be chosen in the fictive situation of deliberation?"* Rawls presents two principles of justice and by so doing, demonstrates their correct placement. For Rawls, self-interest rational human beings behind the *veil of ignorance* would under normal circumstances, choose two general principles of justice to structure society: that is, (1) the *principle of equal liberty;* and (2) the *difference principle.* While the first is more egalitarian − demonstrating that all persons have equal rights to liberty in society, the second principle stipulates that social and economic inequality should be carefully arranged so that they are directed; (1) to the greatest benefits of the disadvantaged in society; and (2) that they ensure equal opportunity for all in society in terms of holding offices and positions. Here, justice as distribution is, "extended to all kinds of advantages capable of being treated as shares to be distributed: rights and duties on the one hand and benefits and burdens on the other."[398] Their purpose is to ensure the establishment of fairness in all segments of society. According to Rawls, just as the content of these principles remains very significant, "so also the rule of priority that ties them together."[399] This rule of priority follows a serial or a lexical order which signifies that, "'a departure from the institution of equal liberty required by the first principle cannot be

396 Paul Ricoeur. *Oneself as Another.* 1992, p.232.
397 Paul Ricoeur. *Oneself as Another.* 1992, p.232.
398 Paul Ricoeur. *Oneself as Another.* 1992, p.233.
399 Paul Ricoeur. *Oneself as Another.* 1992, p.235.

justified ... by greater social and economic advantages'"[400] To put it simply, Rawls' emphasis is that the interest of an individual should never be sacrificed for the benefit of the common good. In other words, society must always be attentive to both the individual's needs and the needs of the wider community.

In response to the third question: "*where the deliberating parties would choose the Rawlsian principle of justice against that of utilitarianism*", Rawls relies on what he calls the "maximin" which is a decision theory in the context of uncertainty where parties are required, "to choose the arrangements that maximize the minimum shares."[401] Situated within the original context of the *veil of ignorance* where no one knows where his place in society is and therefore reasons on the basis of mere possibilities, the contracting parties become committed to each other on the basis of the terms of the contract which are publicly defined and unanimously accepted. In this way, "if two conceptions of justice are in conflict and if one of them makes possible a situation that someone would find unacceptable, whereas the other would exclude this possibility, then the second conception would prevail."[402] Like Kant, the value of Rawls' contractualism makes it impossible to adopt rules to the advantage of some at the expense of others. As David Kaplan put it, "it prohibits forms of treatment that no one would want for themselves."[403]

Having followed Rawls in response to the three questions on the principle of justice, Ricoeur then asked: "does Rawls' pure procedural conception of justice break all ties with the sense of justice that precedes it and follows it all along?" In Ricoeur's view, the procedural conception of justice, at best, formalises the sense of justice that it never ceases to presuppose.[404] As it were, Rawls

---

400 Paul Ricoeur. *Oneself as Another*. 1992, p.245.
401 Paul Ricoeur. *Oneself as Another*. 1992, p.236.
402 Paul Ricoeur. *Oneself as Another*. 1992, p.236.
403 David Kaplan. *Ricoeur's Critical Theory*. 2003, p.109.
404 Paul Ricoeur. *Oneself as Another*. 1992, p.236.

himself even admitted that the argument of the procedural conception of justice rests upon a preunderstanding of what *justice and injustice* are. It is the meanings derived from these concepts which permit us to define and interpret these two principles of justice before considering them as the chosen principles in the original situation behind the "veil of ignorance".[405] What is however noteworthy in the Rawlsian contractual theory is that just like Kant, Rawls' contractualism also makes it impossible to adopt rules which are discriminatory. Within an interreligious dialogue context, Rawls' contractualism forestalls and preserves the value of equality among partners in dialogue. Let us now reflect on the relevance of these ethico-moral components of Ricoeur's ethical intention to the understanding of dialogue as an exercise in learning.

We indicated earlier that the basis for the individual's faith response to Christianity or to Islam emanates from one's esteem for the religion as providing the necessary guidance to living the "good life" – that is, the "life lived in response to God". However, the "life lived in response to God" is not done in isolation. It encompasses a relationship expressed in concern for others (that is, solicitude) who equally aspire to live the "good life". It is this form of relationship which gives rise to the formation of Christian or Muslim communities. In the wider society, Christians and Muslims know that they are not communities living in isolation, but share sometimes the same space, streets, facilities and amenities with each other and with other communities. In other words, many societies today are so multi-faith and multi-cultural that in living the "good life", one is caught up not just with oneself or with members of one's religious community, but with many "anonymous others". These "anonymous others" have to be carefully considered in my desire to live the "good life". This is because, respecting the autonomous other is essentially part of "living the good life". The other deserves respect in my interest to live the "good life" as a life lived in response to God.

---

405 Paul Ricoeur. *Oneself as Another*. 1992, p.237.

The idea of *mutual co-existence,* which is always viewed as the consequence of the reciprocity of respect, is better fostered when one knows and understands that which essentially constitutes the other's sense of the "good life". To know the other demands that we learn from them, and if we are to learn from each other, then this exercise of learning could take place through the medium of dialogue as "the sharing of mutual testimonies". However, for such genuine dialogues to occur, the other must be recognized as an *equal partner* who also possesses a unique understanding of what it means to live the "good life". Viewing the other as an *equal-partner-in-dialogue* is not based on the understanding that they share the same faith principles as we do. It is based on the recognition that just as I have faith principles which form the basis for my beliefs in God, so does the other and if I desire to be listened to and respected, so does the other. In other words, if I desire to find the tranquil space to be able to live my life in response to God's invitation to live the "good life" as perceived in my religious tradition, so does the other. In this way, seeing the other as an equal-partner-in-dialogue then becomes an indispensable quality of "living-the-good-life", expressed in a live lived in God.

3.4 Ricoeur's "Ethical Intention" and Dialogue as An Exercise in Learning

We defined interreligious dialogue in Chapter One as, "the constructive and positive conversation between people of different religious traditions on issues of religious significance, for the purpose of mutual learning, growth and enrichment." In the light of Christian-Muslim dialogue, we proposed Christology as the context for dialogue as an exercise in learning from and about the other. Within this form of dialogue, we indicated that two issues needed to be clarified: (1) "learning about"; and (2) "learning from" the other. The "other" here is used interchangeably to refer to either Christianity or Islam or their respective adherents. In this way, whereas Muslims could be considered *other* to Christians, so also are Christians *other* to Muslims. Having also considered the Ricoeurean hermeneutic fingerprints that support the effective engagement between the self and the other, we indicated that dialogue as an exercise in learning needs to be guided by some necessary conditions which we earlier identified as *dialogical attitudes*.[406]

While these dialogical attitudes include concepts such as *commitment, openness, respect* and *equality,* some scholars indifferent contexts also refers to them as "the necessary conditions" or "the ground rules" for interreligious dialogue.[407] Whereas most of scholarly work in this area only mentions these conditions as providing the appropriate dialogical dispositions that facilitate the process of dialogue, what follows below is the attempt to clearly articulate their meaning and their significance in the light of the ethical and the moral implications of Ricoeur's hermeneutics on narrative identity. These elucidations on what we term here as *dialogical attitudes* are undertaken within the framework of the understanding of dialogue, "as an exercise in learning from and about the other."

3.4.1 Self-esteem and the Value of Commitment

The virtue of *commitment* defines the idea of being dedicated, devoted and faithful to a cause. It conveys a sense of rootedness.

---

406 Many scholars in the interreligious dialogue field consistently indicate that effective dialogues take place when they are guided by conditions that support effective engagement between the self and the other. Some of these necessary conditions to dialogue which we identify as "dialogical attitudes" include *commitment, openness, respect for the other* and *equality.*

407 See, Leonard Swidler. *Faith Meets Faith.* 1988, p.13.

Understood interreligiously, *commitment* highlights one's faithfulness to the doctrines and the practices of the religious tradition to which one belongs. It defines the attitude of believing and belonging to a particular religious community. As Catherine Cornille put it, religious commitment is, "a deliberate identification with the teachings and the practices of a particular tradition. It thus entails assent to the truth-claims of a particular tradition and recognition of the authority of the tradition in matters of doctrine and discipline."[408] Although we indicated earlier that the establishment of *religious commitment* occurs against the background of *critical questioning and reflection* as to whether or not the tradition provides guidance to living a "good life", it must be said here that the process itself is also not devoid of the practice of *inherited faith* – understood here as; the practice of passing on belief-systems, especially within families, from one generation to the other.

Whether established through inherited faith or through critical reflection or both, religious commitment represents the *esteem of the self* for the teachings and practices of a particular religious tradition to which one belongs. If *attestation* is a statement of conviction and confidence in one's religious beliefs, then in an interreligious dialogue context, *attestation* derives its breath from the *commitment* of the believer to the religious tradition. It represents one's commitment to the religious tradition which has contributed to defining who one is – as an *attested to self.* As Dupuis put it, "honesty and sincerity specifically require that the various partners [in dialogue] enter it and commit themselves to it in the integrity of their faith. Any methodical doubt, any mental reservation, is out of place here."[409] This explains why *commitment* is a necessary condition for dialogue as an exercise in learning; because that which the other seeks to learn from oneself,

---

408 Catherine Cornille. *The Im-possibility of Interreligious Dialogue.* 2008, p.66.
409 Jacque Dupuis. *Christianity and the Religious.* 2001, p.228.

157

is that which I believe in and I am committed to. Nevertheless, this form of commitment must be informed by the interlocutors' understanding of the teachings and the practices of their respective religious beliefs. This is because dialogue as an exercise in learning demands that one has full knowledge and understanding of the belief-systems of one's religious tradition and, can faithfully communicate these belief-systems to the understanding of the other. It consists of what Panikkar calls *intra-religious dialogue*[410] – a dialogue where one consciously and critically appropriates beliefs in one's own religious tradition to deeply understand them. Without this deep understanding and commitment to one's own religious tradition, there are simply no grounds for dialogue to proceed.[411]

3.4.2 Respect for Others and the Value of Openness

According to Ricoeur, esteem for oneself and for others is very fundamental for the establishment of meaningful relationships. This is because Ricoeur believes that one cannot have self-esteem without the esteem for others *as myself.* The comparative "as oneself" means that I am also "capable of starting something in the world, of acting for a reason, of hierarchizing your priorities, of evaluating the ends of your actions and, having done this, of holding yourself in esteem as I hold myself in esteem."[412] To understand the other in this way is to recognise and respect their integrity as I would want my integrity respected. It establishes a kind of *solicitude* between oneself and the other based on

---

410 *Intrareligious dialogue* "is an inner dialogue within myself, an encounter in the depths of my personal religiousness." (See Raimon Panikkar. *Intra-Religious Dialogue.* !999, p.73-74).

411 Raimon Panikkar. *Intra-Religious Dialogue.* !999, p.73.

412 Paul Ricoeur. *Oneself as Another.* 1992, p.193.

mutual respect – the kind of respect which goes beyond treating people simply as *means to an end* to treating them as *ends-in-themselves*. While the first exploits and violates the other's integrity, the second recognises and preserves it.

If the virtue of *openness* in dialogue means the willingness to enter into dialogue by sharing my testimonies of faith with the other while listening with generosity to the other's testimonies of faith, then *openness* is founded on the respect one has for the other. Here, the value of openness begins from my recognition and my acknowledgment that the other is an *authentic other* who also possesses unique truths which I desire to learn. As Panikkar put it, the *other* here, "is not just an-other (*alius*) and much less an object of my knowledge (*aliud*), but another self (*alter*) who is a source of self-understanding and also of understanding, is not necessarily reducible to my own."[413] It is on the basis of this sense of respect for the integrity of the other and their religious beliefs and practices that dialogue as an exercise in learning is made possible.

To learn is always to have an encounter with something new, the unfamiliar, the unexpected and the strange. Learning takes place when that which was previously strange now becomes familiar. As an exercise in learning, dialogue always begins with a sense of openness and interest in encountering the unfamiliar and the strange – that which is other. Within Christian–Muslim dialogue on Christology, it involves being open to learn from and about the otherness of each religious tradition in respect of the identity and the mission of Jesus Christ. The purpose is the desire to know the authentic content of the other's belief-systems on Christology, and to be transformed by this knowledge. It is for this reason that the Pontifical Council for Interreligious Dialogue and Proclamation indicated that, "the fullness of truth received in Jesus Christ does not give individual Christians the guarantee that they have grasped that truth fully. In the last analysis truth

---

413 Raimon Panikkar. *Intra-Religious Dialogue*. 1999, p.33–34.

is not a thing we possess, but a person by whom we must allow ourselves to be possessed."[414] In this way, the Council further indicated that, "while keeping their identity intact, Christians must be prepared to learn and to receive from and through others the positive values of their traditions. Through dialogue they may be moved to give up ingrained prejudices, to revise preconceived ideas, and even sometimes to allow the understanding of their faith to be purified."[415]

According to the Council, to cultivate such openness and allow one's faith to be tested, brings together the fruits of dialogue. That is, dialogue as an exercise in learning will help Christians to, "discover with admiration all that God's action through Jesus Christ in his Spirit has accomplished and continues to accomplish in the world and in the whole of humankind. Far from weakening their own faith, true dialogue will deepen it."[416] This is because, just like the other, Christians too will become increasingly aware of the significance of their identity and their faith, thus perceive more clearly its distinctive elements. The enrichment of their faith will stem from the gain of new dimensions to this faith, expressed in their discovery of God's active presence (through the mystery of Jesus Christ) in the lives of people who live beyond the visible boundaries of the Church and of the Christian fold.[417] In other words, dialogue as an exercise in learn-

---

414 Pontifical Council for Interreligious Dialogue and Proclamation: *No. 49* https://astro.temple.edu/~swidler/swidlerbooks/universal_theology.htm (29/02/2020).

415 Pontifical Council for Interreligious Dialogue and Proclamation: *No. 50* https://astro.temple.edu/~swidler/swidlerbooks/universal_theology.htm (29/02/2020).

416 Council for Interreligious Dialogue and Proclamation: *No. 50* https://astro.temple.edu/~swidler/swidlerbooks/universal_theology.htm (29/02/2020).

417 Pontifical Council for Interreligious Dialogue and Proclamation: *No. 50* https://astro.temple.edu/~swidler/swidlerbooks/universal_theology.htm (29/02/2020).

ing begins with an openness to the encounter with otherness. As Moyaert put it, interreligious dialogue begins with, "that which stands in opposition to what is known, and hence questions the naturalness of our own familiar horizons of meaning."[418] As a result, openness to the other forms the starting point for genuine engagement with them; it redefines the space-between selfhood and otherness, and invites the creative negotiation of this space through the exercise of learning. This explains why openness to other is an essential quality to dialogue as an exercise in learning.

3.4.3 The Principle of Equality or Equal-Partners-in-Dialogue

Within the context of Ricoeur's ethical intention, he asserts that *just institutions* use the *principles of justice and equality* to ensure the equitable distribution of benefits and burdens, rewards and tasks among the *different* members of society. Whether understood as the *sense of justice* in the ethical plane or in the Rawlsian conception of *fairness* in the moral plane; the *principle of equality* attempts to regulate, "what is fair to each one as anonymous members of the society."[419] Its distributive principle, "consists in equalizing two relations between, in each case, a person and merit."[420] Consequently, it ensures that the beliefs, needs and aspirations of some are not sacrificed for or violated by the interests of others. In this way, the principle of equality ensures that the views and needs of all members of the society are fairly served.

It is the above sense of *equality* which is at the heart of dialogue as an exercise in learning. In his seventh "Ground Rules for Interreligious Dialogue", Leonard Swidler rightly pointed out

---

418 Marianne Moyaert. *Fragile Identities*. 2011, p.233.
419 David Kaplan. *Ricoeur's Critical Theory*. 2003, p.106.
420 Paul Ricoeur. *Oneself as Another*. 1992, p.201.

that, "dialogue can only take place between equals."[421] This sense of equality is informed by the fact that in dialogue, one does not presume or consider the other's religious tradition or theological views inferior to one's own. Dialogue as an exercise in learning neither glories in absolutist or exclusivist claims which denigrate the other's viewpoints or beliefs, nor does it relativize one's religious beliefs in the face of the other. Here, the principle of *equal-partners-in-dialogue* recognises and respects the other's belief systems as constitutive truths within their original tradition-specific contexts. That which dialogue as an exercise in learning then offers is the opportunity to learn from what the other has to say in respect of their beliefs. In consequence, we could say that *religious commitment* remains the foundation from which authentic interreligious dialogue occurs. It is from one's commitments that one seeks to know the commitments of another. As Dupuis indicates, "it is in the fidelity to these personal non-negotiable convictions, honestly accepted on both sides, that interreligious dialogue takes place 'between equal' – in their differences."[422]

In this way, the tension between *commitment* and *openness* is neither dissipated nor resolved but is kept creative in an on-going process whose interest is learning from and about the other. Learning comes with an open and positive approach to the other's religious believes and traditions. It does not overlook apparent contradictions and incompatibilities between one's beliefs and those of the other, but questions with criticality in the interest to understand. As the Pontifical Council for Interreligious Dialogue and Proclamation indicates, "while entering with an open mind into dialogue with the followers of other religious traditions, Christians may have to also challenge them in a peaceful spirit with regard to the content of their belief. But Christians too must allow themselves to be questioned. Notwithstanding the fullness of God's revelation in Jesus Christ, the way Christians sometimes

---

421 Leonard Swidler. *Towards a Universal Theology of Religion.* 1988, p.15.
422 Dupuis, Jacque. *Christianity and the Religions.* 2003, p.129.

understand their religion and practise may be in need of purification".[423] Within the particular context of Christian-Muslim on Christology, what happens when differences in Christological understandings create dialogical aporias? In response, let us turn to Ricoeur's notion of *practical wisdom* (*phronesis*) which is also understood as the appropriate judgement of situations for the good of the situation.

3.5 The Hermeneutics of the Self and Practical Wisdom

By way of recall, we noted that Ricoeur's "little ethics" or "ethical intention" sought to establish a relationship of subordination and complementarity between ethics and morality. In doing so, Ricoeur proposed three theses: (1) the primacy of ethics over morality; (2) the necessity for the ethical aim to be mediated by the moral norm; and (3) the recourse morality must take to ethics to resolve morally conflictual situations. The exercise we have undertaken so far has been an investigation into the first two theses. This section concentrates on the third thesis – the recourse morality must take to ethics to resolve moral conflicts. Ricoeur calls this approach *practical wisdom* – the appropriate judgement of situations for the best of situations in the effort to live, "the good life with and for others in just institutions."[424]

Ricoeur undertakes this project within the context of *tragic wisdom*. For him, tragedy produces ethico-practical aporias, and Ricoeur cites examples of such aporetic situations in Greek tragedy; in the case of *Antigone* and *Creon* who find themselves in

---

423 Pontifical Council for Interreligious Dialogue and Proclamation: *No. 32* https://astro.temple.edu/~swidler/swidlerbooks/universal_theology.htm (29/02/2020).

424 See, Paul Ricoeur. *Oneself as Another.* 1992, p.172.

conflicting moral obligations.[425] Without intending to recount these stories, what Ricoeur emphasizes in these accounts is the moral obligation which forces Antigone to give her brother a sepulchre in accordance to custom, even though he has become an enemy of the city. For Ricoeur, this act expresses something more than the rights of the family in opposition to those of the city.[426] Here, one finds that the bond between sister and brother supersedes the political distinction between friend and enemy. However, in the case of the city in whose defence *Creon,* "subordinates his family bonds by forbidding the burial of the friend who has now become an enemy, it too receives from its mythical and from its lasting religious structure, a significance that is more than political."[427]

In these two tragic cases, therefore, one finds discordance in the way Antigone and Creon draw the lines between friend and enemy. For Ricoeur, the practical determination of these two cases, "cannot be reduced to simple modalities of choices along the lines described by Aristotle and Kant."[428] Something more is needed and in the light of Sophocles' *Antigone,* Ricoeur relies on *tragic wisdom.*[429] According to Ricoeur, "tragic wisdom" is capable of directing us in conflicts of a different nature – conflicts which are borne out of conflicting moral obligations. Like the tragedy of Antigone, we are also, in some way, caught up with the interminable opposition between man and woman, old age and youth, society and the individual, the living and the dead –

425 For the full story on the relationship between Antigone and Creon, read: Paul Ricoeur. *Oneself as Another.* 1992, p.242-244.

426 Paul Ricoeur. *Oneself as Another.* 1992, p.241-241.

427 Paul Ricoeur. *Oneself as Another.* 1992, p.242.

428 Paul Ricoeur. *Oneself as Another.* 1992, p.242.

429 Sophocles is a tragic Greek playwright who presents a terrifying image of man as a species whose ability to master nature is paralleled only by his failure to master himself. In other words, man seems to be in control of nature, yet uncontrollable (cf. *Antigone,* 368ff).

an opposition whose solution is not to be sought in an *either-or* dialectic. In the same way, the conflicts that arise as a result of our obligations to one thing or another are not merely resolved by recourse to morality or ethics or even a synthesis of the two. For Ricoeur, what is to be sought in such aporetic situations is "practical wisdom".[430]

According to Ricoeur, *practical wisdom* is the appropriate application of universal norms in situations where one is confronted by conflicting moral obligations. It is neither synthetic nor disavows the morality of obligation but is designed to give guidance as to how one can act appropriately and justly in aporetic situations. It is the art of mediating the requirements of the ethical aim and the moral norm so as to be able to act appropriately, and thereby contribute to establishing happiness *with and for others in just institutions.*[431] By taking the triadic components of the ethical aim (just institutions, respect for persons and autonomy), Ricoeur demonstrates how morally conflictual situations arise within these different components.[432] However, we shall only focus attention on two examples of morally conflictual situations within the context of *respect for persons,* and show how Ricoeur proposes their fruitful mediation through *practical wisdom.*

The reasons for this delimitation are as follows: while the reciprocity of respect (solicitude) constitutes the dialogic structure of self-esteem or respect, the principles of justice and equality are the extension of solicitude at the level of just institutions. As Ricoeur put it, "the sense of justice takes nothing away from solicitude but presupposes it to the extent that it holds persons to

---

430 Ricoeur refers to "practical wisdom" as the moral judgement made in particular situations and the convictions that dwell in it. For Ricoeur, if moral judgments indeed develop aporetic situations, then "convictions remain the only available way out." (See, Paul Ricoeur. *Oneself as Another.* 1992, p.240-241).

431 Paul Ricoeur. *Oneself as Another.* 1992, p.240.

432 Paul Ricoeur. *Oneself as Another.* 1992, p.249-282.

be irreplaceable."[433] Since self-respect (*autonomy*) and the principles of justice and equality (*just institutions*) can be derived from *respect for persons* (solicitude), we deem that the focus on two examples of the conflicts generated in solicitude and how practical wisdom mediates between them would, to some extent, provide an implied or inferred sense of how practical wisdom could mediate between morally conflictual situations at the levels of *society* and the *individual*. Apart from this reason, not only is time and space a factor, but the attempt to give a comprehensive treatment to the other components would digress from the thesis of the chapter. Thus, lets us now address the two examples of moral conflicts in solicitude or respect for persons and how practical wisdom mediates between them.

3.5.1 Respect for Persons and Conflicts

Ricoeur's moral principle on *respect for persons* hinges on the second Kantian Categorical Imperative: "treat humanity in one's own person and in the person of others as an end in itself and not as a means."[434] For Ricoeur, one finds in this imperative a fine dividing line between the universalist version of the imperative (represented by the idea of *humanity*) and the pluralist version of it (represented by the idea of *persons* as ends in themselves). Whereas Kant finds no opposition between the two dimensions,[435] Ricoeur asserts that a conflict arises, "as soon as the otherness of persons, inherent in the very idea of human plurality, proves to be … incompatible with the universality of the rules that underlie the idea of humanity."[436] Here, *respect* due to persons splits up "into respect for

---

433 Paul Ricoeur. *Oneself as Another*. 1992, p.202.
434 Paul Ricoeur. *Oneself as Another*. 1992, p.262.
435 Paul Ricoeur. *Oneself as Another*. 1992, p.263.
436 Paul Ricoeur. *Oneself as Another*. 1992, p.262.

the law and respect for persons."[437] Under these competing claims between respect for *persons* and respect for the *law,* practical wisdom may constitute, "giving priority to the respect for persons in the name of the solicitude that is addressed to persons in their irreplaceable singularity."[438]

Ricoeur also examines the idea of *promise-keeping* in the light of the application of the second Kantian Categorical Imperative and those sanctioned by *law.* According to Ricoeur, the Constitutive rule of promising says that; "*A* places himself under the obligation of doing *X* on behalf of *B* in circumstance *Y.*"[439] Here, the *principle of fidelity*[440] defines the obligation to keep one's promises. It begins from the firm intention or the commitment to do what the other expects of me. As a rule of reciprocity it, "establishes the other in the position of someone to whom an obligation is owed, someone who is counting on me and making self-constancy a response to this expectation."[441] In respect of promises sanctioned by *laws, oaths* and *contracts,* Ricoeur says that, "the expectations of others who count on me … becomes a right to require something of me."[442] Although the promise-to-keep-the-law takes us into the area of legal norms which seem to obliterate the relations between the norm and the solicitude when one reconsiders the forms of promise sanctioned by the courts, there still remains a tie between the normative moment and the ethical intentions expressed as: "'from you' says the other, 'I expect that you would keep your word; to you I reply, 'you can count on me.'"[443] So, *counting-on-me,* "connects self-constancy in its moral tenor to the principle of reciprocity founded in solicitude."[444]

---

437 Paul Ricoeur. *Oneself as Another.* 1992, p.262.

438 Paul Ricoeur. *Oneself as Another.* 1992, p.262.

439 Paul Ricoeur. *Oneself as Another.* 1992, p.262.

440 Paul Ricoeur. *Oneself as Another.* 1992, p.262.

441 Paul Ricoeur. *Oneself as Another.* 1992, p.268.

442 Paul Ricoeur. *Oneself as Another.* 1992, p.268.

443 Paul Ricoeur. *Oneself as Another.* 1992, p.268.

444 Paul Ricoeur. *Oneself as Another.* 1992, p.268.

Since the above discourse constitutes the context within which self-constancy is maintained through *promise-keeping* and the *obligation imposed on one by law,* the conflicts of moral duty arise when one makes exceptions to the maxim on behalf of oneself or on behalf of others. Here, Ricoeur cites two examples of morally conflictual situations and how practical wisdom mediates between them to facilitate the path to *living the good life with and for others in just institutions.* Whereas one example is cited from the "beginning of life", the other comes from the "end of life" situations. The first example concerns whether or not to tell the truth to the dying. Here, a breach occurs between two extreme attitudes: either telling the truth to a dying person out of sheer respect for the law, and without the concern for the capacity of the dying person to receive the truth; or consciously lying to the dying person out of fear that the truth might agonise him or her. How does practical wisdom apply in this situation?

For Ricoeur, *practical wisdom* would consist of inventing the *just behaviour* best suited for each case. It considers as false the establishment of rules out of the duty to *lie* to the patient for fear that the truth might cause them more pain. It therefore disallows, "transforming into a rule, the exceptions of the rule."[445] Practical wisdom therefore focuses on *how* to communicate the truth to the patient in the most appropriate way, taking into consideration the condition of the patient. As Ricoeur put it, "it is one thing to name an illness, it is quite another to reveal the degree of seriousness and the slight chances of survival, and yet another to wield the clinical truth as a death sentence."[446] By focusing on the appropriate way to communicate the truth, practical wisdom also takes cognizance of the fact that there are some situations where even telling the truth to the patient, "becomes the opportunity for the exchange of giving and receiving under

---

445 Paul Ricoeur. *Oneself as Another.* 1992, p.269.
446 Paul Ricoeur. *Oneself as Another.* 1992, p.269.

the sign of the acceptance of death."[447] Thus, it demands that we carefully judge the situation with the aid of expert advice. This advice then helps one to take the best suitable step in response to the rule of reciprocity and respect.

The second example relates to respect for persons at the "beginning of life" or the problem of abortions. Abortions cause difficult moral problems because of the ontological questions which are posed at the beginning of life. For instance, what is the nature of the *being* of the embryo and the foetus? If Kant's statement that, "rational beings exist as ends in themselves" is to be taken seriously as the basis for respect due to persons, then the difficult moral question is – what sort of being are the embryo and the foetus? Are they things or persons? If one follows Kant's argument that, "only rational beings exist in themselves", then the implication remains that only fully developed rational beings have moral standing and since the foetus and the embryo are not fully rational, they have no moral standing. Thus, construing the human person based on the Kantian "rational being" proposition contradicts the views of advocates of the *biological criterion* who see human life in terms of the presence and the absence of the human person. For advocates of the biological criterion a, "person and life are indissociable inasmuch as the latter supports the former."[448] For them, the genomics of heredity which signs biologic individuality is constituted at the moment of conception. This means that human life begins at the moment of conception. In this way "the embryo's 'right to life' is a right to a 'chance to live.'"[449] Thus, any practice that does not serve this "presumed ends of the embryo and the foetus, which are the right to live and to develop, is to be prohibited."[450]

Practical wisdom therefore mediates between Kant's rational beings view and the views of the biologic school by stirring a

---

447 Paul Ricoeur. *Oneself as Another.* 1992, p.270.
448 Paul Ricoeur. *Oneself as Another.* 1992, p.270.
449 Paul Ricoeur. *Oneself as Another.* 1992, p.271.
450 Paul Ricoeur. *Oneself as Another.* 1992, p.271.

middle ground between the understanding of persons and things. Here, it focuses on the position of the biological school to determine the phenomenon of the thresholds and the stages of the development of life. This is achieved through a *progressive ontology* which recognizes embryos as *potential human beings* whose rational capacities develop over time.[451] This progressive ontology is then used to defend the rights of foetuses as persons. As a result, practical wisdom affirms that there are different stages of the development of the human person, from the human embryo to the fully developed person. Embryos are therefore potential human beings. So, in each stage of their development, there is a progression of qualitatively different rights and duties: the right not to suffer, the duty to prevent suffering, the right to protection and the obligation to offer it, and the right to respect and the duty to give it. These rights are accorded to the embryo, "once something like an exchange – even dissymmetrical, of proverbial signs is begun between the foetus and its mother."[452] In consequence, *practical wisdom* in these and similar moral conflictual situations has the following features: (1) it upholds the moral norm, though it may apply it differently according to different situations; (2) it searches for a "just mean" or the Aristotelian *mesotēs,* in other words. it searches for a common ground or a negotiation of the broken middle; and (3) as a judgement in situations, practical wisdom always relies on the knowledge of competent and wise experts, in order to traverse the domain of arbitrariness and make appropriate judgements of the situation.[453] As Kaplan put it, a person of practical wisdom, "confers with others in order to arrive at an informed, just and appropriate action."[454]

In considering practical wisdom in the light of Christian-Muslim dialogue, one could say that in the case of the conflict

451 Paul Ricoeur. *Oneself as Another.* 1992, p.271.
452 Paul Ricoeur. *Oneself as Another.* 1992, p.272.
453 Paul Ricoeur. *Oneself as Another.* 1992I, p.273.
454 David Kaplan. *Ricoeur's Critical Theory.* 2003, p.113.

of interpretations concerning the meaning of, for instance, a Christological title like *Messiah* which is common to Islam and Christianity, practical wisdom would first of all consist of understanding its meaning within each tradition and the theological frameworks which give rise to this meaning. Hence, a consideration of the principle of the *Tawhid* and the doctrine of the *Holy Trinity* and how they give meaning to the Christian and the Islamic interpretations of the title is helpful. Furthermore, the views of recognised Islamic and Christian scholars may contribute to giving clarity to the understanding of the concept within the two faith traditions. In the case of Christian-Muslim dialogue on Christology as an exercise in learning, *practical wisdom* would also emphasize on how Christians and Muslims can learn from each other on the basis of the identity and the mission of *Jesus the Christ* and the significance of his *message* in both faith traditions. Here, although the title *Messiah* may be understood differently between the two traditions, practical wisdom does not emphasize on the right claimant of truth about the title, but what can be learnt from the *life, mission* and the *message* of the title bearer (Jesus the Christ) in the desire to *live the good life with and for others in just institutions*? This is the significant question which will guide our deliberations in Chapters Five and Six.

3.6 Conclusion

In conclusion, it must be said that Christology is still, today, a contentious subject in Christian-Muslim conversations. These contentions seem to be worsened by the negative perceptions that both Christians and Muslims have about each other's theologies, religious texts and traditions in response to the identity and the mission of Jesus Christ. Yet, Jesus remains a common historical person shared by both faith traditions but is divided between them. Although differences in religious traditions may be the reason for the deadening apologetics between them, much of these are also the result of unresolved prejudices each has about the other. This explains why dialogue on Christology as an exercise in learning is deemed relevant for clarifying some of these prejudices, preconceptions and stereotypes. In this chapter, we asserted that learning has the capacity to clarify unfounded prejudices and set the dialogical parties on a new form of interrelationship defined by what Ricoeur refers to as *aiming at the good life with and for others in just institutions*. If we consider that in interreligious dialogue the "good life" could also mean "a life lived in submission to God" expressed in the *love of God and love of thy neighbour*; then aiming at the "good life" is not only undertaken in isolation, but together with others through the institutions which shape and guide their respective understandings of the good life.

However, living a good life together with others in just institutions demands that we cultivate certain attitudes or dispositions in respect of our perceptions of the other, and how we relate to them. In other words, the encounter with the other demands *honest, sincere* and *respectful* relationships. We indicated that dialogue as an exercise in learning is made possible under some necessary conditions such as *commitment, openness, respect for others* and the recognition of the other as an *equal-partner-in-dialogue*. In the discourses above, we found that Ricoeur's three components of the ethical intention somehow provided the medium for further reflections on these necessary conditions, also called the *appropriate dialogical attitudes*. Consequently, the thesis of this chapter lies in the claim that: for Christian-Muslim dialogue on Christology to succeed as an exercise in learning, it must take serious considerations of the above necessary conditions to dialogue as an exercise in learning. By so doing, the locus of learning would then lie in what the self and the other have to say about the identity, the mission and the significance of the message of Jesus Christ in their respective faith traditions. For Islam Jesus is a *Prophet* or the *Messenger of Allah*, while for Christianity he is the "Son of God" and the "Saviour of the World". However, what do Christians and Muslims really mean when they construe Jesus Christ in these terms? And what can Christians and Muslims learn from each other about Jesus Christ following these faith constructions? While Chapter Four provides a Christian response to the first question, Chapter Five gives a Muslims response to it. Let us now delve into the essential content of what Christians mean when they describe Jesus as the "Son of God" and the "Saviour of the World". We shall undertake this task following the lens through which the Gospel writers (with a Markan priority) perceived him.

CHAPTER FOUR
THE CHRISTIAN UNDERSTANDINGS
OF CHRISTOLOGY

4.1 Introduction

The thesis of this chapter is built on the argument that Christianity and Islam are religions with different traditions which define their respective understandings of the identity and the mission of Jesus Christ. This suggests that there is something more about Jesus Christ in the other's faith tradition which one can learn in new and better ways through dialogue as an exercise in learning. As we indicated in Chapter Three, respect for the integrity of the *other* must first begin by allowing the *other* to communicate their faith beliefs about Jesus as they pertain to their tradition-specific contexts. This chapter therefore seeks to create the appropriate platform for a systematic presentation of the Christian tradition-specific conception of Christology within the context of dialogue as an exercise in learning. Within this context of these dialogical conversations as Gadamer put it, "what is to be grasped is the substantive rightness of the other's opinion, so that we can be at one with each other on a subject."[455]

"Christology" has its etymological roots from two Greek words: "Χριστός" (Christos) which means "Christ" and "λογία" (logos) which means "word, reason or the study of". Since "Christ" refers to Jesus, we could say that ,"Christology" in the Christian context, means "the study of the person and the mission of Jesus Christ." As Raymond Brown put it, "Christology would discuss how Jesus came to be called the *Messiah* or Christ and what was meant by that designation."[456] From this perspective, Brown

---

455 Gadamer, *Truth and Method*. 1989, p.385.
456 Raymond Brown. *An Introduction to New Testament Christology*. 1994, p.3.

views Christology as that subject which discusses any evaluation of Jesus in respect to who he was, and the role he played in the divine plan.[457] It thus addresses issues relating to Jesus Christ as both God and Man, and how he became such in the incarnation. Whereas the Christian scriptures provide a wealth of evidence in relation to narratives that justify the conceptual pairing of the humanity and the divinity of Jesus Christ, Christology correlates and clarifies how this is made possible in the same person. In other words, we could say that today, Christology represents a renewed response to the question Jesus put to his disciples, "Who do you say I am?"

From the testimony of the synoptic Gospels, we find different responses to this Christological question. For instance, in Mark 8: 27-29, while others said he was John the Baptist, still others said he was Elijah or one of the Ancient prophets, Simon Peter identified him as "the Christ, the son of the living God". So, from the text of Mark 8: 27-29, we could say that these different responses to the Christological question represents the diverse understandings of the early Christians' experience of Jesus, giving rise to what Richard Longenecker called the "multiple Christologies" of the New Testament.[458] In our contemporary context, there is a growing interest among scholars who seek to investigate whether or not there is a correlation between Jesus' self-understanding and the understanding of the disciples. As Raymond Brown rightly interrogated, "to what extent did what his followers said and thought about him correspond to the image reflected in what he himself said and did?"[459] Are these in continuity with Chalcedonian Christology? Responses to these questions have equally precipitated multiple Christological approaches such as *low* Christology (Christology from below) and

---

457 Raymond Brown. *An Introduction to New Testament Christology* 1994, p.3.

458 Richard Longenecker. *Contours of Christology in the New Testament*. 2005, p. xiii.

459 Raymond Brown. *An Introduction to New Testament Christology*. 1994, p.6.

high Christology (Christology from above) – sometimes set in diametrical opposition.

According to Raymond Brown, while "low Christology" covers the evaluation of Jesus in terms that do not *necessarily* imply his divinity; "high Christology" covers the evaluation of Jesus in terms that include *an aspect* of his divinity.[460] Thus, there are variant responses to the Christological question – sometimes very similar with the responses of the immediate disciples of Jesus as demonstrated in Mark 8: 28-29. However, do these different responses defy any possibility of a unified Christological understanding of Jesus Christ for Christian faith and theology? For Longenecker, even though there may be distinctive features in the portrayals of Jesus by the New Testament writers, "there is a certain 'sense of centre' in the various representations and statements about Jesus of Nazareth by the New Testament writers."[461] Trusting the veracity of Longenecker's view in the light of the contemporary argument that, "Christology is pluralistic in both method and content",[462] it could be said that Christian theology nonetheless continues to emphasize on this "sense of centre" as the appropriate Christian response to the Christological question. That is, for Christian faith and theology, Jesus is Christ, the "Son of God" (Mark 8: 29).

In the light of the views that the synoptic Gospels portray Jesus Christ as one who was predominantly concerned with proclaiming the imminence of the Kingdom of God and of its justice, without particular emphasis on himself as God,[463] some scholars seem to battle with the question as to how the *proclaimer* or the *bearer of the Word of God* could suddenly become the *proclaimed* or the *essential*

---

460 Raymond Brown. *An Introduction to New Testament Christology.* 1994, p.4.

461 Richard Longenecker. (editor). *Contours of Christology in the New Testament.* 2005, p. xiii.

462 Roger Haight. *The Future of Christology.* 2007, p.15.

463 Küng *et al. Christianity and World Religions; Paths to dialogue.* 1993, p.116.

content of that Word?[464] They ask whether there is congruence between Jesus' self-understanding and the understanding of the early Christian community. Here, the question Muslims constantly put to Christians remains relevant; how could God become man in Jesus Christ and still retain his divine attributes? These questions point to the Christological challenge which Christian theology is called upon to respond. Consequently, our interest in this section is to investigate into how the Synoptic Gospels, especially the Gospel of Mark, maps out the identity and the mission of Jesus Christ, and how this is articulated in Christian theology today. We choose to take this route into the Christian perspective on Christology because Christology represents an enormous branch of Christian theology whose scope cannot be covered in this limited space.

As we shall see, Jesus Christ is the reason for Christian faith and hence, permeates the entirety of the Christian life and theology. So, a Christology from a Christian perspective cannot be comprehensively addressed given the limited space in this chapter. This is because such a Christology will embrace an account of the protology and the eschatology of Christian faith and life. However, since dialogue as an exercise in learning demands the sharing of mutual testimonies of faith about the life and the mission of Jesus Christ, Christians cannot but present a Christian view of the identity and the mission of Jesus Christ – one which is at once succinct for this purpose and yet represents an authentic Christian perspective. It is in response to this sense of duty to attest to the Christian story about Jesus Christ that we turn to the Christology of the synoptic Gospels, particularly the Gospel of Mark. While it is scholarly acclaimed that the synoptic Gospels "see Jesus Christ with the same eye" and so, tell similar stories about him; our interest in Mark's Gospel is informed by how

---

464 In reference to this notion of the preoccupation of Jesus, Adolf von Harnack said that, "the gospel, as Jesus proclaimed it, has to do with the Father only, not with the Son" (See Adolf von Harnack. *What is Christianity?* 1986, p.144-162).

Mark presents the identity of Jesus Christ through his the "Son of God" and the "Son of Man" motifs.

Consequently, what follows below is a *theological reading or interpretation* of the Gospel of Mark. By "theological interpretation of Scripture", we mean the "readings of Biblical texts that consciously seek to do justice to the theological nature of these texts, and embraces the influence and the direction of theology on the interpreter's enquiry, context, and methods".[465] It is said that the theological interpretations to Biblical texts arise as a result of the "character of the texts" and the "interpreter's commitment" to it. While the character of the texts underscores the theological nature of the text *per se,* some scholars question whether this theological nature of the text is not often spanned by the interpreter's personal perspectives.[466] Even though it is generally agreed that there is no such thing as presuppositionless interpretation of texts, yet the interpreter's honest commitment to comprehend the text's true nature, guards against his or her self-imposed understanding or misunderstanding. Besides, Spinks indicates that, "for theological interpretations, the place and the view of the interpreter often go hand in hand with the nature of the text." This is because, if the interpreter's vantage point is from a Christian stance, with all the conditions that this entails, "then either an implicit or explicit acknowledgment of the theological character of the nature of the biblical texts is at work in the practice of reading and interpreting."[467] In this way, a theological interpretation of biblical texts takes into consideration, the theological nature of the text and the interpreter's worldview of it.

---

465 Christopher Spinks. *The Bible and the Crises of Meaning: Debates on the Theological Interpretation of Scripture.* 2007, p.7.

466 See also, Todd Billings. *The Word of God for the People of God: An Entryway to the Theological Interpretation of Scripture.* 2010; Daniel Trier. *Introduction Theological Interpretation of Scripture: Recovery a Christian Practice.* 2008, p.24-34.

467 Christopher Spinks. *The Bible and the Crises of Meaning.* 2007, p.6.

Consequently, our theological reading and interpretation of the Gospel of Mark is informed by the fact that the theological nature of the text captures a unique Christian worldview on the identity and the mission of Jesus Christ. As a result, following the broad models of interpretations and meanings given to the text by Christian scholars, one is able to reach a better understanding of Mark's Christological intent, which he unmistakably presents in the prologue of the Gospel, and expounds in his two Christological motifs. On the one hand, while this two-nature Christology represents the authentic Christian perspective on the identity of Jesus Christ, on the other hand, it is also the locus of conflict (particularly the "Son of God" motif) between the Christian and the Muslim understanding of Christology. Hence, a clarification on the *metaphoricity* of the "Son of God" designation might contribute to clarifying the Muslim perceptions about the Christian worldview on the matter. Where this occurs, dialogue as an exercise in learning would have been considered successful on the merits of its goal.

4.2 Christology in the Synoptic Gospels: the Markan Priority

The term "synoptic" has its etymology from two Greek words; "*syn*" and "*optic*" which means "together" and "seen" respectively. Hence, "synoptic" literally means "seeing together." When applied to the Gospel material, *synoptic* characterizes those Gospels that "see together" or present the same narratives, in the same sequence and wording about the life and the mission of Jesus Christ. The first three Gospels (Mathew, Mark and Luke) are often defined by this category because of their degree of similarity in content, narrative structure, language and sentence formation. As Paul Haffner pointed out, "when placed side by side and brought in one view, these three Gospels present a striking resemblance and appear as one narrative."[468] Thus, Mathew, Mark, and Luke are said to be so similar to each other that in a sense, they view Jesus Christ "with the same lens" in contrast to the very different picture of Jesus Christ presented in the Johannine Gospel. Yet, as Haffner indicated, there are also many significant differences between the synoptic Gospels.[469] Hence, we consider that a focus on Mark's Christology would, to some degree, speak to the Christological issues raised in the Gospels of Mathew and Luke. Why Mark's Gospel?

The Gospel of Mark is credited to John Mark, a companion of Peter the Apostle (see Acts 12: 12-13; Colossians 4: 10; and 1 Timothy 4: 11). Whereas some scholars like Dominic Crossan think that Mark made use of earlier traditional sources (that is, the Gospel of Saint Thomas or the Gospel of Barnabas) in composing his Gospel,[470] scholarly consensus has it that Mark's Gospel was written between 60-70AD and is regarded as the earliest among the canonical Gospels.[471] Mark's Gospel is the shortest among the canonical Gospels; written in primitive (simple) Greek possibly by an author who clearly has a first language other than Greek.[472] Its language is very direct and vivid. It has no background information about Jesus; especially his ancestry and other relevant

---

468 Paul Haffner. *New Testament Theology: An Introduction.* 2006, p.135.

469 For more information on the differences between the synoptic Gospels, see: Haffner, Paul, M. *New Testament Theology: An Introduction.* 2006.

470 For Dominic Crossan, there are four layers in the Jesus tradition which correspond to four different periods: (1) 30-60 AD, (2) 60-80 AD, (3) 80-120 AD and (4) 120-150 AD. In these layers, Crossan suggests that his work went "beyond the present Gospel of Mark to an earlier layer to which he places the source Q, the Gospel of Thomas, and the genuine letters of Paul." (See, Hans Schwarz. *Christology.* 1998, p.68ff).

471 Raymond Brown. *Introduction to the New Testament.* 1997, p.164; Morna Hooker. "Who Can This Be?" The Christology of Mark's Gospel." 2005, p.79.

472 Richard Burridge & Gould, Graham. *Jesus Now and Then.* 2004, p.54.

biographical information as one might expect. The Gospel is equally stripped of the normal endings of Jesus' appearances after the resurrection, commonly associated with the other synoptics. In this way, its earlier dating is the reason for our preference.

According to Morna Hooker, the best way to discover Mark's Christology is by considering the Gospel as it stands; a narrative Christology which can only be understood by studying the story that Mark tells.[473] If dialogue on Christology demands that we listen carefully to what the other has to say about Jesus Christ, then it is all the more necessary for us to be attentive to the story Mark tells about Jesus Christ. Many scholars agree that the narrative structure of Mark's Gospel consists of the *Prologue* (1: 1 – 15), the *Galilean Ministry* (1: 16 – 8: 26), *the Way of the Cross* (8: 27 – 15: 39) and the *Epilogue* (15: 40 – 16: 8).[474] Kummel and George however indicate that the epilogue (Mark 16: 9 – 20) is not part of the original Mark.[475] From this structure, one could study Mark's Christology in different ways: either by focusing on the healings, the exorcisms and the miracle stories; or by the titles used by Jesus or designated to him. For this study, we propose an entry into Markan Christology through the titles the "Son of God" and the "Son of Man". Here, we shall demonstrate that Mark's authorial intent is unmistakably stated in the prologue of the Gospel; while the rest of the narrative serves as a progressive development of this intent. As we indicated in the introduction, the work here is not an exegetical presentation *per*

473 Morna Hooker. "Who Can This Be?" 2005, p.80.

474 See, Jack Kingsbury. *The Christology of Mark's Gospel*. 1983; English, Donald. *The Message of Mark: The Mystery of Faith*. 1992; Morna Hooker. "Who Can This Be?" 2005.

475 Mark 16: 9 – 20 concerns the resurrection and the post-resurrection experiences. For many scholars, this part of the Gospel is an addition to the oldest manuscript traceable to the author (Kummel, Werner, and George. *Introduction to the New Testament*. 1975, p.96-101; Jack Kingsbury. *The Christology of Mark's Gospel*. 1983, p.47-173).

se, but a theological reading and interpretation of Mark's Gospel – an exercise in learning within which Mark is allowed to walk us through his narrative story about *Jesus Christ,* the *Son of God.*

4.2.1 The Prologue of Mark (1: 1 – 15)

According to Donald English, Mark's purpose is to be found in the prologue, especially in the opening thirteen verses which "sets it out in breath-taking clarity."[476] The prologue to the Gospel begins in Mark 1: 1 – "this is the beginning of the Gospel of *Jesus Christ,* the *Son of God.*"[477] According to Morna Hooker, Mark sees the *Gospel* (the Good News) to be not just about Jesus Christ, but Jesus Christ himself. This is attested to by the fact that from Mark 1: 9 onward, Jesus would become the central figure in the narrative. Furthermore, the fact that Mark describes Jesus as the "Christ" (*Christos*) and as the "Son of God" (*huios Theou*) in Mark 1: 1 it further defines his authorial intent on Jesus' identity and the mission. But what does Mark mean when he uses titles like the "Christ" and the "Son of God" in reference to Jesus? Although one finds the answer to this question in the prologue, it is also located in the main narrative of the Gospel.

In the prologue, Mark first of all, draws continuity between Jesus and God's previous activities in the world (Mark 1: 2 – 3) – "Look, I am sending out my messenger ahead of you to prepare your way…" According to Morna Hooker, Mark attributes this quotation (which is a mixture of Exodus 23: 20, Malachi 3: 1 and Isaiah 40: 3) to the Prophet Isaiah[478] who is a strong pillar in the Old Testament prophetic narratives. By establishing that continuity between Jesus and the Prophet Isaiah, Mark "sees Jesus

---

476 English, Donald. *The Message of Mark: The Mystery of Faith.* 1992, p.15.
477 The *Holy Bible* (Revised Standard Version).
478 Morna Hooker. "Who Can This Be?" 2005, p.82.

as the fulfilment of the Old Testaments hopes and as the one who brings redemption that is, in effect, a new exodus."[479] Secondly, John the Baptist who is the last of the Old Testament prophets is presented in the Gospel as the "voice" that cries in the wilderness (Mark 1: 3). Here, John the Baptist functions as the one who calls the nation to repentance through baptism (Mark 1: 4 – 5) and to some extent, a herald and a witness to the identity of the one he announces (Mark 1: 7 – 8).[480] Thirdly, the voice from heaven which said; "You are my son, the beloved with whom I am well pleased" (Mark 1: 11), seals Mark's Christological intent in that the "heavenly father's" voice is identified as God himself. So, if God calls Jesus His son, what further evidence does the reader need to ascertain Jesus' divine sonship? This breath-taking evidence displayed in the Gospel made Donald English to assert that Mark 1: 11 "provides the closing brackets of the parenthesis which began with the "Son of God" in Mark 1: 1."[481]

In consequence, Mark provides the reader with three veritable testimonies to the identity of Jesus in the prologue: that is, (1) the testimony of the scriptures through the Prophet Isaiah; (2) the witness of John the Baptist as a herald; and (3) the affirmation of a heavenly higher authority (a God-father). As Morna Hooker put it, "whatever answers are given to the question 'who is Jesus?' in the rest of the narrative would certainly have to be judged against this one."[482] Hence, what follows the prologue is the progressive development of Mark's Christology in the main narrative which is built on the motif of Jesus Christ as the "Son of God" and the "Son of Man". These two Christological titles then provide access to a fuller comprehension of Mark's story about Jesus the Christ, and the "Son of God". Without the presumption that the prologue is the summary of the content of the

479 Morna Hooker. "Who Can This Be?" 2005, p.82.
480 Morna Hooker. "Who Can This Be?" 2005, p.82.
481 Donald English. *The Message of Mark*. 1992, p.16.
482 Morna Hooker. "Who Can This Be?" 2005, p.82.

Gospel, it could be said that the prologue in Mark's Gospel gives clarity to the words and the deeds of Jesus which follow from Mark 1: 16 – 15: 47.

The *corpus* of Mark 1: 16 – 15: 47 is divided into two sections which are defined by the density of the two Christological titles: that is, the "Son of God" and the "Son of Man" titles. Peter's *confession* on the way to Caesarea Philippi (Mark 8: 27 – 30) serves as the watershed which separates these two Christological titles, and yet unites them in a holistic narrative on Mark's story about the identity and the mission of Jesus the Christ. Thus, the first section is defined by the density of the "Son of God" sayings and implications (Mark 1: 16 – 8: 26), while the second section has the dominance of the "Son of Man" sayings and implications (Mark 8: 31 – 15: 47). However, it must be said that the two sections are not exclusive to each other in the use of these Christological titles. Occasionally, one finds the title "Son of God" in the second section and vice versa. These fine intertwinements in Christological titles further demonstrates how the titles are linked in one person, and yet separated in him. As a result, what one finds in Mark is a tacit accentuation of the hypostatic union of the humanity and the divinity of Jesus Christ; a form of Christology which the Council of Chalcedon will later develop and promulgate as the official Christian understanding of Christ in 451AD. Let us see how Mark develops his Christology in the Gospel.

4.2.2 Jesus Christ as the "Son of God" in Mark (1: 16 – 8: 26)

Many New Testament scholars have variously noted the conspicuously favoured position Mark gives the title the "Son of God" to Jesus the Christ. The title appears in the following parts of the Gospel: the opening lines of the prologue (Mark 1: 1); the voice from heaven at Jesus' Baptism (Mark 1: 11); it is confessed by the demons as Jesus subdues them (Mark 3: 11 and Mark 5: 7); the "voice from heaven" proclaims it again at the Mount of Transfiguration (Mark 9: 7); Jesus himself claims it at the high priest's interrogation (Mark 14: 61-62); the Centurion confesses it at the foot of the cross (Mark 15: 39); and other instances in which it is insinuated either by word, by deed or by both, where Jesus directly or indirectly associates himself to the use of this title (Mark 13: 32). Even though Jesus is not seen to overtly refer to himself by the "Son of God" title, except in response to the question put to him by the High Priest (Mark14: 61), he nevertheless did not openly object to the title anytime he was referred to by it. As Lewis Hay points out, "Mark had a high regard for the title is not seriously questioned, but the precise meaning of the title to the Evangelist is a matter of sharp debate."[483] What then did Mark mean by use of the title the "Son of God"?

The title the "Son of God" has frequently been used in the Old Testament. So, understanding its meaning and context within the Old Testament might offer us helpful insights into Mark's understanding of the title. According to Cornelius Aherne, "the word 'Son' was employed among the Semites to signify not only filiation, but other close connexions and intimate relationships".[484] In the Old Testament, one finds descriptions such as the "son of strength" (meaning a hero), the "son of Belial" (meaning a wicked man), the "sons of prophets" (meaning the disciples of prophets) and so forth. From the sense of *established relationships*, the title the "Son of God" was applied in the Old Testament to persons who have such special relationships with God. For instance, the title was used for the Old Testament figures such as: The Angels, devout men, and the descendants of Seth, among others. These were equally referred to as "sons of God" (See, Job 1: 6, 2: 1; Psalm 88: 7 and Wisdom 2: 13). The title was also used

---

483 Lewis Hay. "The Son-of-God Christology in Mark." 1964 (2): 106.
484 Cornelius Aherne. "Son of God." *The Catholic Encyclopaedia*. Vol. 14. 2010. http://www.newadvent.org/cathen/14142b.htm (03/03/2013).

in reference to Israel as a nation (See Exodus 4: 22; Deuteronomy 14: 50; Jeremiah 31: 9 and Hosea 11: 1) and to Israel's leaders who owe their authority to God (See 2 Samuel 7: 14; 1 Chronicles 17: 13 and Psalm 2: 7). In the light of Israelite kingship, the title is also used in reference to Yahweh's promise of the Messianic King. Here, James Dunn indicates that, "in the Qumran scrolls, the royal *Messiah* is thought of as God's son."[485] Inferring therefore from the above use of the title, one could surmise that the use of the title in the Old Testament was more analogical and metaphorical than the literal sense of filiation. Could this be the same sense in Mark's identification of Jesus as the "Son of God"?

Before responding to the above question, it might be helpful to try to conceptualize how the designation "Son of God" in Mark relates to Jesus' identity as the *Messiah*. This is significant because: (1) the title the *Messiah* feeds into Mark's identification of Jesus as the "Son of God"; and (2) the Qur'an in many verses also refers to Jesus as the *Messiah* (al-Masih – see Surah 4: 171). As a result, some Christian enthusiasts have the tendency to illegitimately impose Christian views on Islamic contexts when theologizing on *al-Masih*. In dialogue as an exercise in learning, both Christians and Muslims need to know what each means when they refer to Jesus as the *Messiah* or *al-Masih*. This is very significant for the prospects of dialogue as an exercise in learning from and about the other.

As we indicated earlier, Mark's identification of Jesus as the *Messiah* begins in the prologue which has within it the key Greek terms: *'ησοῦ Χριστοῦ υἱοῦ θεοῦ*, transliterated as: "Jesus Christ, the "Son of God" (Mark 1: 1). The word *Christos* (*Messiah* in Aramaic) means "the anointed one." It initially referred to the anointing of a king who is appointed by God (King David being an example). Here, Gerald O'Collins indicates that. "by the ritual act of anointing, Old Testament kings were installed, for example: Saul (1 Samuel 10: 1), David (2 Samuel 2: 4, 5: 3) and Solomon (1 Kings 1: 34). Hence the king could be called the

---

485 James Dunn. *New Testament Theology: An Introduction.* 2009, p.59.

'Lord's anointed'".[486] Gerald O'Collins adds that this practice of anointing kings was later extended to the anointing of Aaronic priesthood; and also to the prophets, although there was no actual rite of anointing for the prophets.[487] However, with time, the term became linked to the expectations of a *kingly Messiah* who would liberate Israel from foreign domination.[488]

From its political context, the concept soon took on a more religious meaning in connection with the establishment of the Kingdom of God. As Dermot Lane put it, "in time, God's promises became centred around the establishment of the Kingdom of God on earth. The leading figure here was the *Messiah* who would be associated with the setting up of the Kingdom of God."[489] Establishing this Kingdom of God no longer entails waging wars of conquests, but leading people to seek repentance and forgiveness of sins. As a result, the enemy would no longer be a foreign power but sin. As the *Messiah,* Jesus' role would be to save fallen humanity from the tyranny of sin and death. Thus, Jesus' particular interest in preaching the reign of the Kingdom of God, together with the miracles that accompanied his teachings convinced his disciples that he was the expected Messiah. Here, Gerald O'Collins does not hesitate to add that while the miracles and the wondrous deeds Jesus performed helped the first Christians to identify him as the promised Messiah, Jesus himself also interpreted his person and activities messianically; in an unregaled and unwarlike fashion.[490]

---

486 Gerald O'Collins. *Christology: A Biblical, Historical and Systematic Study of Jesus.* 2009, p.24.

487 Gerald O'Collins. *Christology: A Biblical, Historical, and Systematic Study of Jesus.* 2009, p.25.

488 According to Gerald O'Collins, the rule of Yahweh is revealed in the rule of this messianic Davidic king who is also symbolized in the "one like the Son of Man." (Ibid, p.27, p.25-28).

489 Dermot Lane. *the Reality of Jesus.* 1975, p.13.

490 Gerald O'Collins. *Christology: A Biblical, Historical, and Systematic Study of Jesus.* 2009, p.27.

Consequently, if Mark ascribes the title the *Messiah* to Jesus, then he was simply expressing the experience of the first Christian community, of which he was constitutively part. Besides, the events of Jesus' baptism and transfiguration in which the voice from heaven calls Jesus "my beloved son" (Mark 1: 11 and Mark 9: 7), goes to confirm the close link between Jesus' *messianism* and his identity as the "Son of God". In this way, the *corpus* of Mark 1: 16 and Mark 8: 26 is a demonstration of the author's attempts to showcase to his readers the truth about Jesus as the *Messiah*, the "Son of God". If Jesus performs miracles and wonders, then it is as a consequence of his being the *Messiah*, the "Son of God". No one ever performed such wondrous deeds in contrast to him, precisely because no one shares his identity as the only begotten "Son of God". So, Jesus' divinity therefore provided the warrants to the miracles and to the wondrous deeds he performed.

As a result, the reader soon discovers that after Jesus' announcement of the imminence of the "Kingdom of God" and the calling of some disciples, what immediately follows in breath-taking succession are exorcisms, healings and the show of supernatural authority. Here, one finds that the *Messiah*, the "Son of God" is seriously at work by healing the man with the unclean spirit (Mark 1: 21ff), the healing of Simon's mother-in-law (Mark 1: 29ff), other healings in Galilee (Mark 1: 35ff), the cleansing of the leper (Mark 1: 40ff), the healing of the paralytic (Mark 2: 1ff), and the man with the withered hand (Mark 3: 1ff), the calming of the storm (Mark 4: 35ff), the deliverance of the Gerasene demoniac (Mark 5: 1ff), the raising of Jairus' daughter back to life (Mark 5: 21ff), the feeding of the five thousand (Mark 6: 30ff), walking on the sea (Mark 6: 45ff), the deliverance of the little girl with the unclean spirit (Mark 7: 24ff), the cure of the deaf man (Mark 7: 31ff), feeding the four thousand (Mark 8: 1ff) and the cure of the blind man (Mark 8: 22ff). These spectacular events by themselves evoked significant questions and responses on the part of the people who experienced or witnessed them. According to Morna Hooker, "the events affect those who observe them with *terror* (Mark 4: 41), *amazement*

(Mark 5: 20) and *astonishment* (Mark 5: 42), for they can find no answer to the question posed in Mark 4: 41, *"who can this be?"*[491] The expressions: "what is this? A new teaching! With authority he commands even unclean spirits and they obey him" (Mark 1: 7); "we have never seen anything like this" (Mark 2: 12); "who then is this, that even the wind and the sea obey him?" (Mark 4: 41) and so forth,[492] somehow points to the extraordinary way the people conceived the actions of Jesus. Thus. the people's amazement and acknowledgement of Jesus' supernatural powers seem to point to the work of the *Messiah* whose picture Mark seeks to accentuate. This explains why Donald English could say that Mark's, "picture of the *Messiah* is made even more compelling by the demonstration, beyond words of preaching, in the miracles Jesus performed."[493]

In effect, it could be said that Mark's reference to Jesus as the "Son of God" is not to be taken literally as the physical generation of a son, but as establishing the intimate relationship which existed between God the Father and Jesus Christ. As James Dunn pointed out, "when Christianity came to grapple with defining Jesus' relationship with God, it was the son of the father that emerged as the consensus way of doing so."[494] The reasons being that: first of all, in the Gospels Jesus expressed the relationship between himself and God in a "father-son" kind of relationship. For instance, he prayed to God as "Abba Father" (Mark 14: 36) which is a language of family intimacy. Secondly, the designation

---

491 Morna D. Hooker. "Who Can This Be?" 2005, p.88-89. The italics are not part of the original quote. Their purpose is for the sake of emphasis.

492 For Morna Hooker, the stilling of the storm presents us with Jesus' extraordinary authority. He controls not only the wind and the waves (4: 35 – 41), but also the whole legion of unclean spirits who addresses him as 'son of the most high God' (5: 7). (See Morna Hooker. "Who Can This Be?" 2005, p.88).

493 Donald English. *The Message of Mark: The Mystery of Faith*. 1992, p.16.

494 James Dunn. *New Testament Theology*. 2009, p.58.

the "Son of God" was used by the early Christians in their prayers and liturgy which supported their conviction that by faith in Jesus, they too were sharing in the same sense of sonship that "Abba" expressed.[495] Thus, the notion of divine sonship is not literal in the sense of God begetting a son.[496]

From the perspective of Christian–Muslim dialogue, the understanding of Jesus as the "Son of God" is perhaps one of the biggest stumbling blocks in their dialogical relations. In Surah 6: 101, the Qur'an says; "people of the Book; do not go to excess in your religion ... God is only one God. He is far above having a son ..." The Qur'an further says in Surah 4: 171; "... how could He (God) have a son when He has no spouse, when he created all things and has full knowledge of all things?"[497] While the designation "People of the Book" popularly refers to Christians, one gets the impression from the two texts above that the Qur'an perceives the Christian designation of Jesus as the "Son of God" in terms of physical generation – that is, the misunderstanding that Christians believe that God has taken the Virgin Mary as His wife and somehow impregnated her, giving birth to His son Jesus Christ. But as can be seen in this Markan *pericope* (Mark 1: 16 and Mark 8: 26), when Christian theology conceives Jesus as the "Son of God", this is viewed in a rather metaphorical sense which captures the special relationship which existed between Jesus and God. While this point shall be further developed in Chapter Five, let us now turn to the meaning of the designation the "Son of Man" in the Gospel of Mark.

---

495 James Dunn. *New Testament Theology*. 2009, p.58-59.
496 Oscar Cullmann. *The Christology of the New Testament*. 1963, p.276.
497 M.A.S. Abdel Haleem. *The Qur'an: A New Translation*. 2010.

4.2.3 Jesus Christ as the "Son of Man" in Mark (8: 31 and 15: 47)

The title the "Son of Man" (ὁ υἱὸς τοῦ ἀνθρώπου in the Greek) appears fourteen (14) times in Mark's Gospel. Out of these fourteen (14) occasions, only two (2) of these references (Mark 2: 10 – 11 and Mark 2: 27 – 28) appear in the "Son of God" narrative section (Mark 1: 16 and Mark 8: 26). The rest of the twelve references can only be located in the second section of the Gospel (Mark 8: 31 and Mark 15: 47). As one will notice, the "Son of Man" sayings are presented in Mark and the other synoptic Gospels as the title Jesus constantly applied in his self-reference. In Mark's Gospel, these self-references appear to gain their frequency and density immediately after Jesus' gathering of the opinion poll from his disciples concerning his identity, demonstrated in the question he put to his disciples: "who do people say I am?" (Mark 8: 27 – 30).

The answers from the poll (Mark 8: 28) and Peter's confession (Mark 8: 29) offered Jesus the hint, at least to the minimum, that the people associated his identity and his mission to God. As Donald English put it, Caesarea Philippi was for Jesus, a turning point in his ministry, and Peter's confession a high point in the revelation of his identity.[498] As a result, Morna Hooker indicates that, "Mark's careful ordering of the material makes it clear that Peter's declaration at Caesarea Philippi marked a break-through in the disciples understanding. For in contrast to those who, like Herod, think of Jesus as a prophet, Peter acknowledges Jesus to be the *Messiah*".[499] Consequently, Donald English asserted that after Peter's break-through, "the Master would from now on, concentrate increasingly on the preparation of the disciples on what lay

---

498 Donald English. *The Message of Mark: The Mystery of Faith.* 1992, p.159.
499 Morna Hooker. "Who Can This Be?" 2005, p.90.

ahead",[500] the paschal mystery (the suffering, the death and the resurrection) – which would later give definitive meaning to Jesus' identity and mission. Here, one begins to see that Mark's use of the "Son of Man" sayings in the second part of the Gospel inaugurates and brings to the fore, the humanity of Jesus as the "suffering servant" who redeems by dying and rising from the death.

The question however is: what is the meaning and significance of the "Son of Man" title in Mark, and how does it contribute to the understanding of his Christology? There are various disputed views as to what the title the "Son of Man" frequently used by Jesus as a self-designation really means. For instance, Brown reports that while Géza Vermes argues that from the Aramaic Targums, the "Son of Man" was used as a circumlocution for 'I,' Barnabas Lindars thinks that the "Son of Man" title is used to mean "a man such as I, or a man in my position".[501] In Jack Kingsbury's view, the title is without content as far as the identity of Jesus is concern. Kingsbury attributes this to the fact that Jesus' self-references as the "Son of Man" does not *break* the secret to his identity. Thus, Kingsbury thinks that the title only functions as a "public title" by means of which Jesus referred to himself in the world. As a result, its meaning in Mark's story captures the force of "this man" or "this human being".[502] For James Dunn however, when seen in such ordinary sense as in the case of G. Vermes, B. Lindars and Jack Kingsbury, the "Son of Man" does not seem to carry great theological or Christological implications.[503] Yet, it conveys a sense deeper than its force as "this man" or "this human being." It relates more specifically to Jesus' second nature as a human being.

---

500 Donald English. *The Message of Mark: The Mystery of Faith*. 1992, p.159.

501 Raymond Brown. *Introduction to New Testament Christology*. 1994, p.97–98.

502 Jack Kingsbury. *The Christology of Mark's Gospel*. 1983, p.159.

503 James Dunn. *New Testament Theology: An Introduction*. 2009, p.57.

Following the above views, Oscar Cullmann indicated that the self-designation of Jesus as the "Son of Man" points to two categories of meaning: firstly, it points to the *eschatological work* that Jesus must fulfil in the future; and secondly, it applies to his *earthly task*. The *eschatological application* represents a pronounced statement of majesty which corresponds to the Jewish view expressed in the Old Testament, especially in Daniel 7: 13 – 14. His primary function here is that of *judgement*. The *earthly application* relates to his incarnation and to his ministry which in themselves inaugurate the future eschatological experience. In this *earthly task*, his primary role is that of the *suffering servant of God*.[504] In this way, Cullmann's *double sense* proposition (eschatological work and earthly task) makes one wonder about the tenability of the views of Lindars, Vermes and Kingsbury among others.[505] This is because its association to Jesus' suffering, death, resurrection and to the future glory of the Kingdom of God gives the title a deeper meaning. Thus, one could say that the Markan use of the title captures Mark's attempt to acknowledge that Jesus, is Christ, the "Son of God", is also a human being defined by his susceptibility to suffering and death like all other human beings. But unlike all other human beings, he will rise from the dead. Let us see how some texts in the Old Testament help us to understand Mark's use of the title.

In the Old Testament, while the title the "Son of Man" in Psalm 8: 5 refers to an ordinary human being,[506] in Ezekiel 2: 1; Ezekiel 3: 1; Ezekiel 4: 1 and Ezekiel 5: 1, it is used as a title for

---

504 Oscar Cullmann. *The Christology of the New Testament*. 1963, p.155-164.

505 Jack D. Kingsbury. *The Christology of Mark's Gospel*. 1983, p. xvi, p.157-166.

506 For James Dunn, if understood as an Aramaic idiom, the title "Son of Man" designates that which is characteristic of humankind. From this perspective, the phrase carries no Christological or theological implications (Dunn, James, D.G. *new Testament Theology: An Introduction*. 2009, p.57).

the prophet. However, in Daniel 7: 13 – 14, it refers to a heavenly exalted figure who receives authority, glory and sovereign power. This *exalted heavenly figure* in Daniel, described as "one like the "Son of Man" would be worshipped by all peoples and nations. His dominion is said to be everlasting and his kingdom is never to be destroyed. According to O'Collins, this image of the "one like the "Son of Man" in Daniel 7: 13 – 14, could refer to the angels and/or the righteous and persecuted Jews who would be vindicated and given authority by God (Daniel 7: 18, 21 – 22).[507] However, its usage in the Gospels as the self-designation of Jesus draws in new contexts, meanings and implications. As his self-designation, O'Collins asserts that Jesus used the title the "Son of Man" in his self-reference in three ways: (1) in his earthly work and its humble condition (Mark 2: 10); (2) in his impending suffering, death and resurrection (Mark 9: 9); and (3) in his future coming in heavenly glory to act with sovereign power at the final judgement (Mark 8: 38).[508]

Following O'Collins view, if the "one like the Son of Man" in Daniel 7 reflects some apocalyptic messianic interpretations, then it suggests that Mark's identification of Jesus as the *Messiah* in the prologue (Mark 1: 1) needs no further elucidation. Should one even argue that the one like the "Son of Man" in Daniel does not represent a *heavenly individual figure*, then the question would be: does the meaning associated to Daniel 7: 13 – 14 prevent Jesus from taking an inherited expression and massively using it in his own way? The "Son of Man" title was Jesus' own way of identifying himself.[509] Consequently, when one relates Mark 1: 1 to the title the "Son of Man", one sees clearly the story

---

507 Gerald O'Collins. *Christology: A Biblical, Historical, and Systematic Study of Jesus.* 2009, p.62.

508 Gerald O'Collins. *Christology: A Biblical, Historical, and Systematic Study of Jesus.* 2009, p.63

509 Gerald O'Collins. *Christology: A Biblical, Historical, and Systematic Study of Jesus.* 2009, p.64-67.

Mark sought to share with his readers. In other words, Mark wanted his readers to know that Jesus, who is the *Messiah*, the "Son of God" walked the face of the earth as a human being (the "Son of Man"). He is not an abstract concept or a myth. Thus, it represents Mark's way of telling his later readers that the "Son of God" walked the face of the earth as the "Son of Man", and this was demonstrated by his susceptibility to death, and his power to rise from the dead on the third day, as he himself predicted. In this way, Mark's work also serves as an attestation to the historicity of the identity and the mission of Jesus Christ, the "Son of God".

In Mark's particular style, his the "Son of Man" motif first of all, fulfils his literary style (the *messianic secrecy*) which we shall take up in the succeeding section. Secondly, it also demonstrates how Gentiles (who form part of Mark's readers) could come to know and believe in the true identity of Jesus as the "Son of God". This is shown from the example of the centurion (a Gentile), at the foot of the cross, who affirms Jesus' divinity (in Mark 15: 39: *truly, this man is the Son of God*) in the same way that God Himself affirmed it at the beginning of the story (Mark 1: 11). Thus, Peter's confession may be the high point of Mark's Christology, but the centurion's confession further demonstrates the depths of faith which Gentiles are capable of attaining in their belief in God. So, while Jesus is misunderstood, rejected and abandoned to die on the cross, even by his closest disciples, one man, a Gentile, still saw God in him (Mark 15: 39).

4.3 The Significance of the "Son of God" and the "Son of Man" Motif

First of all, we indicated that the opening lines of Mark's prologue (1: 1) betrayed his authorial intent. Whereas one can already find the Christological titles of the *Messiah* and the "Son of God" in this verse, its meaning, as a whole, makes it the foundational construct from which every chapter and verse is a further development. Thus, the recognition that the "Gospel" is about no other person but Jesus Christ, the "Son of God" is very significant for Mark. In Mark 1: 2 –3, the author draws continuity between Jesus the *Messiah* and the work of God in the past, as can be found in Isaiah 40: 3 – "a voice cries in the wilderness, prepare a way for our God." By presenting Jesus as the fulfilment of the prophecies of Isaiah, Jesus is undoubtedly identified by Mark as the *Messiah* who fulfils the Old Testament hopes (see 2 Samuel 7: 12 – 16). Secondly, the figure of John the Baptist and the "voice from heaven" further confirms this claim. But how does the "Son of God" and the "Son of Man" motif help in defining and giving shape to the identity and to the mission of Jesus in Mark's Gospel?

When one considers the context of Mark 8: 29 – 30, one realises that it consists of the dual interplay between Peter's confession (Mark 8: 29) and Jesus' response – "tell no one about this" (Mark 8: 30). This call to silence about his identity which Peter divulged, immediately leads to Jesus' statement that the "Son of Man" must suffer and die but would rise on the third day (Mark 8: 31). So, we could deduce that in this *pericope* of Mark 8: 29 – 30, Jesus acknowledges his Messianism by his *affirmative silence*[510] on the matter and his request that they tell no one about it (Mark 8: 30). Convinced that his disciples now know who he is, Mark proceeds to tell his readers the *ultimate earthly task* that Jesus still had to fulfil. That his suffering and his death will show forth his second nature, his humanity expressed in the "Son of Man" motif (Mark 8: 31). That is, since suffering and death are by nature human experiences, Jesus, who is also human, will equally experience these human realities. Only by virtue of his divinity (the "Son of God"), will Jesus,

---

510 We take "affirmative silence" here to mean a silence which is judged to be neither neutral nor disapproving, but one which consents to a popular claim.

unlike all other humans, rise from death on the third day. So, in considering the use of the two titles in the Gospel, one gets the impression that Mark sought to communicate to his readers the message that: "Jesus Christ, the "Son of God" can only fully be understood in the light of his identity also as the "Son of Man". Although this appears to be plausible considering the arguments put forward so far, it is also worth noting that some scholars have identified and presented other points as reasons for Mark's use of these titles in his Christology. Some of these reasons include: (a) Mark's intention to correct an erroneous understanding of the *Messiah* at the time; and (b) to present his story of Jesus Christ as a call to Discipleship.

As a *Corrective Christology,* some scholars agree that Mark's use of the two titles was in his interest to correct an erroneous understanding of the identity of Jesus Christ in the early Church.[511] For instance, Norman Perrin thinks that Mark sought to, "teach the Christians of his day a true Christology in place of the false Christology that he felt they were in danger of accepting."[512] Mark achieved this through his unique style called the *Messianic secrecy*[513] which rests between two poles of early Christian thoughts. One pole expressed the Christian belief that Jesus first became the *Messiah* only after the resurrection (See Acts 2: 36; Romans 1: 4; Philippians 2: 6 – 11). The other pole conceives that Jesus' Messianism is pre-existent in terms expressed in the Johannine Gospel (John 1: 1 – 5).[514] So, the contest between these two poles of Christological thought created an unhealthy tension in the early Church. In Wrede's view therefore, Mark diffuses this

---

511 Morna Hooker. "Who Can This Be?" 2005, p.95.

512 Norman Perrin. *A Modern Pilgrimage in New Testament Christology.* 1974, p.92-93.

513 William Wrede is said to be the originator of the theory of the *Messianic secret* (see, Jack Kingsbury. *The Christology of Mark's Gospel.* 1983, p.2-33).

514 Jack Kingsbury. *The Christology of Mark's Gospel.* 1983, p.2.

tension by situating his Christology between the two poles, and by so doing, welded them together.[515]

In this way, while Mark portrays Jesus as the *Messiah* in the prologue (Mark 1: 1), he is also under the influence of the early Christian view on the post-resurrection experience of Jesus as the *Christ of God*. This makes Mark portray Jesus as keeping his Messiahship secret[516] as is demonstrated by Jesus' "commands of silence" to demons (Mark 1: 25; Mark 3: 4 and Mark 3: 12), to persons he heals (Mark 1: 43 – 45 and Mark 5: 43) and to the disciples (Mark 8: 30 9: 9). In Morna Hooker's view, Mark's use of the *messianic secret* also serves to explain why Israel failed to recognize Jesus as the *Messiah*. 'It serves as a pointer to the truth about Jesus' identity which so many people failed to grasp. This truth is spelt out for us at the *beginning* of the Gospel in the prologue (Mark 1: 1), in the *middle* of the Gospel at the transfiguration (Mark 9: 2 –13) and at the *end* of the Gospel in the words of the centurion (Mark 15: 39).' As a result, Morna Hooker points out that Mark by this rendition, seems to nudge his readers in the rib as if to say; '"and you of course, because I have led you into the secret, would understand precisely what this means!"'[517]

As a *call to Discipleship,* Irenaeus of Lyon reports that after the martyrdom of Peter and Paul, "Mark the companion of Peter, transmitted to us in writing what was preached by Peter."[518] Peter is said to have died around 65AD within the period of the persecution by Nero (64-67AD). If Irenaeus is right, then Mark's Gospel must have been written within this period of persecution (65-70AD). While these persecutions went on in Rome, there were other persecutions in Jerusalem occasioned by the failure of the Jewish revolt which led to the destruction of the temple of

---

515 Jack Kingsbury. *The Christology of Mark's Gospel.* 1983, p.3.

516 Jack Kingsbury. *The Christology of Mark's Gospel.* 1983, p.2-3.

517 Morna Hooker. "Who Can this be?" 2005, p.98.

518 See Irenaeus: *Against Heresies.* 3:1:3. http://www.columbia.edu/cu/augustine/arch/irenaeus/advhaer3.txt (15/01/2013).

Jerusalem (in 70AD). Thus, we could reasonably say that the context within which Mark wrote his Gospel was one of persecution, probably written for Roman readers (Gentile Christians). If his readers experienced persecution, then Mark's work was a radical call to discipleship shaped by the story of Jesus Christ, the "Son of God" and the "Son of Man." As the "Son of God", Jesus has the power and the authority over the forces of nature and evil. But as the "Son of Man", his mission also involved suffering, dying and rising from the dead in obedience to the Father. Thus, Mark's audience who experience persecution now may be given the hope and confidence that like Jesus, they too would experience future glory and victory as persecuted believers.

In consequence, it must be emphasized that the Christology of Mark's Gospel can only be located in his purpose, discerned by reading "Mark's own *expression* of purpose wherever he has tried to make it plain."[519] While one finds this in the first thirteen verses of the prologue, the rest of the narrative, which is a progressive development of the prologue, takes on a two-tier question framework. That is, who is Jesus and how should the reader respond to him? Mark relies on his unique style of the *messianic secret* which involves the dialectic interplay of the two Christological titles to respond to the above questions. We did indicate that by the criterion of density, the two titles divide the main narrative into two parts: Mark 1: 14 – 8: 26 and Mark 8: 31 – 15: 47 – with Peter's confession (Mark 8: 27 – 30) being the watershed. Though divided into two parts, these two sections nonetheless constitute a composite narrative which adequately expresses the identity and the mission of Jesus Christ. For Mark, Jesus is the Christ, the "Son of God" who becomes the "Son of Man" in order to save fallen humanity.

---

519 As Morna Hooker intimated, "Mark's story about Jesus is full of Christological significance, a significance sometimes expressed clearly, but more often only suggested by allusions, hints and the juxtaposition of his material." (Morna Hooker. "Who Can this be?" 2005, p.87).

It is this Christological construct which the Church would continue to clarify in the Christological debates leading to the councils of Nicaea, Chalcedon and beyond. As Alan Spence indicated, once there are evidences of the attempts to conceptually pair the *divinity* and the *humanity* of Jesus in Christian faith and theology, "the church finds itself facing, even as it continues to face today, a whole host of complex and baffling questions about his person",[520] to which she must make appropriate theological responses. Here, the theological task lies in, "providing a coherent theological explanation of Jesus' person in harmony with the scriptural testimony, which is able to account for his role in its worship and faith."[521] As Walter Kasper put it, within Christian theology therefore, "when we say that Jesus is the Christ, we maintain that this unique, irreplaceable Jesus of Nazareth is at one and the same time the Christ sent by God."[522] In other words, as the Christ, Jesus is experienced as the "Saviour of the World" and the eschatological fulfilment of history. For Walter Kasper therefore, the confession that, "Jesus is the Christ is the basic statement of Christian belief, and Christology is no more than the conscientious elucidation of that proposition."[523]

Jesus' identity as the "Son of God" and the "Son of Man" must always be at the heart of Christian faith and theology. Christian theology may be challenged to justify and to make comprehensible this conceptual pairing of Jesus Christ (as the "Son of God" and the "Son of Man"), but this does not entail replacing this tradition-specific conception (the two nature Christology) with some revisionary Christologies. One tends to agree with Walter Kasper's indication that the Church's effort to make Christology relevant to contemporary context may pose a theological problematic. This challenge lies in the fact that; on the one hand, if

520 Alan Spence. *Christology: A Guide for the Perplexed*. 2008, p.6
521 Alan Spence. *Christology: A Guide for the Perplexed*. 2008, p.6
522 Walter Kasper. *Jesus the Christ*. 1977, p.15.
523 Walter Kasper. *Jesus the Christ*. 1977, p.15.

the Church must preserve her identity by articulating her doctrines unambiguously in straightforward terms, she risks the loss
of relevance. Yet on the other hand, if she struggles for relevance, she may end up forfeiting her identity.[524] So, the way out
of this impasse is for the Church to undergo profound reflections on her *real basis, mission and significance* in the world. Since
the Church does not find her *basis* and *mission* in ideas, principles, programmes, moral or doctrinal injunctions, but on a person with a specific name – Jesus Christ,[525] Christian theology
must never lose sight of its task of articulating his identity and
his mission in fidelity to the scriptural testimonies which Mark,
for instance, makes plain.

4.4 Conclusion

In a nutshell, a *Christian-tradition-specific understanding* of the identity
and the mission of Jesus Christ must reflect what Christian faith
and theology has to say about Jesus. From the synoptic Gospels,
Mark tells us that Jesus Christ is the "Son of God" and the "Son of
Man" – the constitutive "Saviour of the World". Although there
were other opinions to the contrary in response to Jesus' question – "who do people say I am?" it was Peter's response which
received Jesus' approval and commendation.[526] Hence, Christian
faith and theology must never lose sight of this inherited faith
and tradition. After all, "if tradition means the passing on of that
which has been received, tradition is not bad. Quite the contrary,

---

524 Walter Kasper. *Jesus the Christ.* 1977, p.15.

525 Walter Kasper. *Jesus the Christ.* !977, p.15.

526 Mathew 16: 17-18 – "And I tell you, you are Peter, and on this rock,
     I will build my church, and the powers of death shall not prevail
     against it" (Revised Standard Version).

it is necessary in order for continuity to be preserved."[527] Christian faith and theology may be called upon to make *tradition* relevant to contemporary situations, but it must never jettison the traditions from which it was formed and founded. Thus, if we assert in dialogue that Jesus Christ "makes salvation possible", this does not "deny that other modes of salvation are possible by other means"[528]. It is simply to insist, as Alister McGrath put it, "that within the Christian tradition, the distinctively Christian understanding of what salvation is can only be realized on the basis of Jesus Christ."[529]

In Chapter Three, we asserted that *commitment, openness, respect* and *equality* together constitute the kind of dispositions that make dialogue as an exercise in learning possible. In this form of interreligious dialogue, the Christian dialogical partner must be convinced of, and thus capable of articulating an authentic Christian understanding the identity and the mission of Jesus Christ as it pertains to Christian faith and theology. By this, we mean that one must be committed to and ready to attest to the two-nature Christology which defines the identity of Jesus Christ within the context of his role as the "Saviour of the World". This is significant for the success of dialogue as an exercise in learning. However, while exercising this aspect of *commitment* to the Christian tradition, the Christian party is also called upon to be *open* to what Muslims have to say about Jesus in their tradition-specific contexts. Hence, what follows below in Chapter Five is the development of an Islamic Christology from a predominantly Qur'anic perspective.

---

527 Hans Schwarz. *Christology.* 1998, p.137.
528 Alister McGrath. *Christian Theology: An Introduction.* 1998, p.325.
529 Alister McGrath. *Christian Theology: An Introduction.* 1998, p.325

CHAPTER FIVE
CHRISTOLOGY IN ISLAM

5.1 Introduction

In the preceding section, one gets the impression that *Christology* connotes a Christian theological articulation of the identity and the mission of Jesus Christ; particularly on how Jesus' divinity and humanity are articulated within the same person as the "Saviour of the World". So, the question then is: if *Christology* is essentially part of Christian theology, then can the notion of an "Islamic Christology" be theologically justified? If yes, what are the grounds for such a Christology? Although it is true that the Qur'an, the Hadiths, and many Islamic scholars and commentators perceive Jesus Christ as a "Prophet" and the "Messenger" of Allah, a human being without any divine attribution, Jesus is nonetheless highly respected in Islam and is given greater mention with honorific titles in the Qur'an than any of the prophets who preceded him.[530] Parrinder affirms that the name *Isa* (Jesus) occurs twenty-five times in the Qur'an and by combining this name with titles such as the *Messiah* and the "Son of Mary" in the Qur'an, "Jesus is spoken of some thirty-five times."[531] From these references to Jesus in the Qur'an one finds that the Qur'an itself contains narratives about Jesus Christ who occupies a central place in Christian faith and theology. The Qur'an provides answers as to who Jesus was, how he came to be, and his mission.

Consequently, if Christology concerns the study of Jesus Christ in respect of his identity and his mission, then Islam also has the resources that provide for this study within its own religious

---

530 Geoffrey Parrinder. *Jesus in the Qur'an.* 1965, p.16.
531 Geoffrey Parrinder. *Jesus in the Qur'an.* 1965, p.18.

context. Hence an "Islamic Christology" focuses on the Islamic understanding of the identity and the role played by Jesus the Christ in the divine plan of Allah. It is from the perspective that Mahmoud Ayoub and other scholars define an *Islamic Christology* as, "an understanding of the role of Christ within the divine plan of human history, of Christ the man, one of the servants of God, but also of Christ, the 'Word of God', His Spirit and exalted friend."[532] For Ayoub therefore, these ideas are clearly stated in the Qur'an and therefore represents the framework within which an Islamic view about Jesus can be conceptualized. Whereas these views are in stark contra-distinction from the Christian understanding of Jesus Christ, the conception that Jesus is a "Prophet" or the "Messenger" of Allah represents the authentic Islamic understanding of him. So, the story that Islam has to share about who Jesus is and the mission he fulfilled is the justifiable ground for an "Islamic Christology."

However, before delving into the issues that speak of this Christological category, it is useful to draw attention to the interest and the focus of this section on Islamic Christology. Since the purpose of this section is to develop a Christology that is uniquely Islam, it will focus on identifying the prophetic role of Jesus within the context of the Qur'an and the Hadiths in the light of the overall Islamic conception of God, humanity and the world. From this standpoint, while Jesus would be identified as a Prophet of Allah, we would seek to answer the questions – how did Jesus fulfil this role as a prophet? and in what ways does he provide guidance to humanity in its response to God? We will therefore commence this section by firstly focusing on the theological framework within which an "Islamic Christology" can be situated. Here, we shall demonstrate how the fundamental Islamic faith principle on the obligation to the *Tawhid* (the Oneness of God) defines and shapes the Islamic theological comprehension

---

532 Irfan Omar (editor). *A Muslim View of Christianity: Essays on Dialogue by Mahmoud Ayoub.* 2007, p.134.

of the identity and the mission of the *Messiah,* Jesus, the "Son of Mary" (Surah 4: 171). Secondly, since Islamic Christology is predominantly centred on Jesus as a "Prophet" and a "Messenger", we shall focus on investigating the concept of prophecy in Islam, the role played by the prophets and the messengers of Allah, and the significant role Jesus plays within this context. Until then, let us briefly examine the meaning of Islam and how the *Tawhid* contributes to defining the theological context for understanding Islamic Christology.

5.2 Understanding the Meaning of Islam

The word "Islam" comes from the Arabic word (*al-'islām*) which literally means "to surrender" or "to submit". In a religious sense, it means "the submission or the surrender of oneself to *Allah* (God)."[533] Murata and Chittick point out that "*Islam*" carries a double connotation: the *universal* and the *particular* sense. From the universal sense, *Islam* means "'submission to God' as an undeniable fact of existence."[534] This means that since God is the creator and the sustainer of the universe, creation only functions properly if it submits itself to the will of the creator (God).[535] Hence, from this universal perspective, every person who submits himself or herself to God is considered a *Muslim*. It is from this perspective that the Qur'an identifies Adam, Abraham, Jacob, Moses, Jesus (Surah 2: 131 – 133) and

---

533 Badru Kateregga & David Shenk. *Islam and Christianity: A Muslim and a Christian in Dialogue.* 1980, p.1.

534 Murata, Sachiko & Chittick, Williams, C. *The Vision of Islam.* 1994, p.3.

535 Murata Sachiko & Chittick Williams, C. *The Vision of Islam.* 1994, p.3.

his disciples as *Muslims* (Surah 5: 111).[536] However, the *particular sense* of the word *Islam,* refers to the specific religion established by Allah through the Prophet Muhammad. All believers in this established religion are thus called *Muslims.* Thus, from the *universal* and the *particular* senses of the word, we could surmise that the word *Islam* implies four basic meanings: (1) the submission of the whole of creation to God; (2) the submission of humanity to God through the guidance of His prophets; (3) the submission of humanity to Allah through the guidance of His Prophet Muhammad, (4) the submission of the followers of Muhammad to the will of Allah. Within these four facets of meaning, the last two senses of the word properly refer to *Islam* with the uppercase *I* as a religion.

From the context of the *Hadith of Gabriel* which concerns the discourse between Muhammad and the Angel Gabriel who assesses Muhammad's understanding about the three *dimensions* of Islam; scholars tend to divide the religious beliefs of Islam into three dimensions: that is, (1) *Islam* (submission); (2) *Iman* (Faith); and (3) *Ihsan* (perfection or excellence). These dimensions sum up the Islamic religious worldview. It must be said here that the use of the word *dimension* is a heuristic device intended for a better understanding of Islam as a complex religious structure.[537] To understand this complex structure theologically, one needs to approach it from its different parts (*Islam, Iman* and *Ihsan*), but be aware that it is the overall constitution of these parts that truly define the religion. Along these lines, the use of *dimension* is an attempt to understand the religion as a whole in respect of its different aspects, and its different aspects within the context of the whole. As Murata and Chittick put it, the parts are "separated only

---

536 Murata Sachiko & Chittick Williams, C. *The Vision of Islam.* 1994, p.4.

537 Murata Sachiko & Chittick Williams, C. *The Vision of Islam.* 1994, p. xxxii.

to suggest that they fit together as a whole."[538] In the discourse between Muhammad and the Angel Gabriel, Gabriel "cross-examines" the prophet about his comprehension of the message of the Qur'an. This cross-examination is found in the *Hadith Jibril*. The aspects of the *Hadith* which concerns these three dimensions read as follows:

"Umar ibn al-khattab said: One day when we were with God's Messenger, a man with very white clothing and very black hair came up to us. No mark of travel was visible on him and none of us recognized him. Sitting down before the Prophet, leaning his knees against his and placing his hands on his thighs, he said, 'Tell me, Muhammad about submission.'

He replied, 'Submission means that you should bear witness that there is no god but God and that Muhammad is God's Messenger, that you should perform the ritual prayer, pay the alms tax, fast during Ramadan and make the pilgrimage to the house if you are able to go there.'

The man said, 'you have spoken the truth.' He said, 'Now tell me about faith.'

He replied, 'Faith means that you have faith in God, his Angels, his Books, his Messengers and the Last Day and that you have faith in the measuring out, both its good and its evil.'

Remarking that he had spoken the truth, he then said, 'Now tell me about doing what is beautiful.'

He replied, 'Doing what is beautiful means that you should worship God as if you see him, for even if you do not see him, He sees you."[539]

In this hadith, *Islam* as the first dimension consists of the confession of the *Shahada,* and observing the *Salat,* the *Zakat, Ramadan* and the *Hajj.* In other words, the first dimension relates to *practice.* It asks the question: "what do Muslims do?" In response, Muslims are supposed to submit themselves to the one and true

---

538 Murata Sachiko & Chittick Williams, C. *The Vision of Islam.* 1994, p. xxxii.
539 Murata, Sachiko & Chittick Williams, C. *The Vision of Islam.* 1994, p. xxv.

God (the *Tawhid*). This form of religious monotheism makes the *Shahada* the most fundamental faith principle in Islamic religiosity. If Muslims see Jesus as the "Prophet of Allah", this would be theologically justified within the context of the *Tawhid*. The second dimension (*Iman*) focuses on the faith of the Muslim. From Muhammad's response to the Angel Gabriel, "Faith means that you have faith in God, his Angels, his Books, his Messengers and the Last Day and that you have faith in the Measuring Out, both its good and its evil."[540] Within these *six articles of faith*, it is the *Tawhid* which gives meaning to them because the rest of the other articles find their relevance in the light of God's oneness. The third dimension (*Ihsan*) focuses on the translation of one's faith into good deeds and action. *Ihsan* is used in the Qur'an as an action verb which means; "to do what is beautiful and good, to do something well, to do something perfectly, to gain perfection and virtuous qualities."[541] Here, perfection and virtuous qualities are measured by one's degree of commitment to the one God.

Consequently, while *Islam* directs one to the right practice of faith, *Iman* focuses on faith and the understanding of it. *Ihsan* however, is a call to perfection and excellence; a sense of virtuous living informed by the religious convictions derived from *Islam* and *Iman*. All these dimensions make no sense if they are devoid of the obligation to the *Tawhid*. As we mentioned earlier, these dimensions only represent the different aspects of Islam as a religion; for the more a person harmoniously integrates *faith*, *works* and *perfection*, the closer the person is drawn to the life of submission to the will of Allah. In short, the emphasis is that Islamic Christology finds its tradition-specific meaning in the light of the *Tawhid*. What precisely is the *Tawhid* and how does it determine the understanding of Qur'anic Christology?

---

540 Murata Sachiko & Chittick Williams, C. *The Vision of Islam*. 1994, p. xxv.

541 Chittick Williams, C. *Faith and Practice of Islam: Three Thirteenth Century Sufi Text*. 1992, p.5.

5.3 Islamic Christology in the Light of the *Tawhid*

The word *Tawhid* has its Arabic roots from *Wahid* which means "God is one". Hence, *Tawhid* takes on the meaning of, "recognizing and acknowledging that God is One." It is "'the assertion of divine unity' or 'the declaration of God's oneness'".[542] This oneness of God is expressed in the first part of the *Shahada* which states that, "there is no god but God." *God* here is seen as the creator and the sustainer of everything that exists. Thus, the confession that, "there is no god but one God" (Surah 5: 73) underscores Islamic monotheism where Allah remains the transcendent Being who is the creator and the source of everything in the world. He created the world in order that creation would submit to Him, by living according to His plan as the "master designer". For God himself said in the Qur'an: "There is no god but *I*, so worship *me*" (Surah 21: 25). The Qur'an further emphasizes that, "God himself bears witness that there is no god but Him, and so do the Angels and those who have knowledge" (Surah 3: 18).

As the creator and the sustainer of the universe, Allah created everything for a purpose. He created humanity for the purpose of worshipping Him alone and being vicegerents to the rest of His creation. Consequently, to worship Allah alone is to have fundamentally fulfilled the purpose for one's creation. In this way, Muslims conceive that all the prophets of Allah including Jesus, provided guidance in respect of the observance of the *Tawhid* – "there is no god but *I*. So, worship me" (Surah 21: 25). *Worship* here captures the sense of the total submission of the believer to Allah. It implies following what Allah commands through the guidance of His prophets. To submit oneself to anything apart from Allah is to follow *misguidance*. So, the statement, "there is no god but God" (Surah 5: 73; 4: 171) means that all *gods* whom people worship other than Allah are false: an act which is vehemently

---

542 Murata Sachiko & Chittick Williams, C. *The Vision of Islam*. 1994, p.43.

condemned in the Qur'an and by Muslims as *Shirk*. Within the Qur'an, *Shirk* means to give God Partners or worship others along with God or exclusive of God.[543] This act is condemned in the Qur'an (see Surah 4: 36, 31: 13, 6:19 and 13: 36). *Shirk* is nothing but the opposite of the *Tawhid*. The *Tawhid* is the first principle and pillar of Islamic faith.

Consequently, the emphasis on the avoidance of, "associating others with God" forms a central tenet of Islamic faith understanding. To associate others with Allah would be to destroy the very foundations on which Islam rests. This explains why *Shirk* is viewed as a *serious sin;* for the Qur'an indicates that, "if someone associates any other with God, God will prohibit paradise to him" (Surah 5: 72). For Islam therefore, humanity was created to know that, "there is no god but God" and so to worship only Allah. Hence the *Tawhid* lies within human nature (*fitra*). Since the purpose of humanity is to worship only Allah, Allah sent His messengers to help humanity to fulfil this purpose. So, to associate others with Allah is to go against the most fundamental instincts of the human species. As Murata and Chittick put it, it is so to speak, "to betray human nature and even leave the domain of human existence."[544] The *Tawhid* therefore leaves no room for any Islamic theologizing about God outside the confines of strict monotheism.

It is in the light of this faith principle (the *Tawhid*) that Jesus is understood as only a "Prophet of Allah". As a "Prophet of Allah" *vis-a-vis* the rest of the other line of prophets, the Qur'an describes Jesus as the "closest *friend* of Allah" (Surah 3: 45), "His *Word* directed to Mary and a *Spirit* from Him" (Surah 4: 171). The Qur'an therefore contain Christological titles such as *Word*

---

543 *Shirk* is not just the question of worshipping idols or physical objects. It also consists of following one's own opinions and feelings apart from the message of Allah (Ibid, p.49–50).

544 Murata Sachiko & Chittick Williams, C. *The Vision of Islam*. 1994, p.50.

of/from *Allah, Spirit of Allah* and the *Messiah* which resonate in Christian Christological discourses. Therefore, the tendency is to read Christian meanings into these titles, and thereby conclude that the Qur'anic ascription of these titles to Jesus is an inevitable admission of Jesus' divinity. For Islamic faith and theology, these honorific titles mean nothing more than the fact that Jesus, the *Messiah*, the "Son of Mary", is nothing more than a "Prophet" and the "Messenger" of Allah. Unlike Christian theology which conceived God within the context of the *Holy Trinity* (that is, three persons in One God), Islam does not admit to such theological constructions because of the obligation to the *Tawhid*. Islam perceives any attempt to articulate the nature of Allah outside His *Oneness* and *transcendence* as misguidance. For Islam, the fundamental truth about God is that He is *One* – "Your God is but one. So, submit to Him" (Surah 22: 34). This understanding (the *Tawhid*) is a non-negotiable faith principle. Hence, when engaging Muslims in dialogue, one must be aware of this aspect of the faith and respect the views which emanate as a consequence of it. However, let us see how the prophets functioned within the context of this divine unicity.

5.4 Prophets, Messengers and Prophetic Guidance

While prophecy forms the second part of the *Shahada* (*Muhammadun rasul Allah*), giving it a more specific context, Muhammad identifies the prophets as constitutively part of the articles of faith in his reply to the Angel Gabriel in the *Hadith Jibril* concerning *Iman* (faith). From this hadith, the Angel said to Muhammad, "Now tell me about faith. He replied: 'faith means that you have faith in *God*, His *Angels*, His *Books*, His *Messengers*, the *last day* and the *measuring out.*'" Whereas the Angel commended Muhammad for getting it right; we can say that between the *Hadith Jibril* and the second part of the *Shahada*, demonstrates the interplay of the universality and particularity of *prophecy* within Islamic theology.

211

But before we address this dialectic, let us first of all understand what "prophet" and "messenger" means in Islam.

The word *"Prophet"* comes from the Arabic word *Nabi* which has two basic meanings: (1) *to utter a word, a sound or to inform or to give news*; and (2) *to be elevated by God*.[545] For Murata and Chittick, both senses of the word *Nabi*, reflect the Islamic understanding of the word *prophet*; since in Islam a *prophet* is a person who is chosen by God and given a message which may either be personal or for an intended audience or both. The Qur'an employs four words to qualify this task: (1) *al-Nabi* (Prophet); (2) *rasul* (Messenger); (3) *mursal* (Envoy); and (4) *ulu'l- 'azm* (possessor of steadfastness). Whereas *envoy* and *messenger* may be synonymous; *prophet, messenger* and the *possessor of steadfastness,* have fine distinctions. These differences are that the *prophets* are persons chosen by God with a message; they only "proclaim Allah's news. They are not given Books."[546] The *messengers* however are the prophets who established religious communities, preserving their message in an oral or in written scripture. Thus, whereas messengers are prophets, not all *prophets* are messengers.[547] The *possessors of steadfastness* are the five messengers who established the major religions in history (namely, Noah, Abraham, Moses, Jesus and Muhammad).[548]

It is relevant to note here that unlike Christianity, Islam admits Adam as the first prophet of Allah in successive line with the prophet Muhammad as the final prophet. The admission of Adam into the line of prophecy contributes significantly to shaping and differentiating the Islamic worldview of human nature, sin and redemption. These views are not the same as the Christian notion of *original sin* (which humanity contracted through the *fall* in Genesis 3: 1-23) and the redemption which Jesus achieved through the

545 Murata, Sachiko & Chittick, Williams, C. *The Vision of Islam.* 1994, p133.

546 Badru Kateregga. & David Shenk. *Islam and Christianity.* 1980, p.34.

547 Mona Siddiqui. *Christians, Muslims & Jesus.* 2013, p.12.

548 Murata, Sachiko & Chittick, Williams. 1994, p.134.

Paschal Mystery. Here, Mona Siddiqui indicates that, Islam's biggest parting with Christian doctrine lies in the fact that, it does not have that sense of alienation from God as in the fall, and the subsequent reconciliation with God through the redemption brought about by the death and the resurrection of Jesus Christ.[549] If Islam rejects the belief that Jesus died on the cross, or that his death and resurrection have no soteriological significance, this is directly influenced by its theology of human nature, sin and redemption. We deem that knowledge of this theological *turn* is very significant for Christian-Muslim dialogue on Christology as an exercise in learning. Let us see how Adam, as the first prophet of Allah, sets the stage for a fundamental distinction between the Christian and the Islamic theology of redemption, and how this contributes in defining the prophetic role of Jesus.

5.4.1 Adam, Iblis and the Fall: The Question of Original Sin

The Qur'an, like the Judeo-Christian scriptures also presents *Adam* as the first human being to be created by God. In Qur'anic usage Adam stands for: (1) what it *means to be human*; (2) the *problem of human nature* in keeping the *Tawhid*; and (3) the *reason for prophetic guidance* to humanity. Murata and Chittick identify the Qur'anic use of the word *Trust (Amana)* as that which sums up the distinctive characteristics between humanity and the rest of creation (Surah 33: 72).[550] *Trust* refers to the task of "care-taking" or the human vocation to be vicegerents to the whole of creation. According to the Qur'an, this "care-taker" task was not only given to Adam but to all his descendants, who unanimously

---

549 Mona Siddiqui. *Christians, Muslims & Jesus*. 2013, p.218.
550 Murata, Sachiko & Chittick, Williams. *The Vision of Islam*. 1994, p.135.

agreed to the divine injunction as they said; "Yes, we bear witness to God as our Lord" (Surah 7: 172). This event is commonly called the "Covenant of Alast",[551] whereby humanity made a compact with God to acknowledge the *Tawhid*. This covenant established an innate disposition in humanity to acknowledge the *Tawhid*. This innate disposition is often referred to as the *fitra*.[552]

However, the verse on *Trust* (Surah 33: 72)[553] concludes that the human being is "ignorant, a great wrongdoer". For Murata and Chittick, this verse "refers to the children of Adam who did not live up to the *Trust*." Although one might agree with this interpretation, it is rather plausible to trace the root of this "wrongdoing" to the events leading to the fall of Adam and Eve in the Garden (Surah 15: 39-43). In this narrative, *Iblis* (Satan) is said to have previously disobeyed God (Surah 2: 34 and 7: 11 − 12) and was to be subjected to punishment (Surah 7: 13). However, *Iblis* who is an *evil spirit* or a *jinni* made a deal with God for the postponement of his punishment until the *Day of Resurrection* (Surah 7: 14 − 15). This postponement seems to buy him time to lead all God's loyal servants astray.[554] According to the Qur'an God

---

551 "The Covenant of Alast" refers to a primordial covenant between each human being and God referred to in Surah 7: 172. (See, Murata, Sachiko & Chittick, Williams, C. 1994, p.136; Lakhani, Ali, M. *The Sacred Foundation of Justice in Islam*. 2006, p.7).

552 "Fitra" is commonly translated as "primordial nature" or "innate disposition" to observe the Tawhid (See, Murata, Sachiko & Chittick, Williams, C. 1994, p.137).

553 "We offered the *Trust* to the heavens, and the Earth and the mountains, but they refused to carry it and were afraid of it. And the human beings carried it. Surely, he is very ignorant and a great wrongdoer."

554 Surah 7: 16 − 18 − "And Iblis said, 'because you have put me in the wrong, I will lie in wait for them all on the straight path. I will come after them at their front and their back, from their right and their left − and you will find that most of them are ungrateful'. And God said, 'get out! You are disgraced and are banished. I swear, I shall fill hell with you and all who follow you.'"

agrees to *Iblis'* deal, aware that, "*Iblis* shall have no authority over them, except those who *choose* to follow him" (Surah 15: 43).

Now, the option of the "choice to follow *Iblis*" in the above text demonstrates that although humanity has the innate disposition to acknowledge the *Tawhid (fitra)*, God's gift of *free will* to humanity also opens up the possibility of human disobedience to the divine will. Thus, the innate disposition to obey God (*fitra*) and the gift of *free will* constitute what it means to be truly *human*; that is, "to be faced with the choice between right and wrong, obedience and disobedience."[555] So one would see that in Surah 7: 20, *Iblis* would lure Adam and Eve into disobedience to the divine command (Surah 7: 19) leading to the *fall*. *Iblis* is said to have deceived Adam and Eve in this way; "your Lord only forbade you this tree to prevent you from becoming angels and immortals." Thus, Allah's question, "did I not prohibit you two from this tree?" (Surah 7: 22), confirmed that "Adam disobeyed his Lord" (Surah 20: 121).

However, there was an immediate response of *regret* and *repentance* from Adam and Eve after the *fall*. Their repentance marked a significant departure from the Christian story in Genesis 3: 14 – 19. The Qur'an testifies that, "they were immediately shocked at what they had done and with one voice the two of them said, 'we have wronged ourselves and unless you forgive us and have mercy on us, we shall surely be among the lost'" (Surah 7: 23). From this act of repentance and the search for forgiveness, Adam and Eve were forgiven by Allah who restored them back to the state of "grace" so to speak – "Then Adam received some words from His Lord, and He accepted his repentance" (Surah 2: 37). This suggests that whereas the Qur'an acknowledges the fall of Adam, it also admits that there was reconciliation in which Adam's state of grace was completely restored to him by Allah. Thus, Murata and Chittick indicate that the fundamental difference between

---

555 Murata, Sachiko & Chittick, Williams, C. *The Vision of Islam.* 1994, p.142.

Adam and *Iblis'* disobedience lies in how each responded to God after the fall. "Whereas *Iblis* refused to admit that he had done something wrong by blaming God for leading him astray (Surah 7: 16), Adam and Eve admitted their fault and asked God to forgive them"[556] and Allah forgave them. In this way, we find two significant differences between the Islamic and the Christian accounts of the event of the fall.

First of all, within the Islamic context, the fall of Adam is not understood in the same way as the Christian doctrine of *Original sin*. For Christianity, the disobedience of Adam and Eve brought irrecoverable damnation on the human race. For instance, Christian theology asserts that, "on account of their disobedience, human beings exist in a state of corruption from which they are unable to extricate themselves. If redemption is to take place, it must be on the basis of a new obedience on the part of humanity."[557] But since humanity is unable to break free from its entanglement to sin, it could only take God in Jesus Christ to set it free from this bond of sin, through Jesus' death and resurrection.[558] However, for Islam there is no such thing as *Original sin*, because God immediately forgave Adam and Eve for their disobedience when they sought for mercy (Surah 2: 37). As the Qur'an affirms, God did not only forgive him, but "His Lord Chose him" (Surah 20: 122).

Consequently, Adam was made a true prophet of Allah and both he and *Hauwa* (Eve) were the first true *Muslims*.[559] For Islam, if Adam was forgiven by God and was made the first true Muslim, then there is no original sin. Without the concept of original sin, the notion of Jesus' death and resurrection as atonement for sin loses its soteriological pertinency. So, the fall underscores God's divine power to restore His creation to normalcy without the need

556 Murata, Sachiko & Chittick, Williams, C. *The Vision of Islam*. 1994, p.145.
557 Alister McGrath. *Christian Theology: An introduction*. 1997, p.338.
558 Alister McGrath. *Christian Theology: An Introduction*. 1997, p.338.
559 Badru Kateregga. & David Shenk. *Islam and Christianity*. 1980, p.16.

to suffer, die and resurrect in order to redeem. In Islam then, the significance of Jesus does not lie in, "a death and resurrection as atonement for original sin". However, his significance lies in the role he played as a "Prophet" and the "Messenger" of Allah in the way he provided guidance in the acknowledgement of the *Tawhid* which defines the Islamic obligation to acknowledge God as One.

Secondly, the "sending out" of Adam and Eve from the Garden is not seen within Islam as constituting a punishment from God for their transgressions. Within the Christian account, the departure from the Garden gives the impression that it is constitutively part of the consequences of the fall. In Genesis 3: 16 – 24, God said to the woman: "because you have done this, I will greatly multiply your pains in childbearing ..." Then God said to the man: "because you have listened to your wife and have eaten of the tree ... cursed is the ground because of you; in toil you shall eat of it ..." The text then says that God subsequently drove the man and his wife out of the Garden of Eden and took measures to prevent them from coming back to the Garden again (Genesis 3: 22 – 24). From the Qur'anic perspective, Adam was intended to be God's vicegerent to the "heavens and the earth and the mountains" (Surah 33: 72). This explains why Allah thought him the names of all created reality (Surah 2: 30 – 33). Hence, living in the Garden of Eden was therefore a preparatory process for his later job as the vicegerent of creation. As a result, Murata and Chittick affirm that, "God put Adam and Eve in the Garden so that they could gain strength for the hardships that would follow once they were placed at a great distance from Him, in the earth."[560] So, whereas in the Christian context, the separation from Eden is seen as part of the punishment meted out to Adam and Eve, for Islam, the separation is not as a consequence of their sin, but a necessary act which commences Adam's task as God's vicegerent.

In consequence, Islam sees man as God's *Khalifa* on earth. Although it acknowledges that humanity is not perfect; for only

---

560 Murata, Sachiko & Chittick, Williams, C. 1994, p.144.

Allah is perfect; it does not have the concept of *original sin*. The question of the *free will* of man and the continual presence of *Iblis* shows that there is the human propensity to *sin* (understood as *heedlessness* or *misguidance*). Although Adam heeded to the allurement of *Iblis,* Adam's repentance reconciled him to God and gained for him his servant role in creation. As Murata and Chittick put it, "Adam's entrance into the earth as vicegerent and prophet is a sign that God's mercy takes precedence over his wrath, and that his guidance overtakes the misguidance of Satan."[561] In this way, if humanity is to accomplish its task of vicegerency and the acknowledgement of the *Tawhid*, then it would need the guidance of the prophets and the messengers of Allah. It is for this reason that God in his kindness provides for the prophets who give the right guidance to humanity. This brings us to the significance of prophetic guidance in Islam.

5.4.2 The Nature and Significance of Prophetic Guidance

Like Christianity, Islam also believes that God sent prophets at various times and in different stages of human history to provide guidance to humanity. The Qur'an testifies that these prophets were raised from among every race and nation – "We sent a Messenger to every community saying, 'worship God and shun false gods'" (Surah 16: 36). The Qur'an further states that: "Muslims say: 'we believe in God and in what was sent down to us and in what was sent down to Abraham, Ishmael, Isaac, Jacob and the tribes and what was given to Moses, Jesus and all the prophets by their Lord'" (Surah 2: 136). As servants of Allah, all the prophets and the messengers are presented by the Qur'an as worthy of

---

561 Murata, Sachiko & Chittick, Williams, C. 1994, p.144.

belief. To "deny the Prophethood of any of them constitutes disbelief",[562] for their message comes from Allah who is all-knowing. Islam conceives each of these prophets as fundamentally communicating the obligation to acknowledge the *Tawhid*. So, as the first prophet of Allah, Adam heeded and submitted himself to Allah as the only true God and Creator of all. However, some of his offspring refused to follow Allah's teachings and committed *shirk*.[563]

As a result, God raised up prophets to give the right guidance to humanity on the straight path to Allah. These prophets accomplished this task through *Dhikr* (remembrance) and *Huda* (guidance).[564] *Dhikr* is not just limited to the sense of "remembering" but it also takes on the meaning of "mentioning" and "reminding". In the *Tawhid,* the work of the prophets as *Dhikr* was not just limited to reminding people about the *Oneness of God and the human obligation to submit to Him,* but it also centred on helping people to confess the *Tawhid* (mention). Those who respond to the prophets appropriately are *Muslims* and those who refuse are the *truth-concealers*. In consequence, *Dhikr* represents the drama of prophecy and the human response to it.[565] *Huda* (guidance) however, defines God's reason and motivation for sending the prophets.

As we saw earlier, since *Iblis'* intention and task were to promote *misguidance* (Surah 7: 16 – 18), God in His Mercy sends the prophets as guides to the actualization of the *fitra*. To actualize the *fitra* is to actualize one's human potential, and the actualization of one's potential is the key to happiness and peace.[566] Hence,

562 Badru Kateregga & David Shenk. *Islam and Christianity.* 1980, p.35.

563 Badru Kateregga & David Shenk. *Islam and Christianity.* 1980, p.36.

564 Murata, Sachiko & Chittick, Williams, C. *The Vision of Islam.* 1994, p.147.

565 Murata, Sachiko & Chittick, Williams, C. *The Vision of Islam.* 1994, p.147.

566 Murata, Sachiko & Chittick, Williams, C. *The Vision of Islam.* 1994, p.151.

the reason for the guidance provided by the prophets from Adam to Muhammad was to lead humanity to a total submission to the will of Allah as expressed in the *Tawhid*. Among these prophets of Allah are Adam, Noah, Moses, Abraham, Ishmael, Isaac, Jacob, Joseph, David, Elijah, Elisha, Jonah, Zachariah, Jesus and Muhammad. Their universal task was to direct humanity to observe the *Tawhid* – "There is no god but one God" (Surah 21: 25). The *Tawhid* is the basic message of each of these prophets. As a result, the Qur'an affirms "… that which was given to Moses and Jesus and the other prophets by their Lord, we make no distinction among any of them" (Surah 2: 136 and 3: 84).

Consequently, it is considered an act of disbelief for a Muslim to despise the message of any of the prophets and the messengers of Allah; for they all served to bring right guidance to humanity in its response to the *Tawhid*. (See Surah 5: 48). Even though Islamic theology views Jesus as a "Prophet" and the "Messenger" of Allah who provided right guidance to the children of Israel with a new Scripture (the Gospels), the Qur'anic texts about the prophets and the messengers of Allah demonstrates that this guidance does not contradict the human obligation to the *Tawhid*. In this way, the message of Jesus is not just significant to Christians only, but significant to Muslims in their response to the *Tawhid* as well. For Islam, faith in one God demands the observation of the *Tawhid* which constitutes the fundamental message of the prophets and the messengers of Allah. The question however is: how does Jesus function within this context of the *Tawhid*?

5.5 Qur'anic Christology: Jesus as the Messenger of Allah

The interest in this area of Qur'anic Christology is to carefully analyse and present the various references concerning the relationship between Jesus, the *Holy Spirit,* and Allah in the Qur'an, and how this relationship contributes in defining the role that Jesus played in Allah's divine plan. Since there are many texts which relate to Jesus in the Qur'an, we shall focus particular attention on Surah 2: 87; 2: 253 and 5: 110. The reasons for selecting these particular texts are that: first of all, these texts capture the identity of Jesus in the Qur'an, asserting his prophetic role within the whole context of Islamic prophecy; secondly, these texts equally highlight a unique relationship between Jesus and the *Holy Spirit* (Ruh al-qudus), who will later provide guidance to the Prophet Muhammad in his reception of the Qur'an. Although there are other texts of equal importance, we reckon that these texts contain, in themselves, the support that we need for a careful reflection on what is today called a "Qur'anic Christology." We shall approach the above texts thematically; by focusing on the unique relationship between Jesus and the *Holy Spirit,* and how this contributes to defining his identity and his mission in the Qur'an.

Our interest in the theme of the *Holy Spirit* is first of all, informed by the argument that the *Holy Spirit* is that significant agent who remains instrumental in the life of Jesus in the Qur'an, right from his birth, his public ministry to his final end. Consequently, a careful study of the relationship between Jesus and the *Holy Spirit* would help elicit his identity, and the role that he played within the divine plan of Allah. It would also provide the appropriate context for a better interpretation and understanding of the Christological titles ascribed to Jesus in the Qur'an. As a significant agent in the life and ministry of Jesus, the *Holy Spirit* teaches Jesus the *Injil* (the Gospel) and communicates the Qur'an to the Prophet Muhammad. So, by virtue of His origin as a "Messenger" of Allah and His involvement in the prophetic missions of Jesus and Muhammad; the *Holy Spirit* in the eyes of Muslims, places a stamp of authenticity on the message received by Jesus and the message of Muhammad in the Qur'an: for both derive their source from Allah. In other words, in the Qur'an, the *Holy Spirit* could be seen as a *principal agent* in the communication of the message of the *Injil* (the Gospel) and the Qur'an.

It will become clearer as the discourse unfolds that the message of Jesus as can be found in the Qur'an is fundamentally about

221

the observance of the *Tawhid*. Jesus in the Qur'an said, "I have come to you to confirm the truth of the Torah which preceded me ... I have come to you with a sign from your Lord. Be mindful of God, obey me. God is my Lord and your Lord, so serve Him – that is the straight path" (Surah 3: 50 – 51). Here, one finds an immediate connection between Jesus' message and the message of the prophets who preceded him. Since it is the *Holy Spirit* who is the *principal agent* through whom Allah communicated His message to His prophets, then the *Holy Spirit* remains an important agent for reflecting on the identity and the mission of Jesus, the Christ. Thus, a significant question that is worthy of note here is: if the *Holy Spirit* is the medium through whom God provides guidance to humanity through the message of His prophets, then how does the message of Jesus in the Qur'an contribute to providing this guidance? We shall commence this section by first considering the identity of the *Holy Spirit* in the Qur'an, and His relationship with Jesus in the light of Surah 2: 87, 2: 253; and 5: 110.

5.5.1 The Identity of the Holy Spirit in the Qur'an

According to O'Shaughnessy, the concept of, "*Spirit* as a symbol of divine power is a term of unique importance in the religions of both the Semitic people, and of the nation's directly influenced by them."[567] It represents the tangible means by which the supreme Deity of both the Judeo-Christian religions and the nature religions of Babylonia, Assyria, Egypt and so forth, exercises control over humanity and the cosmos. For O'Shaughnessy, although this idea of the "Spirit" may be unique to these religions,

---

567 Thomas O'Shaughnessy. *The Development of the Meaning of Spirit in the Koran*. 1953, p.9.

it nonetheless represents a natural solution to the problem of how the divine communicates life force to man. Since *respiration* is universally observed to be coextensive with life, and ceases with its cessation, then *breath* becomes the concrete manifestation of life imparted to humanity through the supreme Deity.[568] Thus, the *Spirit* is viewed as the "Divine breath" and the "unseen power" that moves the cosmic forces and gives life to humanity and the entirety of creation. For the Judeo-Christian religions, *Ruh* is the breath of Yahweh, the life-giving spirit in man and the mysterious power at work in the natural phenomena of the universe. According to O'Shaughnessy, in pre-Islamic Arabic poetry the term *Ruh* means "breath or blow." It was only after the establishment of Islam that *Ruh* took on an additional meaning of the *soul*.[569]

In the Qur'an, the word *Ruh* (Spirit) is used about twenty times.[570] From the chronological study of *Ruh,* William Shellabear asserts that there are different ways in which *Ruh* is used in the Qur'an. Firstly, at the start of Muhammad's mission at Mecca, *Ruh* (*Ruh al-Quddus*) was used to refer to the *Angel Gabriel* (see Surah 70: 4; Surah 78: 38 and Surah 97: 4). Secondly, in the later Meccan Surahs, *Ruh* was used in connection with the creation of Adam (Surah 15: 29; Surah 38: 72; and Surah 32: 8) and the conception of Jesus (Surah 21: 91; Surah 19: 17; and Surah 66: 12). Thirdly, in the Surahs believed to be delivered in Mecca nearer the time of the *Hijra, Ruh* was used in four occasions in connection to the *amr* (a *Command,* an *Order* – Surah 16: 2, 17: 87 and 40: 15).[571] "Finally, in the Medina Surahs it is stated three

568 Thomas O'Shaughnessy. *The Development of the Meaning of Spirit in the Koran*. 1953, p.9.

569 Thomas O'Shaughnessy. *The Development of the Meaning of Spirit in the Koran*. 1953, p.11.

570 Thomas O'Shaughnessy. *The Development of the Meaning of Spirit in the Koran*. 1953, p.13-15.

571 William Shellabear. *The Development of the word 'Spirit' as Used in the Koran*. 1932, p.355.

times that Jesus was aided with the Holy Spirit (*Ruh al-qudus* –
Surah 2: 87; Surah 2: 53; and Surah 5: 110), once that Jesus was
himself a *spirit from Allah* (Surah 4: 171), and once that the believers had been aided with a spirit from Allah (Surah 58: 22).[572]
From these different forms of usage, though the word *Ruh*
appears to mean something distinct from the angels and yet in
some way is associated with them or something associated to
the creation of Adam and Jesus,[573] the *spirit* is that force which
gives life through the command of Allah. When referred to as
Ruh al-Quddus, Samuel Schlorff asserts that without exception,
Muslims identify it with *Gabriel, the Angel of revelation.* Hence,
"when the Qur'an states that Jesus, Muhammad and others, were
strengthened by the *Holy Spirit,* it is clearly referring to the Angel
Gabriel in the process of revelation."[574] Indeed, the word *Spirit*
or *al-Ruh* may be taken to mean the "soul", the "breath of life"
or as "intangibility". However, when specifically mentioned as
"Ruh al-Quddus" in the Qur'an, many scholars are of the view
that it refers to the Angel Gabriel. Let us see how the relationship between Jesus and the Angel Gabriel (the Holy Spirit) helps
us arrive at a better understanding of the identity and the mission of Jesus.

---

572 William Shellabear. *The Development of the word 'Spirit' as Used in the
     Koran.* 1932, p.355.
573 William Shellabear. *The Development of the word 'Spirit' as Used in the
     Koran.* 1932, p.356.
574 The Theological and Apologetical Dimensions of Muslim Evan-
     gelization" in *Westminster Theological Journal.* Vol. 42 (1986), p.335.
     http://www.answering-islam.org/Authors/Schlorff/schlorff1_f.
     html (12/04/2013).

5.5.2 The Relationship between Qur'anic Jesus and the Holy Spirit

The discourse here is centred on three Qur'anic texts: Surah 2: 87; Surah 2: 253; and Surah 5: 110. Whereas each of these three verses state that Jesus was *"strengthened by the Holy Spirit"*, our interest is to investigate what this phrase means within the Qur'an. We shall do this through the exegetical views of three Islamic scholars – namely *Abu Ja'far Muhammad ibn Jarir al-Tabari* (838 – 923AD), *Abu al-Qasim Mahmud ibn Umar al-Zamakhshari* (1075 – 1144AD) and *Abu Abdullah Muhammad ibn Umar ibn al-Husayn al-Taymi al-Bakri al-Tabaristani Fakhr al-Din al-Razi* (1149 – 1209AD). Due to the lengthy nature of their names, we shall adopt their fully recognised shorter forms such as *al-Tabari, al-Zamakhshari* and *al-Razi* for simple referencing.

The reasons for the recourse to these three classical Islamic commentators are that on the one hand, they enjoy some degree of historical proximity to the beginning stages of the development of Islam, and therefore have the privilege of enjoying the title "classical commentators". Yet on the other hand, their commitment to the religion of Islam as Sunni, Mutazilite and Shi'i Muslims coupled with their desire to learn more about the religion through the application of linguistics, philosophical and exegetical tools, brings freshness to issues of textual interpretations of the Qur'an. In other words, these commentators provide the insiders' point of view in respect of the interpretations of the above Qur'anic texts. As Ricoeur indicated in the section on practical wisdom, where there appears to be the conflict of understanding as a result of interpretation, recourse to the opinion of experts in the area is advised. The texts under consideration in this area are:

Surah 2: 87 – *We gave Moses the scriptures and We sent messengers after him in succession. <u>We gave Jesus, the Son of Mary, clear signs</u> and <u>strengthened him with the Holy Spirit</u>. So now, how is it that whenever a messenger brings you something you don't like, you become arrogant, calling some imposters and killing others?*

225

Surah 2: 253 – *We favoured some of the messengers above others.* _We gave Jesus, the Son of Mary our clear signs and strengthened him with_ _the Holy Spirit._

Surah 5: 110 – *Then God will say, 'Jesus, the Son of Mary!* _Remember my favour to you and your mother: how I strengthened you_ _with the Holy Spirit, so that you spoke in your infancy and as a grown_ _man; how I taught you the Scriptures and the wisdom, the Torah and the_ *Gospel; how by My leave, you fashioned the shape of a bird out of clay,* *breathed into it and it became by My leave a bird; how by My leave, you* *brought the dead back to life; how by My leave, I retrained the children* *of Israel from harming you when you brought them the clear signs and* *those of them who disbelieved said, 'This is clearly nothing but sorcery.*[575]

The underlined sentences and phrases will be part of our primary exegetical concern. Let us see how the contributions of al-Tabari, al-Zamakhshari and al-Razi helps us to understand the relationship between Jesus and the Holy Spirit and the identity and the mission that this relationship underscores.

(i) Abu Ja'far Muhammad ibn Jarir al-Tabari (838 – 923AD)

Al-Tabari was an orthodox Muslim of Sunni belonging from Bagdad, Iraq – a renowned Muslim scholar and author of many compendiums of Islamic history and Qur'anic exegesis. Al-Tabari was very scrupulous in his predilections on the type of material he relied on for his commentary on the Qur'an. He was very dogmatic in his thoughts which found intellectual resonance with the Islamic school of *Ibn Hanbal* in Bagdad where he studied.[576] According to Franz Rosenthal, al-Tabari memorized the Qur'an at the age of seven and qualified as a religious leader at the age of eight, and started learning the tradition of the prophets at nine.[577]

---

575 Texts are taken from M.A.S. Abdel Haleem. *The Qur'an: A New Translation.* 2010.

576 Edmund Bosworth. "Al-Tabari" in *the Encyclopedia of Islam.* Vol. 10 (1998), p.12.

577 Rosenthal, Franz (Trans.). *The History of al-Tabari.* Vol. 1 (1989), p.10-12.

From this wealth of knowledge, al-Tabari employed a methodology centred on the collection of disparate traditions and the critical analysis of the chain of transmitters so as to verify the authenticity of the tradition concerned. According to Neal Robinson, al-Tabari "comments on the whole Qur'an in sequence dividing each Surah into subsections which vary in length. He introduces each subsection with a phrase which reminds the reader that it is God's word."[578] He presents the text with its paraphrase and quotes other texts in the Qur'an to explain the meaning of the text. He then renders his personal view based on the analysis. For Jane McAuliffe, this work showcased the classical era of Qur'anic exegesis.[579]

One body of work which is attributed to al-Tabari is: *Jāmi' al-Bayān fī Tafsir al-Qur'an* (Collection of Explanations for Interpretation of the Qur'an). According to Mahmoud Ayoub, al-Tabari's work is the "first major work in the development of traditional Qur'anic sciences."[580] In respect of the relationship between Jesus and the Holy Spirit as expressed in these selected texts (Surah 2: 87 and Surah 2: 253), al-Tabari, indicates that the phrase *strengthen him with the Holy Spirit,* connects Jesus to the Holy Spirit in the two text (Surah 2: 87 and Surah 2: 253). But this phrase is preceded by; "*We gave Jesus, the Son of Mary the sign.*" The *sign* here refers to the miracles that Jesus performed. These were meant to authenticate the truthfulness of his claim to be the "Prophet of Allah".

His power to give life to the dead, to breathe life into clay birds and to heal the sick all add-up as evidence to this prophetic claim. Jesus' ability to inform people about what was happening in their homes testified to his knowledge of the *unseen*. On the question of *strengthening,* al-Tabari suggests two meanings: (1) it could mean that God empowered Jesus with unique characteristics

578 Robinson Neal. *Christ in Islam and Christianity.* 1991, p.71.
579 Jane McAuliffe. *Qur'anic Christians: An Analysis of Classical and Modern Exegesis.* 1991, p.19-20.
580 Mahmoud Ayoub. *The Qur'an and its Interpreters.* 1984, p.3-4.

that supported him in facing challenges of all kinds; and (2) it could also mean that God gave Jesus the *Injil* (the Gospel) since both the Qur'an and the *Injil* are viewed as having their source from God.[581]

In his analysis of Surah 5: 110, al-Tabari concluded that the Holy Spirit could only be identified as the Angel Gabriel because, if in this verse, Jesus is strengthened by the *Holy Spirit* and given the *Injil,* then two things (the Holy Spirit and the Gospel) are given to Jesus and not one. This is because the Holy Spirit and the Gospel could not mean one and the same thing.[582]

Al-Tabari's identification of Gabriel as the Holy Spirit is further sustained by his argument that Gabriel is the Angel of revelation from God to all the other prophets. Hence, Gabriel's primary function was to assists Jesus by teaching him the *Torah,* the *Wisdom,* the *Injil* and endowing him with the power to perform wondrous *signs.*[583] In consequence, al-Tabari concludes that the Holy Spirit is the Angel Gabriel who assisted Jesus in the performance of the miracles. Gabriel's relationship with Jesus therefore remains instrumental in substantiating Jesus' prophetic claims. Having seen what al-Tabari makes of these texts (Surah 2: 87, 2: 253 and 5: 110), let us seek the views of al-Zamakhshari on the matter.

---

581 *Abū* Ja' far Muhammad b. Jarir al-Tabari. *Jāmi 'al-bayān fí ta'wíl al_ Qur'an.* Beirut, Lebanon. Vol. 1, p.448-149.

582 *Abū* Ja' far Muhammad b. Jarir al-Tabari. *Jāmi 'al-bayān fí ta'wíl al_ Qur'an.* Beirut, Lebanon. Vol. 1, p.450.

583 *Abū* Ja' far Muhammad b. Jarir al-Tabari. *Jāmi 'al-bayān fí ta'wíl al_ Qur'an.* Beirut, Lebanon. Vol. 1, p.450.

(ii) Abu al-Qasim Mahmud ibn Umar al-Zamakhshari (1075 – 1144AD)

Umar al-Zamakhshari is an Iranian Muslim who belongs to the *Mu'tazillite theological school.*[584] He was a renowned philologist who considered Arabic as the queen of languages. According to Mohammad Khaleel, "he journeyed to Mecca, studied there for a while … It was in this city, on a second visit that he wrote his famous *Tafsir,* completing the work in two years attributable, he said, to the spiritual influence of his environs."[585] Despite his Mu'tazillite persuasion, Mahmoud Ayoub intimates that the *Tafsir of* al-Zamakhshari is even regarded by the Sunni *ulama* as one of the most significant works of *Tafsir.*[586] Islamic scholars of every rank and file have tremendous respect for him, even though some disagree with some of his ideas because of their hint of Mu'tazillite theology.[587] It is said that al-Zamakhshari steers his Islamic theological concepts and opinions carefully, bringing out a sense of novelty and freshness and opening up windows to alternative interpretations of Qur'anic texts.

In his interpretation of *sign* in the three texts named above, al-Zamakhshari indicates that *sign* here refers to the miracles Jesus performed and the disputations he engaged in as he tried to point

---

584 The *Mu'tazillite School* is an Islamic school of theology based on rational philosophy. It asserts that, the perfect unity and eternal nature of Allah does not allow for the claim that the Qur'an is co-eternal with God. Hence, Qur'an is created. Once it is created, it can be subjected to the rigor of human reason. Thus, knowledge becomes the final arbiter in the question of right and wrong. (See, Abdullah Saeed. *The Qur'an: An Introduction.* 2008, p.203).

585 Khaleel Mohammad. *David in the Muslim Tradition.* 2015, p.63.

586 Mahmoud Ayoub. *The Qur'an and Its Interpreters.*1984, p.5.

587 Mohammad Khaleel indicates that, while Ibn *Khallikān* praised al-Zamakhshari's work noting that "nothing like it has been written before," Taimiyya rather thought that the work was full of heretical innovations. (See Mohammad, Khaleel. *David in the Muslim Tradition.* 2015, p.63).

out the right way to worship Allah. Like al-Tabari, al-Zamakhshari contends that these *signs* authenticated the prophetic identity of Jesus.[588] Jesus is therefore *strengthened by the Holy Spirit* who emanates from God, for the purpose of carrying out the divine will. In terms of the relationship between Jesus and the Holy Spirit, al-Zamakhshari indicates that there is no fusion or unity of substance in the relationship between them.[589] The Spirit is only Allah's living breath which animates the life of Jesus through Allah's favour.[590] Al-Zamakhshari views the interpretation of Surah 2: 253 as practically meaning the same as Surah 2: 87.

In respect of Surah 5: 110, he observes that the discourse between Jesus and Allah is not about Jesus *per se*, but it is meant to re-orientate the people of Israel to the right path as a result of their rejection of Jesus and his message. In Surah 5: 110, while some rejected Jesus' prophetic claims, others interpreted the *signs* he performed as pure *sorcery*. Yet others even went to the extreme end to divinize him. So, by questioning Jesus on his *divine status* in the text, Allah sought to correct the wrongdoers who divinised him as God or "Son of God". Al-Zamakhshari then concludes that since Jesus was animated by *Ruh al-Quddus* from birth, his whole life is marked by *purity* from sin and wrongdoing.[591] Thus, the understanding of Jesus as the *spirit of Allah* only points to the fact that Jesus came into being through a special intervention of Allah, without human seed or substance.[592]

Like al-Tabari, al-Zamakhshari also asserts that the Holy Spirit refers to the Angel Gabriel. Consequently, in al-Zamakhshari, we

---

588 Al-Zamakhshari. *Al-Kashshāf.* 4 Vols. (Beirut: *Dār* al-kutub al-ilmi-yah, 2006), vol. 1, p.162.

589 Al-Zamakhshari. *Al-Kashshāf.* 4 Vols. (Beirut: *Dār* al-kutub al-ilmi-yah, 2006), vol. 1, p.163.

590 Thomas O'Shaughnessy. *The Koranic Concept of the Word of God* (Table II – Spirit) 1953, p.32; and (Table IV – Spirit Sense group D), p.52.

591 Al-Zamakhshari. *Al-Kashshaf.* vol. 1, p.675-676.

592 Thomas O'Shaughnessy. (Table V – Spirit Sense group E) 1953, p.65.

find two significant interpretive assertions which introduce some freshness to Qur'anic Christology: (1) al-Zamakhshari's second association of the *Holy Spirit* as the pure breath of Allah. Since the *Holy Spirit* symbolises *purity,* then His presence in the life of Jesus from the beginning to the end suggests that Jesus' whole life was marked by *purity* (the absence of sin and wrongdoing); and (2) al-Zamakhshari asserts that the dialogue between Jesus and Allah in Surah 5: 110 was meant to re-orientate the people of Israel to right guidance on the identity and prophetic task of Jesus. If one pieces together the element of his *purity* with his task as a *Prophet of Allah,* one finds a fine prophet who demonstrates an unwavering commitment to providing guidance in the acknowledgement of the *Tawhid.* The continual presence of the Holy Spirit in Jesus' life, from beginning to end, further attests to the success of his mission.

(iii) Abu Abdullah Muhammad ibn Umar Fakhr al-Din al-Razi (1149 – 1209AD)

Commonly known as *Fakhruddin Razi,* al-Razi was a Persian Sunni theologian and philosopher. He was born in 1149 in Iran and died in 1209 in Afghanistan. His commentaries on the Qur'an are known to be unique because of their context of varied and multi-sided approach to the text. Two of his major works are the *Tafsir-e Kabir* (The Great Commentary) and the *Mafatih al-Ghayb* (The Keys to the Unknown). Al-Razi was a rationalist who believed in the "self-sufficiency of the human intellect" and its power to unravel truths. Even though he considered that proofs based on the *hadiths* only lead to *presumptions,* he nonetheless gradually acknowledged the primacy of the truths of the Qur'an. In al-Razi then, one finds the harmonization of reason and revelation in the interpretation of the Qur'anic texts.[593]

---

593 John Cooper. "al-Razi Fakhr al-Din (1149-1209)" in *Routledge Encyclopaedia of Philosophy.* 1998 http://www.muslimphilosophy.com/ip/rep/H044.htm (09/09/2014).

Unlike al-Tabari who was very orthodox – restricting himself to the hadiths and to other recognised Islamic traditions in his interpretations, al-Razi approaches these verses (Surah 2: 87, Surah 2: 253 and Surah 5: 110) from a more philosophical perspective, rendering his exegetical style in layers of arguments and counter-arguments.[594] In doing this, al-Razi does not only seek evidence of meaning in the texts, but also seeks to discern the deeper meaning of the texts. He starts by first providing a translation of a *Qur'anic* paragraph, followed by the disputes surrounding its meaning and status, abrogated or otherwise. He then correlates the various positions of the earliest Arabic Qur'anic commentators, seeking knowledge of the reasons for the revelation of the verse, and knowledge of what God intended as its meaning. According to Mahmoud Ayoub, al-Razi's work is one of *Tafsir* and *Ta'wil* where "*Tafsir* concerns the translation of tradition, while *Ta'wil* seeks a deeper comprehension of the inner meaning of the sacred text.[595] Ayoub indicates that one finds in al-Razi's work, an effective play of these exegetical styles in his *Tafsir al-Kabir (The Great Commentary)* and *Mafatih al-Ghayb (Keys to the Unknown)*.[596]

In respect of the interpretation of the above three verses, al-Razi first draws a link of continuity between the prophet Moses and Jesus from the beginning statement of Surah 2: 87 – "We gave Moses the scriptures and We sent messengers after him in succession." Here, al-Razi asserts that divine guidance was given by Allah for the Jews through Moses. However, the Jews later disagreed among themselves leading to civil strife and the general perversion of their faith. Consequently, Allah sent successive messengers to remind them about the message of Moses and to provide them with the right guidance. This

594 Mahmoud Ayoub. *The Qur'an and Its Interpreters.* 1984, p.5.
595 Mahmoud Ayoub. *The Qur'an and Its Interpreters.* 1984, p.21.
596 Mahmoud Ayoub. *The Qur'an and Its Interpreters.* 1984, p.5.

continued until the advent of Jesus.[597] According to al-Razi, while all the other prophets after Moses were committed to the content of the Mosaic message, Jesus brought in a new *shari'a* (that is, a new law and path) – the *Injil*. This new law had to be proven through the miracles Jesus performed in his infancy and in public ministry.[598]

In his interpretations of *Ruh al-Quddus*, al-Razi does not differ from the views of al-Tabari and al-Zamakhshari. For him the *Holy Spirit* is the same as the Angel *Gabriel* who emanates from Allah but is not part of Allah.[599] Gabriel is created by God as His messenger who animates Allah's servants. Al-Razi also views *Ruh al-Quddus* as Allah's life-giving breath, breathed into man.[600] The Angel Gabriel is created by Allah to obey Allah's commands and carry them out.[601] Al-Razi intimates that Gabriel as an Angel is exulted above the rest of the Angels on the basis of two realities: (1) he is the intermediary between Allah and all the messengers of Allah, communicating the revelation of Allah to them.[602] It is Gabriel who teaches Jesus the *Torah,* the *wisdom* and the *Injil* (Surah 5: 110);[603] and (2) Gabriel brought the spirit of Jesus to Mary through the agency of his breath – *nafkh*.[604] Thus, it is the Holy Spirit who brings the truths of Allah to the prophets. This is supported by Surah 16: 102 where the Qur'an says, "Say, the Holy Spirit has brought the revelation with the Truth step by step from your Lord to strengthen the believers and as guidance and good news to the devout."

597 Fakhr al-Razi. *Tafsir al-Kabir.* Dar al-Kutub Al- 'imiyyah, n.d. Tehran. Vol.3, p.175-176.

598 Fakhr al-Razi. *Tafsir al-Kabir.* Dar al-Kutub Al- 'imiyyah, n.d. Tehran. Vol.3, p.176.

599 Thomas O'Shaughnessy. (Table I – Spirit Sense group A) 1953, p.24.

600 Thomas O'Shaughnessy. (Table I – Spirit Sense group A) 1953, p.32.

601 Thomas O'Shaughnessy. (Table I – Spirit Sense group A) 1953, p.43.

602 Fakhr al-Razi. *al-Tafsir al-Kabir.* Vol. 3, p.177.

603 Fakhr al-Razi. *al-Tafsir al-Kabir.* Vol. 3, p.177.

604 Fakhr al-Razi. *al-Tafsir al-Kabir.* Vol. 3, p.178.

Similar to the views of al-Zamakhshari, al-Razi also asserts that the verse in Surah 5: 110 is the consequence of the two modes of misunderstanding connected to the association of *divinity* to Jesus. The first mode of misapprehension is the Jewish disbelief in Jesus as a "Prophet of Allah" despite the *signs* he performed to prove his prophetic calling. The second mode of misunderstanding is the later Christian deification of Jesus.[605] In his esoteric interpretation of the *ta'wil* of Surah 5: 110, al-Razi intimates that *Ruh* or *Spirit* essentially has two natures: (1) the pure and luminous spirit; and (2) the wicked and the tyrannical spirit" who have the power to rule over an individual or be a means by which others are ruled. *Ruh* can therefore be luminous or dark. So, if Jesus is referred to as "a Spirit from Allah" it is because he is a Spirit that is *wholly pure* and *luminous* from Allah. His ontological constitution as a pure *spirit from Allah* establishes the relationship between him and Gabriel,[606] for Gabriel was identified as *al-Quddus* because he is created from pure light.[607] By connecting the purity of Gabriel with that of Jesus, al-Razi then concluded that in the history of prophecy, no prophet ever possessed the qualities that Jesus had. In al-Razi therefore, one sees a sustained argument for the unparalleled uniqueness of Jesus *vis-a-vis* the other prophets who preceded him.

Thus, when one considers the views of the above three Islamic commentators on Surah 2 :87, Surah 2: 253 and Surah 5: 110, one is given a clearer understanding of what Muslims mean when they talk about the *Holy Spirit* and the sort of relationship that existed between him and *Jesus*. Here, all three commentators (al-Tabari, al-Zamakhshari and al-Razi) concur that the *Holy Spirit* is the same as the Angel Gabriel. Islam views the Angel Gabriel as over-ranking the other angels and as the agent who

---

605 Fakhr al-Razi. *Tafsir al-Kabir.* Dar al-Kutub Al- 'imiyyah, n.d. Tehran, Vol. 12, p.122-124

606 Fakhr al-Razi. *al-Tafsir al-Kabir.* Vol. 3, Vol. 12, p.125.

607 Fakhr al-Razi. *al-Tafsir al-Kabir.* Vol. 3, p.178.

communicates God's revealed message to His messengers. The commentators also agree that *Gabriel* is referred to as *al-Quddus* (purity) because he is created from pure light.[608] In this way, we could say that if Jesus is referred to as *a spirit from Allah,* it could be because of his *life of purity and holiness.*

Furthermore, from all three commentators one realizes that it is the Angel Gabriel who constantly assisted Jesus in the performance of his miracles, and these miracles were *signs* intended to authenticate Jesus' role as the "Messenger" of Allah. Only al-Razi indicates that Jesus remains unique from the other prophets who preceded him because he inaugurated a new *Shariah, a new law* for the people of Israel. Al-Zamakhshari and al-Razi also agree that the dialogue between Allah and Jesus (in Surah 5: 110) was meant to correct a wrong "Christology" in practice among the Jews and the Christians. Firstly, while the Jews rejected the authenticity of Jesus' prophetic calling, and rejected the miracles he performed as pure sorcery, Allah's dialogue with Jesus in Surah 5: 110 had the purpose of re-orienting them to the authenticity of Jesus' claim as His (Allah's) prophet. Secondly, while Christians accepted Jesus' miracles as authentic, they nonetheless interpreted these miracles as *signs* which pointed to his divinity as God's Son, with divine status equal to that of Allah. For al-Zamakhshari and al-Razi, the dialogue in Surah 5: 110 was meant to correct this Christian deification of Jesus.

In short, one could say that the Christology of the Qur'an is built on the relationship between Jesus and the Holy Spirit identified as the Angel Gabriel. From the views of the Islamic Scholars above, it is Gabriel who teaches, guides, strengthens, and assists Jesus in doing what he was sent to do as the "Messenger" of Allah. As al-Tabarsi later puts it, if it is asked why Jesus was specially mentioned among all the prophets as being supported by Gabriel even though every prophet was also supported by

---

608 Murata, Sachiko & Chittick, Williams, C. *The Vision of Islam.* 1994, p.85–89.

him, it is because, "Gabriel accompanied him from his youth to his manhood. He was with him wherever he went, so that when the Jews conspired to kill him, He the Holy Spirit did not leave him until he took him to heaven."[609] Any Qur'anic Christology must find its breath and life in this intimate relationship between Jesus and the Holy Spirit.

5.6 Conclusion

Both the Qur'an and the Bible respectively shape the way faithful Muslims and Christians understand the nature of God and interpret reality. For in Islam as a religion, "there is no god but One God" (*Tawhid*). The one God is the creator and the sustainer of everything that exists. As the creator, He transcends His creation (*Tanzih*) and yet is immanent to His creation (*Tashbih*). He created humanity for one sole purpose – to worship Him and to be good vicegerents to the rest of creation. To help humanity fulfil this purpose, God sent messengers to provide them with the right guidance against the misguidance of *Iblis* and his agents. Among these messengers was Jesus, the *Messiah*, the "Son of Mary". From the context of the *Tawhid*, although Jesus is given reverential designations such as *Messiah, Spirit of God, Spirit from God, Word of God, Word from God* and *the friend of God* among others, these titles only define his role as a "Prophet" or as the "Messenger" of Allah. Here, Islamic commentators are unanimous on the view that Jesus succeeded in performing his prophetic task through his intimate relationship with the Holy Spirit, also identified as the Angel Gabriel.

From a particularly Christian front, although God is one, Jesus Christ is the second person of the triune God (the *Holy Trinity*)

---

609 Al-Tabarsi Vol. 1, p.249 in Ayoub, Mahmoud. *The Qur'an and Its Interpreters*.1984, p.124-125.

who took on human nature through the incarnation in order to redeem fallen humanity from its bondage of sin and death. Through his death and resurrection Jesus Christ atoned for the sins of fallen humanity (see Genesis 3: 1 – 24) and therefore made salvation possible for all believers. Although he walked the face of the earth as a human being (the "Son of Man"), he was nonetheless God (the "Son of God"). This explains why it is impossible to speak of God within the parameters of Christian theology without relating such statements to the life, death and resurrection of Jesus Christ.[610] In consequence, the Christian and the Islamic tradition-specific understandings of Christology demonstrate that each religious tradition has a theological framework which supports a coherent articulation of their respective perspectives (*Tawhid* and *Holy Trinity*) on the identity and the mission of Jesus Christ.

So far, we have consistently emphasized that dialogue as an exercise in learning from and about the other must focus on the faithful and on the fruitful communication of these Christian and Islamic tradition-specific understandings of the identity and the mission of Jesus. As different systems of belief (expressed in the *Tawhid* and in the *Holy Trinity*), it is obvious that one system cannot be used as the standard of measurement for the truthfulness of the other. What is rather possible and beneficial, is the sense of dialogue whose purpose is the desire to learn from and about the other, and to be enriched by this learning. In this way, Chapter Six will focus on the critically correlation of some Christian and Islamic Christological themes and titles which we have all along "passed-over" in defined silence. The purpose is to understand their deeper meaning within each tradition and how they offer learning examples for Christian-Muslim dialogue of life and the dialogue of common action.

---

610 Alister McGrath. *Christian Theology.* 1997, p.324.

CHAPTER SIX
CORRELATIONS OF COMMON CHRISTOLOGICAL THEMES

6.1 Introduction

The fact that Jesus Christ remains the central figure in Christian faith and theology, and yet is significantly referenced in the Qur'an; presents common grounds for undertaking a deeper analyses of certain common Christological themes expressed both in the Synoptic Gospels and the Qur'an. The interest is to learn and to understand their deeper meanings and significance within each religious tradition, and how this learning can facilitate better relationships between adherents of each religious tradition. In his assessment of earlier researches on Christian-Muslim dialogue on Christology, Mahmoud Ayoub indicated that, "earlier research on the subject of Jesus in Islam has been comparative and usually, the yardstick being the New Testament record of the life, teachings and significance of Jesus, the Christ. Useful as this research may have been … it had often harboured old prejudices and fostered new hostilities."[611] For Hamilton Gibb, the reason for these hostilities is because such comparative assessments do not do justice to Islam as, "an autonomous expression of religious thoughts and experiences which must be viewed in and through its own principles and standards."[612]

In our contemporary context, it is no longer acceptable to give Christian interpretations to theological themes and concepts which are particularly Islamic. In the same way, one cannot read

---

611 Mahmoud Ayoub. "Towards an Islamic Christology" in the *Muslim World*. 1976, p.165.

612 Gibb, Hamilton, A.R. *Muhammadanism*. 1962, p. vii.

the Synoptic Gospels with an Islamic bias.[613] To do so, is to ig-nore the fact that the Bible and the Qur'an have different histor-ical contexts and modes of revelation; and as such, have different theological frameworks within which the identity and the mission of Jesus are construed. Thus, for Christian–Muslim dialogue on Christology to be successful as an exercise in learning, the *other* must be viewed as an original source of self-understanding, ca-pable of communicating a unique experience.[614]

Following the views of Gadamer which we earlier on indi-cated, it is important to reiterate that, in dialogical-conversa-tions, we need to open ourselves to experience the *other* truly as a *thou*, not overlooking their claims, but allowing them to truly say something to us about themselves.[615] The interest in learning from and about the other can genuinely take place only when we allow the other to say something to us about themselves. As Panikkar did intimate, "to cross the boundaries of one's culture without realizing that the other may have a radically different ap-proach to reality is today no longer admissible. If still consciously done, it would be philosophically naïve, politically outrageous and religiously sinful."[616]

In consequence, this current chapter is a development of that which preceded it. It is an attempt to learn and to understand the deeper meanings and significance of the Christological ti-tles and themes which were glossily overlooked in Chapters Four and Five. These titles or themes include: *Messiah, Word of/from God, Spirit of/from God, Son of God, the Trinity, the death and res-urrection, the virginal conception, the ascension* and *the second coming of Jesus*. The critical correlations of these themes and titles may

---

613 Heikki Räisänen. "The Portrait of Jesus in the Qur'an: Reflections of a Biblical Scholars", in *The Muslim World*. 1980, p.123.

614 Raimon Panikkar. *The Cosmotheandric Experience*. 1993, p.60. & *In-tra-Religious Dialogue*. 1999, p.34.

615 Gadamer. *Truth and Methods. 1989, p.361.*

616 Raimon Panikkar. *Myth, Faith and Hermeneutics*. 1979, p.9.

disclose the significant place Jesus occupies in each tradition, and how this context of "Jesus–significance" points to certain religious values within each tradition. While Chapter Seven shall focus on the common values Jesus espouses in both religious traditions, the purpose would be to see how these religious values (espoused by the life and the mission of Jesus), could become contexts for Christian–Muslim dialogue of life and the dialogue of common action.

6.2 The Correlation of Key Christological titles

Just as the New Testament designates multiple Christological titles to Jesus Christ,[617] so also the Qur'anic portrait of Jesus accord him some honorific titles,[618] some of which appear to be similar to the New Testament designations of him. It will be the task of this section to try to understand these titles or themes within their Christian and Islamic tradition-specific contexts. It is worth reiterating that while Jesus Christ is construed as God and the "Son of God" in Christianity, he is considered a "Prophet" or as the "Messenger" of Allah in Islam. Thus, the work of critical correlation would focus on clarifying the meanings of the titles ascribed to Jesus Christ in Christianity and Islam in the light of the *Holy Trinity* and *the Tawhid* respectively. We shall focus here on three of these Christological titles – namely *Messiah, Spirit of/from God* and *Word of/from God*.

---

617 Some of these titles include: Lord, *Messiah*, Son of God, Son of Man, Word of God, Redeemer, and God.

618 Some of these titles include: The *Messiah*, the *Son of Mary*, the *Messenger*, the *Prophet*, the *Word of God*, and the *Spirit of God*. (See Geoffrey Parrinder. *Jesus in the Qur'an*. 1965, p.16).

6.2.1 Jesus as Al-Masih (the Messiah or the Christ)

According to Parrinder, Jesus is referred to as *al-Masih* eleven (11) times in the Qur'an. All these verses appear in the Medinan Surahs.[619] But the meaning it associates with this title is different from the heavily loaded soteriological implications it carries within Christian theology.[620] In Surah 3: 45, which concerns the annunciation of Jesus' birth, Jesus is referred to as the *Messiah* – "the Angel said to Mary, God gives you news of a Word from Him, whose name will be the *Messiah*, Jesus, the 'Son of Mary' ..." In Surah 5: 72, the title is used as a personal name for Jesus – "the *Messiah* himself said; children of Israel, worship God, my Lord and your Lord." So, the title the *Messiah* is used in reference to Jesus at all periods of his life from his birth to his final exaltation.[621] However, although Parrinder asserts that there seems to be no explanation as to what this title conceptually means, the title nonetheless appears to have a particular sense, demonstrated by the injunction in Surah 4: 171 – "people of the Book, do not go to excess in your religion and do not say anything about God except the truth; the *Messiah,* Jesus, the "Son of Mary", was nothing more than a "Messenger of God". To reaffirm this claim, the Qur'an in Surah 5: 17 also says – "those who say God is the *Messiah*, the "Son of Mary", are defying the truth."

Consequently, Parrinder intimates that, "while there is no Qur'anic etymological explanation of the word *Masih,* it was not difficult for the commentators to find a number of meanings"[622] associated with the term. Although there seems to be no specific etymology about the concept in Islam, other than the understanding that it means "anointing", what one can emphatically say about the title the *Messiah* in Islam is that

---

619 Geoffrey Parrinder. *Jesus in the Qur'an.* 1965, p.30.

620 Gerald O'Collins. *Christology.* 2009, p.42–28.

621 Geoffrey Parrinder. *Jesus in the Qur'an.* 1965, p.30.

622 Geoffrey Parrinder. *Jesus in the Qur'an.* 1965, p.31.

the title has no divine connotations. It simply means Jesus was "anointed"[623] by Allah from birth for a special mission as Allah's prophet and his messenger. If one takes serious considerations of the claims in Surah 4: 171, then one could say that the title the *Messiah* as designated in the Qur'an, is the personal name of Jesus who is the anointed "Prophet" and the "Messenger" of Allah. However, while Islamic commentators like al-Zamakhshari and al-Baydawi concede that the title the *Messiah* is foreign in Arabic,[624] some later Islamic commentators considered the Arabic *al-Masih* to mean "King" (al-malik), "righteous" (al-siddik), "pure" (al-quddus) or "one anointed with sacred oil from birth." In Moucarry's view, *al-malik* (King) and *al-siddik* (righteous one) might be more appropriate in reference to the meaning of the title the *Messiah*.[625]

Having said this, it is worth mentioning that although the title the *messiah* does not add divine connotations to the identity of Jesus, Shi'i Islam seems to present what Ayoub calls a "quasi soteriological Christology in the doctrine and role of the Imams, the spiritual heads of the community."[626] According to Ayoub, Ali the first Imam compared himself to Jesus in Shi'i Islam.

623 The Hadith *Bukhari* reports that Jesus was constantly seen with wet hair which looked as if water was dripping from his head all the time. This signified that Jesus was naturally "anointed" as a Prophet of Allah. (See Sahih Muslim Book 001, Hadith number 0323). http://hadithcollection.com/sahihmuslim/129-Sahih%20Muslim%20Book%2001.%20Faith/8461-sahih-muslim-book-001-hadith-number-0323.html (16/03/2015).

624 See, Geoffrey Parrinder. *Jesus in the Qur'an*. 1965, p.31.

625 George Moucarry. *The Prophet and the Messiah: An Arab Christian Perspective on Islam and Christianity*. 2002, p.179–180.

626 Mahmoud Ayoub. "Towards an Islamic Christology." 1978, p.167.

By first declaring God as One, Ali talks about himself and his descendants (the remaining eleven Imams) as being created by God's word.[627] What is significant here is that these twelve Imams are seen as the mediators between God and humanity. As Ayoub put it, "they are a source of salvation on the Day of Reckoning for those who accept their status as the friends of God and true heirs of the prophets."[628] These Imams are supposed to return at the end of time and the twelfth Imam would be the *Messiah* who would establish divine rule over the earth, with Jesus assisting him in his final act of redemption and judgement.[629] Even though Ayoub acknowledges that Islam really has no concept of sin and redemption analogous to the Christian view, he nonetheless asserts that as a "Messenger of God", Jesus could be viewed as "a saviour in that he, by his message, helped to guide humanity from error and to guide its footsteps on the path to God."[630] This notwithstanding, one must always be reminded that nowhere in Islam, does the title the *Messiah* carry divine connotations.

Within the context of the synoptic Gospels (as we saw in Chapter Four), Mark from the onset declares his Christological intent in the prologue of the Gospel – "the beginning of the Gospel of Jesus Christ, the "Son of God" (Mark 1: 1). Whereas we know that the title the *Messiah* is a Hebrew term which means the "anointed one", the use of *Christos* (Christ) here is the Greek equivalent of the Hebrew *Messiah*. This title has a history beginning from the time of Abraham through to the time of the

---

627 God "uttered a Word which became a light. From that light he cre-
     ated me and my progeny. Then God uttered another Word which
     became a Spirit, and from that spirit he made me to dwell in the light.
     The light he made to dwell in our bodies. Thus, we are the *Spirit of
     God* and the *Word of God*". (See, Mahmoud Ayoub. "Towards an
     Islamic Christology." 1978, p.167).

628 Mahmoud Ayoub. "Towards an Islamic Christology." 1978, p.168.

629 Mahmoud Ayoub. "Towards an Islamic Christology." 1978, p.168.

630 Mahmoud Ayoub. "Towards an Islamic Christology." 1978, p.167.

post-exilic prophets and John the Baptist. In this history, God brought Israel's attention to certain expectations in terms of different strands of future divine actions that will establish justice and peace. With Abraham, God established a covenant, stating that all the people of the earth shall be blessed in him (Genesis 22: 15 − 18). Here, the Messianic promise is more-or-less the awaiting of the *messianic era* than the promise of the *person of the Messiah*.

However, the expectation of this future divine event became associated with some of Abraham's descendants, namely the *Davidic line of kings*.[631] King David (1 Samuel 16: 1ff) was known for his excellent kingship. After King David and Solomon, God promises Israel an Ideal Davidic king who will establish perfect peace and justice. This longing for the ideal Davidic king became associated with the prophecies of the *anointed one* who will destroy the enemies of Israel.[632] Later on, these messianic utterances became intertwined with popular consciousness (the unfaithfulness of Israel's kings) leading to the prophecies which indicated that God himself was going to be their liberator.[633] In time, these prophecies gave rise to the association of divinity to the status of the *Messiah* (Isaiah 9: 5 − 6), the virginity of his mother (Isaiah 7: 14), and his place of birth (Micah 5: 2 − 3). From then on, Israel awaited the coming of this *Messiah* even to the time of the Apostles.

Consequently, after having experienced Jesus personally, Peter made a breakthrough on the way to Caesarea-Philippi by identifying Jesus as the *Christ* (Mark 8: 29). Without having to repeat what was said in Chapter Four, what is worth noting here is that in Christian faith and theology, the ascription of the title the *Messiah* to Jesus points to the fact that this very Jesus is the "Son of God" and the "Saviour of the World". Following this

---

631 Kaiser, Walter, C. *The Messiah in the Old Testament*. 1995, p.77-83.

632 Mahmoud Ayoub. "Towards an Islamic Christology." 1978, p.151.

633 Mahmoud Ayoub. "Towards an Islamic Christology." 1978, p.191-194.

line of thought, Alistair McGrath earlier on indicated that within the Christian tradition, it is impossible to talk about salvation without relating this to Jesus Christ.[634] So, while prophecies in the Old Testament (See Isaiah 7: 14, 9: 5-6, Isaiah 52: 13 – 53: 12 and Daniel 7: 13-14) predicted the coming of *the anointed one* who will bring liberation to the people of Israel,[635] the Synoptic Gospels see Jesus Christ as the fulfilment of these prophecies. In consequence, while the *Messiah* in Islam depicts the identity of Jesus as a "Prophet of Allah" in the light of the obligation to acknowledge the *Tawhid*, in Christianity, this title has a soteriological import. It identifies Jesus as the "Son of God" and the "Saviour of the World".

Yet, there is something to take home here. Within the context of Qur'an, Jesus as the *Messiah* suggests that Jesus is: (1) blessed and honoured by God (Surah 19: 31 – 32); (2) he is protected from Satan from birth (Surah 3: 31); and (3) he is blessed with a special birth (Surah 7: 171 – 172). Furthermore, the Arabic word *msh* which means "to touch" implies that the *Messiah* is seen as "one whose touch purifies from all faults, being himself provided with protection from the divine and anointed with the blessed oil" (Surah 3: 43, 49).[636] With the above text, one could say that the title the *Messiah* in the Qur'an is not just a loose title but conveys the precise identity of Jesus as the anointed "Prophet of Allah" who was very faithful to the task given to him by Allah. In the discourse concerning *Adam*, *Iblis*, and the *fall;* we indicated that Allah forgave Adam after the fall and made him his first prophet. Islam therefore has no concept of original sin and redemption similar to the fundamental Christian view of fallen humanity and its need for redemption.[637] So, with the fall of Adam

---

634 Alister McGrath. *Christian Theology.* 1997, p.324.

635 Walter Kaiser. *The Messiah in the Old Testament.* 1995, p.155-199.

636 Geoffrey Parrinder. *Jesus in the Qur'an.* 1965, p.31.

637 Irfan Omar (ed). *A Muslim View of Christianity: Essays on Dialogue by Mahmoud Ayoub.* 2007, p.137.

and his immediate reconciliation with Allah, there seem to be nothing for Jesus to save except to provide guidance to his descendant on following the straight path to Allah. In Christianity however, the fall of Adam (*original sin*) brought depravity to the entirety of humanity, from which sinful humanity could not save itself unless through a sinless one. It therefore took the sinlessness of Jesus, the Christ to save sinful humanity. This gives the title a soteriological significance in Christianity.

Yet as Ayoub conceives, one can still see some salvific elements in Jesus' role as a "Prophet of Allah", in that; "by his message, he helped to save humanity from all error and to guide its steps further on the path to God, to whom all belong and to whom we shall all return" (Surah 2: 1, 56).[638] In this way, Ayoub concludes that, "the Christ of Muslim piety has continued to be a living personality, humble and pious, forever thundering against the wrongs of society."[639] The question then is: what can be learnt from the identity of Jesus as the *Messiah* in Islam and in Christianity? It is here that a focus on the message of Jesus in the Qur'an and in the New Testament becomes significant. As a prophet in Islam, Jesus' message contributes to providing guidance to humanity from the misguidance of Iblis and his agents. He is a living example of commitment to the practice of acknowledging the *Tawhid* and submitting oneself in worship to the One God. As the "Son of God" in Christianity, Jesus' message in the New Testament does not only provide guidance to living morally good lives, but his death and his resurrection brought about redemption for all Christians. In this way, how can the messages of Jesus the *Messiah* be a context for Christian–Muslim dialogue of life and dialogue of common action? Chapter Seven will provide an effective response to this question.

---

638 Irfan Omar (ed). *A Muslim View of Christianity: Essays on Dialogue by Mahmoud Ayoub*. 2007, p.137.

639 Mahmoud Ayoub. "Towards an Islamic Christology," 1976, p.163.

6.2.2 Jesus as Ruh (Spirit) of/from Allah

According to Parrinder, even though the encyclopaedia of Islam reports that the Qur'anic use of the term *Spirit* is a bit obscure, *Spirit* is used seven (7) times in the Qur'an (some examples are Surah 2: 87, 4: 171, 5: 110, 19: 17 and Surah 21: 91) in reference to Jesus.[640] In some of these verses, Jesus is referred to as *a Spirit from Allah*. Among the six prophets who are dignified with special titles,[641] Jesus is identified as the "Spirit of God". What does this designation mean in Islam? For the modern Islamic commentator Yusuf Ali, it means, "Christ was a spirit proceeding from God."[642] For S.M. Seale, "It means the spirit was sent to him by divine command."[643] But, in Samuel Schlorff's view, "Spirit from Allah" should not be seen in divine terms because the Qur'anic understanding of the *Holy Spirit* is different from the Biblical deification of him. According to Schlorff, even though the Qur'an makes references to the *Spirit* in terms such as the, "*Holy Spirit*" (*Ruh-al-Quddus* – Surah 2: 87), "*a Spirit from Allah*" (Surah 4: 171), "*a Faithful Spirit*" (*al-Ruh-al-almin* – Surah 26: 193), these are not symmetrical to Christian theological understanding of the *Holy Spirit*.[644] As al-Tabari, al-Zamakhshari and al-Razi earlier indicated in Chapter Five, the *Holy Spirit* refers to Gabriel, the Angel of revelation who strengthens and guides the prophets and the messengers of Allah.

---

640   Geoffrey Parrinder. *Jesus in the Qur'an*. 1965, p.48.

641   According to Parrinder, the six were dignified prophets with special titles which are: Adam is the "Chosen of God" (*Safiy Allah*), Noah is the "Prophet of God" (*Nabi Allah*), Abraham is the "Friend of God" (*Khalil Allah*), Moses is the "Converser with God" (*Kalim Allah*), and Jesus is the "Spirit of God" (*Ruh Allah*) (Ibid, p.40).

642   Yusuf Abdullah. "Commentary on the Qur'an." Lahore, 1934, p.234.

643   M.S. Seale. *Muslim Theology: A Study of Origins with Reference to Church Fathers*. 1964, p.111.

644   Samuel Schlorff. "The Theological and Apologetical Dimensions of Muslim Evangelization" in *Westminster Theological Journal*. Vol. 42 (1986), p.352-353.

In the commentaries presented on Surah 2: 87, 2: 253 and Surah 5: 110 in Chapter Five, al-Tabari, al-Zamakhshari and al-Razi helped us to understand the relationship between Jesus and the Holy Spirit (the *Angel Gabriel*), who is God's messenger of revelation. In Islam, Angels are not divine beings but are created by God from pure light, to serve God as his messengers.[645] Consequently, the Angel Gabriel is not a divine being, but a messenger of God's revelation to his prophets. Since the Qur'an reports that Jesus was supported by the *Holy Spirit* from the cradle to his final end, one would imagine that Allah's favour was continuously with him from the moment of his birth to his final exaltation. Hence, al-Tabarsi could state emphatically that if it is asked why Jesus was specially mentioned among all the prophets as being supported by Gabriel, even though every prophet was also supported by him, it is because, "Gabriel accompanied him from his youth to his final end."[646]

Consequently, to say that Jesus is the "Spirit of God" carries no divine connotations. It rather emphasizes on the one hand, how Jesus came to be born through Allah's express command ("Be! and he was" − Surah 19: 35), and on the other, how he was continually supported by the Angel Gabriel from the cradle to his final exaltation. As al-Zamakhshari indicated, the understanding of Jesus as the *spirit of Allah* only points to the fact that Jesus came into being through a special intervention of Allah without human seed or substance.[647] In al-Zamakhshari's view, since the *Holy Spirit* is the *pure breath of Allah* (symbolizing *purity*), then His presence in the life of Jesus from beginning to end suggests that Jesus' whole life was marked by *purity* (the absence of sin and wrongdoing) and hence could be called the *Spirit of God*.

---

645 Murata, Sachiko & Chittick, Williams, C. 1994, p.84–89.

646 Al-Tabarsi Vol. 1, p.249 quoted in Ayoub, Mahmoud. 1984, p.124-125.

647 Thomas O'Shaughnessy. (Table V − Spirit Sense group E) 1953, p.65.

From the perspective of Christian faith and theology, even though one does not find references to Jesus as *a Spirit from God*, the Synoptic Gospels also present a picture of Jesus Christ which depicts his relationship with the *Holy Spirit*. For instance, Matthew 1: 18 reports how through the power of the Holy Spirit, Mary was to conceive and bear a son. Although the Gospel of Mark has no narrative on the annunciation, it does report of the descent of the *Holy Spirit* on Jesus at his baptism (Mark 1: 10). It was the same *Holy Spirit* who drove Jesus into the wilderness and supported him during his temptation (Mark 1: 12 − 13). Thus, Mona Hooker indicates that although Mark does not report of the outcome of the temptation in the way Mathew and Luke do, what is clear is that Jesus was victorious over the devil through the support he received from the Holy Spirit. In this way, "his future actions and words would be governed by the Spirit, not by Satan."[648] As a result, the descent of the Holy Spirit on Jesus at his Baptism (Luke 3: 22) and the working of the Holy Spirit in his ministry (Luke 4: 14 − 18), demonstrates that the Holy Spirit was continually active in the ministry of Jesus Christ from the beginning to the end.

However, unlike Islam which identifies the Holy Spirit as the Angel Gabriel, Christian faith and theology identifies the *Holy Spirit* as a divine being, the third person of the Holy Trinity. Whereas the Islamic obligation to the *Tawhid* asserts the unity and the transcendence of God and forbids the association of God to other beings, the Christian experience of God as Creator (the Father), as Redeemer (Jesus Christ), and as Sanctifier (the Holy Spirit), provides the context for conceptualizing God as One, and yet experienced in three divine persons. Thus, for Christian faith and theology, the Holy Spirit who is active in the ministry of Jesus Christ from the beginning to the end was none other than the third person of the Holy Trinity, a *Divine Being*. It could therefore be said that in Islam, the understanding that the

---

648 Mona Hooker. "Who Can This Be?" 2005, p.83.

Holy Spirit who emanates from God was constantly at work in Jesus' life and ministry is worth noting, although the *Holy Spirit* is identified as the Angel Gabriel. In Christianity too, even though the *Holy Spirit* is identified as the third person of the *Holy Trinity,* one nonetheless finds him actively involved in the ministry of Jesus, the *Messiah*, the "Son of God". So, in both the Qur'an and in the New Testament, one finds that the Holy Spirit although understood differently, nonetheless emanated from God and supported Jesus in the task he performed as a "Prophet of Allah" in Islam and as the "Son of God" in Christianity. If the Holy Spirit emanates from God (as a messenger in Islam and as proceeding from God as the third person of the Trinity); then it could be said that all that Jesus said and did in the Qur'an and in the New Testament had God's divine approval. In this way, what then can Muslims and Christians learn from the exemplary life of Jesus (as a Prophet and as the "Son of God") for their living relationships?

6.2.3 Jesus as the "Word from God" or "Word of God"

Two of the texts that refer to Jesus as "a Word from Allah" are: *"the Angel said, Mary, God gives you news of <u>a Word from Him</u>, whose name will be the Messiah, Jesus, the Son of Mary who will be held in honour in this world and the next …"* (Surah 3: 45); and *"People of the Book, do not go to excess in your religion and do not say anything about God except the truth: the Messiah, Jesus, the Son of Mary, was nothing more than a "Messenger of God", <u>His Word directed to Mary</u> and a Spirit from Him"* (Surah 4: 171). The key word for our interest here is: *Kalimatuhun* (His Word). What does this mean?

From the ordinary sense of the phrase – if "His" here refers to Allah, then "His Word" means that Jesus is in some unique way, God's own Word. This sense of the word becomes clearer when Surah 3: 45 is considered in the light of Surah 3: 39: "the Angel called out to him (Zachariah), while he stood praying in the sanctuary: God gives you news of John (Yahya) who will confirm a

Word from God" (*kalimatim–minallah*). In this text, if the same Angel announces the conception of Jesus to Mary as *"kalima-tim-minhu"* (a Word from Him) in Surah 3: 45, then one could say that Jesus is God's Word whom John heralds. But what does Jesus as *"kalimatim-minallah"* (A Word from God) mean in Islam?

It must be said that the Qur'anic understanding of Jesus as *a Word from Allah or the Word of God* is not synonymous to the Johannine *logos* Christological understanding.[649] Although the tendency is for some Christian scholars to conclude that the title, *"Word from God or Word of God"* (Surah 3: 39 and Surah 3: 45) means that Jesus is the incarnate "Word of God."[650] Jesus as "a Word from God" must be understood in the light of Surah 4: 171. In this text (Surah 4: 171), the Qur'an is unequivocal in its position on the identity of Jesus — *"People of the Book, do not go to excess in your religion and do not say anything about God except the truth: the Messiah, Jesus, the Son of Mary, was nothing more than a Messenger of God..."* This text, coupled with the overall Islamic obligation to the *Tawhid,* implies that the title of Jesus as "a Word from God" or the "Word of God" could not be construed in *logos Christological terms.* Having said this, what interpretations do Muslim commentators give to this dense Christological title?

Among the Qur'anic interpreters, Yusuf Ali focuses attention on Surah 3:39 and Surah 3: 45 in the attempt to find explanations to the designation of Jesus as "a Word from God". In Surah 3: 59, the Qur'an says: "In God's eyes, Jesus is just like Adam. He created him from dust and said to him, "'Be,' and he was" (*Kun fayakuun*). According to Yusuf, this text implies that Adam and Jesus were both created by the single "Word of God".[651] Hence, if divinity can be derived from this notion of Jesus as the "Word from God", then Adam could be considered divine as well. In

---

649 See, John 1: 1 – 3.

650 See, Thomas O'Shaughnessy. *The Koranic Concept of the Word of God*, 1948, p.56.

651 Yusuf Abdullah. *The Holy Qur'an.* 2001, p.132.

this way, Yusuf indicates that to say that Jesus is a "Word from Allah" does not imply that he is the pre-existent "Word of God" per the Johannine Logos Christology. It means that Jesus is a "Messenger of God", created for a special purpose. According to al-Baydawi, Jesus is referred to as the "Word from God" because he came into being without a father. For al-Razi, Jesus was called the "Word of God" because he was created by the express command of Allah: "Be and he was." Furthermore, as the "Word of God" he is the fulfilment of the words spoken to the prophets.[652] Other commentators also think that Jesus is referred to as the "Word from God" because he came as the effect of the "Word of God" which He cast upon Mary. Thus, al-Tabari remarked that, "'God calls this son which is in thy womb his word.'"[653]

In consequence, although there may be divergent views as on the exact interpretation of the phrase "Word of God" or "Word from God", it is noteworthy that each of these views renders an interpretation that honours and respects the uniqueness of Jesus devoid of divine overtones. Hence, many Islamic commentaries on the designation of Jesus as the "Word from God" centres on the meaning associated to Surah 19: 35 in which God creates by simply saying: "'Be!' and it is". In other words, Jesus is referred to as the "Word from God" because he came into being through the *creative Word of God* – through Allah's divine command which is symptomatic of Adam's creation (see, Surah 3: 59). However, Jesus stands in contradistinction from Adam in that whereas Adam is created from the dust of the earth and disobeyed God at some point in history (Surah 7: 19 – 23), Jesus was created by the exclusive *Word of God* cast upon Mary and never disobeyed the will of Allah. Besides, nowhere in the Qur'an is the designation "Word from God" or "Word of God" used to describe any of the prophets except for Jesus. The exclusive use of these phrases

652 Baydawi and Al-Razi quoted in Parrinder, G. *Jesus in the Qur'an*. 1965, p.45–46.

653 Al-Tabari quoted in Parrinder, G. 1965, p.47.

in reference to Jesus suggests that there must be something more about the identity of Jesus which warrants the exclusive use of the phrase. In some sense, could it be because Jesus is the only "Prophet of Allah" who is known to have been gifted with the *Injil,* the *Torah* and the *Wisdom* (Surah 3: 48) at the same time? In the Qur'an, none of the messengers of God is known to have taught these scriptures which are known to be from God (God's Word). Hence, if the Qur'an (Surah 3: 48) reports that, "God will teach him (Jesus) the Scriptures and Wisdom, the Torah and the Gospel", then Jesus by this very fact, possessed in considerable measure the "Word from God" or "Word of God" in a unique way. What then can Muslims learn from Jesus as the "Word from Allah"? We shall take this up in Chapter Seven.

Within the context of the New Testament, the phrase, "Word of God" (the *Logos*) is one of the most significant titles designated to Jesus Christ. Although Jesus as the *logos* is not used elaborately in the Synoptic Gospels, the Gospel of John uses this title in very unequivocal terms: "In the beginning was the Word. And the Word was with God. And the Word was God. He was in the beginning with God. All things came to be through him" (John 1: 1 – 2). According to Parrinder, linking the *Logos* to creation takes us back to the creation story in the book of Genesis where creation came into being through the *creative Word of God*.[654] Although the word *Logos* is the Greek derivative of the Hebrew *Dābār* (Word), *Logos* was first used by Philo of Alexandria to refer to "the Divine Reason, intermediate between God and the world."[655] However, in the Johannine account, *logos* is not an intermediary in the "Philonian sense" but refers to God himself who pre-existed creation. Here, *Logos* does not belong to the created order, but the divine order. It is this *Word* who became incarnated in Jesus Christ – "And the *Word* became flesh and dwelt among us, full of grace and truth" (John 1: 14).

---

654 "And God said, let there be..." (Genesis 1: 3 – 25).

655 Geoffrey Parrinder. *Jesus in the Qur'an.* 1965, p.47.

In consequence, Christian faith and theology holds that by virtue of the incarnation, the *Word of God* (Jesus) became flesh through the conception of the Virgin Mary. After the incarnation Jesus Christ as the "Word of God", retained two natures: the human and the divine, in one prosopon (person). As McGrath intimated, within Christian faith and theology, "the importance of the confession that 'Jesus is Lord' is not only that Jesus is divine, but that God is Christ-like."[656] For Abdul-Haqq, there is no doubt as to the identity of Jesus as the "Word from God" whom John came to announce to Israel. In the expression "Word from Him", the participle (from) "*Min*" signifies a generic relationship between the noun and pronoun linked together by it. Therefore, it implies that "the Word" is of the same divine essence as Him (*hun*) – God.[657] For Samuel Zwemer, if Christ in Christianity were a mere "Word from God", then it would be clear that He was only one expression of God's will. But since God Himself calls Him the "Word of God", it is clear that He must be the one and only perfect expression of God's will and the only perfect manifestation of God.[658] Thus, in Christian faith and theology, to say that Jesus Christ is the "Word of God", is to admit that this Jesus is divine: truly God and truly Man, the second person of the most *Holy Trinity*.

Having considered the Islamic and the Christian interpretations of the Christological title: "Word from God" or "Word of God", we could conclude that the title is exclusively designated to Jesus in both the Qur'an and in the Gospels (particularly the Johannine Gospel). However, while it is interpreted in Islam as emphasizing the unique coming to be of Jesus through Allah's divine command – "Be and it is", (Surah 19: 35), in the Christian faith and in theology, Jesus Christ as the "Word of

---

656 Alister McGrath. *Christian Theology*. 1997, p.323.

657 Abdul-Haqq, Adbiyah Akhbar. *Sharing Your Faith with a Muslim*. 1980, p.68.

658 Samuel Zwemer. *The Muslim Christ*. 1912, p.37.

God" relates to the incarnation in which in his pre-existence, Jesus took on human nature and was born of the Blessed Virgin Mary (Philippians 2: 6 – 11). Here, he is not created by God but predates creation and is the source of it. Having said this, what can we learn from these two forms of christologising about Jesus in Islam and in Christianity?

Within the context of Islam, Jesus is conceived as a "Messenger of Allah". We know that every "Messenger of Allah" is sent with a message which is very often summarized in the *Tawhid*.[659] So, whether understood as a bearer of God's Word (the messenger in Islam) or the content of that very Word (the Incarnation of the Word as per the Christian notion), Jesus still provides guidance to all who seek to submit themselves to God. As the "Word from God" in Islam and the "Word of God" in Christianity, if Jesus communicates the divine message in the Gospels and in the Qur'an, then what is the central tenet of this message for Christians and Muslims? Does it provide a context for Christian-Muslim dialogue of life and the dialogue of common action?

While the responses to the above questions will be taken up in Chapter Seven, they nonetheless demonstrate the potentiality of the identity and the mission of Jesus the *Messiah* in stimulating Christians-Muslim conversations about the call to submit oneself to the will of God and the believer's response to it. In considering the designation "Word of God" from a Christian and a Muslim perspective, Christian Troll indicates that Christians and Muslims are unanimous on the understanding that God took the first initiative to speak to humanity through His Word. While adherents from both religions consider themselves to be the privileged beneficiaries of this "Word of God", Muslims believe that the Qur'an is the unique and final "Word of God" to humanity through the Prophet Muhammad (Surah 42: 53). For Christians

---

659 See V.G. Cornell. "Tawhid: The Recognition of the One in Islam," in Hans Küng and Jürgen Moltmann (eds). *Islam: A Challenge for Christianity.* 1994, p.61.

however, God has in many and diverse ways spoken to our ancestors through the prophets. But in these last days, he has spoken to us through his son – Jesus Christ (see, Hebrew 1: 1 – 2).[660]

Following the two perspectives, while Muslims identify the Qur'an as the "Word of God" communicated to Muhammad in the Arabic language, Christians see Jesus Christ as that incarnate "Word of God" – God's unique, definitive and universal self-communication to humanity.[661] Christian Troll therefore draws a distinction between the two textual traditions: whereas the Qur'an is the concrete "Word of God" for Muslims, Jesus Christ is the concrete "Word of God" for Christians. Yet, the question is: what about the "Word of God" as found in the Old Testament and in the New Testament? For Troll, although sacred, these books are, "jointly the work of God, and the divinely inspired authors, are only one means, albeit an exceptional and normative means, of coming to know the "Word of God" in life's experience".[662] In this way, Troll indicates that Christians and Muslims need to know these profound differences between their respective scriptures in order to avoid irrelevant conflicts. But Troll's distinctions undercut the Christian understanding of the Bible as the "Word of God" – a Sacred Book.

While it is true that for Muslims, the "Word of God" became a Book (as in the Qur'an), it is also true that for Christians, Jesus is the concrete manifestation of the "Word of God". Yet, before the incarnation, the "Word of God" as represented in the Old Testament was also communicated to our ancestors through the

660 Christian Troll. "The Bible and the Qur'an in Dialogue". 79/80. https://www.sankt-georgen.de/fileadmin/user_upload/personen/Troll/troll37.pdf (11/03/2020), p.31.

661 Walter Kasper. "The Uniqueness and Universality of Jesus Christ". 2004, p.16.

662 Christian Troll. "The Bible and the Qur'an in Dialogue". 79/80. https://www.sankt-georgen.de/fileadmin/user_upload/personen/Troll/troll37.pdf (11/03/2020).

prophets (see, Hebrews 1: 1 – 2). Upon breaking into human history through the incarnation, Jesus Christ did not cease to communicate the "Word of God" to His followers (as represented in the Gospels) who later continued the mission of communicating this same Word to others (as expressed in the epistles). This explains why the New Testament is seen as the fulfilment of "God's Word" communicated in the Old Testament. In this way, the Old Testament and the New Testament are seen as the Sacred "Word of God" (a sacred Book) given to Christians despite its enfleshment in the person of Jesus Christ. So, the embodiment of the "Word of God" in Jesus Christ does reduce the Sacred Book of the Bible to just the mere expressions of the work of God as Troll indicated. The Bible (the Old Testament and the New Testament) is the "Word of God" for Christians, just as the "Word of God" became a Book (the Qur'an) for Muslims. It is on the basis of this very understanding that the Qur'an even refers to Christians as "people of the Book" (Surah 9: 29 – 30) or "People of the Gospel (Surah 5: 47). This honest understanding must be at the heart of Christian–Muslim dialogue on their sacred texts.

6.3 Jesus Christ as a Bridge and a Barrier to Christian-Muslim Dialogue

So far, we have learnt some distinctive differences in the Christian and the Islamic conceptualizations of the identity and the mission of Jesus Christ. While for Christians, Jesus Christ is the "Son of God" and the "Saviour of the World", Muslims view him as a "Prophet" and a "Messenger" of Allah whose task was to provide right guidance to the people of the Book. These two notions of the "Son of God" and "prophet" presents a context of "claim and counterclaim" between the two traditions on the identity and the mission of Jesus Christ. This explains why the structuring of Christian–Muslim dialogue on Christology on this context of claim and counterclaim makes such dialogues a daunting task. As a result, Mark Beaumont indicated that unless Muslims develop a more dynamic concept of the transcendence of God, they will never admit to the Christian notion of the divinity of Christ. And yet, "Muslims for their part are pleased when Christians give up the idea of divine presence in Christ and presumably hope that more Christians will follow John Hick's example."[663]

Due to the contentious nature of Christology in Christian-Muslim conversations, some scholars propose that a focus on the ethics of Jesus would help to lighten the tensions that exist between Christians and Muslims when it comes to dialogue about him. But Christian-Muslim dialogue on the ethics of Jesus will not be more straightforward than dialogue on his status. This is because the authority of Jesus' teachings may have to be faced when a clash between his teachings and Islamic tradition emerges. As Mark Beaumont put it, "whether Muslims will be prepared to grant him the authority to challenge Islamic norms is a difficult question to answer."[664] Thus, an honest dialogue on Christology must begin first from the status of Jesus and then proceed to his ethics. Jesus did what he succeeded in doing because of who he was. As indicated earlier, the benefit of learning from and about the other supports a constructive dialogue between Christians and Muslims on Christology.

Islam may deny the doctrines of the incarnation, the death and the resurrection of Jesus but Qur'an also contains accounts which attest to the "Virginal Conception", the "miracles Jesus performed", the "Ascension" and the "Parousia". Since these accounts resonate in the Christian understanding of Christology, one could say that between Islam and Christianity, Jesus Christ is both a *barrier* and a *bridge* in their relationships. Whereas the concept of a *barrier* represents that which divides them christologically, the idea of a *bridge* underscores the common Christological themes they appear to share. To engage in dialogue as an exercise in learning,

663 Mark Beaumont. *Christology in Dialogue with Muslims*. 2005, p.210.
664 Mark Beaumont. *Christology in Dialogue with Muslims*. 2005, p.211.

there is need for further clarity on the meanings and the theological understandings of some of these Christological themes that serve as both a bridge and a barrier to Christian-Muslim relations. The purpose is to learn and to be enriched by this learning. By enrichment, we mean the extent to which these Christological issues may also create contexts for Christian-Muslim dialogue of life and the dialogue of common action. Let us now investigate some of the Christological themes heuristically referred to here as a *bridge* and a *barrier* to Christian-Muslim relations.

6.4 Jesus as a "Barrier" to Christian-Muslim Dialogue

The meaning of the concept *barrier* can either be seen in physical or non-physical terms. It is viewed in a physical sense when it refers to "a set of objects used to separate, demarcate or barricade a passage from one point to another."[665] From this sense, we can think of a fence, a highway barrier, a high wall or a roadblock. From the non-physical perspective, a *barrier* can also mean, "a regulation that is intended to set apart and differentiate one thing from another." Here, we can think of the ethics of a profession, rules of courtesy, civil laws, religious rules and doctrines and so forth. From these two definitions we could say that the goal of every *barrier* is: to maintain the status-quo; to regulate conduct; to maintain law and order; or to ensure the maintenance of originality or particularity. Hence, *barriers* pose no problems once one respects and observes that which they seek to preserve. Situating this within the context of Christian-Muslim dialogue on Christology, a *barrier* here is used as a heuristic device intended to help us to understand the Christological issues which seem to set a dividing line between the Christian and the Muslim way of theologizing about Jesus.

---

665 Agnes Michael. *Webster's New World College Dictionary.* 2007.

As a result, to say that Jesus remains a *barrier* to Christian-Muslim dialogue is to mean that there are stark differences in the way Christians and Muslims theologize about Jesus of Nazareth. These differences need to be respected. As we indicated in Chapters Four and Five, while Islamic Christology is guided by its obligation to the *Tawhid,* the Christian view of Jesus Christ as the "Son of God" finds its expression in the Christian experience of God as *Trinity.* Thus, the context of *Tawhid* and *Trinity* set the parenthesis within which Christology finds its articulation in Islam and Christianity respectively. That is, the *Tawhid* and the *Trinity* define the *barriers* within which the Qur'anic Jesus and Jesus of the New Testament are to be understood. Some of the Christological themes considered as *barriers* here include Jesus as the *Son of God,* Jesus' *passion* and *death* and the *resurrection.* For Christian-Muslim dialogue to be an exercise in learning, this form of dialogue must recognize and respect these *barriers* as essentially part of the exercise of learning.[666]

6.4.1 The Most Holy Trinity and The Tawhid

The doctrine of the *Holy Trinity* is a theological articulation of the Christian experience of God as One God in three divine persons – that is, God the Father, God the Son and God the Holy Spirit. These three divine persons are *distinct*, but are *one substance*, one *essence* or one *nature.* The Catechism of the Catholic Church indicates that while their *personhood* focuses on *who* they are, their *nature* defines *what* they are.[667] These three divine persons of the Holy Trinity are said to be distinct from one another in their relations of origin but co-equal, consubstantial and co-eternal

---

666 See Jacque Dupuis. *Towards a Christian Theology of Religious Pluralism.* 1997, p.378.

667 The Catechism of the Catholic Church, # 252.

in their nature.[668] In conceptualising this theological complexity, the basic question however is: how can God be *One* and at the same time *Three*? How can Jesus be human and God at the same time? What takes precedence in him? His humanity or his divinity? It is some of these questions that Muslim often bring to the dialogical table,[669] questions which continue to vex every theological discourse on the doctrine of the Holy Trinity and Jesus' place within it. In this subsection, the interest is to briefly attest to how God revealed himself through the mystery of the *Most Holy Trinity,* and how the Church articulated this revelation.

First of all, it must be said that the Christian experience and knowledge of God is informed by two premises: "the knowledge of who God is" and "what God has done". In the Catechism of the Catholic Church, these two poles of the divine encounter are defined by the Greek words: *theologia* (theology) and *oikonomia* (economy). Whereas *theologia* refers to the knowledge attained through the revelation of the mystery of God's innermost life, *oikonomia* refers to the experiential encounter of the work by which God reveals and communicates his life. In this way, The Catechism of the Catholic Church indicates that, "God's works reveal who he is in himself, and the mystery of his inmost being enlightens our understanding of all his works."[670] In the encounter between people which leads to the gradual revelation of the character of oneself to another, we understand that "a person discloses himself in his actions, and the better we know a person, the better we understand his actions."[671] Thus, through the *oikonomia* of God, the *theologia* is revealed to us, while the *theologia* illuminates the whole *oikonomia*.

---

668 The Catechism of the Catholic Church, #253.

669 For more information on the questions raised by Muslim scholars on the authenticity of the incarnation and its relation to the Holy Trinity, see Mark Beaumont. *Christology in Dialogue with Muslims.* 2005, p.93–112.

670 The Catechism of the Catholic Church # 236.

671 Catechism of the Catholic Church (hereafter CCC), # 236

Following the above method of the attainment of knowledge of God, it could be asked: how did God reveal himself to us as *Trinity*? And how did the Church articulate this revelation? From the onset, it must be said that *God* is *Holy Mystery* and that is His nature. This sense of *mystery* implies that God cannot be fully and absolutely comprehended by the human mind (reason). His incomprehensibility defines his nature as God. Consequently, Christian faith and theology perceives the *Holy Trinity* (the Father, the Son and the Holy Spirit) as part of the *mystery of God* who he is, and how He chooses to reveal himself to humanity. Thus, the *Holy Trinity* comes as part of that which God chose to make known to the Christian Church. Just as in some religions God is called *father,* so also in the Old Testament, Israel referred to God as *Father* because he created the world and sustains it (Deuteronomy 32: 6). By the establishment of the covenant between God and Israel, Israel was known as God's "first born son" (Exodus 4: 22). God was also known as the *father* of the kings of Israel, as *father* to the poor, the widowed and orphans.[672] So by calling God "Father", the language of faith indicates two main implications: (1) that God is the source of origin of everything that exists; and (2) that He transcends everything that exists.[673]

Through earlier prophecies and the testimonies of Jesus Christ, God is further revealed not only as *father* in the sense of being *creator,* but also as *father* in the sense of being *eternally father* in relation to his son who is also the eternally son in relation to his father.[674] Through the testimonies of Jesus, this relationship is affirmed when he said during his public ministry; "No one knows the Son except the Father, and no one knows the Father except the Son, and any one to whom the Son chooses to reveal him" (Matthew 11: 27). Here, not only does Jesus express the connection between him and the father as based on his knowledge

672 CCC, # 238.
673 CCC, # 239.
674 CCC, # 240.

of him, but also in John 10: 30 and John 17: 21, Jesus further asserts that he and the father are one. It is this unique unicity of the eternal being of the *Father* and the *Son* which is expressed in the prologue of John's Gospel (John 1: 1) — "In the beginning was the Word and the Word was with God and the Word was God." In reflecting on John 10: 30 and John 17: 21, while Michael Mullins affirms that Jesus' priestly prayer in John 17: 21 was an expression of the life of intimacy between him and God, intended as a special gift for his disciples, this gift nonetheless reflects the communion between Jesus himself and his Father. For Mullins, this communion is, "not a matter then, of simple union of a moral kind, but a unity at the level of being — a unity that has as its model and permanent source, the oneness of the father and the son."[675]

Consequently, it is on the basis of articulating this attested-to *Oneness* (consubstantiation) between Jesus Christ and God the *Father* that the councils of Nicaea (325) and Constantinople (381)[676] affirmed Christ as, "eternally begotten of the Father, light from light, true God from true God, begotten not made, consubstantial with the Father."[677] In Christian faith and theology therefore, even though it is acknowledged that God has revealed himself in many and diverse ways, Jesus Christ is known to be the definitive revelation of God to humanity. As Walter Kasper put it, "the fact that the one God has once only, yet wholly, definitively and unreservedly communicated himself historically in Jesus Christ is the basic conviction of the fathers of the church

---

675 See, Michael Mullins. *The Gospel of John.* 2003, p.351.

676 For more information on the Christological debates from Nicaea to Chalcedon and beyond, see: J.D.N. Kelly. Early Christian Doctrines.1977; p.223-243; Cairns, E.E. *Christianity Through the Centuries. A History of the Christian Church.* 1984; Anthony Thiselton. *The Hermeneutics of doctrine.* 2007.

677 See Stevenson, J. Creeds, Councils and Controversies. 2003, p.114-115.

reflected in the church's ancient tradition."[678] Following the deposit of faith borne from the experience of Jesus of Nazareth, the Apostles and first century Christians encountered Jesus Christ as the promised *Messiah* who was truly God and Truly man in his nature and actions.

In John 14: 16, shortly before the Passover, Jesus announced the coming of the Holy Spirit as *Paraclete* (Advocate) to the disciples – "I will ask the father and he will give you another Paraclete to be with you forever." According to Mullins, when Jesus promised to send another *Paraclete,* he spoke in terms of "another Paraclete", which suggests that the latter *Paraclete* will be performing the same function or carrying out the same agenda as the former.[679] Who is the *former Paraclete* and what was his function? For Mullins, the concept *Paraclete* has different meanings in the Hebrew and in the Greco-Roman traditions. In the Hebrew sense, it refers to Biblical tradition in which God is said to be the *comforter* or the *consoler of Israel* (See Isaiah 52: 12). Jesus also introduces himself as the one who offers this comfort when he said; "the Spirit of the Lord is upon me, he has anointed me and sent me to bring good news to the poor, to bind up hearts that are broken" (Luke 4: 18 – 25). So, for Mullins, *paraclêsis* means "comforting actions, words and writings."[680] Here, if "God is the first *Paraclete,* comforting the people through word and deed, then Jesus is by implication, a Paraclete in his acting and speaking on behalf of the father."[681]

From the Greco-Roman sense, Mullins asserts that, "a *Paraclete* is seen in terms of a legal advisor, helper or advocate in court."[682] For Mullins, as Jesus encountered trials and called witnesses like the father, John the Baptist and the Scriptures to his defence, so

---

678 Walter Kasper. "The Uniqueness and Universality of Jesus Christ." 2004, p.16.

679 Michael Mullins. *The Gospel of John.* 2003, p.324.

680 Michael Mullins. *The Gospel of John.* 2003, p.325.

681 Michael Mullins. *The Gospel of John.* 2003, p.325.

682 Michael Mullins. *The Gospel of John.* 2003, p.325-326.

he envisaged that his disciples would also encounter trials and would need the support of a helper or an advocate. Jesus' promise of this helper, whom he called the *Spirit of truth*, shall come from the father (John 14: 26), just as he came from the father. His task will not just be to comfort them but also "to prepare and instruct them for their role as disciples and witnesses after Jesus' lifetime."[683] In this way, Mullins affirmed that the use of paraclete in the Johannine presentation conveyed both senses. That is, the phrase "another Paraclete" implies that the Holy Spirit was going to perform the same function or carry out the same agenda as Jesus did (i.e. to comfort, advice, and help). Hence, the Catechism of the Catholic Church says: "having previously 'spoken through the prophets,' the Spirit will now be with and in the disciples, to teach them and guide them 'into all the truth.'"[684] If the Holy Spirit is equal to this task, then he must share the same being with God the *Father* and God the *Son* to possess such equal capability. And since the being of God the Father and God the Son are divine, by inference, the Holy Spirit also possesses this life of divinity (another Paraclete) in the same nature as Jesus and the Father. It is for this reason the Catechism of the Catholic Church asserts that, "the eternal origin of the Holy Spirit is revealed in his mission in time. The Spirit is sent to the apostles and to the Church both by the Father in the name of the Son and by the Son in person, once he had returned to the Father" (CCC # 244).

In this way, one begins to see a clearer picture of the *mystery of the Holy Trinity* in the faith experience of the Church, even though the *Holy Trinity* as a concept, is not explicitly stated in the Christian Scriptures.[685] However, the Christian experience of God as three persons in one God, supports the use of the Latin term *Trinitas* (meaning *triad* or *threefold*) as a means of conceptualising

---

683 Michael Mullins. *The Gospel of John*. 2003, p.327.

684 Catechism of the Catholic Church (CCC) # 243.

685 W.R.E. Browning. *The Oxford Dictionary of the Bible*. 1996, p.187.

and communicating this Christian faith encounter with the triune God. From the perspective of *oikonomia* (the functions of the Holy Trinity), God the father is said to be the creator of all things, God the Son (Jesus Christ) is the redeemer of creation and God the Holy Spirit is the sanctifier of creation; and yet the whole drama of creation, redemption and sanctification is seen as a single operation common to them.[686] As Browning put it, "each is God but each is a distinct Person" defined by their roles in the whole drama of creation, redemption and sanctification. This experience of God as *Holy Trinity* in the early Church reflected its usage of the trinitarian formulation in blessings and baptisms (Matthew 28: 19; 1 Corinthians 12: 4ff; 2 Corinthians 13: 13).

Evidence of God working as *Trinity* in the Christian Scriptures goes back to the beginning of creation in the Genesis account where God created the world by His *Word*. In doing so, Genesis 1: 2 says; the "Spirit of God" hovered over the waters." In this creation story of the book of Genesis, the "creative Word" and the "hovering Spirit" are like the "two hands of God" the Creator.[687] In this account, the Church sees the *Creator* as God the father, the creative *Word* as God the Son and the *hovering Spirit* as God the Holy Spirit – with each as distinct in persona but One God.

---

686 "From the beginning, the revealed truth of the Holy Trinity has always been at the very heart of the Church's living faith, principally, by means of baptism, It finds its expression in the rule of baptismal faith, formulated in the preaching, catechesis and prayers of the church" (see, CCC # 249).

687 Genesis 1: 2: "The Spirit of God hovered over the waters". We know that in the Hebrew, "Spirit" is also represented by "wind" or "breath". In this text, it appears "Word" and "Spirit" are the two hands of God the creator. This is professed in the creed that "the Holy Spirit has spoken through the prophets". Worthy of note is that God creates through His Word and the Spirit (see, commentary on the *Christian Community Bible*. 2014, p.67). Curious readers might like to investigate further by reading exegetical works to gain deeper meaning on Genesis 1: 2.

There are other Biblical evidence which further supports the Church's belief in the Holy Trinity. For instance, at the baptism of Jesus in the prologue of Mark 1: 9 – 11, the Holy Spirit came upon him in the form of a dove and a voice from heaven said; "this is my beloved Son in whom I am well pleased." The event of Jesus' baptism therefore demonstrated the manifestation of the Holy Trinity in quite unmissable terms. As we indicated earlier, the mystery of the *Holy Trinity* is the central mystery of the Christian life and faith. Christians are baptized "in the name of the *Father* and of the *Son* and of *the Holy Spirit*" not because this formula is fanciful but because it emanates from the express command of Jesus Christ to the Apostles at the Great Commissioning: "Go therefore and make disciples of all nations, baptising them in the name of the Father, and of the Son, and of the Holy Spirit" (Matthew 28: 19). Hence, Christian faith rests on the veracity of the revelation of God as Holy Trinity; that is the experience of God as the Father, as the Son, and as the Holy Spirit.

However, within the Islamic context, the Obligation to the *Tawhid* (there is no god but one God – Surah 5: 73) expresses the Islamic monotheistic conception of God. For Islam, God is the source of creation and transcends everything in the world. Everything is nothing but subject to Him as His creatures. Thus, the first part of the *Shahada* which contains the sentence of the *Tawhid* states that "there is no god but God" (*La ilaha illa Allah* – in the Arabic). For Murata and Chittick, this proclamation means that there is only a single true and worthy object of worship, God. All other objects of worship and service are false. Worship should exclusively be directed to Allah. To worship anything else is to fall into error and misguidance.[688] For Muslims therefore, to worship anything or conceive it as equal to Allah is to commit *Shirk*. Here, the Qur'an states that, "Do not associate others with Allah; to associate others with Allah is a mighty wrong" (Surah 31: 13).

---

688 Murata, Sachiko & Chittick, Williams, C. *The Vision of Islam.* 1994, p.49.

So, the avoidance of associating others with Allah is a central nerve in the message of the Qur'an. *Shirk* is therefore nothing but the reversal of the *Tawhid,* and any reversal of the *Tawhid* leads to the annihilation of Islam. In this way, the obligation to acknowledge the *Tawhid* is the reason why the theological formulation of God as *Holy Trinity* is perceived by Muslims as unacceptable. Thus, the Qur'an says: "Those who say that God is a third of three are truth-concealers" (Surah 5: 73). In relation to Jesus the Qur'an also warns, "the *Messiah*, Jesus, the 'Son of Mary' is only the "Messenger of God" ... So have faith in God and do not say, 'Three'. Refrain ... God is only One God" (Surah 4: 171). These texts reaffirm the fundamental Islamic faith principle which lies at the heart of the *Tawhid*. One would even find in the Qur'anic Jesus affirming this oneness of God when he said: "God is my Lord and your Lord, so serve Him – that is the straight path" (Surah 3: 51).

In consequence, when the Qur'an criticises followers of other religions as unbelievers, it very often does so on the basis of a perceived distortion to the *Tawhid*. Here, the Christian concept of Holy Trinity is but one of such examples. Since the *Trinity* and the *Tawhid* touch the core of the Christian and the Islamic belief respectively, Christian–Muslim dialogue as an exercise in learning offers the opportunity for the two faith traditions to understand why each tradition construes Jesus the way it does, and the significance of such constructions in the life of the believer. Reaching such mutual understanding as a result of dialogue as an exercise in learning, the interlocutors of the two faith traditions may find themselves in a better position to respect and appreciate the religious views of the other. The assent to genuine respect and appreciation for the religious beliefs of the other as a consequence of dialogue as an exercise in learning, points to its goal of transformation and enrichment.

6.4.2 Jesus as the "Son of God"

In our discourse in Chapter Four on the identity of Jesus as the "Son of God", we asserted that this designation is not to be taken literally as God physically generating a son, but metaphorically as establishing the intimate relationship between Jesus Christ and God the Father. Yet, the significant question often posed in respect of Jesus' designation as the "Son of God" is: did Jesus understand himself to be the "Son of God"? Was the "Son of God" title his self-reference? Was it closely connected to the Jewish and/or Hellenistic use of the title? Was it an alternative to the title *Messiah*? Is it not possible that in using the title the "Son of God", the early Christians or Jesus himself adopted an old Jewish or Hellenistic concept and gave it a new meaning? Was the title simply functional (that is, Jesus was the "Son of God" because he revealed God)[689] Following the analyses of some scholars,[690] it is good to assert that while the use of the "Son of God' title affirms the divinity of Jesus Christ and His oneness with the Father, it also points to His obedience to the will of the Father.[691] Let us attempt a very succinct response to the aforementioned questions on the Hellenistic and the Jewish derivative of the "Son of God" concept, and whether or not Jesus used the concept as his self-reference.

In respect of the presence of the title the "Son of God" in oriental and Hellenistic cultures, G.P. Wetter's studies on

---

689 Gerald O'Collins explores questions like: (1) How early was the "Son of God" title used by Jesus? (2) Was it introduced by the Hellenistic church in the 40ADs (like the church in Antioch)? Or does it go back to Palestine in the 30ADs? Or to Jesus himself? Identical to this sense of dating is also the question on the source of origin of the title and that which led the early Christians to call Jesus by this designation (see, Gerald O'Collins. *Christology.* 2009, p.120).

690 See, Oscar Cullmann. *The Christology of the New Testament.* 1963; Gerald O'Collins. *Christology: A Biblical, Historical and Systematic Study of Jesus.* 2009; Dunn, James, D.G. *New Testament Theology.* 2009.

691 Oscar Cullmann. *The Christology of the New Testament.* 1963, p.270.

comparative religions indicate the presence of this concept in these cultures.[692] Within these religious cultures, the title the "Son of God" was associated with their kings who were thought to be the "begotten sons of gods" like the Pharaohs of Egypt who were considered the "sons of the sun god Re".[693] Although these associations were not very prevalent with the rulers of the kingdoms of Persia and Babylon, emperors of the Roman empire were also called *divi filius*.[694] Furthermore, the title the "Son of God" was not only limited to the kings or to the rulers in Hellenistic culture, but it was also used to refer to people endowed with supernatural divine powers. It was common to find men with such rare miraculous powers referred to as "sons of God".[695]

In Cullmann's view, even though these references were prevalent in Hellenistic cultures, their polytheistic overtones made it impossible for their effective transfer into monotheistic contexts. For instance, in the case of the New Testament, its reference to Jesus expresses, "the intense consciousness of complete, unique unity of will with the One God in executing the divine plan of salvation."[696] The distinction lies in the fact that "God acts not only through him but with him".[697] In tracing

---

692 For references to G.P. Wetter's study on the "Son of God", see Oscar Cullmann. *The Christology of the New Testament*. 1963, p.271.

693 See, Oscar Cullmann. *The Christology of the New Testament*. 1963, p271; Gerald O'Collins. *Christology*. 2009, p.122-126.

694 Oscar Cullmann. *The Christology of the New Testament*. 1963, p.271

695 Cullmann cites Apollonius of Tyana who was described by Philostratus as the "Son of God" for his miraculous powers; and Alexander of Abonoteichus who was considered likewise. Besides, from Origen's work *Against Celsus* (7.9) indicates that there were people in Syria and Palestine who made claims such as: "I am God; "I am the Son of God"; "I am the Divine Spirit"; and "I wish to save you". (See, Oscar Cullmann. *The Christology of the New Testament*. 1963, p.272).

696 Oscar Cullmann. *The Christology of the New Testament*. 1963, p.272.

697 Oscar Cullmann. *The Christology of the New Testament*. 1963, p.282.

the earliest use of the title the "Son of God", Gerald O'Collins indicates that the oldest Christian document (1 Thessalonians 1: 10) already referred to Jesus as the "Son of God", and St Paul in his letters referred to Jesus seventeen (17) times as the "Son of God" (see, examples in 1 Corinthians 15: 28; 2 Corinthians 1: 19; Galatians 2: 20; Romans 1: 3 – 4, etc).[698] In this way, O'Collins concluded that not only does the data from Saint Paul and other early Christian writers rule out the possibility that the "Son of God" title had a later Hellenistic origin, but even the Semitic nature of some of the references to the title in the Gospels (see, Mark 5: 7 and Matthew 11: 27) rules out that possibility as well.[699]

In terms of the Jewish use of the concept the "Son of God", we indicated in Chapter Four that the Old Testament used the concept in three ways: (1) the people of Israel seen as the "Son of God"; (2) their Kings referred to as the "Son of God"; and (3) the *Messiah* and the Angels (persons with special divine commissioning). Examples of references to the "people of Israel" as the "Son of God" are seen in Exodus 4: 22 (Moses is commanded by God to tell Pharaoh: "Israel is my first born son"); Hosea 11: 1 (Yahweh says: "out of Egypt I called my first born son"); Isaiah 1: 2 (the people of Israel are called sons); Jeremiah 3: 22 (the people are called faithless sons). Cullmann indicates that in all these texts, the reference of the people of Israel as a "Son of God" is intended to communicate the idea that they are the chosen people of God, who in turn, owe God their obedience.[700] For O'Collins, "the divine choice and deliverance begot Israel (Deuteronomy 35: 19) as a people, and made Israel God's children" (Isaiah. 45: 11) ... Hosea's classical words about divine

698 Gerald O'Collins. *Christology: A Biblical, Historical and Systematic Study of Jesus.* 2009, p.122.

699 Gerald O'Collins. *Christology: A Biblical, Historical and Systematic Study of Jesus.* 2009, p.122.

700 Oscar Cullmann. *The Christology of the New Testament.* 1963, p.273.

sonship stated: "when Israel was a child, I loved him, and out of Egypt I called my son" (Hosea 11: 1).[701]

While this sense of collective sonship was dominant in pre-Christian Judaistic culture of the Old Testament, the title the "Son of God" was also applied to their Kings who were chosen by God to rule the people, and thus, were answerable to him. O'Collins indicates that while a righteous person could be called a "Son of God" in the Old Testament (see, Wisdom 2: 13; and 5: 5), royal persons like the kings of Israel were also referred to as God's sons. In the royal Psalms (Psalm 2: 7; 89: 3 − 4 and 18 − 37), the anointed king was also considered as the "Son of God" − "you are my son, today I have begotten you" (Psalm 2: 7).[702] For O'Collins, this sense of sonship was neither one of literal generation of offspring nor the sense of being divinised. It implies that the king was legitimated by God to faithfully perform a task.

In regard to the relationship between the *Messiah* and the "Son of God" title, O'Collins indicates that even though the Messianic expectations were linked to the Davidic king, and the Davidic king further connected to the "Son of God" title, this title had connections to the messianic expectations as represented in the Old Testament.[703] Cullmann further affirms the uncertainty surrounding the connection between the two title in the Old Testament. Cullmann suggest that as a royal attribute, it is possible that the "Son of God" title could occasionally be applied to the *Messiah* when one considers the close relations between the Jewish expectations of the *Messiah* and the idea of

---

701 Gerald O'Collins. *Christology: A Biblical, Historical and Systematic Study of Jesus.* 2009, p.122.

702 Gerald O'Collins. *Christology: A Biblical, Historical and Systematic Study of Jesus.* 2009, p.123.

703 For O'Collins, evidence of the connection between the *Messiah* and the "Son of God" title only started to appear at the time of Jesus (See, G. O'Collins. *Christology: A Biblical, Historical and Systematic Study of Jesus.* 2009, p.123).

the king. This is supported by the relationship between the royal Psalms (see, Psalm 2) as we saw earlier. In this way, Cullmann concludes that if the Jewish designation of the *Messiah* was possibly associated to the idea of the "Son of God", this could have happened only in connection with the same idea of the election which is of constitutive significance for the "Son of God" designation of the king".[704] Judaism and the Old Testament idea of the "Son of God" is only related to the notion of *election* to participate in the work of God and one's *obedience* to the God who elects. It has nothing to do with one's relationship with God by virtue of divine conception.[705]

In consequence, we could conclude that the designation of Jesus as the "Son of God" has no Hellenistic influence. Jesus was not a miracle worker through whom God acted. God acted not only through Jesus but with him. The distinction of the title from the Jewish conception of it in the Old Testament also lies in the fact that; unlike the eventual Jewish notion of the militarised and conquering the *Messiah*, Jesus' sonship (*ebed Yahweh*) is derived from his absolute obedience to the father even unto death. Nonetheless, some scholars indicate that the "Son of God" title is more ubiquitous in the Old Testament than it is in the synoptic Gospels.[706] It is also observed that Jesus rarely used this title in his self-designation. O'Collins indicates that hardly does one find in synoptic Gospels a text where Jesus comes out cleanly to say, "I am the Son of God". Yet, in the synoptic Gospels, Jesus speaks of "father", "my heavenly father", "our father", "your heavenly father" fifty-one (51) times.[707] If all these references imply some

---

704 Oscar Cullmann. *The Christology of the New Testament.* 1963, p.274.

705 Scholars like G. Dalman and G. Bousset flatly deny the connection between the two (see, Oscar Cullmann. *The Christology of the New Testament.* 1963, p.274, p.275).

706 See, Gerald O'Collins. *Christology: A Biblical, Historical and Systematic Study of Jesus.* 2009, p.128.

707 Gerald O'Collins. *Christology.* 2009, p.129.

kind of filiation, then what sort of "sonship" where they intended to communicate? Understanding the identity of the "Father" here is significant in helping us to ascertain whether or not Jesus' relationship with the father is qualitative or functional.

In the synoptic Gospels (Matthew 11: 25 – 30 or Luke 10: 21 – 22), Jesus identifies the "father" as "Lord of Heaven and Earth", and indicates the unique and exclusive knowledge the son (Jesus himself) possesses as a consequence of this father-son relationship: "All things have been delivered to me by my Father, and no one knows the Son except the Father, and no one knows the Father except the Son, and those to whom the Son chooses to reveal him."[708] This sense of exclusivity in knowledge and the deliverance of heaven and earth (all things) unto the Son by the "Lord of Heaven and Earth" demonstrates a unique kind of filiation that points to some degree of intimacy and equality. This sense of intimacy is affirmed by the significant way Jesus constantly refers to the father as "Abba" (see, Mark 14: 36; Matthew 6: 9; Luke 11: 2). As O'Collins indicates, "Abba was the characteristic and significantly distinctive feature of Jesus' prayer life".[709] This reference to God as "Abba" in a direct familial way was unique to Jesus, but less common in the Old Testaments Judaism.[710] In this way, O'Collins indicates that Jesus' example encouraged his followers to also pray to God in such direct familial way.

It is in this same sense that James Dunn indicates, "when Christianity came to grapple with defining Jesus' relationship with God, it was *son of the father* that emerged as the consensus way of doing so."[711] James Dunn asserts that the reasons for this Christological designation were, first of all, because Jesus saw the relationship between him and God as a "father-son" one. His prayer to God as "Abba Father" (Mark 14: 36) is evocative of the

---

708 Gerald O'Collins. *Christology.* 2009, p.127.

709 Gerald O'Collins. *Christology.* 2009, p.128

710 Gerald O'Collins. *Christology.* 2009, p.122-126.

711 James Dunn. *New Testament Theology.* 2009, p.58.

language of family intimacy. Further references to this "father-son relationship" are very dense in John 17: 1-24. Secondly, Dunn intimates that the designation the "Son of God" was used by the early Christians in their prayers and liturgy. Here, it became a source of inspiration to them in the sense that by their faith in Jesus, they believed that they too were sharing in the same sense of *sonship* that "Abba" expressed.[712] In following James Dunn's position, the conclusion one may reach is that the designation the "Son of God" was Jesus' way of expressing his relationship with God, as well as a unique way in which the early Christians interpreted their faith relationship with God (Romans 8: 17).

So, having significantly spoken of God as "my Father", O'Collins indicates that Jesus did not only speak like "the Son", but acted as "the Son" who knows and reveals the truth about God his father; one who is capable of changing the divine law, forgiving sins, serving as the channel through whom others could become the children of God, and one who acted in total obedience as the agent for God's final kingdom.[713] In this way, Jesus had to be the "Son of God" to be able to play this role which lies in the domain of the divine. So, the notion of divine sonship is not literal in the sense of God begetting a son. It communicates the intimate relationship between Jesus and God the Father in a metaphorical way. The Christian Church unequivocally declared its stand on this matter against the Arians in the Council of Nicaea (325 AD). In Nicaea, the Church categorically declaimed the non-orthodoxy of any theological constructions that suggest the physical *generation* of Jesus by the father.[714]

In a particularly Islamic context, the charge of Islam against Christianity on Jesus as the "Son of God" in the Qur'an is that: "The *Messiah*, Jesus, the 'Son of Mary', was only the "Messenger

---

712 James Dunn. *New Testament Theology*. 2009, p.58-59.

713 Gerald O'Collins. *Christology: A Biblical, Historical and Systematic Study of Jesus*. 2009, p.131.

714 J.N.D. Kelly. *Early Christian Doctrines*. 2007, p.232.

of Allah" ... God is only *one*; He is far above having a son" (Surah 4: 171). A clearer Qur'anic charge on this designation is also found in Surah 9: 30.[715] It is significant to note here that the *Tawhid* remains the bedrock against which the designation of Jesus as the "Son of God" is interpreted. As al-Tabari (923 AD) put it, "the naming of Jesus as God's son undermines the unity of God. By introducing concepts of fatherhood and sonship, Christians ... reduce God's freedom and power."[716] For al-Razi, the understanding of Jesus as the "Son of God" takes away, "some of the greatness from God because he would have to carry some of the seed of his father."[717] Hence, al-Razi suggests that it might be more appropriate to refer to Jesus as "the servant of God" instead of "God's son". The Prophet Muhammad also stated his disbelief in the divine sonship when he said in the Qur'an: "if the Lord of Mercy had a son, I will be the first to worship him, but blessed be the Lord ... He is far above their false descriptions" (Surah 43: 81 – 82).

From the above verses, one gets the strong impression that Muslims understand the Christian conception of the "divine sonship of Jesus" not in metaphoric terms, but in the sense of biological generation. In Surah 6: 101, the Qur'an further interrogates: "how should He (Allah) have a son, seeing that He has no female companion, and He created all things, and He has knowledge of everything?" It is therefore in no doubt that Islam perceives the Christian belief in the divine sonship of Jesus Christ to be based on biological generation. In attempting to negate the Christian

---

715 "The Jews say, 'Ezra is the son of Allah' and the Christians say, 'The *Messiah* is the son of Allah.' That is their statement from their mouths; they imitate the sayings of those who disbelieved [before them]. May Allah destroy them; they are deluded."

716 Al-Tabari quoted in Beaumont, Mark. *Christology in Dialogue with Islam*. 2005, p.8.

717 Al-Razi quoted in Beaumont, Mark. *Christology in Dialogue with Islam*. 2005, p.8.

conception of the divine sonship, the Qur'an not only rebuts this idea, but it also attempts to invalidate the whole idea of the divine son being equal to the father: *say, He is God, One God, the Everlasting Refuge. He did not give birth, nor was He given birth to. He has no equal.*[718] If Christians present texts in the Gospels which portray the Father–Son relationship between Jesus and God the Father, many Muslims are quick to dismiss these texts as borne from the falsifications or the alterations of the true Scriptures.[719] Although the controversies surrounding the scriptural authenticity of both the Qur'an and the Bible remain unresolved, dialogue as an exercise in learning does not seek a resolution of these controversies but learning from the other despite them. Yet, the exercise of learning and its transformative dimension is capable of eradicating prejudices that are borne out of the exclusive claims to religious truth.

Thus, even though Muslims interpret the Christian view of Jesus' identity as the "Son of God" to imply biological generation, dialogue as an exercise in learning offers Christians the opportunity to clarify their beliefs in the divine sonship of Jesus Christ to Muslims, and for Muslims to learn and be enriched by these clarifications. Through these forms of dialogue, the Muslim who learns from the metaphoricity of the Christian notion of the "divine sonship" may find himself or herself in a completely different place than those who have settled for its literal interpretations. Mahmoud Ayoub reached this form of understanding, and thus, challenged the Islamic interpretation of the Christian belief in the divine sonship of Jesus. Ayoub asserts that the Qur'an does not use the term *walad* (offspring)[720] to refer to Jesus but uses *it-*

---

718 Murata, Sachiko & Chittick, Williams, C. *The Vision of Islam.* 1994, p.171.

719 See, Louay Fatoohi. *The Mystery of the Historical Jesus.* 2007, p.38–39.

720 Irfan Omar. *A Muslim View of Christianity: Essays on Dialogue.* 2007, p.118.

takhadha (took unto himself).[721] This term (that is, *ittakhadha*) does not suggest the physical generation of Jesus but a relationship of adoption.[722] In this way, Ayoub concludes that, "the Qur'an nowhere accuses Christians of calling Jesus the *walad* of God."[723] If Muslims cling to this interpretation, it does not find support in the Qur'an. While Ayoub's contribution appears to resolve the matter by repositioning the Islamic stand on the Christian understanding of Jesus as the "Son of God", one wonders whether the majority of Muslims share this understanding, and whether it truly captures the Qur'anic presentation of Jesus' divine sonship today (Surah 4: 171 and Surah 19: 35). This explains why dialogue as an exercise in learning offers Christians the opportunity to clarify their claims on Jesus as the "Son of God".

In conclusion, Christian faith and theology understands the reality of Jesus' divine sonship as an expression of the intimate relationship between him and God. This relationship is fully expressed in the *Trinity,* in what Christian theology calls the *trinitarian koinonia* (the communion of the trinity). So, a dialogue that seeks mutual understanding will invite Christians to respect the Islamic obligation to the *Tawhid* which forbids divine sonship interpretations. This form of dialogue also offers Muslims the opportunity to understand what Christians mean when the talk about the divine sonship of Jesus and its implications for Christian faith and life. In the final analysis, when this form of dialogue leads to mutual respect and appreciation of the religious beliefs of the other, then dialogue is considered successful on the basis of its interest; that is, learning from and about the other and being enriched as a consequence of this learning.

---

721 Irfan Omar. *A Muslim View of Christianity.* 2007, p.125.

722 Irfan Omar. *A Muslim View of Christianity.* 2007, p.118.

723 Irfan Omar. *A Muslim View of Christianity.* 2007, p.118.

6.4.3 The Suffering, Death, and Resurrection of Jesus

The event of Jesus' suffering, death and Resurrection, also referred to as the *Paschal Mystery*, is central to Christian faith and theology. Its centrality hinges on both the *soteriological* and the *eschatological* implications it has for Christian faith and hope. As Alister McGrath indicated, "at the *soteriological* level, Christ's death on the cross is interpreted as God's victory over death and the coalition of other allied forces and powers. At the *eschatological* level, the paschal mystery gives both foundation and substance to the Christian hope of eternal life."[724] In a sense, Jesus' death and resurrection is for Christians a source of God's saving grace and the means to eternal life with God. That is, within the context of original sin, Jesus' death on the cross is viewed as that perfect *sacrifice* that restores humanity back to God (Romans 3: 25).[725] By His death and His resurrection Jesus gained *victory* over sin, eternal death and Satan.[726] Thus, McGrath attests that the effect of the victory of the cross is that it provides the basis by which God is enabled to *forgive* sins.[727] It is also a *moral example* for Christians in the way Jesus demonstrates a selfless love of God for humanity. As a result, the cross evokes a Christian response of love, guided by this act of selflessness.[728] In this way, McGrath indicates that for Christian faith and theology, salvation is, "manifested in and through and constituted on the basis of the life, death and resurrection of Jesus Christ."[729]

In terms of the veracity of the event of the death and resurrection of Jesus Christ, all the Synoptic Gospels give detailed accounts of the event (see Mark 14: 32 – 16: 12, Mathew 26: 47 – 28:

---

724 Alister McGrath. *Christian Theology: An Introduction.* 1997, p.384.

725 Alister McGrath. *Christian Theology.* 1997, p.391-394.

726 Alister McGrath. *Christian Theology.* 1997, p.395-399.

727 Alister McGrath. *Christian Theology.* 1997, p.399-406.

728 Alister McGrath. *Christian Theology.* 1997, p.407-412.

729 Alister McGrath. *Christian Theology.* 1997, p.324.

16 and Luke 22: 47 – 24: 50). The entire New Testament consistently attests to the reality of the death and the resurrection of Jesus Christ, especially in the Pauline letters. For instance, Paul lays claim to this significant event when he states in his four-part formula about Jesus Christ's *death, burial, resurrection* and *appearances*. Paul writes: "In the first place, I have passed to you what I, myself, received: that Christ died for our sins as scripture says; that he was buried; that he was raised on the third day in accordance to the scriptures; that he appeared to Cephas and then to the twelve" (1 Corinthians 15: 3 – 5).[730] Gerald O'Collins interrogates this Pauline formula when he said, "what does Paul mean in this formula? Does he intend to provide facts about the event of the resurrection or is he merely stating it to encourage a fresh understanding and a new way of perceiving it?[731] In other words, does the Christian claim the event of the resurrection of Jesus Christ to be a reality? If yes, what is its foundation and its purpose?"

As indicated earlier, scriptural attestations to the event of the death and the resurrection of Jesus Christ are not hard to find. In the synoptic accounts of the event (see, Mark 14: 32; Mark 16: 12; Mathew 26: 47; Matthew 28: 16; Luke 22: 47; Luke 24: 50; and John 18: 1; John 21: 23). Even though each of the Gospel writers reported the event with slight nuance differences, their unanimity in attesting to the reality of the event is unhindered. This is because their singular purpose for recounting what took place, as Saint John the Evangelist indicated, was to testify to the truth of these events (John 21: 24) surrounding Jesus of Nazareth – "Jesus performed many other signs in the presence of his disciples, which are not recorded in this book. But these are written that you may believe that Jesus is the *Messiah*, the "Son of God", and that by believing you may have life in his name" (John 20: 30 – 31).

---

730 Text taken from "The Christian Community Bible" (62nd Edition).

731 Gerald O'Collins. *Christology: A Biblical, Historical and Systematic Study of Jesus.* 2009, p.83.

In other words, the interest of the evangelists was not providing a document that answers questions of historical accuracy, theological validity and hermeneutic preciseness of the events. Their main goal was to enable their readers to believe that Jesus is the *Messiah*, the "Son of God", and by so doing, find life through him. In this way, O'Collins asserts that Paul's four-part kerygmatic formula in 1 Corinthians 15: 3 – 5 (that is, Jesus *died*, he was *buried*, he *rose* and he *appeared*) was intended to convey factual information about what happened to Jesus on the one hand, and on the other, to express its significance for the believer.

In expressing the spiritual transformation that is enacted by the event of the death and the resurrection of Christ, Paul informs the early Christians that, "their baptism meant 'dying' and 'being buried' with Christ, so as to walk with him in newness of life" (Romans 6: 3 – 4).[732] Death and burial now take on new meanings in that the waters of baptism now re-enact dying and burying, which in a sense, presupposes the facticity of the actual death and burial. For Paul therefore, the vast testimonies to the resurrection of Christ presupposes the facticity of death and burial, and the new life the believers attain as a consequence of their life in Christ. As he indicates; "Well then, if Christ is preached as risen from the dead, how can some of you say that there is no resurrection of the dead? If there is no resurrection from the dead, then Christ has not been raised. And if Christ has not been raised, our preaching is empty and so is your faith … your faith is futile, and you are still in your sins … But Christ has indeed been raised from the dead, the first fruits of those who have fallen asleep" (1 Corinthians 15: 12 – 20). Thus, in following the Pauline four-part kerygmatic formula, O'Collins indicates that while Jesus Christ is certainly the subject of the four-part formula, one gets to know that, "Christ died because he was buried. The experience of burial is a certain pointer to death, and so,

---

732 Gerald O'Collins. *Christology: A Biblical, Historical and Systematic Study of Jesus.* 2009, p.84.

we know that Christ has been raised because he appeared bodily alive (in glory) to a number of individuals and groups; dead persons do not appear like that."[733] And certainly, "dead men don't talk", to quote an old saying.

While the above points to the early Christians' attestations to the reality of the resurrection, how did they come to the certainty of it? As O'Collins put it, "what grounds did they have for making their claims about the transformed personal life and activity of Jesus after the death?"[734] While the disciples were by this time fascinated by the extraordinary nature of the life and the ministry of Jesus Christ, most of these experiences eventually led to their faith-experience of Jesus as "the Christ, the Son of the living God" (Mark 8: 27; Matthew 16: 16). From this moment, other encounters and experiences will be measured against the backdrop of the revelation of Jesus Christ as the "Son of God". As O'Collins intimated, every new experience of the disciples will then be received and interpreted in the light of the factors already effective in the lives of the disciples. Thus, the grounds for the disciples' claim to the death and the resurrection of Jesus Christ are found in their experiences of the appearances of the risen Christ (see, Matthew 28: 1 – 19; Mark 16: 13 – 114; Luke 24: 36 – 40; John 21: 1 – 18), the discovery of the empty tomb (see, Mark 16: 1 – 8; Matthew 28: 1 – 8; Luke 24: 1 – 8; John 20: 1 – 18), the gift of the Holy Spirit (Acts 2: 1 – 13), and the success of their ministry (Acts 2: 14 – 40).[735] In this way, the claim on the resurrection of Jesus Christ is founded on the above indubitable accounts.

However, from an Islamic point of view, Jesus the *Messiah,* the "Son of Mary" never died. The Islamic belief on the fate of

733 Gerald O'Collins. *Christology.* 2009, p.85.

734 Gerald O'Collins. *Christology.* 2009, p.90.

735 For more information about the explications of the above events (the appearances, the empty tomb, the gift of the Spirit and the success of the disciples' ministry, see Gerald O'Collins. *Christology: A Biblical, Historical and Systematic Study of Jesus.* 2009, p.90-93).

Jesus reflects the Qur'anic verse on the Jewish claim to have killed Jesus: "We (the Jews) have killed the *Messiah*, Jesus, the 'Son of Mary', the "Messenger of God". They did not kill him nor crucified him, though it was made to appear like that to them … No! God raised him to Himself" (Surah 4: 157). The Qur'an further indicates God's personal communication to Jesus: "God said, Jesus, I will take you back and raise you up to me. I will purify you of the unbelievers" (Surah 3: 55). Another Qur'anic text of remarkable importance here is where Jesus himself said; "Peace was on me the day I was born, and peace will be on me the day I die and the day I am raised to life again" (Surah 19: 33). The Qur'anic Jesus also said of himself: "I was a witness to them as long as I was with them. But ever since you took my soul, you were their overseer" (Surah 5: 117). From these texts, it is evident that there are different claims as to whether Jesus actually died or not. Thus, the controversies surrounding the Qur'anic texts on the death and the resurrection of Jesus have gingered the interests of both Islamic scholars and commentators to investigate what actually happened to Jesus according to the Qur'anic narratives.[736]

While some Christian apologists attempt to justify the claim that the Qur'an does not actually reject the crucifixion of Jesus Christ, Leirvik provides *exegetical*, *theological* and *political* reasons for the standard Muslim rejection of the crucifixion of Jesus on the *cross*.[737] Exegetically, Leirvik intimates that, "what the Qur'an actually says about the crucifixion remains unresolved".[738] Muslim interpreters are said to hold different interpretations on the matter. Theologically, Leirvik asserts that the

---

736 See, Omar Irfan A. *A Muslim View of Christianity: Essays on Dialogue.* 2007, p.156-179; Leirvik, Oddbjørn. *Images of Jesus in Islam.* 2010, p.238-240; Mark Beaumont. *Christology in Dialogue with Islam.* 2005, p.9-10; Cragg, Kenneth. *Jesus and The Muslim.* 1999, p.166-188.

737 Oddbjørn Leirvik. *Images of Jesus in Islam.* 2010, p.239.

738 Oddbjørn Leirvik. *Images of Jesus in Islam.* 2010, p.239.

question of the crucifixion seems to be, "inseparable from what Muslims have perceived as the non-acceptable implications of the cross as a religious symbol, like the idea of vicarious suffering and redemption."[739] And politically, Leirvik intimates that the cross was the symbol of the rising Byzantine Empire in its formative period with the *cross* later becoming the symbol of the invading crusaders.[740] Although the above views may represent reasons for the standard Muslim rejections of the crucifixion, how did classical Islamic commentators interpret some of the text listed above in respect to the many claims about the death and the resurrection of Jesus?

Let us consider the commentaries of some classical Islamic scholars like al-Tabari, al-Razi, al-Zamakhshari and al-Baydawi on the final end of Jesus. The views of these scholars revolve around the *substitution theory* or the *swoon theory*. As we intimated in Chapter Five, when al-Tabari undertakes a project on the interpretations of Qur'anic verses which are open to multiple interpretations, his frequent practice is, "to list in order, each of the options which are presented in the traditions of which he is aware of. Then, having listed these legitimate options, he then states which of them is most likely or have the greater weight of evidence in its favour."[741] In his analysis of the meaning of *mutawaffi* (meaning "taken away") in Surah 3: 55, al-Tabari says that Islamic exegetes have differed on the meaning of *tawaffa* ("death"). While some scholars consider that *tawaffa* means *"sleep"* (i.e. I am causing you to sleep and raising you to myself in your sleep"), others consider *tawaffa* to mean *"seizing"* (i.e. "I am seizing you to myself and raising you to heaven"). Yet, others

---

739 Oddbjørn Leirvik. *Images of Jesus in Islam.* 2010, p.239.

740 Oddbjørn Leirvik. *Images of Jesus in Islam.* 2010, p.139.

741 Joseph Cumming. "Did Jesus die on the Cross? The History of Reflection on Jesus' Death in Sunni Tafsir Literature" (unpublished). 2001, p.7 http://www.learningace.com/doc/997971/e22490e3729bc1bdc-ca5495a3f68ca09/didjesusdieenglish (09/10/14).

still think that *tawaffa* really means *"real death"* (i.e. "I am causing you to really die").[742]

Having considered these varied meanings of *tawaffa*, Al-Tabari
indicates that since some commentators think that *"death"* here
has no chronological order, *tawaffa* could mean, "I am raising you
to myself and cleansing you of the unbelievers and I will cause
you to die after I send you back to earth at the end of time."[743]
In this way, al-Tabari concluded that the theory that gains legitimate support in Islamic exegesis about whether or not Jesus died
is the *seizing* theory that is: "I am seizing you from the earth alive
to be close to me and taking you to be with me without death
and raising you from the unbelievers."[744] With his interpretation
of Surah 4: 157, al-Tabari said that it was not Jesus who died on
the cross, but God transformed someone to look like him and it
was this person who died on the cross.[745]

In considering whether or not Jesus really died on the cross,
al-Razi focused attention on Surah 4: 157 where the Jews seem
to claim that they killed the *Messiah*. In its refutation of the death
of Jesus, the *Messiah* on the cross, the Qur'an says – "they did not
kill him, nor did they crucify him, though it was made to appear like that to them ..." From this text, al-Razi supported the
substitution theory, listing five different possibilities by which the
substitution could have occurred: (1) it is possible that the Jews
crucified someone like Jesus and lied about it; (2) it is possible

742 Joseph Cumming. "Did Jesus die on the Cross? The History of Reflec-
     tion on Jesus' Death in Sunni Tafsir Literature" (unpublished). 2001,
     p.7 http://www.learningace.com/doc/997971/e22490e3729bc1bdc-
     ca5495a3f68ca09/didjesusdieenglish (09/10/14).

743 See Abu Ja'far Muhammad ibn Jarir al-Tabari in Cumming, Joseph.
     "Did Jesus die on the Cross? 2001, p.8.

744 Abu Ja'far Muhammad ibn Jarir al-Tabari in Cumming, Joseph. "Did
     Jesus die on the Cross? 2001, p.7-8.

745 Irfan Omar. *A Muslim View of Christianity: Essays on Dialogue.* 2007,
     p.160 & Cumming, Joseph. "Did Jesus die on the Cross? The History
     of Reflection on Jesus' Death in Sunni Tafsir Literature." 2001, p.7-10.

that Judas sent Titanus to kill Jesus and Titanus was arrested and crucified instead; (3) or maybe a man who was guarding Jesus was transformed to look like him and it was him they killed; (4) or Jesus asked one of his disciples to volunteer and one of them did; (5) or a hypocritical disciple who sought to betray Jesus was made to look like him and killed.[746] Having considered these possibilities in the light of the exegetical considerations of "I am causing you to die" (*mutawaffika*) in Surah 3: 55,[747] al-Razi concluded that the text of Surah 4: 157 implies that some kind of substitution must have taken place.[748] Hence, Jesus did not die. Allah took him to himself.

Al-Baydawi also provides his interpretations on the death of Jesus. In Joseph Cumming's view, the commentaries of al-Baydawi "are among the most popular and well trusted in the world today."[749] Yet, like al-Tabari and al-Razi, al-Baydawi also list various legitimate interpretations of a given verse, without indicating their origins or his particular preferences. In his commentary on Surah 3: 55, al-Baydawi provides five interpretations to the clause "I am causing you to die" (*mutawaffika*): (1) bringing an end to your lifespan; (2) seizing you from the earth; (3) causing you to sleep; (4) causing you to die to earthly desires; and (5) causing you to actually die.[750] In his commentary on Surah 4: 157, al-Baydawi provides two substitution theories to the text: (1) Jesus asked a volunteer to take his place when he knew that the Jews were coming to kill him in revenge for God turning a band of Jewish revilers into apes and pigs; and (2) a Jew named Titanus was the victim.[751] Although al-Baydawi seems to have

746 Joseph Cumming. "Did Jesus die on the Cross? The History of Reflection on Jesus' Death in Sunni Tafsir Literature." 2001, p.17.

747 Joseph Cumming. "Did Jesus die on the Cross?" 2001, p.11-12.

748 Joseph Cumming. "Did Jesus die on the Cross?" 2001, p.14.

749 Joseph Cumming. "Did Jesus die on the Cross?" 2001, p.21.

750 Joseph Cumming. "Did Jesus die on the Cross?" 2001, p.21-22.

751 Joseph Cumming. "Did Jesus die on the Cross?" 2001, p.22.

problems with the substitution theory[752] he nonetheless believes like most Islamic scholars do, that God could not possibly have allowed his prophet to die such a shameful death. Hence, God took him to himself.

From the views of the three commentators above, one would realise there are different Islamic scholarly interpretations of the Qur'an regarding whether or not Jesus died on the cross. Yet, standard Muslim belief has it that Jesus, the *Messiah* did not die on the cross. God took him to himself. While many of the scholars do agree that there were attempts to crucify Jesus, these attempts were completely smothered by the all-knowing and all-powerful Allah. Merad explains that the reason for this *turn* is because; "in the Qur'an, everything is aimed at convincing the believer that he will experience victory over the forces of evil." Islam therefore refuses to accept the tragic image of the passion, because "the passion implies in its eyes that God had failed".[753] In his study on "The Cross and Islam", Edwin Calverley also intimates that for Muslims, "the prevention of the death of Jesus was another marked proof of Allah's care for His prophets, His apostle, His word and His Spirit."[754]

Consequently, we could conclude that all the three commentators (al-Tabari, al-Razi and al-Baydawi) converge on the claim that Jesus did not die and was certainly not crucified. God raised him to himself. In this way, if there was no death of Jesus, then

---

752 Al-Baydawi finds two problems with the substitution theory: the theological and the grammatical. On the theological plain, al-Baydawi finds it difficult to understand how one may predicate *deceit* as an attribute of God. From the grammatical point of view, he thinks that Islamic commentators have confused the subject of the passive verb *shubbiha*. (See, Cumming, Joseph. "Did Jesus die on the Cross?" 2001, p.23).

753 See, Merad M.A. "Christ According to the Qur'an". 1980, p.96; as cited in Leirvik, Oddbjørn. *Images of Jesus in Islam*. 2010, p.4.

754 Edwin Calverley. "The Cross and Islam," in *the Muslim World Vol. XXVII No. 2*. 1937, p.108.

there was no resurrection either. It must be reiterated here again that while Christians believe in Jesus' death and resurrection that it is situated within the Christian understanding of redemption – with its soteriological and eschatological significance (that is, the salvation of fallen humanity from the depravity of *original sin* and the hope of eternal life with God). Islam has no concept of *original sin* because Allah forgave Adam and Eve after the *fall*. So, even if Jesus died and rose from the dead, this act bears no soteriological significance for Islam. In this way, one can see that the idea of the death and the resurrection of Jesus Christ sets a separation between the Christian view and the Muslim perspective. As Mona Siddiqui pointed out, it is perhaps on this theology of redemption that Islam parts company with Christianity in that, "it does not have those defining moments of alienation from God as in the *fall* and subsequent reconciliation with God, redemption through the death and the resurrection of Christ."[755]

Yet, within the distinctive differences that set apart the Christian and the Muslim perspectives on the *death and the resurrection of Jesus,* dialogue as an exercise in learning still offers greater prospects for the enrichment of the interlocutors in dialogue. This sense of enrichment lies in the fact that although Christians believe that Jesus died and rose from the dead, and Muslims hold that Jesus did not die at all; what remains significant between the two faith traditions is that: whether or not the crucifixion took place, they both acknowledge that Jesus ascended to heaven by virtue of God's divine intervention. For Islam, this intervention raised Jesus to heaven without dying on the cross. For Christianity, the same divine intervention raised him to life after his death, and the same divine intervention was instrumental at his ascension.[756] In other words, both religious communities agree that there was God's divine power working with, and in the life of Jesus which prevented him from experiencing the *shamefulness*

---

755 Mona Siddiqui. *Christians, Muslims & Jesus*. 2013, p.218.
756 Oddjøørn Leirvik. *Images of Jesus Christ in Islam*. 2010, p.165.

of death. For Islam, death did not occur as a consequence of this, and for Christianity he died but rose from the dead as a consequence of this divine power. Thus, if God's divine power enabled Jesus to accomplish the divine will in this remarkable way, how can Jesus' life and teachings provide learning examples for the living relationships between Muslims and Christians? While this question will be taken up in Chapter Seven, let us turn to the Christological issues that serve as a *bridge* to Christian–Muslim dialogue on Christology.

6.5 Jesus as a "Bridge" to Christian-Muslim Dialogue

The concept *bridge* connotes the sense of a structure built for the purpose of providing passage over physical obstacles such as water, roads, valleys, rifts or a fracture in relationships of some sort and so on. Thus, it serves the purpose of linking two points that were initially separated or alienated by a perceived abyss, a ditch or a perception. Within the context of Christian–Muslim dialogue on Christology, *bridge* is used here heuristically to capture some of the narrative accounts about Jesus, the *Messiah* in the Qur'an and in the New Testament which appears to bear some similarities. It is widely acknowledged that among all the world religions, Christianity and Islam are the only two religions which have narratives about the life and the mission of Jesus the *Messiah*, the "Son of Mary". Accounts such as the *virginal conception,* the *miracles of Jesus, the ascension and the Second Coming* are a few examples. The symmetrical relationships between texts in the Qur'an and in the New Testament regarding the aforementioned events in the life of Jesus demonstrates that Christians and Muslims have so much to share about Jesus. It is these accounts which we consider as building *bridges* in Christian–Muslim conversations. Let us see how some of these Christological themes serve as fruitful contexts for Christian–Muslim conversations within the context of learning from and about the other.

6.5.1 The Virginal Conception and Birth

The *Virginal Conception* and the *Virginal Birth* of Jesus are essentially part of the Christian story about the life of Jesus. Although many people seem to use one to refer to the other, there are nonetheless nuance differences between them. While the *virginal conception* means that Mary conceived Jesus without the aid of a human father (*virginitas in partu*); the *Virginal Birth* means that Mary remained a *virgin* after the birth of Jesus (*virginitas post-partum* meaning perpetual virginity). In other words, Jesus' birth did not cause a rupture of the hymen or bodily lesions.[757] Whereas these two concepts define the *pre* and *post* parturient state of Mary's virginity within a particularly orthodox Christian understanding, they are both indicative of two separate realities: that is, while the *virginal conception* conveys the Christian belief that the Blessed Virgin Mary conceived Jesus Christ through the power of the Holy Spirit (the incarnation) without the involvement of a human father, the *virginal birth* asserts that Mary gave birth to Jesus without the loss of her virginity.[758] For easy comprehension of this subject matter, we shall limit ourselves to the use of the term *virginal conception* which implies *virginitas in partu* without the *virginitas post-partum* implications of it. In other words, by use of the *virginal conception,* we mean that Mary conceived Jesus Christ while still a virgin. Yet, what is the basis for this Christian belief? What religious significance does the virginal conception bring to Christian faith and theology?

---

757 Joseph Fitzmyer. "The Virginal Conception of Jesus Christ in the New Testament." 1973, p.541–542.

758 For O'Collins, the *Virginal Conception* is the Christian belief that "Christ's incarnation did not follow the ordinary, inner worldly laws of procreation but was the fruit of a special intervention by the Holy Spirit". In this way, the virginal conception focuses on the way Christ was conceived while the virginal birth focuses on how he was born (Gerald O'Collins. *Christology: A Biblical, Historical and Systematic Study of Jesus.* 2009, p.286).

Belief in the *virginal conception* finds expression in the Scriptures (the Christian Bible) — first foretold in the Old Testament by the Prophet Isaiah (Isaiah 7: 14 — 16) and finds its fulfilment in the New Testament in the synoptic Gospels' nativity narratives (see, Matthew 1: 18 — 25 and Luke 1: 26 — 38). First among his ten fulfilment formulas, Matthew indicates; "All this (the virginal conception) happened in order to fulfil what the Lord had said through His prophets; 'Look, the Virgin will conceive and bear a son, and he will be called *Emmanuel,* which means; God-is-with-us'" (Matthew 1: 22 — 23). Many scholars have consistently indicated that the Old Testament text Matthew quoted in his Gospel was Isaiah 7: 14.[759] Whiles the Gospels of Matthew and Luke present in detail the events leading to Jesus' birth, the Gospels of Mark and John together with the letters of Saint Paul are silent on the matter. Coupled with this *silence* are also some differences in the way that Matthew and Luke present their accounts. For instance, while Matthew's account includes the betrothal, Luke's account does not make reference to it (see Matthew 1: 18 — 25 and Luke 1: 26 — 35).

Furthermore, while the virginal conception is communicated to Saint Joseph (the foster father of Jesus) in Matthew's account (Matthew 1: 21 — 23), in Luke's account it is communicated to Mary herself (Luke 1: 31). So, O'Collins indicates that it is difficult to harmonise the two different standpoints taken by Matthew and Luke. This is because the traditions on which they draw, and the ways in which they develop them, the Old Testament language and motifs which they adapt differ markedly".[760] As a consequence, some scholars tend to question the historical legitimacy or veracity of their accounts of the virginal

---

759 See, Gerald O'Collins. *Christology: A Biblical, Historical and Systematic Study of Jesus.* 2009, p.290.

760 Gerald O'Collins. *Christology: A Biblical, Historical and Systematic Study of Jesus.* 2009, p.291.

conception.[761] However, for Raymond Brown, the two evangelists were presenting a historical account of how once upon a time,
the Virgin Mary conceived Jesus Christ by the special intervention of the Holy Spirit, and without sexual intercourse.[762] In this
way, what is shared in Matthew and Luke's account is the common acceptance and affirmation that the "virginal conception"
was the work of God through the power of the Holy Spirit, exclusive of any form of human intercourse or marital conjugation.

It is the above understanding which received universal recognition, and acceptance in the Christian Church by the turn
of the second century, and was incorporated into the Apostles'
Creed, and later in the Nicene Creed. In the Roman Catholicism
of the West and in the Eastern Orthodox Church and protestant circles, the "Virginal Conception" was never strongly disputed, although some protestant thinkers see it as not relevant
for Christian faith.[763] The claim on the universal acceptability of
the *virginal conception* of Jesus Christ does not however side-line
or overlook the fact that there were already *Psilanthropists*[764] at

---

761 See, Fitzmyer, Joseph, A. "The Virginal Conception of Jesus Christ
in the New Testament." 1973, p.541 & Fatoohi, Louay. *The Mystery
of the Historical Jesus.* 2007, p.99-112. Fatoohi particularly provides
scientific, historical, rational and Scriptural reasons for which the
virginal conception is objected to today.

762 Raymond Brown. *The Birth of the Messiah.* 1993; as intimated in Gerald O'Collins. *Christology: A Biblical, Historical and Systematic Study of
Jesus.* 2009, p.291-292.

763 According to Joseph Fitzmyer, "The notion of the virginal parturi-
tion has no basis in Scripture and comes from post-New Testament
and patristic writings". (See, Fitzmyer, Joseph, A. "The Virginal
Conception of Jesus Christ in the New Testament." 1973, p.541 &
Filson, F.S. *A New Testament History.* 1965, p.86).

764 "Psilanthropism" comes from two Greek words: "*psilós* meaning
"plain, mere or bare" and "*ánthrōpos*" meaning "man, human being". Hence, "Psilanthropism" is an approach to Christology which
rejects the divinity of Jesus Christ and presents him as a mere human
being, the literal son of human parents (Mary and Joseph). This heresy was rejected in the Council of Nicaea in the fourth century.

the time, whose views were a challenge to the virginal birth of Jesus in the second century, and such views still linger on even in our time. For example, Celsus the Greek philosopher contested the virginal birth in the second century, as did Samuel Taylor Coleridge in the eighteenth century.[765] In other words, the belief in the virginal conception still faces what Gerald O'Collins refers to as philosophical, historical, hermeneutic and theological difficulties.[766] We revisit a few of these schools below.

From a philosophical and scientific point of view, proponents of this position hold that the virginal conception contravenes the laws of nature. People like Richard Dawkins reject this belief on the basis that it cannot be biologically proven.[767] In other words, even if Mary conceived Jesus through parthenogenesis, or the reproduction from the ovum without fertilization by the sperm, her offspring would have been a female baby, not male. This is because, "left to their resources, women do not have the Y chromosome necessary to produce a male child".[768] Yet, we know that God is not defined by the laws of nature. God surpasses the law because he is their source of origin. So, for good reasons best known to him, God can override natural law in order to bring about the fulfilment of his plans and his purposes. There is no self-contradiction here because God is not equal to nature but transcends nature; and there is no violation here, because God's desire to advance and transform the laws of nature for the redemption of nature cannot be undercut by nature itself.

There is also the hermeneutical school which indicates that the Christian view of the virginal conception is a misinterpretation

765 See McClintock, John. & Strong, James. *Cyclopedia of Biblical, Theological and Ecclesiastical Literature.* Vol. 2. 1994, p.404.

766 See, Gerald O'Collins. *Christology: A Biblical, Historical and Systematic Study of Jesus.* 2009, p.287-291.

767 Dawkins, Richard. *The God Delusion.* 2006, p.93-94.

768 Gerald O'Collins. *Christology: A Biblical, Historical and Systematic Study of Jesus.* 2009, p.287-288.

of the intentions behind Matthew and Luke's infancy narratives. For instance, Wolfhart Pannenberg asserts that belief in the virginal conception of Jesus contradicts belief in the incarnation of the pre-existent logos found in John's Gospel. For him, it is impossible to say in the same breath that Jesus is the pre-existent "Son of God" and at the same time entertain the thoughts that he was conceived by the Blessed Virgin Mary. Virginal conception and pre-existence cannot be connected without contradiction. But as O'Collins interrogated, "when a pre-existent, divine person acquires a human nature, why could this not happen through the virginal conception?"[769] The incarnation occurred as a consequence of the pre-existent "Son of God" taking flesh in the womb of the Blessed Virgin Mary through the special intervention of the Holy Spirit. For "nothing is impossible to God," said the Angel to Mary (Luke 1: 37).

In objecting to the reality of the virginal conception, Edward Schillebeeck also indicated that the accounts of Luke and Matthew on the virginal conception only offer truths about revelation. They were not intended to impart empirical truths or secret information about family history. That is, the different accounts of Matthew and Luke offer opportunities for theological reflections about the coming to be of Jesus. They do not offer empirically apprehensible truth.[770] Yet, as a counter to Schillebeeck, we know that in Christian faith and theology, theological reflections are very often based on man's experience of God through the truths of revelation. And revelation is a source of informative data about the revealed. So, Schillebeeck's dissociation of the link between theological reflections and revealed truths about God is foreign to the task of theology. To follow Schillebeeck's opinion, is to limit Christian faith and theology to a speculative endeavour.

---

769 Gerald O'Collins. *Christology: A Biblical, Historical and Systematic Study of Jesus.* 2009, p.287-287.

770 See, Gerald O'Collins. *Christology: A Biblical, Historical and Systematic Study of Jesus.* 2009, p.287-289.

Consequently, irrespective of the position people take regarding the *virginal conception,* the Church continues to unequivocally define its stand on the matter.[771] For Michael Schmaus, the Church believes that Mary conceived Jesus of the Holy Spirit without a human principle of generation. The virginal conception remains the constant teaching of the church from the beginning, "that she gave birth to Jesus without violation of her integrity and that she remained ever virgin."[772] This is indeed part of the Church's profession of faith as it is clearly stated in the Catechism of the Catholic Church.[773] This faith is not just an abstract theological construction without its basis in Scripture, since the Gospels of Luke and Mathew do testify to it. However, what is the significance of the virginal conception to Christian faith and theology?

From a particularly Lukan perspective, O'Collins offers some points on the significance of the virginal conception of Jesus Christ. First of all, Luke situates Mary's virginal conception within the extraordinary conceptions of other women of the Old Testament to demonstrate the special place Jesus' conception occupies. In following the genealogy of Jesus, Sarah conceives Isaac in extraordinary circumstance (Genesis 21: 1 – 7); Rebecca conceives Jacob in similar circumstances (Genesis 25: 21 – 26); although barren, Hannah conceives Samuel (1 Samuel 1: 1 – 28). For Luke, these women were old and barren but gave birth to children who played remarkable roles in the history of salvation. The birth of John the Baptist by Elizabeth then becomes the climax of these

---

771 Vatican II on *Lumen Gentium,* No. 52-67.

772 Karl Rahner (Editor). *Encyclopedia of Theology.* 1999, p.898.

773 Catechism of Catholic Church (CCC) # 490: "To become the mother of the Saviour, Mary was enriched by God with gifts appropriate to such a role". This was attested to by the Angel Gabriel when He saluted her saying: "Hail Mary, full of grace" (Luke 1: 28). In this way, "from the first formulation of faith, the Church has confessed that Jesus was conceived by the power of the Holy Spirit in the womb of the Virgin Mary" (CCC # 496).

extraordinary births. So, the virginal conception then becomes a quantum leap for Luke.[774] If God will do such extraordinary deeds in the lives of those women, how much will he not do for the birth of his only son. This is where the Magnificat (Luke 1: 46 – 55) finds its place: "… All generations will call me blessed. The Almighty has done great things for me, Holy is his name". So, the virginal conception of Jesus is as O'Collins put it, "a unique action of God that may never be repeated."[775]

Secondly, the virginal conception points to the *double generation* of the "Son of God" (that is, the divinity and the humanity of Jesus Christ). While this two nature Christology was clearly defined and promulgated in the Council of Chalcedon (451AD), themes of the double-nature of Jesus Christ were already developed among the early church fathers like Irenaeus, Cyril of Alexandria, Leo the Great, Cyril of Jerusalem among others.[776] They demonstrated the origin of the divinity and the humanity of Jesus Christ. In this way, O'Collins concludes that, "the fact that Jesus was conceived and born of a woman points to his humanity. The fact that he was conceived and born of the virgin Mary points to his divinity and eternal, personal origin as the *Son of God*."[777] In this way, to understand the Christology of Luke's Gospel, is to be conscious of this double.

Thirdly, the virginal conception of Jesus also provides the context for a better understanding of the *relationship between Jesus Christ and the Holy Spirit*. In the annunciation story, the Angel Gabriel said to the Blessed Virgin Mary when she pointed to

---

774 See, Gerald O'Collins. *Christology: A Biblical, Historical and Systematic Study of Jesus.* 2009, p.287-293.

775 Gerald O'Collins. *Christology: A Biblical, Historical and Systematic Study of Jesus.* 2009, p.293.

776 Gerald O'Collins. *Christology: A Biblical, Historical and Systematic Study of Jesus.* 2009, p.294.

777 Gerald O'Collins. *Christology: A Biblical, Historical and Systematic Study of Jesus.* 2009, p.294.

her life of virginity and innocence; "the Holy Spirit will come upon, and the power of the Most High will overshadow you" (Luke 1: 25). Thus, we can see that the Holy Spirit was there even at the point of the incarnation. The same Spirit will equally manifest itself at the baptism of Jesus by John the Baptist (Luke 3: 21 – 22) and at the temptation before the commencement of his public ministry (Luke 4: 1 – 13). The Holy Spirit will continue to be actively present in the life and in the ministry of Jesus, and in several areas, Jesus himself will promise the disciples, the Holy Spirit who will teach them the complete truth; "But the Advocate, the Holy Spirit, whom the Father will send in my name, will teach you all things and will remind you of everything I have said to you" (John 14: 26). In this way, O'Collins indicates that the virginal conception contributes to revealing and clarifying the central truth that the Holy Trinity was actively present in the life of Jesus from the beginning to the end. As he put it, Jesus' "total history discloses the God who is Father, Son, and the Holy Spirit."[778]

Fourthly, the significance of the virginal conception lies in the fact that through it, we are able to understand that God took the primary initiative to break into human history in order to redeem it. This is demonstrated by the presence of the Angel Gabriel with Mary and the message he conveyed to her. In the Book of Daniel, the Angel Gabriel appears to announce the hour of salvation (Daniel 8: 16 and Daniel 9: 21). So, the reference to the Angel Gabriel here implies that, "for Mary, everything begins with the assurance that this was the moment when the destiny of the world was being decided."[779] For O'Collins, the virginal conception of Christ demonstrates that the salvation is a pure divine gift. "Human beings cannot inaugurate and carry through their own redemption. Like the original creation of the

---

778 Gerald O'Collins. *Christology: A Biblical, Historical and Systematic Study of Jesus.* 2009, p.295.

779 Christian Community Bible, 2014, p.1449.

universe, the new creation is a divine work and pure grace – to be received on the human side, just as Mary received the new life of her womb."[780] In this way, while the disobedience of the first Eve led to the damnation of the human race, through the obedience of the second Eve, grace and peace has been restored to it through the virginal conception of Jesus. However, where does Islam stand in respect of the belief in the virginal conception of Jesus?

The Qur'an also has its narratives about the virginal conception of Jesus and the virginal state of Mary after his birth. It accepts the virginal conception as a historical reality but denies the incarnation. In other words, it accepts that Mary conceived Jesus in an extraordinary way through the power or command of Allah without the intervention of a human father. However, it does not agree like Christians, that the child Mary conceived is God or the "Son of God". That is, Islam does not support the doctrine of the incarnation. According to Fatoohi, the Qur'an makes it explicitly clear that, "Mary conceived Jesus without having a relation with a man. This is clear in the story of the annunciation, the story of the birth of Jesus and some other verses."[781] We find some of these affirmations in the two annunciation narratives in the Qur'an in Surah 3: 42 – 47 and Surah 19: 16 – 22, where the Angel Gabriel is said to have told Mary about God's intended plans for her. Thus, the Qur'an says, "the Angel said to Mary, 'Mary, God has chosen you and made you pure. He has truly chosen you above all women" (Surah 3: 42). In Surah 3: 45, "The Angel said, 'Mary, God gives you news of a Word from Him, whose name will be the *Messiah*, Jesus, the 'Son of Mary'." In Surah 19: 19 – 22 the Angel Gabriel testifies; "'I am but a Messenger from your Lord, to announce to you the gift of a pure son.' She said, 'how can I have a son when

780 Gerald O'Collins. *Christology: A Biblical, Historical and Systematic Study of Jesus.* 2009, p.295.
781 See, Louay Fatoohi. *The Mystery of the Historical Jesus.* 2007, p.117-119.

no man has touched me? I have not been unchaste,' and he said, 'This is what your Lord said; 'it is easy for me.'"

The above texts demonstrate a Qur'anic narrative of the account of the *annunciation*. While Jackson Montell contends that the accounts of Surah 19: 16 – 22 share similarities with the Lukan account of the annunciation and the birth of Jesus,[782] one finds that the two texts are not exactly the same. For instance, while the Qur'an reports that Mary first secluded herself from her family before her encounter with the Angel (Surah 19: 16 – 17), the report in Luke's Gospel (Luke 1: 26 – 27) is silent on the exact location where the encounter occurred except for the mention of Nazareth where she comes from. In terms of where exactly in Nazareth, the text is silent on the matter. Secondly, Surah 19: 16 – 22 does not have the opening greetings of the Angel as expressed in the Gospel of Luke – "Hail Mary full of grace, the Lord is with you" (Luke 1: 28). Apart from these differences, which some scholars may consider insignificant, the rest of the message of the *annunciation* narrative in Surah 19: 16 – 22 seems to find resonance in Luke 1: 26 – 31. To make this claim is by no means intended to imply that they are the same. For Parrinder, although similar to the canonical Gospels, the Qur'anic narratives on the annunciation are more linked to the apocryphal sources.[783]

Although the tendency may be to overlook the subtle or the refined differences between the two narratives, Leirvik Oddbjørn cautions that one must always be sensitive to the functions of these texts in their respective contexts.[784] This is because as Leirvik put it, "superficial similarities between two signs may conceal

---

782 Montell presents a Christian Apologetical view in the bid to discredit Islam and Muhammad. It is understood that his work is not dialogue friendly. However, he acknowledges this point of closeness in the story of Jesus' birth in the Bible and in the Qur'an. (See, Montell Jackson, R. *Islam Revealed*. 2003, p.71-79, 73).

783 Geoffrey Parrinder. *Jesus in the Qur'an*. 1965, p.76.

784 Oddbjørn Leirvik. *The Image of Jesus in the Qur'an*. 2010, p.15.

profound differences in the meaning that a certain conception is attributed within the different systems of meaning."[785] Thus, it could only be proper to say that although *different*, Christians and Muslims could identify with the Biblical and the Qur'anic narratives about the "virginal conception"; in that, not only do they agree that the Angel Gabriel is the announcer of God's intended purpose for Mary, their respective texts also show that God himself was going to aid Mary accomplish his purpose without the need for human intervention. Here, both accounts confirm that Jesus' birth was an express act of God: In Surah 3: 47, God himself issued the command; "Be! And He was". In Surah 21: 91 and Surah 66: 12, the Qur'an reports that God "breathed His Spirit" into Mary while she was still chaste. In Mathew's Gospel, the Angel said to Joseph; "what is conceived in her (Mary) is by the Holy Spirit" (Matthew 1: 20). In Luke 1: 35, The Angel said to Mary; "The Holy Spirit will come upon you and the power of the Most High will overshadow you; therefore, the child to be born shall be called the Son of God".

In their interpretations to the above Qur'anic texts, many Islamic commentators consistently support the claim that the Qur'an affirms the Virginal Conception of Jesus. For instance, Fakhr al-Din al-Razi (1210 AD) intimates that there was no question of a human father involved in Jesus' conception, for either God breathed His Spirit into Mary or the Angel Gabriel did. There was no human father involved in her conception.[786] For Yusuf Ali, "Mary the mother of Jesus was unique in that she gave birth to a son by a special miracle without the intervention of the customary physical means."[787] In consequence, while there are also other dissenting voices in Islam concerning the virginal

---

785 Oddbjørn Leirvik. *The Image of Jesus in the Qur'an.* 2010, p.15.

786 Al-Razi quoted in Mark Beaumont. *Christology in Dialogue with Islam.* 2005, p.2.

787 See, Yusuf Ali. *The Meaning of the Holy Qur'an.* 1934 (as cited in Mark Beaumont. *Christology in Dialogue with Islam.* 2005, p.2).

birth of Jesus,[788] Islam as a whole affirms the *virginal conception and the virginal birth* of Jesus, it must be said that, to quickly read divine implications into the Islamic stand on the matter finds no place in the religion. This is because of the Islamic obligation to acknowledge the *Tawhid*. In Islam, there is only one God and Jesus is his prophet. Hence the Qur'an says: "in God's eyes, Jesus is just like Adam: He created him from the dust and said to him, "'Be,' and he was" (Surah 3: 59). It is said that Christians from Najran and Ethiopia argued with the Prophet Muhammad about the divinity of Jesus, basing their claim on his exceptional birth. In response, Muhammad indicated that God also created Adam without human parents.[789] Yet, as indicated before, unlike Adam, Qur'anic Jesus was not created from the soil of the earth and never disobeyed the will of Allah.

Consequently, what could be said about the Qur'anic and Biblical accounts about the "virginal conception" is that although different, there is a sense of common resonance in the message each account offers in its own context. That is, there are perceived equivalences between the two accounts informed by the following: (1) the common admission of the Angel Gabriel as the conveyer of the good news to Mary; (2) the acknowledgement of the extraordinary nature of the conception; (3) Jesus as the child to be born; and (4) the intimate relationship between Jesus and the Holy Spirit (also known as Gabriel in Islam). These commonalities offer a convenient ground for Christian–Muslim conversations about the identity and mission of Jesus Christ, and how the message of Jesus Christ can inspire believers in both faith traditions in their response to God and to issues of human

---

788 One finds the dissenting voice of Ahmadi commentator Muhammad Ali who insists that Jesus was conceived in the womb of Mary in the same way as all other women do. (See, Mark Beaumont. *Christology in Dialogue with Islam.* 2005, p.2; Muhammad Ali. *The Holy Qur'an.* 1917. See, Surah 19: 22).

789 See, Mark Beaumont. *Christology in Dialogue with Islam.* 2005, p.2.

flourishing. Both traditions admit that the extraordinary birth of Jesus was for an extraordinary purpose. What is this purpose in both the Qur'an and in the Christian Gospels? While this purpose can be discerned in his message as proclaimed in the Qur'an in and in the Gospel, how does it essentially differ from God's fundamental call to Muslims and Christians and their expected response to this call? Addressing these practical questions bring us face to face with Christian–Muslim dialogue of life and of common action. It is through these forms of dialogue that Christians and Muslims can together discern common values between them and take steps to promote these values. Chapter Seven addresses this area of dialogue.

6.5.2 The Miracles of Jesus Christ

In his *The Reality of Jesus*,[790] Dermot Lane asserts that within the self-consciousness or experiences of the *disciples,* Jesus' divinity was fully realized at the Resurrection. But before they came to this point, they understood Jesus Christ initially as a *prophet, a Rabbi and* the *Messiah*. The accounts of Mark 8: 27 – 29 and Luke 9: 18 – 20 demonstrate the varied perceptions the disciples of Jesus had about him and the mission he fulfilled in their midst. That is, the conviction with which Jesus preached his message and the signs and the wonders that accompanied his preaching, initially, provoked the thinking of the disciples that Jesus was not just an ordinary Jewish man, like the rest, but that God was with him affirming his message through the signs and the wonders he performed. Géza Vermes indicates that Luke's Gospel shows that Jesus himself defined the nature of his ministry through these healings and exorcisms. These wondrous deeds of Christ

---

790 Dermot Lane. *The Reality of Jesus: An Essay in Christology.* 1975, p.66–80.

are consistently demonstrated in varied forms in the whole synoptic tradition.[791] But what are miracles? Do the signs and the wonders performed by Jesus necessarily imply that he was God or the "Son of God"? In other words, does the outward show of miracles necessarily imply divinity?

In studying the miracle traditions of the Gospels, while some scholars begin their studies by providing various definitions of the word *miracle*, it is good to assess some of these definitions in the attempt to delve into our study of the miracles of Jesus Christ, and their theological implications for the Christian faith and theology within the context of dialogue as an exercise in learning. For instance, Walter Kasper provides a Christian apologetic conception of a miracle and systematically points out the loopholes in such an approach to it. For the apologetics, a miracle is, "a perceivable event outside the possibilities of nature, one brought about by God's almighty power in contravention or at least circumvention of natural causality, for the purpose of confirming verbal revelation".[792] In other words, a miracle is that extraordinary or supernatural power which contravenes or interrupts the laws of nature for a good effect. If miracles are known to be set against the laws of nature, Kasper indicates that one then needs to know all the laws of nature and their operations to be able to establish whether or not an event is a miracle.[793] While this apologetic conception of a miracle was set up against the modern scientific attitudes of causality and determinism, it fails to serve the Biblical and the theological conception of a miracle, from which Christian faith is derived and nourished.

Within the Christian Scriptures, miracles are seen as God's acts of power defined by their extraordinary and unexpected nature. These acts which appear in visible signs evoke responses of amazement and wonder in those who perceive them. In this way,

---

791 Géza Vermes. *Jesus the Jew.* 1973, p.58.

792 Walter Kasper. *Jesus The Christ.* 1977, p.91.

793 Walter Kasper. *Jesus The Christ.* 1977, p.92.

miracles are not necessarily set against the laws of nature but are viewed as God's extraordinary intervention in particular human experiences or situations in order to redeem them.[794] From this Biblical point of view, Kasper indicates that miracles are characterised by the following features: (1) miracles always involve the extraordinary, the unusual and the amazing. While these are reached through faith, their interpretations are made possible through the preaching that accompanies them; (2) miracles are the personal initiatives of God. God is always behind the powers and the actions that are demonstrated in physical and symbolic signs; (3) they can only be seen as God's actions through faith. Miracles do not force faith but challenge it and make it credible. In Goethe's words, "miracles are 'faith's favourite children.'"[795]

Following Kasper's designations above, we can necessarily conclude that a person who performs such extraordinary and wondrous deeds from God is necessarily divine? Are the miracles that Jesus performed a necessary affirmation of his divinity? History shows that the performance of miracles is very often part of the experiences of religious communities. Oddbjorn Leirvik affirmed this point when he indicated that, "expectation of bodily healing and visible miracles in general are integral parts of popular religiosity in most faith communities".[796] While these miracles often demonstrate in the eyes of their perceivers, the credibility of their religious leader, they also point to the presence of a higher power in whom the miracles find their source. From this perspective, Kasper indicates that there are rabbinic and Hellenistic stories of miracles in various forms such as; cures from sicknesses, expulsions of demons, raising from the dead, quelling of storms among others.[797] For instance, within Judaism, Moses is known to have performed many

---

794 Walter Kasper. *Jesus The Christ*. 1977, p.92

795 Walter Kasper. *Jesus The Christ*. 1977, p.89, 94-95.

796 Oddbjørn Leirvik. *The Image of Jesus in the Qur'an*. 2010, p.245.

797 Walter Kasper. *Jesus The Christ*. 1977, p.90.

wondrous deeds demonstrated by the ten (10) plagues (Exodus 7: 19 and Exodus 10: 27), the crossing of the Red Sea (Exodus 14: 5 – 12), and the squeezing of water from the rock (Exodus 17: 1 – 7) among others. The Prophet Elijah is also known to have raised the dead son of the widow of Zarephath (1 Kings 17: 17 – 23). These miracles point to the power of God working through Moses and Elijah among others.

However, in the case of Jesus Christ, one finds a different picture. As we indicated in Chapter Four on "Markan Christology", Mark presented the wondrous signs performed by Jesus as affirmations of his status as the "Son of God". Here, Walter Kasper indicates that Mark reported the first miracle (Mark 1: 21ff) right after Jesus' announcement of the imminence of the Kingdom of God. In this way, he presents Jesus' miracles, "as signs of the arrival of the Kingdom of God. Their coming means the beginning of the end of Satan's kingdom."[798] Thus, the reader in Mark's Gospel soon discovers that as the "Son of God" (Mark 1: 16 and Mark 8: 26), the announcement of the imminence of the Kingdom of God and the calling of some disciples is immediately followed by successive miracles of exorcisms, healings, deliverances and the show of supernatural authority. Here one sees Jesus, the *Messiah*, the "Son of God", actively at work: healing the man with the unclean spirit (Mark 1: 21ff), healing Simon Peter's mother-in-law (Mark 1: 29ff), walking on the sea (Mark 6: 45ff), the deliverance of the little girl with the unclean spirit (Mark 7: 24ff), the cure of the deaf man (Mark 7: 31ff) and the cure of the blind man (Mark 8: 22ff). As Donald English intimates, these signs and wonders made Mark's picture of the *Messiah* more compelling because Jesus did not only preach to the people, but he accompanied his preaching with miracles of healing, deliverance and raising people from the dead.[799]

---

798 Walter Kasper. *Jesus The Christ*. 1977, p.95.

799 Donald English. *The Message of Mark*. 1992, p.17-18.

In his review of these successive miracles, Walter Kasper asserts that these miracles are, "signs that the well-being that the Kingdom of God brings has already arrived. They are an expression of the physical and the visible dimension of the Kingdom of God."[800] So, demonstrating the imminence of the reign of the Kingdom of God was at the centre of the miracles Jesus performed. This explains why when the Pharisees accused him of performing miracles through the power of Beelzebul, Jesus asserted; "... but if it is through the 'Spirit of God' I cast out demons, then know that the Kingdom of God has already come upon you" (Matthew 12: 25 – 28). While the Kingdom of God is an eschatological one (pointing to the future), Jesus' miracles serve as its present inauguration and guarantee of man's hope of liberation from the bondages of sin and eternal death. As Kasper put it, "it is to this hope in man, and not to his observing and recording intellect, that the miracles speak."[801]

So, the goal of inaugurating the reign of the Kingdom of God therefore sets apart the miracles that Jesus performed. This explains why Jesus did not systematically heal all the sick in the world or cast out all demons in it in order to make the world a better place. He was not interested in a better world, but the new world defined and shaped by God's Kingdom.[802] Being potent signs of the introduction of the Kingdom of God, Jesus' miracles also function as attestations to his own eschatological *exousia* (authority and power) – demonstrated by the way he taught with authority (Matthew 7: 29), his power even to forgive sins (Matthew 9: 6), and the people's realisation of his *exousia* (Matthew 9: 8). Thus, in demonstrating the authority and the power which accompanied his message, Jesus did so not as a show-off (Matthew 12: 38) or in the manner exhibited by worldly authorities (Matthew 20: 28), but as a representation of the nature of the future glory which he now inaugurates.

---

800 Walter Kasper. *Jesus The Christ*. 1977, p.95.

801 Walter Kasper. *Jesus The Christ*. 1977, p.95.

802 Walter Kasper. *Jesus The Christ*. 1977, p.96.

In this way, Kasper indicates that Jesus' miracles can be viewed in these three ways: (1) they are a fulfilment of the Old Testament demonstrated by the messianic mission plan (Luke 4: 16 – 21). He says, "this scripture is being fulfilled even as you listen" (Luke 4: 21). This implied that in Jesus' miracles, the will of God as communicated in the Old Testament is being fulfilled.[803] His miracles are therefore an act of obedience to God the Father. According to Kasper, this sets Jesus' miracles apart from those performed by magicians or Hellenistic wonderworkers;[804] (2) the miracles of Jesus reveal God's power through human lowliness. That is, his miracles are not a necessary pointer to his divinity, but a sign of the lowliness of God in Jesus of Nazareth. The miracles then become scenes of the hidden epiphany of God's power;[805] (3) the goal of the miracles of Jesus was to release men for God through discipleship.[806] If the devil was cast out from them, the reason was for them to follow Jesus, and this call to discipleship also implied mission – demonstrated by the empowerment of the disciples to also perform such miracles (Matthew 10: 1ff; Luke 9: 1ff; and Mark 3: 22ff). So, Kasper indicates that the miracles of Jesus were also an inauguration of the eschatological gathering of God's people. Through these miracles, the sick, the poor, the lame, the lost

803 Donald English indicates that by placing Jesus Christ at the centre of the miracle events, Mark wanted to make it clear that the person at the centre of the events was establishing continuity with God's previous activity in the world as established in the Old Testament. (See, Donald English. *The Message of Mark.* 1992, p.15).

804 See, Walter Kasper. *Jesus The Christ.* 1977, p.97.

805 See, Walter Kasper. *Jesus The Christ.* 1977, p.97.

806 As Donald English intimated, at the outset of Jesus' preaching and performance of miracles, was Jesus' call not just to hear the message about the imminence of the Kingdom of God, and marvel at the miracles that accompanied it, "but to do something about it. They should repent and believe in the Good News". (See, Donald English. *The Message of Mark.* 1992, p.16).

and the sinful symbolically experience salvation and the love of God now, so that they too can bear witness to it.[807]

In consequence, we can say that the miracles that Jesus performed were not necessarily indicative of his divinity. In themselves, miracles are completely open to any interpretation, and can even be performed by the devil (Matthew 12: 27 and Mark 3: 22). However, what differentiates Jesus' miracles and all other forms of miracles was that his miracles served as an inauguration of the reign of the Kingdom of God and his place in it. In this way, not only were his miracles a fulfilment of the Old Testament, but demonstrated how God manifests his power through human lowliness. In performing them, Jesus' miracles lead to the formation of discipleship and the bringing together of the eschatological gathering of God's people, the church. For Christian faith and theology therefore, Jesus succeeded in accomplishing this task because of who he was: the *Christ,* the son of the living God (Mark 8: 29). God was not working *through* him, but he was God at work.[808] While these miracles simply bowl men over, their purpose was to lead them to faith – that "God's power does not end when human possibilities are exhausted."[809]

In a particularly Islamic context, God is seen as the sole source of Jesus' miraculous powers. This is copiously acknowledged in the Qur'an when the Angel told Mary, *"God will teach Jesus, the Messiah the Wisdom, the Torah and the Gospel, He will send him as a Messenger to the people of Israel. I have come to you with a sign from your Lord … I will heal the blind, the leper and bring the dead back to life with God's permission"* (Surah 3: 48 – 49). This text is a prediction of the future mission of Jesus, the *Messiah.* This mission

---

807 See, Walter Kasper. *Jesus The Christ.* 1977, p.97.

808 Kasper intimates that what Jesus' miracles were ultimately communicating was that "in Jesus God was carrying out his plan, and that God acted in him for the salvation of humankind and the world". (See, Walter Kasper. *Jesus The Christ.* 1977, p.98).

809 See, Walter Kasper. *Jesus The Christ.* 1977, p.98.

will significantly involve the performance of healings and raising the dead to life. In Surah 19: 30, Jesus, the *Messiah* is said to testify in defence of his mother from the cradle: *"But he said; I am a servant of the God. He has granted me the Scriptures; made me a prophet; made me blessed wherever I may be."* While the family of Mary doubted the legitimacy of the birth of her son Jesus, he rises to her defence by inviting Mary's family to rather honour her for his birth. Following these two texts, Mark Beaumont indicates that, "Jesus is a precocious personality in the Qur'an; not only is his birth seen as spectacular, but his maturity of thought is beyond compare for such a young child."[810]

The Qur'an also says: *"Then God will say, Jesus, the Son of Mary! Remember my favour to you and to your mother: how I strengthened you with the Holy Spirit … How by my leave, you fashioned the shape of a bird out of clay, breathed into it and it became a bird; how by my leave, you healed the blind and the leper; how by my leave, you brought the dead back to life"* (Surah 5: 110). From the preceding texts, the Qur'an explicitly affirms that Jesus succeeded in doing what he did because God's favour was with him – for by God's leave, he healed the blind, the lepers and raised the dead to life. In other words, in Surah 5: 110, Jesus, the *Messiah* solemnly followed God's command and accomplished the mission for which he was sent. So, what was predicted in Surah 3: 48 – 49 is confirmed by the divine review of his mission as demonstrated in Surah 5: 110: you fashioned a bird out of clay and breathed into it and it lived *by my permission*; you healed the blind man and the leper *by my permission*; you raised the dead to life *by my permission*.[811]

Following the implications of the three Qur'anic texts above, we could say that, among all the prophets of Allah, only Jesus is known to have had such an extraordinary life-pattern: the announcement of the nature of his birth by the Angel Gabriel;

810 See, Mark Beaumont. *Christology in Dialogue with Muslims.* 2005, p.3.
811 See, Mark Beaumont. *Christology in Dialogue with Muslims.* 2005, p.4.

his actual birth as announced; the defence of his mother from the cradle; the prediction of his mission; and his fulfilment of it. While Adam is known to have come into the world without a human father and mother, he nevertheless cannot be compared to the Qur'anic Jesus, because Adam was fashioned from dust (or clay) and subsequently disobeyed Allah.[812] Even though the Qur'an also indicates that other prophets of Allah performed miracles, a combination of the events surrounding Jesus' conception, birth, and the unique nature in which he accomplished his mission, seem to set him apart. No wonder the Qur'an indicates that Jesus will be held in honour in this world and in the next,[813] and one of those brought nearer to Allah, as testified to by Gabriel: *"The angels said: 'O Mary! Allah gives you the glad tidings of a command from Him: his name shall be Messiah, Jesus, the Son of Mary. He shall be highly honoured in this world and in the next and shall be one of those nearest to Allah"* (Surah 3: 45).

In Islam, the Qur'anic Jesus' miraculous powers raise questions as to whether the power he possessed was given to him by God or was he merely a channel used by God to accomplish his task? In other words, did Jesus have creative power in himself or he was he merely a channel for God's creative work?[814] As indicated in Chapter Five in the section on "the relationship between

---

812 Oddbjørn indicates that even in Muslim apologetics (both classical and modern), the characterisation of Jesus and the miracles he performed, present him in more distinct terms than even the magic of Moses and the eloquence of Muhammad. (See, Oddbjørn Leirvik. *The Image of Jesus in the Qur'an.* 2010, p.245).

813 For Oddbjørn, even though the image of Jesus as the healer of bodies seems to be far spread even in Islamic folktales, from the time of the prophets to present day popular religiosity in places like Persia and indo–Pakistan, Jesus' miracles both for Christians and for Muslims are the sole basis for establishing divinity. (See, Oddbjørn Leirvik. *The Image of Jesus in the Qur'an.* 2010, p.245).

814 See, Mark Beaumont. *Christology in Dialogue with Muslims.* 2005, p.4.

Jesus and the Holy Spirit,"[815] we saw that the intimate relationship between Jesus and the Holy Spirit accounts for the Qur'anic Jesus' ability to function as an outstanding "Prophet" and the "Messenger" of Allah. Even though the Holy Spirit is identified as the Angel Gabriel, Gabriel is also known to be a "Messenger of Allah". We saw that al-Tabari, al-Zamakhshari and al-Razi unanimously asserted that Jesus' miracles were *signs* which authenticate his status as the "Prophet of Allah".[816] So, in response to the above question, al-Razi for instance, indicates that, the phrase; *by my permission* means that the Qur'anic Jesus did not possess creative powers in himself. He was able to do what he did through God's consent. For instance, the breathing of life into the clay bird does not belong to the inherent power of Jesus but emanates from God.[817] Jesus was only a means through whom Allah accomplished his plans and his purposes.

Consequently, even though the Qur'an itself contains evidence of the special place that Jesus occupies in the divine plan of Allah, both the Qur'an and the religion of Islam do not interpret these texts and events in divine terms. Irrespective of the spectacularity of the events surrounding the miracles of Jesus, they are in no way, a pointer to any divine status. The Islamic obligation to acknowledge the *Tawhid* does not entertain the association of divinity to any servant of Allah. For Islam, the unicity and the absolute divinity of Allah is unparalleled. So, by correlating the two theological positions on the miracles of the Qur'anic Jesus and Jesus the "Son of God", one realises that whereas Christianity asserts that Jesus performed his miracles as a consequence of who

---

815 See Chapter Five on "The Relationship between Jesus and the Holy Spirit," interpreted against the background of the three Qur'anic texts (Surah 2: 87, Surah 2: 253, and Surah 5: 110).

816 See Chapter Five of this current study on the views of al-Tabari, al-Razi and al-Zamakhshari.

817 See, Fakhr al-Din al-Razi. *Tasfsir al-Kabir,* on Surah 3: 48: as in Mark Beaumont. *Christology in Dialogue with Muslims.* 2005, p.5.

he was (the "Son of God"), for Islam, Jesus performed these miracles through God's power invested in him.

In dialogue as an exercise in learning, we can discern that both religions, first of all acknowledge that Jesus indeed performed these miracles. Secondly, both religions equally agree that the mission of Jesus was a fulfilment of God's divine plan. As part of the Godhead, Christians perceive the miracles of Jesus as essentially part of his redemptive role as the second person of the Holy Trinity. These acts of healing and deliverance brought relief and life to those who experienced them. From an Islamic context, the Holy Spirit is known for being instrumental in the life and in the mission of the Qur'anic Jesus. With his presence, Jesus was able to fulfil the divine command of Allah. Understood as the Angel Gabriel, it is the Holy Spirit who *teaches*, *guides*, *strengthens* and *assists* Jesus in doing what he was sent to do as a "Messenger of Allah". This means that God was instrumental in helping Jesus accomplish his mission through the aid of the Angel Gabriel. In this way, since Jesus performed the miracles by Allah's permission, Allah was in a sense alleviating the suffering, the alienation through death and the pain of his people through Jesus, the *Messiah*. The question then is: how can Jesus' life and mission inspire Christians and Muslims to collectively undertake acts that would promote human flourishing?

6.5.3 The Ascension and the Second Coming of Jesus Christ

The ascension of Jesus Christ is the Christian belief that after the resurrection, Jesus was taken up into heaven in His glorious resurrected body. This event is said to have occurred forty (40) days after the resurrection (Acts 1: 3). According to Walter Kasper, Luke inserts a period of forty (40) days between the resurrection and the ascension. Hence, the ascension occurred within the context of a post-resurrection appearance. As Kasper understands, Luke's *Forty (40) days* is a sacred number (representing the Israelites journey in the wilderness; Jesus' sojourn in the wilderness). It designates a holy period of a considerable length of time; the time during which Jesus appeared to the disciples after the resurrection. It is not to be taken as an exact historical period of time but as a round figure; designating a considerable period of time within which Jesus appeared to the disciples after the resurrection.[818] Where did the appearances occur and what is the significance of the ascension to Christian faith and to theology?

In Luke's Gospel, the ascension is said to occur in Bethany not far from Jerusalem (Luke 24: 50). In the Acts of the Apostles, Luke provides the precise location where it occurred – "on the Mount of Olives" (Acts 1: 12). While Luke 24: 50 – 53 and Mark 16: 19 presents a succinct description of the event, the Acts of the Apostles (especially Acts 1: 9 – 11), present a more picturesque account of Jesus' ascension into heaven.[819] In the Gospel, Luke 24: 51, we are told that; "as he blessed them, he withdrew from them and was taken up to heaven". In the Acts of the Apostles (1: 9), Luke mentions a vision: "He was taken up before their eyes, and a cloud hid him from their sight. While they were still looking up to heaven, where he went, suddenly two men dressed in white stood beside them and said, "'men of Galilee, why do you stand here looking up at the sky? This Jesus who has been taken up from you into heaven will return in the same way you have seen him go'" (Acts 1: 9 – 11). This account of the ascension marks the final encounter between the resurrected Christ and the apostles. Having come from the Father, he returns to the Father by being *taken up* into space in the presence of his disciples and *disappears into the clouds*. According to Walter Kasper, the cloud which bears Jesus away in the sight of his astonished disciples is not

---

818 Walter Kasper. *Jesus the Christ*. 1977, p.148.

819 Walter Kasper. *Jesus the Christ*. 1977, p.148.

intended to be a meteorological phenomenon, but a theological symbol of God's vehicle.[820]

According to the Gospel of Mark, the ascension occurred after a meal (Mark 16: 19). One finds a series of brief references to Jesus appearing to some disciples after the resurrection (Mark 16: 9, 12, 14). But the arranged meeting between Jesus and the Apostles in Galilee which was communicated to Mary Magdalene is not reported (Mark 16: 7: Matt. 28: 10). Here, Donald English explains that the reason for this inconsistency in Mark's concluding chapter (Mark 16) is because of the differences between Mark 16: 1 – 8 and Mark 16: 9 – 20. In considering Mark 16: 8 (*Trembling and bewildered, the women went out and fled from the tomb. They said nothing to anyone because they were afraid*) alongside Mark's Good News in Mark 1: 1 (*This is the beginning of the Good News of Jesus Christ, the Son of God*), some scholars found it odd that Mark's proclamation of the Good News about Jesus Christ should end with some women saying *nothing about it (Jesus' resurrection) to anyone because they were afraid*. Since the young man at the tomb (who is supposed to be an angel) told them that Jesus had risen, and was going before them to Galilee, where they will see him (Mark 16: 5 – 7), one would expect Mark to continue with a description of this promised encounter.[821] The absence of this Galilean encounter after the resurrection presents an anomaly (Mark 16: 8) in Mark's conclusion. For English, this anomaly led earlier Scribes to attempt to fill the lacunae in the Gospel.

---

820 In the Old Testament, "the cloud" has always been presented as God's vehicle and the sign of his all-powerful presence. So, in the ascension account, the cloud means nothing more than that Jesus was taken up into the sphere of the divine glory and the divine life. (Eee, Walter Kasper. *Jesus the Christ*. 1977, p.148).

821 Donald English. *The Message of Mark*. 1992, p.239.

As a result, two attempts survived: (1) the shorter ending (Mark 16: 1 – 8) and the longer ending (Mark 16: 9 – 20).[822] Yet, the whole purpose of Mark was to proclaim the singular truth that, Jesus Christ, the "Son of God" ascended to heaven after his crucifixion, death and resurrection. In this way, the paschal mystery becomes part of the Good News which Mark sought to proclaim.

Although the Evangelists seem to present different accounts about Jesus' ascension, what remains significantly common to them is that each of them confirms the fact that indeed the ascension did occur. For Christian faith and theology, the significance of this fact of the ascension lies in the fact that whereas the resurrection presupposed the crucifixion and death of Christ, it also serves as the foundation from which the ascension finds its authenticity; for if Jesus did not die, he could not have risen from the dead; and if he did not rise from the dead, he could not have ascended to heaven. In reverse, if the ascension did occur, then Jesus was resurrected from the dead before he ascended to heaven. If all these took place (that is, the crucifixion, death, resurrection and ascension), then they contribute to affirming the Christian belief that Jesus is the pre–existent "Son of God" who took on human nature (the incarnation) in order to redeem it from its decrepit state due to sin. Having ascended into heaven, it is the Church's belief as attested by the two Angels (Acts 1: 11) that this same Jesus "will come again in glory to judge the living and the dead."[823] This notion of the *Return* brings to the fore the Church's doctrine of the *Second Coming of Jesus Christ*.

---

822 In considering the longer ending, Donald English indicates that the scribe who added this version did well by taking up Mark's theme of belief and unbelief. Yet, verse 9-16 appears to be an inauthentic part of the Gospel (See, Donald English. *The Message of Mark*. 1992, p.240).

823 This statement – "He will come again in glory to judge the living and the dead," is part of the Church's profession of faith, articulated in the Nicene Creed.

Known in Christian theology as the *Parousia,* the *Second Coming of Jesus* Christ is an eschatological event recounted in both Christianity and in Islam. Within the context of the New Testament the word *Parousia* is used eighteen (18) times in the sense of "the Second Coming of Jesus Christ" or "the Day of the Lord."[824] Apart from the name *Parousia,* the "Second coming of Jesus Christ" is also referred to as the *epiphany* (2 Thessalonians 2: 8) or the *apocalypse* (1 Peter 4: 13). As Alister McGrath pointed out, the event of the *Second Coming of Jesus Christ* is "closely connected to the execution of final judgement."[825] This is fully expressed in the Nicene Creed which says: "*He will come again in glory to judge the living and the dead, and his kingdom will have no end.*" From the Gospel accounts, Jesus did not only predict this event, but he also presented a graphic picture of the nature of this event and how it will occur (Matthew 24: 29 – 41; Mark 13: 28ff; Luke 17: 20ff).

As we indicated earlier, the Qur'an denies the crucifixion and the death of Jesus (Surah 4: 157 – 159). For orthodox Islamic commentators like al-Tabari and al-Razi, while the Jews plotted to kill Jesus, God raised him to Himself in heaven; making one to appear like Jesus who was crucified instead of him.[826] Many Islamic scholars and commentators concur that the phrase, "raising Jesus unto himself" means that God took Jesus bodily into heaven.[827] So, Jesus' ascension to heaven is widely attested to,

---

824 The word *Parousia* can be found in the following verses: Matthew 24: 3, 27, 37, 39; 1 Corinthians 15: 23.

825 See, McGrath, Alister, E. *Christian Theology.* 1992, p.543.

826 See the Islamic exegetical support for the *Substitution Theory* expressed in the views of al-Tabari, al-Razi and al-Baydawi in Cumming, Joseph. "Did Jesus die on the Cross? The History of Reflection on Jesus' Death in Sunni Tafsir Literature." 2001, p.7-22.

827 See Chapter Five on the death and the resurrection of the Qur'anic Jesus.

in both the Qur'an and in *Tafsir* literature.[828] As Mark Beaumont intimated, the consequence of the denial of the death of Jesus on the cross has been the assumption of many scholars that, "Jesus was raised up without going through the process of death. This is seen in al-Tabari's interpretation that God raised Jesus to himself before the one like him was seized and crucified."[829] Hence, in the denial of the crucifixion and the death of Jesus on the cross, is the affirmation of the fact of the *ascension* narrative. Here, the Qur'an and the post-Qur'anic literature like the Hadiths acknowledge the *ascension* and *Second Coming of Jesus* (Surah 4: 158 and Surah 43: 61).

In Surah 4: 158, concerning the *ascension*, the Qur'an says: "No! God raised him (Jesus) to himself, and God is almighty and wise," In Surah 43: 61 in reference to the *Hour*, the Qur'anic Jesus says: "This is knowledge for the *Hour*, do not doubt it. Follow me for this is the right path." Whereas the *Hour* (al-Saa'ah) in Islam refers to the *Day of Judgement* or the *Time of Reckoning* (see, Surah 80: 33 – 43), this day has a twofold dimension: (1) personal reckoning immediately after death; and (2) universal reckoning which will occur after the final resurrection. Thus, while the two Qur'anic texts above are indicative of the "Second Coming of Jesus" at the *Last Hour*, the hadiths also give a clearer account on the matter, with some hadiths even indicating where and how the "Second Coming of Jesus" will occur. For instance, according to the Hadith *Sahih al-Bukhari*, "the *Hour* will not be established until Jesus descends as a ruler."[830] The "Day of Judgement" will

---

828 This assertion is presupposed in al-Tabari, al-Razi and al-Badawi's arguments that Jesus was not crucified, but God raised him to himself in heaven, and only allowed one who looked like him to be crucified. (See, Beaumont, Mark. *Christology in Dialogue with Islam.* 2005, p.9).

829 Beaumont, Mark. *Christology in Dialogue with Islam.* 2005, p.10.

830 Sahih al-Bukhari. Vol. 3, p.656. Its full title is "Kitab-ul-`Ilm (Book of Knowledge). http://sunnah.com/search/?q=jesus+and+the+hour (16/03/2015).

only occur after Jesus' *Second Coming*. This elicits the significance of Jesus' Second Coming in Islamic eschatology.

According to the Hadith *Sahih al-Bukhari*,[831] the *second coming of Jesus* will be in the midst of wars that are fought by the *Mahdi* (the righteous) against the Anti-Christ (*Dajjal* or false Messiah) and all his followers. During these wars, the Qur'anic Jesus is expected to descend on the East of Damascus and be anointed while wearing yellow robes. He will then join the *Mahdi* in the fight against the Anti-Christ. He will follow the Islamic teachings as a Muslim. His conquests over the Anti-Christ and his followers will be a *sign* to the "People of the Book" who will then believe in him, leading to the formation of one community, the community of *Islam*.[832] Jesus will assume leadership of this community bringing about *universal peace*.[833] In this *Second Coming*, the Qur'anic Jesus will pray as a Muslim, and Allah in response to His prayers, will kill Gog and Magog (the gods responsible for disharmony in the Universe).[834] Having ruled his *Islamic community* for forty (40) years, the Qur'anic Jesus will die and will be buried as a Muslim in Mecca in an empty tomb prepared for him beside Muhammad and his immediate companions (Abu Bakr and Umar).[835]

---

831 According to the Dictionary of Islam, the word "Sahih" means "authentic" or "correct". Put together, *Sahih al-Bukhari* is one of the six (6) major editions of Hadith collections (*Kutub al-Sittah*) of Sunni Islam. The Hadith was written by the classical Islamic scholar called Muhammad al-Bukhari around 846 AD. This Hadith is said to be the second most authentic hadiths in Sunni circles.

832 *Ṣaḥīḥ Muslim*, 41: 7043. Its full title is: "Al-Musnadu Al-Sahihu bi Naklil Adli". http://www.usc.edu/org/cmje/religious-texts/hadith/muslim/041-smt.php#041.7023 (27-05-2013).

833 Harun Yahya. *Portents and Features of The Mahdi's Coming*. Global Publishing (Kindle Edition). 2010.

834 Tamar Sonn. *A Brief History in Islam,* 2004, p.209.

835 See, "Isa" in Cyril Glassé. *The New Encyclopedia of Islam*. 2002, p.239-240.

Even though *Sahih al-Bukhari* has a Sunni orientation and so may not speak for the entire Islamic world, this Hadith is also known to be among the two most authentic Hadiths in Sunni tradition. Of course, it may not represent the views of Muslims in other traditions, nonetheless it allows us to understand the significant role that the Qur'anic Jesus plays in Islamic eschatology. As we intimated earlier, Jesus' *Second Coming* which is directly connected to *the Hour* is a significant eschatological concept for Muslims and for Christians. In Islam, *the Hour* is directly linked to "*Yawm al-Qiyāmah*" (the Day of Resurrection) or "*Yawm ad-Dīn*" (the Day of Judgement). These eschatological events constitute the "end time" for all life, followed by the resurrection and Allah's assessment of the conduct of every human person (Judgement).[836] For the Hadith Sahih al-Bukhari, this *Hour* will not be established without Jesus' *Second Coming* – demonstrating the significance of the event.

As an eschatological event, Christians and Muslims believe that, associated to the "Second Coming of Jesus" is the "last hour", the "Day of Judgement." The judgement of the individual believer will centre on how one submitted oneself to the will of God. While Muslims believe that God will be the final judge in this event and Jesus will only be a witness, Christians on the other hand, believe that Jesus as the "Son of God" will judge both the living and the dead. Consequently, from a correlational perspective, we could say that at the *Second Coming* Jesus would either be the judge for Christians, or he would be a witness in judgement for Muslims. In either way, Jesus would play a significant role in determining the fate of every believer (either as judge or as a witness in judgement) in respect of their faith and their commitment to God. For both Islam and Christianity, it is those who remain faithful and committed to God to the end who would find God's mercies. In this way, how can Muslims and Christians focus on the exemplary life of Jesus as a context

---

836 See, Surah 6: 57, 10: 45, 28: 88 and 33: 63.

for collectively responding to issues of social justice and human flourishing?

6.6 Conclusion

Having engaged in these Christological themes and titles within the context of Christian-Muslim dialogue as an exercise in learning, we could, to some extent say that Jesus is both a *bridge* and a *barrier* to Christian-Muslim dialogue. This is because the Qur'an both affirms and denies aspect of his life which are sacrosanct in the accounts of the Gospels. As Mark Beaumont conceptualizes, the *Virginal Conception* may be accepted as true but the Christian interpretation of the incarnation as a consequence of it is denied. The *Miracles of Jesus* are affirmed but the Christian understanding of these miracles as a consequence of his divinity is denied.[837] Furthermore, while Jesus' *ascension* to heaven and His *Second Coming* is affirmed in both the Qur'an and in some of the Hadiths, the Christian interpretations of these events as intrinsically linked to the mystery of his death and his resurrection is denied. We also discovered that there are references to Jesus as the *Word of God*, the *Messiah* and the *Spirit of God* in the Qur'an, but the Christian interpretations of these titles as evocative of his divinity are categorically denied. As it were, the basis for these denials is the Islamic faith principle of the *Tawhid* (*There is no god but one God*, Surah 5: 73). The *Tawhid* is a non-negotiable faith principle in Islam.

Although the doctrines of the *Holy Trinity*, the *divine sonship* of Jesus and his *death and his resurrection* are seen as *barriers* to Christian-Muslim dialogue in the light of the Islamic obligation to the *Tawhid,* Islam and Christianity have Christological themes which serve as a *bridge* in their dialogical relations. These

---

837 Beaumont, Mark. *Christology in Dialogue with Muslims*. 2005, p.10.

themes include the *virginal conception,* the *miracles of Jesus,* the *ascension and* the *second coming.* Whereas there are subtle differences to the interpretations given to these themes in Christian and in Islamic circles, there are also stark similarities in the way these Christological themes are construed. Consequently, in a project of dialogue as an exercise in learning from and about the other, how can the Jesus of the Qur'an and the Jesus of the New Testament be the context for Christian–Muslim dialogue of life and the dialogue of common action? Here, the focus is on the dimension of enrichment which is fundamentally part of the character of this form of dialogue as an exercise in learning. In other words, if submission to the will of God as expressed in the "love of God and in the love of a neighbour" is central to authentic Christian or Muslim living, how does the life and the mission of Jesus Christ, who completely fulfils this will of God, become learning examples for Christian–Muslim dialogue of life and common action?

We reckon that a critical response to the above question and those that preceded it, could contribute to further reflections on how Christians and Muslims can embark on projects such as; Christian–Muslim *prayers for world peace; the call to promote peace and peaceful co-existence, promoting the value of marriage and family life; collective actions in response to climate change; and collective actions in response to the poor* and *the marginalized in society.* We consider these values as significant issues (values) which touch the core of both religions. In the chapter that follows, we hope to analyse some of these "values" in the light of how the life and the mission of Jesus Christ contributes to espousing their significance as expressed in the Qur'an and in the Hadiths on the one hand, and on the other, the New Testament and social teachings of the Catholic church. The purpose will be to invite Christian–Muslim collective action in response to these values.

CHAPTER SEVEN
DIALOGUE FOR THE PROMOTION OF COMMON VALUES

7.1 Introduction

From the discourses in Chapters Four, Five, and Six; we by now appreciate the claim that it is not just enough to merely allude to the Christian and to the Muslim designations of Jesus Christ (that is, the "Son of God" and the "Messenger" or the "Prophet" of Allah respectively) without careful reflections on their deeper meanings and implications within their tradition-specific contexts, and the theological frameworks which support these meanings. As we discovered in Chapter Six, the Qur'an makes references to Jesus with various titles such as the *Messiah* (Surah 5: 72), "*Word of Allah or Word from Allah*" (Surah 3: 45), a "*Spirit from Allah*" (Surah 4: 171), and the "*closest friend of Allah* who will be held in honour in this world and the next*" (Surah 3: 45). Even though these designations present the Qur'anic Jesus as highly honoured in the sight of Allah, the meanings and the interpretations of these concepts do not approximate to the divine interpretations associated to them within Christian faith and theology. In this way, it was evinced in Chapter Five that the *Tawhid* (Surah 5: 73: "There is only One God") provides the theological framework for a better comprehension of the Islamic tradition-specific conception of Jesus Christ. Islamic faith and theology are built on the knowledge of the unicity and transcendence of Allah. The life of every good Muslim is guided by the belief in God's uniqueness and transcendence. Consequently, to turn the *Tawhid* on its head would amount to destroying the very foundation which Islam as a religion is built. For this reason, despite the honorific titles that are ascribed to Jesus in the Qur'an, the Qur'anic Jesus can only function as a "Prophet" or as a "Messenger" of Allah.

From the perspective of Christian faith and theology, the understanding of Jesus Christ as the "Son of God" is part of the Christian experience of God. Jesus' divine sonship finds its theological articulation in the doctrine of the *Holy Trinity*. The *Holy Trinity* defines the Christian experience of God's revelation as *three persons in One God*. God the father created the world, God the Son (Jesus Christ) redeemed the world and God the Holy Spirit sanctifies the world. Here, while the Father is revealed by the Son, the Father and the Son together revealed the Holy Spirit. Christian faith and theology gets its source and its life from the experience of Jesus Christ as the "Son of God" and the "Saviour of the World", which Jesus accomplished this salvific act through his life, his death and his resurrection. This explains Alistair McGrath's assertion that, "it is impossible to speak of 'God' within the parameters of the Christian tradition without relating such statements to the person and to the work of Jesus Christ."[838] So, the *Tawhid* and the *Holy Trinity* respectively define and shape the Islamic and the Christian understanding of the identity and the mission of Jesus Christ.

However, by engaging the two religions on the theological discourses that capture their respective perspectives on the identity and the mission of Jesus Christ, we found that there are some degrees of common Christological reverberation in each tradition. That is, the Qur'anic narratives Muslims tell about the life and the mission of Jesus Christ appear to share some similarities with those of Christianity. In Chapter Five, we saw examples of such Christological themes such as: "the virginal conception" (Luke 1: 26 – 35 versus Surah 19: 16 – 22), "the miracles of Jesus" (Mark 1: 21 and Mark 8: 22 versus Surah 3: 48 – 49 and Surah 5: 110), and "the ascension and Second coming of Jesus" (Mark 16: 19 versus Surah 4: 158).[839] However, although these themes appear

---

838 Alister McGrath. *Christian Theology.* 1997, p.324.
839 See, Chapter Five of this current study on "Jesus as a Bridge to Christian-Muslim Dialogue."

to be similar, their subtle differences in meaning and interpretation must not be discounted. What is evident is that the Qur'an both affirms and denies aspects of the life of Jesus Christ in the Gospels. This explains why Mark Beaumont earlier on indicated that; in the Qur'an, the virginal conception is accepted as true, but the Christian interpretation of the incarnation as a result of it is ruled out. The Qur'an affirms the miraculous powers of Jesus, but not the Christian reading that they are proofs of his divinity.[840]

Yet, the crucial question for dialogue as an exercise in learning within this context is: how can these Christological affirmations and denials become fruitful contexts for Christian-Muslim dialogue for the promotion of issues of human flourishing? In other words, we find that within the Qur'an and the Gospels, Jesus Christ proclaimed a unique *message* about the will of God, and the need for an urgent human response to it. The task for dialogue as an exercise in learning also lies in uncovering the central tenet of this *message* of the "Prophet" and the "Messenger" of Allah on the one hand, and the "Son of God" on the other. It also seeks disclosure on how this message of Jesus can bring Muslims and Christians to a collective response to God, and to issues of social justice? We know that God calls His messengers and sends them. And we also know that in the history of prophecy, there has never been any Prophet or Messenger of God without a message, and no message without an intended audience.

The saying that, "Islam is the Qur'an, and the Qur'an is Islam",[841] serves to underscore the significant place that the Qur'an occupies in the life of the Muslim. This Qur'an is the "Word of God"; and as Christian Troll indicates, the Qur'an is for the Muslims, "a final, unique, and fully authentic manifestation of the "Word of God" addressed to humankind through the ministry of Muhammad".[842]

---

840 Mark Beaumont. *Christology in Dialogue with Muslims*. 2005, p.10.

841 Murata and Chittick. *The Vision of Islam*. 1994, p. xvii.

842 Christian Troll. "The Bible and the Qur'an in Dialogue. *Bulletin Dei Verbum,* 79/80, p.31.

As the "Word of Allah", the Qur'an issues instructions on how Muslims must live lives that are pleasing to God. It tells them that they need to pray, fast, and be attentive to the needs of the poor and the needy in society.[843] Fundamentally, the Qur'an is the final "Word of Allah", given to Muhammad through the Angel Gabriel, as a source of guidance to the Muslim in his or her response to the will of the One God. As Murata and Chittick put it, the Qur'an "tells people that they should obey God's instructions purely for God's sake, not for worldly gains."[844] It is in this "Word of God" that the message of Jesus, the "Prophet" and the "Messenger" of Allah is situated. With the obligation to obey God's instructions as received and transmitted by his Prophet in the Qur'an, what is the message of Jesus the "Prophet of Allah" in the Qur'an? What can Muslims learn from the message of Jesus in their religious response to the will of Allah, also expressed in the call to pray, fast, and to care for the needs of the poor and the marginalised? As we saw earlier, the Qur'an asserts that; all the messages of the prophets were intended to lead humanity in their submission to God.[845] If so, how does the message of Jesus in the Qur'an contribute to this process?

Within the context of Christianity, even though at various times and in different ways, God spoke his *Word* through the prophets (Hebrews 1: 1 − 2), but in the last days, our own time, Jesus Christ came as the unique, final, definitive and unequivocal self-communication of God to humanity. In other words, for Christian faith and theology, Jesus is the incarnate "Word of God" who definitively reveals God. Yet in time, Jesus Christ as the incarnate "Word of God" on the one hand, made explicit "God's Word" which was spoken before him through the prophets, and on the other, brings freshness and completion to this *Word*; which he himself *is,* and communicates. So, in the Christian notion of

843 Murata and Chittick. *The Vision of Islam.* 1994, p. xvii.

844 Murata and Chittick. *The Vision of Islam.* 1994, p. xvii.

845 Mona Siddiqui. *Christians, Muslims & Jesus.* 2013, p.12.

the "Word of God", one finds a double valence which asserts its authenticity; that is, the spoken or the written Word and its affirmation and fulfilment in the incarnation. Thus, what is the central message of Jesus, the incarnate "Word of God", for Christians? How can this serve as a context for Christian–Muslim collective response to the will of God, also expressed in issues of human flourishing? What follows below is therefore a succinct investigation into the significant place that Jesus occupies in Christianity and in Islam. The purpose is to pry open the door to better understanding of the centrality of the message of Jesus the "Prophet" or as the "Messenger" of Allah in the Qur'an, and the message of Jesus Christ the "Son of God" in the New Testament. We deem that such an approach is necessary for further disclosures on how this message of the "prophet" and the "Son of God" could provide guidance to both Christians and Muslims in their response to God and to issues of human flourishing.

7.2 The Significance of Jesus in Christianity

Jesus Christ is the reason for Christianity. Without him there is no Christianity. In other words, for Christian faith and theology, Jesus Christ does not just reveal something of importance to Christians, but he achieves it – something without which salvation would be impossible and Christianity would never have come into existence. As we indicated in Chapter Four of this study, Jesus is the "Son of God" and the "Saviour of the World". By his identity as the "Son of God", he communicates and reveals God. By his role as the "Saviour of the World", Jesus is the source and the summit of the redeemed life. Hence, it is an altogether impossible task to capture comprehensively the significance of Jesus Christ for Christianity in this rather limited space. Nonetheless, for the purpose of stating the Christian claim on the significant place that Jesus occupies in Christianity, it is necessary to reiterate the fact that Jesus Christ is the *reason* for the existence of Christianity as a religion. He is the historical point of departure and the culmination for Christian faith and theology. As McGrath put it, Christianity represents a "sustained response to the questions raised by the life, the death and the resurrection of Jesus Christ."[846] McGrath presents the following propositions as underscoring the central place of Jesus Christ in Christian faith and theology: (1) Jesus as the revelation of God for Christianity; (2) Jesus as the bearer of salvation; and (3) Jesus as defining the shape of the redeemed life. What do these tripartite propositions of the significance of Jesus Christ in Christianity entail?

First of all, to say that *Jesus reveals God* means that Jesus makes God known in a particular and in a specific manner distinctive to Christianity. To say that "Jesus Christ makes God known" means that he is God, and to see him is to have seen God. As Jesus himself indicated; "If you know me, you will know the Father also … To see me is to have seen the Father" (John 14: 7, 9). The assertion, "I am in the Father and the father is in me" (John 14: 11, 20) underscores the unique relationship between Jesus and God the Father by which he definitively, unreservedly and irrevocably reveals God. This explains why McGrath asserts that, "the confession that 'Jesus is Lord,' is not only that Jesus is divine, but that God is Christ-like."[847] Although scholars indicate that this universality and uniqueness of Christ does not imply that all other conceptions of God outside Christ are wrong,[848] yet, it is to affirm that within Christian faith and theology, "it is impossible to speak of 'God' within the parameters of the Christian tradition without relating such statements to the person and to the mission of Jesus Christ."[849] This explains why Dermot Lane

---

846 Alister McGrath. *Christian Theology: An Introduction*. 1997, p.322.

847 Alister McGrath. *Christian Theology: An Introduction*. 1997, p.323.

848 Walter Kasper. "The Uniqueness and Universality of Jesus Christ". 2004, p.17; Alister McGrath. *Christian Theology: An Introduction*. 1997, p.324.

849 Alister McGrath. *Christian Theology: An Introduction*. 1997, p.324.

indicated that Jesus is the historical point of departure and the culmination for Christian faith and theology. Jesus is seen as the "definitive visitation of God to mankind in history."[850]

Secondly, when we say that *Jesus Christ is the bearer of salvation,* it means Jesus makes salvation possible. He is the source of salvation for the Christian. As McGrath put it, it means salvation is, "manifested in and through and constituted on the basis of the life, the death and the resurrection of Jesus Christ."[851] It conveys the sense of what Jesus said to Martha in John's Gospel: "I am the resurrection and the life. Whoever believes in me will live, even though he dies; and whoever lives and believes in me will never die" (John 11: 25 – 26). While the Words and the Deeds of Jesus uniquely marked him out as distinct from the history of religious figures in Judaism, Dermot Lane indicates that the events leading to the resurrection of Christ explicitly demonstrated the, "divine seal of approval, recognition, and confirmation of everything Jesus had said and done. The ambiguity that surrounded the life of Christ and the challenge of the cross was displaced."[852]

Even though the death of Jesus on the cross was an expiatory death for the sins of humankind (as foretold in the Song of the Suffering Servant (Isaiah 53: 1 – 12),[853] it was not initially understood by them in this way.[854] Notwithstanding the events of the Last Supper which point to the soteriological implications of his self-sacrifice (Mark 14: 22 – 25; Luke 22: 19 – 20), the events

---

850 Dermot Lane. *The Reality of Jesus.* 1975, p.10.

851 Alister McGrath. *Christian Theology.* 1997, p.324.

852 Dermot Lane. *The Reality of Jesus.* 1975, p.71.

853 Walter Kasper. *Jesus the Christ.* 1976, p.119.

854 As Dermot Lane indicates, "For the Disciples of Jesus, His death on the cross spelt failure. It was a supreme crises moment for them. Their hopes had been dashed and their faith shattered. A deep sense of loss, a disappointment, and an exasperation ensued. The cross was indeed both a stumbling block and a scandal" (Dermot Lane, *The Reality of Jesus.* 195, p.43).

of the resurrection and the experience of Pentecost completely clarified the Disciples' experience of Jesus as the source and the bearer of salvation. This new ascent to faith in Jesus is reflected in Peter's address to the crowds in Jerusalem (Acts 2: 14 – 36), citing texts in the Old Testament about the promised *Messiah* and demonstrating how they are fulfilled in Jesus. As Peter put it, "This *Messiah* is Jesus; and we are all witnesses that God raised him to life" (Acts 2: 32). Peter's assertion that, "there is no salvation in anyone else; for there is no other name given to humankind, all over the world by which we may be saved" (Acts 4: 12) except the name of Jesus, underscores the early Church's locus of soteriology.

The experience of the resurrected Christ and the Pentecostal event which completely transformed the faith and the understanding of the disciples led to the formation of the Christian Church. And as Walter Kasper put it, "the basis and the meaning of the Church is not an idea, a principle or a programme. It is not comprised in so many dogmas or moral injunctions ... the basis and the meaning of the Church is a person. And not a vague person, but one with a specific name: Jesus Christ".[855] In other words, to say that Jesus is the Christ, is to mean that Jesus makes salvation possible.[856] And to say that "'Jesus makes salvation possible' is not to deny that other modes of salvation may be accessible by other means; it is simply to insist that within the Christian tradition, that the Christian understanding of what salvation is, can only be realised on the basis of Jesus Christ."[857] It

---

855   Walter Kasper. *Jesus The Christ*. 1976, p.15.

856   According to Kasper, "when we say that Jesus is the Christ, we maintain that this unique, irreplaceable Jesus of Nazareth is at once and at the same time the Christ sent by God; that is, the *Messiah*, anointed of the Holy Spirit, the salvation of the world, and the eschatological fulfilment of history". (See, Walter Kasper. *Jesus The Christ*. 1976, p.15-16).

857   Alister McGrath. *Christian Theology: An Introduction*. 1997, p.324.

is as Saint Paul declared, "if Christ had not risen from the dead, our faith would have been in vain and we would have remained in our sins" (1 Corinthians 15: 17).

Thirdly, to say that *Jesus defines the shape of the redeemed life* means that not only does Jesus Christ make the redeemed life possible or determines it, but he is its source. In a carefully measured way, one could say that the "redeemed life" entails the following: (1) the salvation brought about by the death and the resurrection of Jesus Christ; (2) the inauguration of a new life by the Christ-event; and (3) the believer's commitment to living this life. Paul asserts the significance of the Christ-event when he said that Sin entered the world through the disobedience of one man (Adam), and through sin, death. But the obedience of one man (Jesus Christ), has brought the grace of righteousness, and through it, life (Romans 5: 12 – 17). So, Jesus Christ not only reconciles sinners to God, but he saves them as well. By so doing, he institutes a new way of life defined by man's new relationship with God. In his work on the "Redeemer", O'Collins also identifies three aspects of the human experience of sin or evil as the focus of the redemptive work enacted by the Christ-event: (1) sin or evil as the *alienation* from oneself, from others, from the world and from God; (2) the experience of sin as all *forms of death* such as biological death, sickness, wars, spiritual or physical bondages, and any evil force from which we long to be saved; and (3) the *loss* of meaning and the truth through ignorance, false beliefs and the feeling of absurdity.[858]

While the human experience of ruptured relationships, the annihilation of being, and the absence of meaning and truth, are evils which consistently plague the human condition to the point of depravity, they find their origins in sin. It is Christ's redemptive action which emancipates the human condition from its bondage to sin and offers it the freedom to enjoy the privilege of life

---

858 Gerald O'Collins. *Christology: A Biblical, Historical and Systematic Study of Jesus.* 2009, p.298.

now lived in God. Understood "as a personal and an intentional transgression of the divine",[859] sin always destroys good relationships, causes loss of being and relativizes meaning and truth to the point of falsehood. However, through the paschal mystery, Jesus introduces divine love into the human condition and thus, mends the personal and the intentional transgressions of the divine will be occasioned by sin. As O'Collins put it, "Divine love bestows on us our personal value and identity so that each of us can say, 'I am the person God loves.'"[860] Once a person is able to find himself or herself in the sweet and soothing pool of God's divine love, everything changes including one's understanding of oneself and others, the meaning and the purpose of life and living.

The divine love is fully expressed in the Johannine Gospel in Jesus' own words: "God so loved the world that in the fullness of time He sent His only begotten Son, so that whoever believes in Him may not perish but may have eternal life (John 3: 16); "I have come that you may have life and have it to the full" (John 10: 10); "Greater love has no one than for a man to lay down his life for his friends, and you are my friends if you do what I command you" (John 15: 13). Although there are deeper exegetical meanings of the texts above, what is sacrosanct in each text is Jesus' concrete demonstration of the full length and breadth of divine love expressed in the "paschal mystery"[861] by which humanity is redeemed. In this way, the "redeemed life" becomes a life lived outside of sin and evil. As Saint Paul would later

---

859 Gerald O'Collins. *Christology: A Biblical, Historical and Systematic Study of Jesus.* 2009, p.299.

860 See, Gerald O'Collins. *Christology: A Biblical, Historical and Systematic Study of Jesus.* 2009, p.299.

861 O'Collins indicates that Christ's death and resurrection took place during the days when the Jews celebrated their exodus from Egypt, God delivering them from slavery to freedom. This was meant to show that through Christ redemptive act, God was also saving humanity from slavery to sin (Gerald O'Collins. *Christology: A Biblical, Historical and Systematic Study of Jesus.* 2009, p.301).

understand, "Anyone who is in Christ Jesus is a new creation. The old order has gone, and the new has come" (2 Corinthians 5: 17). By this profound transformation, Paul tells the Christian community in Corinthians that by their new birth in Christ, it is no longer human desires that guide them but the "Spirit of God" who recreates them.[862] In consequence, the redeemed life is guided by the Christian response to the message of Jesus. That is, having become a Christian, the believer now sees Christ and his message as defining and providing insight into the kind of life and relationship he or she is called to develop with God and with others. While this new life is shaped by the constant efforts to avoid sin and evil, this new relationship is lived in one's love for God and for others (Mark 12: 30 – 31). In this way, living the *redeemed life* is shaped by following the message and the exemplary life of Jesus Christ (Romans 12: 1 – 2).[863]

However, within the context of dialogue as an exercise in learning, the question one might ask is: "what is the significance of the Qur'anic Jesus in Islamic faith and theology? While Qur'anic Jesus is considered second in significance to the Prophet Muhammad in Islam, what significant role does he play as a "Prophet of Allah" in Islam? In which way does the Qur'anic Jesus model the life of the Muslim in terms of the response to the *Tawhid* and to issues of human flourishing?" By focusing attention on the significance of Jesus in Islam, the purpose is to find strong foundations from which the case can be made on how Jesus Christ espouses common values between Christianity and Islam.

---

862 See, Christian Community Bible (62nd Edition). 2014, p.1709.

863 To some extent, conformity to the *way of Christ* may reflect what Thomas a Kempis sought to do in *The Imitation of Christ*. Though from a more Catholic perspective, his emphasis on the human responsibility to conform to the example set by Christ seems to apply to all Christians who seek to live the Christian life. (a Kempis, Thomas. *The Imitation of Christ*. 1940, p.12).

7.3 The Significance of Jesus in the Qur'an

There are stark doctrinal and theological differences which exist between the Christian and the Islamic understanding of the identity and the mission of Jesus, the Christ. While these differences are acknowledged, many Muslims and Muslim scholars who carefully study the evidence, do recognize that the Qur'anic Jesus is a unique "Prophet" or a "Messenger" of Allah. He is seen as Allah's closest friend (Surah 3: 45), a Spirit from Him and His Word sent to Mary (Surah 4: 171). For instance, Mahmoud Ayoub asserts that Jesus is seen as a great teacher, a great leader, and one of the greatest influences for good the world has ever known among the line of prophets.[864] According to the Qur'an, "... the *Messiah* Jesus, the 'Son of Mary', will be held in honour above all in this world and in the next" (Surah 3: 45). While these honorific titles such as the *Messiah,* the *Spirit of God, Allah's closest friend* among others, ascribed to the Qur'anic Jesus, what could be his significance in Islam? As a prophet or messenger, how does the message of the Qur'anic Jesus provide guidance in response to the obligation to acknowledge the *Tawhid*? To what extent does he model the life of the Muslim in terms of a *life lived in submission to the will of Allah*? Let us investigate this area from the perspective of some of the titles designated to Jesus in the Qur'an.

7.3.1 The Significance of Jesus as the "Messenger of Allah"

... the Messiah, Jesus, the Son of Mary, was nothing more than a <u>*Messenger of God*</u> *... and a Spirit from Him. So, believe in God and in His messengers"* (Surah 4: 171).

---

864 Mahmoud Ayoub. *A Muslim View of Christianity.* 2007, p.136.

We indicated in Chapter Five that the word "*Islam*" means submission to the will of God revealed through His prophets and messengers. The Qur'an names some of these prophets and messengers as: Abraham, Ishmael, Isaac, Jacob, Moses, Jesus and Muhammad among others (Surah 3: 84). Concerning the place of Jesus as messenger, Allah in the Qur'an said that; "We sent Jesus, the 'Son of Mary' in their footsteps to confirm the Torah that had been sent before him: we gave him the Gospels with guidance and light for those who take heed of God" (Surah 5: 46). Hence, if to be truly "*Muslim*" is to be a committed follower of the message of revelation given to the prophets and the messengers, among whom is Jesus; then the message of Jesus in the Qur'an could provide "guidance" to all who desire to submit themselves to the will of God. The Islamic understanding that Adam is the first messenger of Allah and Muhammad the final messenger is very significant to the religion; for in Adam God established the *Trust* (*amana*) for all humanity and in Muhammad, God brings to conclusion the communication of His message to humanity through prophetic guidance. As Mona Siddiqui indicated, Muhammad is viewed by Muslims as the final prophet in prophetic chronology, but his message is essentially the same as that of his predecessors. "Once distilled to its fundamentals, the message is of the oneness, the mercy and the sovereignty of God."[865] Thus, if the message of Jesus in the Qur'an contributes to giving guidance on the obligation to the *Tawhid* (see Surah 3: 51), then although secondary to the Prophet Muhammad, the Qur'anic Jesus still contributes to pointing to the right way, that straight path which leads to Allah (Surah 19: 30).

While the Qur'an indicates that the details of the message of the prophets and the messengers differ, it nevertheless mentions in several verses that the message of succeeding prophets or messengers confirm those of the past: "step by step, He has sent the Scriptures down to you with the Truth, confirming what went

---

865 Mona Siddiqui. *Christians, Muslims & Jesus*. 2013, p.12.

before: He sent down the Torah and the Gospel earlier as a guide for the people and He has sent down the distinction between right and wrong" (Surah 3: 3 – 4). It is this sense of continuity in the validity of the message of successive prophets of Allah that Mona Siddiqui indicates that, "despite the unique place of Muhammad in Muslim piety and veneration, Muhammad's prophecy in the Qur'an lies in the wider context and mission of previous prophets."[866] Their central mission was to provide guidance in the acknowledgement of the *Tawhid* – "there is only One God" (Surah 5: 73), worship him. As a "Messenger of Allah", Jesus first of all stands as that pivotal point that links Muhammad to the rest of the prophets and to the messengers of Allah who preceded him. He is that significant part of the chain of prophecy, from which the prophethood of Muhammad finds its authenticity; for after the Qur'anic Jesus comes the Prophet Muhammad. In consequence, the Qur'an does not only see Jesus as preceding the Prophet Muhammad, but it also conceives him as the precursor and the guarantor of the coming of Muhammad – thus, "Jesus, the 'Son of Mary' said, 'children of Israel, I am sent to you by God confirming the Torah that came before me and bringing good news of a messenger to follow me whose name will be Ahmad'" (Surah 61: 6).

Secondly, as a "Messenger of Allah", Jesus in the Qur'an also proclaimed the Gospel by inviting all to submit to the will of God – "I have come to confirm the truth of the Torah which preceded me, and to make some things lawful to you which used to be forbidden. I have come to you with a sign from my Lord. Be mindful of God, obey me. God is my Lord and your Lord, so serve Him. That is the straight path" (Surah 3: 50 – 51). Hence, one sees that the message and the life of Jesus provides guidance to living the *Tawhid,* and hence, models the life of the good Muslim. It is therefore not out of place that Qur'an and the Prophet Muhammad consider those who despise the message of

---

866 Mona Siddiqui. *Christians, Muslims & Jesus.* 2013, p.12.

the prophets as an act of disbelief – for he said to Muslims in the Qur'an, "We believe in God and in what has been sent down to us and to Abraham, Ishmael, Isaac, Jacob and to the tribes. We believe in what has been given to Moses, Jesus and the prophets from their Lord. We do not make a distinction between any of them. It is to Allah that we devote ourselves" (Surah 3: 84). So, to jettison the prophetic teachings of any of the prophets of Allah is considered disbelief or misguidance in Islam. It is through this honest recognition of the significance of the message of the prophets of Allah that Muslims can find guidance in the message of the Qur'anic Jesus.

7.3.2 The Significance of Jesus as the "Servant of Allah"

He [Jesus] said; 'I am a servant of God. He has granted me the Scripture; made me a prophet, made me blessed wherever I may be ... (Surah 19: 30 – 32).

As a "Messenger of Allah", the Qur'an further refers to Jesus as the "Servant of Allah" (*abd-allah*) as we can see in the above text. Other references to this title include Surah 4: 172 and Surah 43: 59. According to Parrinder, the word *abd* means a *servant* as to imply one who gives total *submission* to the will of God.[867] The submission of oneself totally to God is what is referred to as *Islam and* the person who conducts himself or herself this way is referred to as a *Muslim*. As Murata and Chittick put it, while "such a person is called a servant (*abd*) of God, servanthood is looked upon as the highest and the most praiseworthy human condition. In a sense, it is even higher than vicegerency and prophecy, since being God's messenger depends on being his servant."[868] To be

---

867 Geoffrey Parrinder. *Jesus in the Qur'an*. 1965, p.34.

868 Murata, Sachiko & Chittick, Williams, C. *The Vision of Islam*. 1994, p.124.

a servant of God is to worship, obey, show humility and be submissive to God (*ibada*).[869]

According to Parrinder, "to be an *abd* does not imply the harsh bondage that is associated with slavery, but a complete surrender or worship of God."[870] Here, the relationship is considered religious rather than social. This explains why one finds the use of *abd* in Muslim personal and family names (such as abd-Allah, Abdul-Fattah, Abdul-Hafiz, Abdul-Jamil, Abdul-Khalil). The purpose is to identify the bearer as one who desires to serve Allah with true devotion. Parrinder also indicates that the Beautiful Names of Allah are also used in construct form with the word *abd* (like *abd* al-Malik, *abd* al-Rahim).[871] While Muhammad is referred to as the "servant of God" (Surah 72: 19) in the Qur'an about five (5) times more than any of the prophets of Allah, Jesus also referred to himself as Allah's servant in the Qur'an: "I am the servant of God, He has given me the Book and made me a prophet" (Surah 19: 30). Here, Jesus is seen as a "servant of God" who truly dedicated his life in complete devotion and service to God. As the Qur'an says, "He (Jesus) is a servant we favoured and have made an example for the children of Israel" (Surah 43: 59). Commenting on this text, Muhammad Ali indicated that not only was Jesus a righteous servant of God who received divine favours, but he was also an example of virtue for the Israelites.[872]

The title of Qur'anic Jesus as the "servant of God" (*abd*) is very often associated with his humanity. This dovetails the Christian

---

869   The word "*ibada*" means servitude or service. It therefore involves the religious duty of worship or acts of devotion expected of the Muslim. These duties involve observing the five pillars of the religion' that is, the Shahada, Salat, Zakat, Ramadan and Hajj. (See, Geoffrey Parrinder. *Jesus in the Qur'an*. 1965, p.34; Murata, Sachiko & Chittick, Williams, C. *The Vision of Islam*. 1994, p.125).

870   Geoffrey Parrinder. *Jesus in the Qur'an*. 1965, p.35.

871   Geoffrey Parrinder. *Jesus in the Qur'an*. 1965, p.35.

872   Ali Muhammad. *The Holy Qur'an,* p.276 in Parrinder, Geoffrey. 1965, p.37.

understanding of the humanity of Jesus as the "Son of Man" expressed in the figure of the Suffering Servant of Yahweh (*ebed Yahweh*) as expressed in Isaiah 53: 12[873]. Thus, the identification of the Qur'anic Jesus as the "Servant of God" is for a particular purpose and significance defined by his absolute and unequivocal surrender and commitment to the will of Allah. It communicates that; "true worship", is the principal thread that links the fidelity of the Qur'anic Jesus to both the prophets who preceded him and to Muhammad who succeeded him. In this way, the life of the Qur'anic Jesus could be seen as an example of virtue to Muslims. This is because, "to be a servant of God is to do His bidding, and His bidding is set down in the Scriptures and in the words of His prophets. Hence, to be a servant of God is to submit oneself freely to God."[874] This form of submission is necessary for one to be a *good Muslim* and many Muslims aspire to live this form of holiness. If many Muslim names today are prefixed with the word *abd,* the motivation for taking on these names is derived from the desire to live out the implications of their names – being Allah's servant. The life of Jesus in this context could be an example for them.

7.3.3. The Significance of Jesus as a "Sign from God"

"… I have come to you with a <u>sign from your Lord</u>. Be mindful of God, obey me. God is your Lord and my Lord, so serve Him – that is the straight path" (Surah 3: 50 – 51)

Other references to Jesus as a *sign* in the Qur'an can be found in Surah 19: 21; Surah 21: 91; and Surah 23: 50. Murata and Chittick indicate that the word *sign* appears in the Qur'an about

---

873 Geoffrey Parrinder. *Jesus in the Qur'an.* 1965, p.35.

874 Murata, Sachiko & Chittick, Williams, C. *The Vision of Islam.* 1994, p.125.

four hundred (400) times, with three different usages.[875] These different meanings range from: (1) a *more general sense* such as anything which gives news of something else (Surah 51: 20 – 21); (2) to a *slightly specific sense* such as the miracles and the scriptures that are given to the prophets as proof of the authenticity of their message (Surah 11: 96 – 97); and (3) in a *more specific sense* in that, "the Qur'an refers to its own words as signs (*aya*), with the term being applied technically to each of the subunits of the Surah" (Surah 12: 1 – 2).[876] Hence, an *aya* (a divine sign) is a proof of God's presence in His creation, in His message to the prophets and in His *Word* (the Scriptures). Parrinder indicates that the Qur'anic Jesus was not only seen as a sign to the Israelites but also to the world as well – "We made him (Jesus) a sign to the people (Surah 19: 21) and "We appointed the 'Son of Mary' and His Mother to be a sign" (Surah 23: 50).

Consequently, if Jesus in the Qur'an is referred to as a *sign from God,* it goes without saying that by that very designation, the Qur'anic Jesus remains a veritable pointer to the existence of God and proof that the message of the *Injil* is not his own creation but from God. There is great convergence of opinion among Islamic commentators like al-Tabari, al-Zamakhshari, and al-Razi, who indicate that the designation of Jesus as a *sign from God* refers to the miracles that he performed which were meant to authenticate his claim to prophecy. As al-Tabari put it, the *sign* refers to the miracles Jesus performed to demonstrate to the people the truthfulness of his claim that he is the "Prophet of Allah". His power to raise the dead to life, to breathe life into clay birds and to heal the sick all add up as *evidence* to this claim.[877] According to Murata and

---

875 Murata, Sachiko & Chittick, Williams, C. *The Vision of Islam*. 1994, p.52.

876 For more information on the four levels of the Qur'anic meaning of the word "sign," See Murata, Sachiko & Chittick, Williams, C. *The Vision of Islam*. 1994, p.52-53.

877 See, Chapter Four on the Classical Islamic commentaries on Surah 2: 87, Surah 2: 253 and Surah 5: 110.

Chittick, the Qur'an itself is perceived by Muslims as the speech of God, as a direct divine *sign* of God to humanity; for whatever God says in the Qur'an is an expression of Himself.[878] Thus, to understand the Qur'an, is to understand what Allah is saying to humanity. Hence, every chapter, every verse, every word, and even every letter of the Qur'an is seen as God's self-expression.[879] If the same Qur'an affirms Jesus as a *sign from God* (*ayatollah*) in some of its chapters and verses, then what message is the *sign* communicating? This message centres on the *Oneness of God* and the human obligation to submit to him. It is here that the message of the Qur'anic Jesus provides guidance to living one's life as a Muslim.

In conclusion, it could be said that although construed differently as the "Son of God" (in Christianity) and the "Prophet" or the "Messenger" of Allah (in Islam), Jesus Christ continuous to tower in significance within the context of Christian-Muslim dialogical relations. As God and the "Son of God" in Christianity, Jesus is not only *the revelation of God and the bearer of salvation,* but he also *defines and shapes the redeemed life.* As the "Prophet" or the "Messenger" of Allah in Islam, the Qur'anic Jesus contributes to giving guidance to all who seek to submit themselves entirely to the will of Allah. He does not only achieve this through his message, but also through his exemplary life. Consequently, the discourses above in relation to the significance of Jesus in the two faith traditions, bring to the fore, new disclosures to the commonalities of virtue which the Qur'anic Jesus and the Jesus of the Synoptic Gospels espouse. From this perspective, they offer common grounds for Christian-Muslim collective actions in response to these virtues. As we stated earlier, the purpose for investigating the significance of Jesus in both faith traditions was to establish a foundation from which we can speak about

---

878 Murata, Sachiko & Chittick, Williams, C. *The Vision of Islam.* 1994, p.52.

879 Murata, Sachiko & Chittick, Williams, C. *The Vision of Islam.* 1994, p.52.

the values that Jesus espouses in each tradition, and how their possible commonality could be a context for Christian-Muslim dialogues of life and of common action. While Beaumont describes it as dialogue on "the ethics of Jesus",[880] Leirvik sees it as "the ethical connection"[881] of Christology to Christian-Muslim dialogue. Before we undertake this task of dialogue on the ethics of Jesus for the promotion of common values, let us first of all unpick the meanings and the parameters of the *dialogue of life* and the *dialogue of common action*.

7.4 The Dialogue of Life and the Dialogue of Common Action

In Chapter One, we defined interreligious dialogue as, "the constructive and the positive conversation between people of different religious traditions on issues of religious significance for the purpose of mutual understanding, learning and enrichment." Even though there are five different types engaging in dialogue with the other such as: (1) the informational; (2) the confessional; (3) the experiential; (4) the relational; and (5) the practical,[882] these

---

880 Mark Beaumont. *Christology in Dialogue with Muslims.* 2005, p.211.

881 Oddbjørn Leirvik. *Images of Jesus Christ in Islam.* 2010, p.246.

882 These types of dialogues include: (1) the informational type where one seeks to acquire the religious history, basic belief and understanding of the scriptures of the other; (2) the confessional deals with the other's assessments on the significance of their religious beliefs and practices in their lives; (3) the experiential involves entering into the traditions of the other and experiencing the rituals, the practices and the forms of worship as they pertain to the tradition; (4) the relational concerns the development of friendship beyond the business of dialogue; and (5) the practical dimension of dialogue deals with developing collaborative efforts in response to issues of social justice and human flourishing. (See, https://www.scarboromissions.ca/interfaith-dialogue/principles-and-guidelines-for-interfaith-dialogue (21/04/20).

only occur in contexts where the interlocutors develop the interest to dialogue. For developing the good-will dialogue is necessary for deciding on the aspect of dialogue to focus on. From Chapters Two and Three, we discovered that Christian-Muslim dialogue on Christology as an exercise in learning from and about the other, is positive, constructive and attractive because; it centres on the dialectics of sharing and learning made possible by the interlocutors' commitments to their religious beliefs and their practices. It is *positive and constructive* because it involves a form of conversation in which one opens oneself to the other, and truly accepts his points of view as valid and seeks to grasp the substantive rightness of the other's views on the subject matter of the dialogue. This placed dialogue as an exercise in learning, over and above the traditional models of interreligious dialogue.

In considering the different forms of dialogue, the "Pontifical Council for Interreligious Dialogue" listed the following: (1) *dialogue of life;* (2) *the dialogue of common action;* (3) *the dialogue of theological exchanges;* and (4) *the dialogue of religious experience.*[883] While the Council views the *dialogue of life* as the context where people strive to live in an open and in a neighbourly spirit, sharing together their joys and their sorrows, their human problems and their preoccupations; it is considered the *dialogue of common action* as that area of interreligious endeavour where the religions collaborate on issues of integral development and human flourishing. Whereas the *dialogue of theological exchanges* concerns the work of specialists who seek to deepen their understanding of their respective religious heritages and those of the other through theological exchanges in conferences and colloquia; the *dialogue of religious experience* relates to contexts where persons who are rooted in their own religious traditions, share their spiritual riches

---

883 "Pontifical Council for Interreligious Dialogue: Dialogue and Proclamation." # 42 (06/04/2015). http://www.vatican.va/roman_curia/pontifical_councils/interelg/documents/rc_pc_interelg_doc_19051991_dialogue-and-proclamatio_en.html (06/04/2015).

(for example how they pray, methods of contemplation, experiences of faith and the ways of searching for God) with others.[884]

While the preceding discourses on Christian-Muslim dialogue on Christology are more akin to the dialogue of theological exchanges on the identity and the mission of Jesus Christ, the interest was to see how these theological exchanges provided the appropriate contexts for the *dialogue of life* and the *dialogue of common action*. In other words, our explicit focus is on how the *life and the message of Jesus* the "Prophet of Allah" (in Islam) and the "Son of God" (in Christianity) provides the appropriate contexts for the discernment and the promotion of Christian-Muslim common values. Whereas the praxis of dialogue is often associated with the dialogue of common action, this form of dialogue is also intrinsically linked to the other forms of dialogue, lest it loses not only its theological foundations, but also its connections to the believer's experience of God and reality. In other words, a Christian-Muslim common response to issues of human flourishing would bear little fruit if these actions are neither sustained nor inspired by the adherents' knowledge and experience of God and the forms of life that these experiences inspire. In this way, while the dialogue of theological exchanges provides the foundation from which authentic and well-informed common actions are undertaken and sustained, the dialogues of life and common action in turn, gives life and breath to the dialogue of theological exchanges.

This interconnection between the different forms of interreligious dialogue is affirmed by the Pontifical Council for Interreligious Dialogue when it asserted that the different forms of dialogue are interconnected such that contacts in daily life and common commitment to action sometimes open up to co-operation in promoting ethical and spiritual values. This "eventually leads to the dialogue of religious experience in response

---

884 "Pontifical Council for Interreligious Dialogue: Dialogue and Proclamation." # 42 (06/04/2015).

to the great questions which the circumstances of life do not fail to arouse in the minds of people."[885] Furthermore, "exchanges at the level of religious experience can give more life to theological discussions. These in turn can enlighten experience and encourage closer contacts."[886] Thus, what follows below is a demonstration on how the identity and the mission of Jesus Christ in both the Qur'an and in the New Testament Gospels provide the context for Christian-Muslim common actions in response to God and to issues of human flourishing.

It is known that for Muslims, Muhammad and the Qur'an provide the decisive guidelines for faith and conduct, life and death of the Muslim. If these two sources are so decisive in the life of the Muslim, why should Muslims look to Jesus for inspiration to be good Muslims or to collaborate with Christians? As indicated earlier, in the Qur'an are records of the life and teachings of Jesus who is also referred to as the "Word of/from God" and purveyor of the "Gospel".[887] Thus, dialogue as an exercise in learning enables Muslims to re-examine the Qur'anic testimonies about the life and the mission of Jesus, and how these conform and contribute to the teachings of the religion. Such an approach does not diminish the decisiveness of the Qur'an and the place of Muhammad in the religion. It rather helps Muslims to gain broader understandings of the message of the prophets and the messengers of Allah, and how they contribute to providing guidance in the acknowledgement of the *Tawhid*.

Although Muslims may equally claim that the message of Jesus in the Qur'an is fundamentally for Christians and for Jews, this

---

885 "Pontifical Council for Interreligious Dialogue: Dialogue and Proclamation." # 42 (06/04/2015).

886 "Pontifical Council for Interreligious Dialogue: Dialogue and Proclamation." # 42 (06/04/2015).

887 See, Hans Küng. Christianity and World Religions: Dialogue with Islam, in Leonard Swidler. *Towards a Universal Theology of Religion*. 1988, p.209.

message as recorded in the Qur'an is equally relevant for Muslims on two counts. First of all, Muslims believe that the Qur'an is the revealed "Word of Allah "to the Prophet Muhammad through the Angel Gabriel. As the revealed "Word of Allah", the Qur'an provides divine guidance to all who seek to submit themselves to the will of Allah. As Murata and Chittick put it, "the Koran possesses an obvious power to transform those who try to approach it on its own terms. This is precisely what Islam is all about – submission to the will of God as revealed in the Koran."[888] It is in this revealed Book of Allah that one finds the message of Jesus which is equally centred on total submission to the will of Allah – "God is my Lord and your Lord, so serve Him – that is the straight path" (Surah 3: 51). That is why the message of Jesus could be relevant for Muslims since it also focuses on *submission of the believer to the will of Allah*.

Secondly, the Qur'an emphasizes that Muslims should not differentiate among the prophets of Allah since each prophet was sent by Allah with the same message about the submission of believers to the will of Allah (Surah 2: 136; Surah 2: 285; and Surah 3: 84). In Surah 2: 285, the Prophet Muhammad said; "The Messenger (Muhammad) believes in what has been sent down to him by his Lord, and as do the faithful. They all believe in God, in His Angels, His Scriptures and in His Messengers. 'We make no distinctions between any of the Messengers,' they say, 'We hear and obey. Grant us Your forgiveness, our Lord. To You we all return'". Based on this and other Qur'anic text, if Jesus is numbered as one of these messengers of Allah, then his message is useful to the *good Muslim* whose religious obligation is also, to not make distinction among the messengers of Allah, but to "hear and obey" their prophetic call to serve only Allah. And so, the questions then are: (1) what values can be learnt from the *person and message of Jesus the Christ* in the Qur'an and in the New

---

888 Murata, Sachiko & Chittick, Williams, C. *The Vision of Islam*. 1994, p. xvi.

Testament Gospels? In which ways can Christians and Muslims collaborate in promoting these values?

7.5 Dialogue for the Promotion of Common Values

The acknowledgement that Jesus Christ towers in significance in both Christianity and Islam brings us closer to the values he inspires by his way of life and his teachings as represented in the Qur'an and in the New Testament. From the discourses in Chapters Four and Five, we discovered that the overarching mission of Jesus the Christ was to accomplish the will of God through his message and his actions. Most of Jesus' actions were undertaken in response to issues of human flourishing. Both the Qur'an and the New Testament Gospels contain records of his message on the need for the submission of the believer to the will of God on the one hand (Surah 3: 51 and Mark 1: 15 or Matthew 3: 2), and on the other, his attentiveness to the needs of the less privileged, demonstrated in the feeding of the hungry, and in his healing and his deliverance miracles which brought relief to their beneficiaries (Surah 5: 112 – 114; Surah 3: 49 and Mark 6: 3 – 44; Mark 7: 31ff; Mark 8: 22ff).

For this reason, discerning common values based on Jesus' words and deeds as found in the Qur'an and in the Gospels proves to be a viable enterprise. It is on the basis of the viability of this form of dialogue that led David Kerr to propose an ethical approach to Christology as the first priority in Christian-Muslim dialogue. For Kerr, its focus on both the core of Jesus' teachings and the application of their ethical standards to issues of human life and society is good for Christian-Muslim relations.[889] Hence, the interest in this section is to see how the person and the message of Jesus Christ elicits common values for Christian-Muslim

---

889 David Kerr. "Christology in Muslim-Christian Dialogue." 1993, p.215.

dialogue of the life and the dialogue of common action. By *dialogue of life* we mean the interest of Christians and Muslims to live in an open and friendly atmosphere which supports the sharing of their joys and sorrows, their human problems and their preoccupations. By *dialogue of common action,* we refer to the collective endeavour where Christians and Muslims work together in response to issues of social justice and integral human development.

7.5.1 The Value of Prayer and Submission to God

As shown in Chapter Five, *Islam* is a religion of belief which essentially centres on the *submission of the believer to the will of God.* Here, the oneness of God remains the key focus in all Muslim religiosity. To take the *Oneness of God* (the *Tawhid*) out of the doctrinal equation of the religion is to totally annihilate *Islam.* In the *Shahada* (which means to testify or to bear witness) therefore, one finds the fundamental act by which all Islamic activities depend. In the *Shahada* the believer affirms that, "there is no god but one God (*la ilaha illa'llah*) and that Muhammad is God's messenger (*Muhammadun rasul Allah*)." Here, Murata and Chittick point out that the primary importance of the *Shahada* lies in the fact that reciting it, "is the ritual whereby one submits oneself to God, that is, becomes a Muslim."[890] Although, theoretically one is obliged to recite the *Shahada* once in one's lifetime, practically the *Shahada* is incorporated into the daily required prayers (*Salat*) such that observing these prayers defines the daily life of the *Muslim.* Thus, pronouncing the *Shahada* maybe all that is obligatory for one's *Islam* to be acceptable to God,[891] but performing the *Salat* (that is, the ritual prayers) is also perceived as very pivotal to the religious life of the believer.

---

890 Murata, S. & Chittick, W.C. *The Vision of Islam.* 1994, p.11.
891 Murata, S. & Chittick, W.C. *The Vision of Islam.* 1994, p.11.

Murata and Chittick accentuated this significance of the *Salat* in the life of the Muslim when they said that, "the Koran commands performance of the *Salat* more than it commands any other activity and the prophetic sayings suggest that God loves the *Salat* more than every other human act."[892] *Salat* here means "to pray or bless". As a *pillar of Islam, Salat* concerns the five daily ritual prayers which every good Muslim must perform every day. Because of the central place *Salat* occupies in Islam, Murata and Chittick indicate that "the rhythm of life in a traditional Islamic society is largely determined by the five daily prayers".[893] According to the Islamic time-reckoning, the first prayer begins at Sunset (in the evening) and the last ends in the afternoon. This means that the whole day in the Muslim's life is a constant submission to the will of Allah through prayer. Not only does the Muslim submit himself or herself to the will of God through the daily prayers, but these prayers also set the Muslim on the path to holiness, in that, it purifies him or her from evil (Surah 11: 114); shields him or her against evil (Surah 29: 45); enriches the soul (Surah 13: 28), and so, must be performed at the required time (Surah 2: 238). All the prophets are said to have performed the *Salat* (Surah 21: 71 – 73).

Having seen the significant place prayer occupies in the life of the Muslim, what can be learnt from the Qur'anic Jesus in respect of prayer and submission to the will of God? Prayer and submission to the will of God was central to the life of Jesus in the Qur'an. He says in the Qur'an; "Be mindful of God and obey me. God is my Lord and your Lord, so worship Him – that is the straight path" (Surah 3: 50 – 51 and Surah 19: 36). In these texts, Jesus affirms the central place God occupies in human life and the human obligation to submit to him. He demonstrates this by his own submission to the will of God which he considered as "the straight path" (Surah 19: 36). Hence, in the Qur'anic

---

892 Murata, S. & Chittick, W.C. *The Vision of Islam.* 1994, p.11.

893 Murata, S. & Chittick, W.C. *The Vision of Islam.* 1994, p.15.

Jesus, we find one who surrendered himself to God and invited others to do likewise. He achieved this through his commitment to his prophetic role, his life of prayer and works of charity. This is confirmed in the Qur'an when he said, "I am a servant of God. He has granted me the Scriptures and made me a prophet … He commanded me to pray, and to give alms as long as I live" (Surah 19: 30 − 31).

Jesus is therefore presented in the Qur'an as one who perfectly fulfils his role as the "Prophet" or the "Messenger" of Allah, especially, in his submission to God and in his provision of guidance for those who also seek to submit themselves to the will of God. Since the ultimate goal of the religion of Islam is to lead the whole of mankind to submit themselves to the will of the one God *(Muslims)* through acts of prayer and charity, Jesus therefore functions as an example par excellence to all who wish to be good *Muslims*. As Ayoub put it, "indeed the Christ of Muslim piety has continued to be a living personality, humble and pious, forever thundering against the wrongs of society and full of wisdom and the Holy Spirit."[894] The Jesus of the Qur'an is apparently not only a holy "Prophet" and a "Messenger" of Allah, but he is also a model and an archetype of the Muslim's life. As the Qur'an itself affirms; "the *Messiah*, Jesus, the 'Son of Mary' will be held in honour in this world and the next" (Surah 3: 45).

Within Christianity, Jesus Christ is recognised as God or the "Son of God" and the "Saviour of the World". For this reason, he instructs Christians in respect of the appropriate way to worship and love God and to love one's neighbour. At the start of his public ministry, Jesus' central message was "repent, for the Kingdom of God is close at hand" (Mark 1: 15). Apart from the proclamation of the Kingdom of God where one finds that intimate connection between Jesus and God the Father, the Gospels also present a picture of Jesus Christ who is very committed to prayer and underscores its relevance to the life of the disciples.

---

894 Irfan Omar. (editor). *A Muslim View of Christianity.* 2007, p.134.

For instance, in the prologue of Mark's Gospel one sees the intimate connection between Jesus Christ, the Holy Spirit, and God the Father (Mark 1: 9 – 11). In this text, the voice from heaven which says, "this is my son, the beloved, in whom I am well pleased" (Mark 1: 11) demonstrates how committed Jesus was to the divine plan as conceived by the Godhead.

After the baptism, Jesus goes to the desert and spends forty (40) days and forty (40) nights alone with God in fasting and in prayer (Mark 1: 12 – 13). This will prepare him for his victorious encounter with Satan in the wilderness. After overcoming the devil's temptations at the beginning of his ministry, Jesus always found time in solitary places to pray (Mark 1: 35; Luke 5: 16). Before choosing the twelve apostles, Jesus went to the mountains to pray about this decision (Mark 3: 13 and Luke 6: 12 – 16). Although there are many other occasions when Jesus Christ is found praying to God the Father (John 17: 1 – 24), one also realises that in his agony in the garden of Gethsemane, before the arrest and the crucifixion, Jesus prayed intensely to God the Father for the grace to accomplish the Father's mission (Luke 23: 46). Hence, one sees in the Gospel that Jesus always found time to pray before making every significant decision, or in undertaking every significant task in his mission to accomplish the Father's will. By so doing, not only did he demonstrate to his disciples the significance of prayer – "watch and pray so that you do not fall into temptation" (Matthew 26: 41), but he also taught his disciples how to pray (Luke 11: 1 – 4).

Through his constant recourse to prayer at every significant stage of his ministry, and by teaching and encouraging the disciples to pray, Jesus Christ demonstrates the significance of prayer in the Christian life. From this context, Jesus demonstrates that, not only is daily prayer the best medium of communication between the Christian and God, but it also reaps benefits for the Christian in many ways: first of all, it is a means of placing the needs and the concerns of the Christian before God (supplication and intercession) who has the power to grant them; secondly, prayer is a means of showing gratitude to God for all the graces and the blessings received (thanksgiving); thirdly, prayer provides the platform for living a virtuous life through the confession of one's sins and seeking God's grace to live a good Christian life; fourthly, the daily prayer of the Christian is a way of acknowledging the importance of God in his or her life. As a result, one can say that prayer is an essential component of the life of the Christian. Hence, Saint Paul would tell the Thessalonians to "pray at all times" (1 Thessalonians 5: 17).

From the above discussions on the importance of prayer in Islam and in Christianity *vis-a-vis* how Jesus models it within the two faith traditions, one could say that prayer is a keystone in the life of the Muslim and the Christian. Its significance for the Christian and for the Muslim cannot be discounted. For instance, we discovered that in Islam, while *submission to Allah* is the essence of religion, prayer (the *Salat*) is one of the concrete means of demonstrating this *submission to God*. Not only does prayer purify the soul of the Muslim, it also protects him or her from evil and serves as the channel through which Allah blesses those who are faithful to him. In Christianity, prayer is not just the key that unlocks the blessings of God to the believer, but it also demonstrates the believer's acknowledgement of God as his or her source of being and provident provider. Prayer connects the believer to the ultimate source of his or her being. This explains why Saint Paul said, "it is in him we live and move and have our being" (Acts 17: 28). Jesus Christ as a Prophet in Islam and as the "Son of God" in Christianity, demonstrates in the Qur'an and in the Gospels the significance of prayer and the submission of the believer to the will of God. In both traditions, Jesus achieves this through the message he proclaimed (Surah 19: 36 and Mark 1: 15), and through his exemplary life (Surah 19: 31 and Mark 3: 13). Having lived a life worthy of emulation as a "Prophet of Allah" and as the "Son of God", Jesus Christ, in both Islam and in Christianity, demonstrates that belief in God and fidelity to him through prayer, brings the best out of Muslims and Christians. Through the grace of God, Christians and Muslims find the appropriate insights and strength to work in ways that contribute to transforming human life and the world in better ways.

However, within our contemporary context, there is the strong force of *secularism*[895] which seeks to undermine the place of God and *the relevance of prayer* in contemporary societies. While in the past, *secularism* emerged through the demand for freedom from any imposition of religious beliefs and practices on those who do not necessarily share them, it has today become an aggressive contender against everything religious.[896] Today, what secularism seeks to achieve is a Godless society – an interest that has been carefully and systematically calibrated in today's modern society, particularly those in Western countries like Europe and America. In his considerations of C.G. Brown's book on *The Death of Christian Britain,* Hakim Murad emphasized that the fact that he finds himself tragically part of this Godless society hurts him deeply, because "what is dying is a set of monotheistic convictions and a life of prayer and human giving."[897] For Murad, *secularism* is the reason for the death of Christianity in Europe. Despite the fact that Christianity and Islam are explicitly different in respect of their histories, their founders and religious doctrines and practices, Murad asserts that a Christian Europe would be a better place for Islam than a secular Europe. This is because a Christian Europe offers the space for religious beliefs while a

---

895 While we admit that, "secularism" is not completely the same as "atheism" on the basis that, a secularist is not necessarily an atheist, we can say that they both serve to limit or eradicate the possibility of religious relevance in the shaping of society; for while one seeks freedom from religion, the other disbelieves and seeks its annihilation. Thus, the common ideal to both positions is the call for a society where there is no trace of God.

896 In Britain for instance, the National Secular Society (NSS) has fought to scrap off Council prayers before and after meetings, the wearing of religious articles in hospitals, the teaching of Religious Education (RE) in schools and so forth [see, http://www.secularism.org.uk/ (03/06/2013)].

897 Abdal Hakim Murad. "Human Dignity and Mutual Respect", in *A Common Word: Texts and Reflections.* 2011, p.66.

secular Europe seeks to erase the trace of God in it.[898] Secularism does not entertain believe in God and submission to him. Yet, believe in God and submission to His will is the frame of reference from which honest and faithful Christians and Muslims relate to the world and contribute to it. For Murad therefore, secularism poses a mutual challenge to Christianity and Islam and these two communities need to work together to confront what he calls "the new barbarians."[899]

Douglas Pratt equally noted that secularism with its sequel constitutes a mutual challenge to Christianity and to Islam today.[900] This challenge lies in how first of all, it systematically denies Christians, Muslims and other religious communities the opportunity to openly express their faith and contribute to public discourse on the meaning of life and our place in it. Consider for instance, how the National Secular Society (NSS – Britain) recently fought to scrap Council Prayers before and after meetings and to abolish the wearing of religious articles in public space. Examples in this area are not hard to find. For instance, quite recently, a British Airways employee (Nadia Eweida) suffered severe discrimination over her Christian beliefs regarding the crucifix which she wore at work. It took seven years for the European Court of Justice to lift her suspension. Other victims of similar discrimination include: Shirley Chaplin (a nurse) whose employers stopped her wearing a cross at work; Gary McFarlane (a marriage counsellor) who was forced to give sex therapy to gay people against his religious beliefs; Lillian Ladele (a registrar) who was disciplined for refusing to conduct same-sex marriages.[901]

---

898 Abdal Hakim Murad. "Human Dignity and Mutual Respect", in *A Common Word: Texts and Reflections*. 2011, p.66.

899 Abdal Hakim Murad. "Human Dignity and Mutual Respect", in *A Common Word: Texts and Reflections*. 2011, p.66.

900 Douglas Pratt. *The Challenge of Islam*. 2005, p.207.

901 BBC NEWS online: https://www.bbc.co.uk/news/uk-21025332 (21/04/20).

Following their religious beliefs, the Ashers' Baking Company in County Antrim in Northern Ireland was taken to court for refusing to bake a cake with the slogan, *support gay marriages* (July 2014).[902] It took repeated court appeals for the company to win the case in October 2018. In June 2017, Tim Farron (the leader of the Liberal `Democrats Party in Britain) was forced to resign because of the aggressive way he was attacked as a result of expressing his Christian views about marriage.[903]

The examples above underscore the powerful influence of a secular society and its ability to limit the contribution of religion to the public discourse. In furtherance to this secularist agenda, the British National Secularist Society has strenuously campaigned against the teaching of Religious Education (RE) in schools.[904] Here, religions like Christianity and Islam are being denied the opportunity to participate in public discourse and thereby contribute to the transformation of society. Secularism poses a challenge to the existence of Christianity and Islam. Secularism is brainwashing the minds of many young and older people in society through the use of the media. It has created the loss of faith in the goodness of the religions through negative reportage – by highlighting and accentuating certain pitfalls in religious practices and under reporting the transformation of society enacted and sustained by the religious traditions.

It is often said that not only do the religions inculcate and promote *social virtues* and *solidarity* in society, but they also promote

---

902 BBC NEWS online: https://www.bbc.co.uk/news/uk-northern-ireland-32065233 (22/04/20).

903 Tim Farron felt that to remain faithful to Christ was incompatible with his position as a political leader. He added; "The consequence of the focus on my faith is that I have found myself torn between living as a faithful Christian and serving as a political leader". (See, The Guardian Online: https://www.theguardian.com/politics/2017/jun/14/tim-farron-quits-as-lib-dem-leader) (21/04/20).

904 See, The National Secularists Society – Britain: http://www.secularism.org.uk/ (03/06/2013).

socialization and social control, welfare and social cohesion. So, religions are invaluably part of the life of man and contribute significantly in bringing about transformation to society through the virtues and the values that they inculcate in the lives of their adherents. To meet the challenge of secularism against the belief in God will demand Christian-Muslim mutual efforts and collaboration. Apart from being good citizens and demonstrating the goodness and the virtue that is inherent in their respective religious traditions, today there is need for Christian-Muslim collective action in response to certain needs in society. Taking cue from the fidelity to God and the prayer life of Jesus, a Christian-Muslim interfaith prayer action in response to issues of peace in a world completely riddled by war and conflicts might be a viable enterprise. While we shall develop this area of Christian-Muslim *interreligious prayers* in the succeeding section on the value of "peace and peaceful co-existence", it is apposite to note here that "Christian-Muslim interreligious prayers for peace" implies the setting aside a period of time to be together to pray for the peace of their society and for the world. It is about being together to pray for world peace.

In this way, when the two religions are seen to be visibly working together in practical contributions to issues of public concern (praying together for peace between themselves and for their society and world peace), they would be reasserting their significance in society, thereby counteracting the secularist propaganda about the irrelevance of God in human society. One might intuit that such a process could be done without recourse to Jesus Christ, but when the life and the mission of Jesus Christ (as one finds in the Qur'an and in the Gospels) becomes the inspiration for undertaking this kind of inter-faith action, it not only reduces the tensions between the two communities as a result of their Christological perspectival differentials, but it also introduce a sense of respect and trust in the other who shares the same prayer intentions with oneself, with both presenting this intention to God on behalf of society and the world. Such a Christian-Muslim assent to "being together to pray for peace" could be the greatest source of inter-faith witnessing to the goodness of these religions.

7.5.2 The Value of Peace and Peaceful Co-existence

The word "peace" comes from the Latin word "*Pax*" which means "freedom from civil disturbance." Used differently, the word "peace" could be a form of personal greeting as in the Hebrew *Shalom* or the Arabic *Salaam*. In these usages, "peace" reinforces the sense of establishing harmony in relationships between those who share it. Thus today, the concept "peace" is used variously to suggest a sense of harmony in personal relationships, the absence of conflict or violence, a state of tranquillity, a formal pact to end war between two enemy factions and so forth. In all its interpersonal, institutional or international usages, what the concept defines is a state of tranquillity and harmony that is informed by a mutual trust and confidence in the other.

Whereas the above understanding of "peace" involves the absence of war, conflict, and violence, it is also grounded on the goodwill to promote tranquillity, cordiality and amity. In this way, if "co-existence" means "the willingness to live together despite fundamental differences", then "peaceful co-existence" denotes the willingness to live together in harmony, tranquillity, cordiality and amity despite the differences that may exist between oneself and another. Christianity and Islam are two different religions of belief. How is this understanding of "peace" upheld in the two traditions? How does Jesus Christ espouse this sense of peace in the Qur'an and in the New Testament Gospels? And how does he provide the contexts for Christian-Muslim collaborations for the promotion of peace and peaceful co-existence? These are the questions which will engage the discourse in this section.

Islam is a religion of "peace". This is partly because the word *Islam* which is derived from the Arabic *Salama* (Š-L-M) means "to be safe, secure or at peace." Although religiously, "Islam" is taken to mean "submission to the will of Allah",[905] when one

---

905 See, Murata and Chittick. *The Vision of Islam*. 1994, p.3.

considers its Arabic roots, it also connotes the sense of "purity or wholeness", "security" and "peacefulness". However, it appears that the concepts "submission" and "peace" are more popular in the use of the term than other alternative meanings. Their popularity lies in the fact that as a religion, the word "Islam" refers to the submission of the believer to the will of Allah. However, within the domain of interpersonal relationships, "Islam" as *Salama* finds its popularity in the Muslim greetings *al-Salamu 'alaykum* (Peace be upon you). Here, one could interpret this form of greetings as a reminder to the *Muslim* of his or her fundamental duty as an agent of peace. But what does "peace" imply here?

According to Admet Akgunduz,[906] in Islam, the concept "peace" connotes three senses: (1) the *eschatological;* (2) the *psychological;* (3) and the *universal.* In the *eschatological sense,* "peace" refers to the ultimate goal of human life, almost synonymous with salvation (Surah 10: 25 − 27). In the *psychological* sense, "peace" means the "tranquillity and peace of mind, an inner confidence born of faith that enables the religious believer to face adversity without anxiety or despair."[907] From the *universal sense*, it reflects the widespread conviction that a time will come when all sorts of evil and destruction in the world will give way to prosperity and human flourishing.[908] These three distinctions of peace can only be realized, as it were, by the utter submission of oneself to the will of God. It is in submitting oneself to the will of God that the individual finds happiness and peace.[909]

---

906 Admet Akgunduz is a professor of Islamic studies in Rotterdam, Holland. He is currently the rector of the Islamic University of Rotterdam.

907 Admet Akgunduz. "Norms and Values in Islam." http://islam.uga.edu/norms_values.html (09/05/2013).

908 Admet Akgunduz. "Norms and Values in Islam." http://islam.uga.edu/norms_values.html (09/05/2015).

909 See, Murata, Sachiko & Chittick, Williams, C. 1994, p.3.

Even though some people conceive that the Qur'an perceives the ideal society to be *Dar as-Salam* (the House of peace), many Muslims nonetheless understand that the "house of peace" is the abode of all who submit themselves to the will of Allah.[910]

If in Islam "ideal peace" consists in submitting oneself to the will of Allah, then Jesus was a man of peace par excellence. In the Qur'an one sees that Jesus' preoccupation was both on his *submission to the will of God* and his proclamation on the human need to *submit to God* (Surah 19: 36 and Surah 3: 50 − 51). In other words, as a "Prophet of Allah", he provided guidance on the need to submit oneself to God as a means of attaining peace.[911] Thus, Jesus is presented by the Qur'an as the epitome of *peacefulness* because it affirms that his entire life was marked by peace: "peace was on me the day I was born and will be on me the day I will die and the day I am raised to life again" (Surah 19: 33). In this way, although the miracles that the Qur'anic Jesus performed were meant as signs which authenticated his prophetic and emissarial calling, these miracles nonetheless contributed to re-establishing harmony and peace in the lives of their beneficiaries (Surah 3: 49 and Surah 19: 31). In the Qur'anic Jesus, one finds an "icon of peace" and a promoter of it.

From a particularly Christian perspective, "peace" is an essential hallmark of Christian virtue. To be a "Christian" means to be a follower of Jesus Christ (who is the "Son of God" and the "Saviour of the World"). In the New Testament Gospels, Jesus Christ demonstrates in both word and deed, his desire to bring peace to the world and to the hearts of all who are troubled. He said: "Come to me all you who labour and are overburdened,

---

910 "God invites everyone to the Home of Peace, and guides whoever he wills to the straight path" (Surah 10: 25).

911 Jesus says in the Qur'an: "I have come to you with a sign from your Lord. Be mindful of God, obey me: God is my Lord and your Lord, so obey him − that is a straight path" (Surah 3: 50 − 51).

and I will give you rest. Shoulder my yoke and learn from me; for I am gentle and humble of heart; and you will find rest" (Matthew 11: 28). While labour and the overburden-ness of human life disturbs its tranquillity and its harmony, Jesus offers in replacement the "restfulness" of the human heart which is synonymous to peace. Referred to as the "Prince of Peace" (Isaiah 9: 6), Jesus Christ was preoccupied with proclaiming and establishing the Kingdom of God through repentance (Matthew 4: 12 – 17). The purpose was to establish a state of relationships wherein persons, societies and nations can live together in harmony and in tranquillity. For Saint Paul says, "He himself is our peace" (Ephesians 2:14).

Consequently, from the accounts of the Gospels, one sees many instances in which Jesus Christ overwhelmingly demonstrates his love for peace, his promotion of peace and the giver of it. He says in John's Gospel: "peace I bequeath to you, my own peace I give you, a peace the world cannot give, this is my gift to you" (John 14: 28). As indicated earlier, Jesus' message of repentance and forgiveness in the Gospels was meant to re-establish the peace destroyed by sin and evil. Through his deeds, Jesus healed the sick, set captives free, raised the dead and stood against the oppressive structures of society. The purpose of these acts of kindness and miracles was to re-establish the harmony, the cordiality and the tranquillity destroyed by sin and death. After his resurrection from the dead his first gift to the disciples was peace: "peace be with you," he said (John 20: 19 – 21). For this reason, Christianity conceives living peacefully and promoting peace in society as essentially part of its evangelizing mission. As Pope John Paul II put it in his address at the Assisi World Day of Prayer for peace; "in Jesus Christ, as Saviour of all, true peace is to be found, 'peace to those who are far off and peace to those who are near.' His birth was greeted by the angels' song: 'Glory to God in the highest and peace among men with whom he is pleased.' He preached love among all, even among foes, proclaimed blessed those who work for peace and through his death and his resurrection he brought about reconciliation between heaven and earth."[912]

In response to the call to promote peace in the world, the Roman Catholic Church continues to preach the message of peace in the manner laid out in the Gospels. Through the Church's interpretations of the *signs of the times,* she continues to provide the road map to world peace and peaceful co-existence by her way of life and her vision for world peace. One finds some of these peace proposals in papal encyclicals such as *Pacem in Terris* (Peace on Earth – 1963) and *Populorum Progressio* (The Development of Peoples – 1967)[913] among others. In *Pacem in Terris,* Pope Saint John XXIII outlined the blueprint of peace for the world. According to him, if we want peace for the world, then there is a moral order which we must all strive to pursue.[914] This moral order which prevails in society is to be: "grounded as it is on truth, it must function according to the norms of justice, it should be inspired and perfected by mutual love and finally it should be brought to an ever more refined and human balance in freedom."[915] This moral order: "whose principles are universal, absolute and unchangeable has its ultimate source in

---

912 Pope John Paul II: "Address to the Representatives of the Christian Churches and to the Ecclesial Communities and to the World Religions" (October 27, 1986). http://w2.vatican.va/content/john-paul-ii/en/speeches/1986/october/documents/hf_jp-ii_spe_19861027_prayer-peace-assisi-final.html (14/04/2015).

913 See, Pope Paul VI. *Populorum Progressio* #1). Essentially, the emphasis of this encyclical is that: building peace means pursuing development. Pursuing development means pursuing justice for all and pursuing justice for all means following a moral order.

914 "Peace on Earth – which man throughout the ages has so longed for and sought after – can never be established, never guaranteed, except by the diligent observance of the divinely established order." (See John XXIII. *Pacem in Terris: Encyclical on Establishing Universal in Truth, Justice and Liberty* (1963). 2002, p.3).

915 Pope Saint John XXIII. *Pacem in Terris* (Peace on Earth, 1963) # 37.

the one true God, who is personal and transcends human nature."[916] If human society is to find a lasting peace, it would need to order its ways according to the ways of God who has made himself known in Jesus Christ. So, as followers of Christ, Christians are called both to live and to promote peace according to the example of Jesus Christ.

From the above discourses on "peace", it is obvious that Islam and Christianity are *religions of peace*. although each tradition understands "the gift of peace" as essentially the part of faith practice, the history of conflicts between the two traditions has emasculated their default positions as religions of peace. According to Pratt, "all too often it seems that religions, especially – but not only – Christianity and Islam, are caught in an apparent hypocrisy. For even as religions actively promote peace, they nevertheless can be found endorsing and blessing the battle-tanks of military might."[917] Indeed, there are records of significant sizes, the conflicts and the wars sanctioned by Muslims and Christians, sometimes directly or indirectly.[918] There are instances aplenty where Muslims and Christians engage in very destructive conflicts and violence against each other, all in the name of God. Consider in recent times, the oppression of Christians in places like Pakistan and the burning of Christian Churches in places like Egypt and Iraq. In Sub-Saharan Africa for instance, one needs only to look at Sudan where Arab Muslims in the North slaughtered more than one million black Christians from the South.[919]

The statistics in Nigeria are even more alarming. More recently, a renewed wave of conflicts between Christians and Muslims in central Nigeria has claimed the lives of thousands of people. For instance, Angela Kariuki reports that, from January 2010 to 2015, more than ten thousand people lost their lives through

916 Pope Saint John XXIII. *Pacem in Terris* (Peace on Earth, 1963), # 38.
917 Douglas Pratt. *The Challenge of Islam*. 2005, p.189.
918 Douglas Pratt. *The Challenge of Islam*. 2005, p.101-116.
919 John Pontifex (editor). *Roll Back the Stone of Fear*. 2005, p.56-58.

Christian–Muslim conflicts in Nigeria.[920] Apart from the many lives that have been lost in Jos, Abuja, and Bauchi, the atrocities committed by Boko Haram are still a big scar in the memories of many. Their multiple attacks on Christians in the North have led to counter attacks of Muslims in the South. It is reported that in July 2013, an Islamic classroom in which 5 to 8-year-olds were studying Arabic and the Qur'an in Southern Nigeria was bombed. Seven pupils were injured. What about the massacre of the 147 Christian students in the Kenyan University College (Garissa) by al-Shabaab militants on April 6th, 2015? While the suggestion that most of these conflicts have political motivation is contestable, it is nonetheless Christians and Muslims who are the agents of these conflicts and wars.

The active involvement of Christians and Muslims in wars against each other and against the human family, raises questions on the essence of the two religions and their adherents' commitments to the teachings and to the practices of their belief-systems. As Pratt put it, "the world looks on aghast at the terror and the havoc that are once again wrought in the name of religion or a religious ideology".[921] Christianity and Islam are supposed to be religions of peace. Hence, conflicts orchestrated and executed by members of the two faith traditions serve as colossal dents (counter-witnesses) to the image of the two faith traditions. Thus, in following the secularist agenda, some scholars believe that, "if there is ever to be a lasting peaceful cohabitation of human communities, not to mention the prospects of a just and ecologically sustainable future for all, then religion is going to have to back off."[922] Yet, we know that Christianity and Islam constitute more than half of the world's population. So, if there

---

920 Angela Kariuki. "Violence begets Violence: Nigeria's Deadly Religious History. http://www.consultancyafrica.com/index.php?option=com_content&view=article&id=367&Itemid=218 (14/04/2015).

921 Douglas Pratt. *The Challenge of Islam*. 2005, p.189.

922 Douglas Pratt. *The Challenge of Islam*. 2005, p.189.

is going to be significant progress made towards world peace, these two religions will need to be active players in these efforts. As Küng observed; there can be, "no world peace without peace among the religions, no peace among the religions without dialogue between the religions, and no dialogue between the religions without accurate knowledge of one another."[923] According to Lejla Demiri too, "Without peace and justice between these two faith communities, there can be no meaningful peace in the world. The future of the world depends on peace between Christians and Muslims."[924]

Consequently, there is growing need to embark on dialogical projects that contribute to engaging the two faith communities in ways that promote peace and peaceful co-existence between them and others. While this goal could be addressed in many and diverse ways through academic scholarships and interfaith actions, we propose the person and the mission of Jesus Christ as the context for these peace initiatives. From the image of the Qur'anic Jesus and that of Jesus Christ in the New Testament Gospels, we find common elements of the espousal of peace and the promotion of it. Not only did Jesus say in the Qur'an that, "peace was on me the day I was born, and will be on me the day I will die, and the day I am raised to life again" (Surah 19: 33); in the New Testament Gospels, He gave peace to the those who were bereft of it. To the Apostles who locked themselves in the upper room for fear of the Jews, he said to them; "peace be with you" (John 20: 19). Hence, what we find common between the Qur'anic Jesus and the Jesus of the New Testament is his emphasis on the significance of peace, and the need to promote it in all aspects of human life. In today's world where there is growing injustice, ethnic and religious conflicts, civil wars, terrorism, national and

923 Leonard, Swidler (editor). *Towards a Universal Theology of Religion.* 1988, p.194.
924 Lejla Demiri (Editor). *A Common Word: Texts and Reflections.* 2011, p. xix.

international conflicts within which Christians and Muslims are sometimes the protagonists, the message and the person of Jesus becomes a wakeup call to adherents of these two religions. It invites them to rethink their essence and their relevance as *religions of peace* and to demonstrate this sense of peace between themselves and in the world. How then can the life and the message of Jesus Christ provide a context for Christian–Muslim collaborations in response to the need for peace and a peaceful co-existence?

In response, we propose *interreligious prayers for peace* as a common context for Christian–Muslim action for world peace. By "interreligious prayer", we mean Christians and Muslims coming together to pray for the needs of the human society and for world peace. It takes on the theme of the 1986 World Day of Prayer in Assisi: "Being Together to Pray". As Pope John Paul II indicated, "being together to pray does not mean praying in one voice, but being present to pray with others."[925] In other words, unlike George Dardess and Krier Mich who worked out the possibility of Christian–Muslim common prayers (praying in one voice) through the Encounter between Saint Francis and the Sultan of Egypt; where the authors eliminated the significance of Jesus Christ in the process,[926] we emphasize that Christian–Muslim prayers cannot be said in one voice.[927] Praying in one voice – the kind proposed by Dardess and Krier Mich – is rather problematic. As Robert Afayori put it, such prayers demand a unitary content, a common form and language which is impossible considering the

---

925 See, Jacque Dupuis. *Christianity and the Other Religions.* 2001, p.236.

926 According to Dardess, G. & Krier Mich, M., to pray in one voice, "all Muslims and Christians have to do is address them to the One God the creator, omitting all references to Jesus". (See, Dardess, George & Krier Mich, Marvin. *In the Spirit of St. Francis and the Sultan.* 2011, p.47, p.48-64).

927 See, Robert Afayori. Book Review: "George Dardess and Marvin L. Krier Mich. In the Spirit of St. Francis & the Sultan: Catholics and Muslims Working Together for the Common Good. 2012, p.207.

fact that there are stark differences between Christian and Muslim ways of praying. Whereas Christian prayers (for instance Roman Catholic) are very often made through Jesus Christ as the "Son of God", Muslims do not believe in the divinity of Jesus Christ. Secondly, Arabic is the medium of prayer in Islam. So, what becomes of those who do not understand Arabic, and do not know the mode and the format of the other's prayers?[928]

Consequently, in talking about Christian-Muslim interreligious prayers, we mean the engagement of Christians and Muslims following their respective liturgical prayers, but with a common prayer intention: that is praying for peace in their communities, peace between the two faith communities and for world peace. Here, Christians and Muslims can set aside a day, a place and a time for praying for these intentions of peace. While sharing the same space and prayer intention, they can either pray differently at their organized comfort zones or pray in turns. As Pope John Paul II indicated, being together to pray in this manner "takes on a particularly deep and eloquent meaning, insofar as, all will be there, one next to the other to implore God for the gift that all of humankind needs most today in order to survive, peace."[929] Whereas this kind of interreligious prayer could be done without Muslims having to find inspiration in the life and the mission of Jesus Christ; it however offers Christians and Muslims the rare opportunity to engage together more fruitfully, especially on the subject of Christology, which has often been a hotbed for confrontations and conflicts.[930]

Fostering these forms of Christian-Muslim inter-faith actions could contribute to establishing peaceful co-existence between

---

928 See, Robert Afayori. Book Review: "George Dardess and Marvin L. Krier Mich. *In the Spirit of St. Francis & the Sultan: Catholics and Muslims Working Together for the Common Good.* 2012, p.208.

929 Jacque Dupuis. *Christianity and the Religions.* 2001, p.236.

930 See, Oddbjorn Leirvik. *The Image of Jesus Christ in Islam.* 2010, p.1; Douglas Pratt. *The Challenge of Islam.* 2005.

them and in the wider society, and hence, contribute to transforming the world. As Pope John Paul II put it, by being together to pray, we "manifest our respect for the prayers of the others and the stance of the others towards the divine. At the same time, we offer them the humble and sincere testimony of our faith."[931] Praying together for peace also contributes to the nurturing of trust and respect between Christians and Muslims. Their long history of conflicts on the basis of their different perspectives on Christology has contributed to fermenting so much mistrust and misapprehensions between the two faith communities.[932] For Christian-Muslim engagement to proceed on this productive course is in itself significant for their living relationships. Additionally, when Christians and Muslims are seen to share a common space with common prayer intentions for peace in the world, it contributes to erasing the accusations levelled against the very essence of their existence as religions of peace.

7.5.3 The Value of Solidarity with the Poor and the Marginalized

The concept *solidarity* generally refers to ties which bind people together whether as a group, as a community or as a society. The bases for these social ties vary from kinship to shared values. Anselm Min identifies the idea of "human solidarity" as something that is "inherent and intrinsic to human existence … It is not something we have to artificially invent … [it] is something already rooted deep in the sociality of human nature which alone makes it something human and profound."[933] Human solidarity has its basis in human nature, and human nature finds its concrete

---

931 Dupuis, Jacques. *Christianity and the Religions*. 2001, p.236.

932 See, Douglas Pratt. *The Challenge of Islam*. 2005, p.191.

933 Anselm Min. *The Solidarity of Others in a Divided World*. 2004, p.79.

expression in our historicity and sociality, and in our differences and our interdependence. So, actions undertaken in response to "human solidarity" are often realized in the mutual agreement, support and collaborative endeavours undertaken by people in response to the *common good* (often arrived at through the collective discernment of shared values, needs, benefits or interests for all).

Anselm Min further asserts that, whereas the great imperative today is to be awakened to this reality of human solidarity and to develop it in the best way possible, this imperative needs to equally undergo a disciplined cultivation so as to avoid creating ethnocentric views and perspectives that are self-contained and immune from interaction with other perspectives and views. Such disciplined cultivation must focus on creating the awareness that though different, peoples, religions, cultures, and perspectives are not frozen realities that are fixed and incapable of engaging in constructive conversations with others. Different groups and cultures can interact in common spaces, challenging each other, modifying and broadening their respective horizons of intelligibility and knowledge, in the desire to work for and to contribute to the common good.[934] It is this understanding of human solidarity that allows Christians and Muslims to work together in response to the needs of the poor and the marginalized in society.

In using this understanding of the concept in relation to offering support to the poor and to the marginalized, the concept "solidarity" finds its basis from "our common humanity."[935] *Our*

934 See, Anselm Min. *The Solidarity of others in a Divided World*. 2004, p.78-79.

935 "Our Common Humanity" refers to the understanding that we are all one family created by God and placed in the world. Hence, building a community or communities that empower each individual to realize their full human potential is seen as our common responsibility. This culture of solidarity is more urgent today in the face of the many situations of inequality, poverty and injustice. (See John Paul II. *Sollicitudo rei socialis* – "On Social Concern" 1987, # 37).

367

common humanity conveys the sense of one's responsibility of valuing other people and respecting their dignity and their integrity as human beings just like us. In his encyclical letter "*Sollicitudo Rei Socialis* – 'On Social Concern' (1987)", Pope John Paul II indicated that this sense of *solidarity* "is not a feeling of vague compassion or shallow distress at the misfortunes of so many people, both near and far. On the contrary, it is a firm and persevering determination to commit oneself to the common good; that is to say, to the good of all and of each individual, because we are all really responsible for all."[936] In connection with this understanding of *human solidarity, Gaudium et Spes* also emphasizes that, "the joy and the hope, the grief and the anguish of men of our time, especially of those who are poor or afflicted in any way, are the joy and the hope, the grief and the anguish of the followers of Christ as well."[937] Here, the focus is that nothing that is genuinely human should fail to find an echo in the hearts of all. It is a quest centred on actions for human flourishing.

The understanding of human solidarity in Islam is not contextually different from the sense of solidarity explicated above. The Prophet Muhammad once said: "in the sight of God, all people are equal like the teeth of a comb and nobody may be deemed better than another except based on piety and good works."[938] In this Sunnah of the prophet one finds an explicit and vivid accentuation of the equality and the universality of the dignity of the human person in Islam. While on the one hand, this sense of equality and universality emanates from God's breath of life given to Adam (Surah 7: 11), on the other hand, God's appointment of Adam as the vicegerent (Khalifa) to the rest of creation (Surah 2: 30 – 33) confers on him the intrinsic responsibility of upholding the dignity of the human person. Adam and Eve are known to be the first

---

936 John Paul II. *Sollicitudo rei socialis* – "On Social Concern" 1987, # 38.

937 Austin Flannery (Ed.). *Vatican Council II*: "Gaudium et Spes" # 1.

938 See, "Human Solidarity in Islam." http://www.islamforchristians.com/human-solidarity-islam/ (10/04/2015).

human beings God created – the prototype of the human race. Hence, what is expected of them in the Qur'an, in effect, is also expected of the whole of humanity.[939] So, Allah did not only create them, but he also entrusted the care of creation to them and to their descendants (*Amana*). They were given the duty of stewardship to creation, preserving and perpetuating its dignity and integrity. Hence, whereas the dignity and the equality of human life comes from this "common humanity" as creatures of Allah, the duty to preserve and to promote this dignity and integrity finds its expression in the command of Allah. As Mona Siddiqui put it, "in the Qur'an, at least human beings carry an inherit dignity and honour conveyed in the very manner of their creation."[940]

In Islam therefore, through Adam and Eve, Allah bestows a common dignity (the gift of life) and vocation (*Amana*)[941] to the rest of humanity. As Allah declared in the Qur'an: "We have bestowed dignity on the progeny of Adam (*wa laqad karramna bani Adama*) and conferred on them special favours above a great part of our creation" (Surah 17: 70). This sense of dignity is seen as the basis of human solidarity. In Islam, although solidarity begins from *kinship* and extends to *neighbours*,[942] the aim is nonethe-

---

939 Murata, S. & Chittick, W.C. *The Vision of Islam*. 1994, p.135.

940 Mona Siddiqui. "Being Human in Islam," in *Humanity: Texts and Contexts*. 2011, p.17.

941 The concept "*Amana*" refers to "the Trust" i.e. the moral responsibility of fulfilling one's obligations due to Allah and fulfilling one's obligations due to the rest of creation (Surah 33: 72). (See, Murata, S. & Chittick, W,C. *The Vision of Islam*. 1994, p.134-137).

942 Whereas *kinship* connotes blood affinity, *Tafsir al-Manar* quotes a *Hadith* which says: "There are three kinds of neighbours. A neighbour who enjoys three rights: neighbourhood rights, kinship rights and the rights of Islam; a neighbour who enjoys two rights: neighbourhood rights and the rights of Islam; and the neighbour who enjoys only the rights of neighbourhood". (See Bouhdiha, Abdelwahab & Muhammad Ma'ruf al-Dawalibi (editors). *The Different Aspects of Islamic Culture: The Individual and the Society in Islam*. 1998, p.238).

less the recognition of the ties that bind us together and bear on us the responsibility of taking care of the other as a consequence of these human ties. In Islam, when human solidarity is directed towards providing support to others, by alleviating their poverty and achieving shared prosperity, it is concretely expressed through *Zakat* – the third pillar of the religion. In respect to Christian–Muslim dialogue on Christology, Christian–Muslim solidarity, in support of the poor and the marginalized in society, could therefore focus on retrieving internal resources from the words and the deeds of Jesus as the basis for collective actions in response to the needs and the concerns of the poor and the marginalized. From this approach, two relevant questions are formulated to guide this discourse: (1) what are the Qur'anic testimonies of the responses of Jesus to the needs of the poor and the marginalized; and (2) how might these accounts stimulate a religious response to the needs of the poor and the marginalized? While these questions also apply to Christians, the intention is to demonstrate how Jesus' fundamental option for the sick, the poor, and the marginalized in the Qur'an and the Gospels provides a compelling force for Christian–Muslim collective action in response to issues of human flourishing.

The Islamic institutional action in response to the needs of the poor and the marginalized in society is captured in *Zakat* or almsgiving. *Zakat* is the payment of some percentage of an individual's wealth, property or profits in lieu of helping the poor and the needy in the community. According to the Qur'an, beneficiaries of this charity include: the needy, the poor, the collectors of the *Zakat,* those whose hearts are to be reconciled to Islam, captives, debtors, those fighting in God's path and travellers (Surah 9: 60). To emphasize the importance of this religious exercise, the Qur'an indicates that; "goodness does not consist in turning your face to the East or to the West. The truly good are those who believe in God and the Last Day ... those who give away some of their wealth to orphans, the needy, the traveller and beggars and to liberate those in bondage" (Surah 2: 177). As a consequence, to be a good Muslim does not only consist in confessing the *Shahada* and observing the ritual daily prayers (*Salat*), but it also consists in helping the poor and the needy in society through the payments of the Zakat. Here, *Zakat* makes it possible to achieve two goals simultaneously: (1) *the material and immediate* (that is the economic autonomy of the individual); and (2) *the spiritual and long term* (that is helping the individual beneficiary to become a fully-fledged Muslim who can in turn pay the Zakat).[943] To emphasize the effects of the Zakat in the lives of the beneficiaries of it, Bouhdiha and al-Dawalibi indicate that, *Zakat* "introduces a new form of solidarity which maintains social peace while upholding the dignity of man".[944]

Due to this Islamic religious responsibility to support the poor and the marginalized, one finds today so many Islamic charities all over world.[945] How does this form of solidarity play out in the life of the Qur'anic Jesus? Jesus in the Qur'an states quite categorically that; "I am a servant of God ... He commanded me to pray, to give alms as long as I live ..." (Surah 19: 30 – 31). Furthermore, even though the Qur'anic interpretations of the miracles of Jesus (Surah 3: 49) are construed by Islamic commentators as *signs* intended to authenticate his claim as a "Messenger of Allah", these miracles were nonetheless the concrete expressions of Jesus' response to the needs of those who benefited from them (Surah 10: 28 – 30). Here, he provides *food* for the hungry (Surah 5: 113 – 115 and Surah 19: 23 – 26), *sight* to the blind, *healing* to the leprous and *life* to the dead (Surah 3: 49 – 50). Thus, according to Ayoub, "the miracles that the Qur'an attributes to Jesus during his ministry are

---

943 Bouhdiha, Abdelwahab & Muhammad Ma'ruf al-Dawalibi (editors). *The Different Aspects of Islamic Culture.* 1998, p.245.

944 Bouhdiha, Abdelwahab & Muhammad Ma'ruf al-Dawalibi (editors). *The Different Aspects of Islamic Culture.* 1998, p.245.

945 Some of these charities include the "Red Crescent," "Islamic Relief," "Muslim Aid," "Islamic Children Relief Fund," "Helping Hands for the Needy".

miracles of life and healing ... The Qur'an credits Jesus alone among the prophets with raising the dead, giving sight to those born blind and healing the lepers and the sick".[946] One sees that the effects of these miracles were directed towards the expression of love, the healing of sicknesses, and the transmission of life; all undertaken in view of promoting and preserving the dignity and the integrity of human life.

From a Roman Catholic perspective, *man* (the prototype of humanity) is viewed as created in "the image and likeness of God" (*imago Dei* – Genesis 1: 27).[947] As a community of beings, man is by nature a social being who realizes himself by living in solidarity with others.[948] According to *Gaudium et Spes,* by his fatherly care for all of us: "God desired that all men should form one family and deal with each other in a spirit of brotherhood ... since they have been created in the likeness of God."[949] Consequently, in the Christian tradition, the love of God, also expressed in the tangible acts of love for one's neighbour remains an essential hallmark of Christian identity. Christian love is not conveyed in mere theoretical expression without practical orientations. Christian love is a love based on self-sacrifice for the sake of the beloved. It is a love expressed in self-giving – one that is measured by the standards set by Jesus Christ; "Greater love has no man than this, that a man lays down his life for his friends" (John 15: 13). Jesus will later demonstrate this by his own self-sacrifice on the cross.

From the section concerning Jesus as the "Son of God" in Chapter Four, we indicated that most of the miracles that Jesus performed were not just for the sake of demonstrating his divine

---

946 Mahmoud Ayoub. *A Muslim View of Christianity.* 2007, p.114.

947 The Book of Genesis in the Christian Bible says: "God created man in the image of himself, in the image of God he created him, male and female he created them" (Genesis 1: 27).

948 Vatican Council II: Gaudium et Spes # 12.

949 Vatican Council II: *Gaudium et Spes*, # 24.

sonship but were also therapeutic; validated by the way they provided restoration to the debilitating conditions experienced by their beneficiaries. This is ascertained by Jesus' own attestations to his "mission statement" in Luke's Gospel: "The Spirit of the Lord is upon me, because he has anointed me to proclaim good news to the poor. He has sent me to proclaim freedom for the prisoners and recovery of sight for the blind, to set the oppressed free, to proclaim the year of the Lord's favour" (Luke 4: 18 – 19; see also Isaiah 61: 1 – 2). In this text and through his actions, Jesus Christ confirms that he is the fulfilment of this prophecy of Isaiah (Luke 4: 21). As a result, one finds that the whole life and mission of Jesus was predominantly marked by this attention to the needs of the less privileged, the outcast and the down trodden (Mark 1: 29, 40; Mark 3: 1; Mark 4: 35 and Mark 5: 1).[950] As followers of Christ, Jesus' fundamental option for the poor and the marginalized in society as expressed in his mission statement, also permeates and gives direction to the mission statement of the Christian Church. That is, Christians are also called: "to proclaim the good news to the poor, to bring liberty to the captives, sight to the blind, to set the downtrodden free and to proclaim God's year of favour." This responsibility finds concrete expressions in the many Christian missionaries and charities all over the world. While the missionaries continue to proclaim the *Lord's year of favour*, the diverse charities also provide sundry help and support to the under privileged and the marginalized in society.[951]

Today, poverty and disease have become globalized and threaten the very survival of the human race. As our communities

---

950 In these texts (Mark 1: 29, 40; Mark 3: 1; Mark 4: 35 and Mark 5: 1), Jesus is said to have healed the blind, cleansed lepers, calmed the storm at sea and healed the Gerasene demoniac.

951 Christian charities such as Aid to Church in Need, SCIAF, CAFOD, Pontifical Mission Society (Mission), Mission without Borders are but few examples.

and societies are fast becoming multicultural and multi-religious, so is poverty and disease sweeping through these communities, societies, countries and continents – reducing many families and communities to subhuman lives.[952] As Knitter put it, "if Jesus reminded us that the poor are always among us (Matthew 26: 11), then they are with us today in ever greater and staggering numbers and with a presence that insists on having a place in our awareness."[953] Christians and Muslims have continued to work separately in support of the needs of the poor and the marginalized in society. Sometimes, most of these charitable works are directed at people who share their respective beliefs.

However, in multicultural societies where Christians and Muslims find themselves living cheek by jowl – sharing the same space and being confronted by similar economic, social and political challenges, they need to work together to be able to meet these shared challenges. The cry of the poor and the marginalized is one of such challenges. Whereas it is true that each religious community unremittingly embarks on such social action projects in response to the needs of the poor, the gigantic nature of this social need invites both communities to join forces in response to a problem that is today a shared challenge.

It is in response to this shared challenge that the life and the mission of Jesus Christ provides the common ground for Christian-Muslim collective action. As we saw earlier, Jesus in both the Qur'an and in the Gospels was resolute in his response to the needs of the poor, the afflicted, the distressed and the marginalized in society. He fed them, healed them and gave them life. If Jesus was so attentive to these needs in both the Qur'an and in

---

952 The glaring situations in some countries in Africa, Asia and South America cannot be overlooked. The homeless and the destitute in the big cities of the West are a challenge to well-minded people.

953 Knitter, Paul, F. *One Earth Many Religions*. 1996, p.58.

the Gospels, then Christians and Muslims (who make up more than 50 percent of the world's population)[954] can find inspiration from his action and work in partnership in response to these social needs which are today behemothic in proportion.

Such concerted efforts have the potential to effect positive changes in the lives of the adherents of the two religions and the beneficiaries of their collaborative actions. That is, by these collective actions, not only will Christians and Muslims be fulfilling their responsibility of caring for the suffering other as *per* the divine expectation, these actions will also bring help and relief to the underprivileged and the marginalised. These unified actions could further lead to the establishment of *trust* and *respect* between followers of the two religions, and contribute to changing the negative perceptions that have been long held about Christian-Muslim relations.[955] In society today, the fast-growing numbers of the poor and the marginalized demand such mutual and concerted efforts.

Based on their fundamental faith principles, Christians and Muslims have the religious and moral obligation to support the poor, the marginalized, and the suffering other in society. While Islamic obligation is borne from *Zakat* which is the third pillar of faith in Islam, Jesus the "Son of God" in Matthew 25: 31 – 46 indicates that the life of the Christian is judged by their response

---

954 It is estimated that there are 2.3 billion Christians and 1.6 billion Muslims in the world; representing about 54 percent of the world's population.

955 Centuries of Christian-Muslim polemics on the nature of God and the place of Jesus in it has muddied the waters in their relationships giving the impression that the only form of legitimate conversation between them on Christology is one of claim and counterclaim, and in the end, the mutual dismissal of the other's beliefs on the matter (see, Mark Beaumont. *Christology in Dialogue with Muslims.* 2005, p. xxi; Douglas Pratt. *The Challenge of Islam.* 2005, p.102; George Dardess & Krier Mich. *St Francis and the Sultan.* 2011, p.53).

to the plight of the needy.[956] In this Matthean text, the sick, the hungry, the naked, the stranger, the imprisoned, and the thirsty are presented as the self-reflection of the king (Jesus Christ) who will later occupy the throne of judgement. So, this parable in effect demonstrates that every Christian response to the needs of the poor and the needy is in effect, a response to Christ.[957] From these perspectives, and considering the growing diversity and the enormity of the needs of the poor, what is needed today is a Christian–Muslim collective action. Such collective efforts could also serve as means of *witnessing* to the world about the rights of the poor and the needy, and our human obligation to respond to these needs. As Saint Pope John Paul II put it, "the obligation to commit oneself to the development of peoples is not just an individual duty and still less an individualistic one, as if it was possible to achieve this development through the isolated efforts of each individual."[958] Collective actions have greater force of effect than isolated ones.

It is true that this form of Christian–Muslim inter-faith action could be undertaken without recourse to the "Jesus–catalyst" or to the conscious efforts to see such actions as inspired by Jesus. Yet, the successes of such inter-faith actions have the potential to further smoothen the already fractured relationships between the two religions as a result of their difficult past. In other words, such actions could become another source of witnessing to the world about the goodness of these two religions expressed in their willingness to work together despite their differences in

---

956 Even though Matthew 25: 31 – 46 is a parable depicting the scene of Judgment in which Gentiles are assessed according to their deeds, this scene of judgment is actually intended for the whole of humanity. Each person is judged based on the way they treated "these least brothers of mine" who were sick, hungry, thirsty, a stranger, naked, and imprisoned (see, Daniel Harrington. *The Gospel of Matthew.* 1991, p.358).

957 Daniel Harrington. *The Gospel of Matthew.* 1991, p.359.

958 Pope John Paul II. *Sollicitudo rei socialis* – "On Social Concern" 1987, # 32.

Christological appropriations. Jesus may be a barrier to Christian-Muslim relations, but he also provides a sturdy and a formidable bridge to Christian-Muslim response to issues of human flourishing. In our contemporary context, the face of the suffering other may not only be a Muslim or Christian face. In the same way, the capacity to provide support to the suffering other does not always fall within the domains of Muslims or those of Christians; and even where this may hold true, these resources are never sufficient considering the growing needs of the poor and the marginalized in society today. This makes the case for Christian-Muslim collective actions in response to the needs of the poor. Such concerted actions have the potential to succeed where isolated actions fail.

7.6 Conclusion

Leirvik Oddbjørn asserted that in Christian-Muslim dialogue on Christology, "what is called for is rather a dialogue among partners who are willing to dive into the depths of the other's well-spring, not for the rebirth of some kind of universal religion, but for the sake of deeper understanding not only of the other, but equally of oneself."[959] While Leirvik's assertion is true, we identify dialogue as an exercise in learning from and about the other as the framework for engaging Christians and Muslims in dialogue on Christology. The reason is that this form of dialogue not only lead to a deeper understanding of oneself as another, but it also has the potential to lead the two communities to embark on collective actions for the promotion of common values inspired by the identity and the mission of Jesus in the Qur'an and in the New Testament.

Even though Jesus Christ is differently construed in Islam and in Christianity, he nonetheless plays significant roles in both their

---

959 Oddbjørn Leirvik. *The Image of Jesus Christ in Islam*. 2010, p.4.

scriptures and their religious traditions. For instance, not only is the Qur'anic Jesus held in honour in this world and in the next (Surah 3: 45), he also functions as the precursor and the guarantor of the coming of the Prophet Muhammad (Surah 61: 6). On the Christian plane, even though Jesus Christ is understood as the historical point of departure and the culmination of Christian faith and theology, he not only reveals God, but he is also the bearer of salvation and defines the shape of the redeemed life. As a consequence, McGrath would assert that: "it is impossible to speak of 'God' within the parameters of the Christian tradition without relating such statements to the person and the work of Jesus Christ."[960] It was acknowledged that the differences in Christian–Muslim Christological constructions that inevitably set Jesus as a "barrier to their relations. Examples of these stark differences were identified with the concept of the *Holy Trinity,* the *Incarnation*, the *Son of God*, the *Crucifixion, Death* and the *Resurrection.* These were considered barriers in Christian–Muslim relations because of the Islamic denials of them.

We equally indicated that the Islamic rendition of Jesus Christ as the "Prophet of Allah", bereft of his divinity, is considered heretical for Christians. This is because the above Islamic denials undermined the developed foundations on which the Christian faith is built. Despite these stark *differences,* Jesus also serves as a robust *bridge* to Christian–Muslim relations because of the common Christological themes the two faith communities share. Some of these themes include: the *"Annunciation and Virginal birth"*, the *"Miracles Jesus performed"*, the *"Ascension"* and the *"Second coming of Jesus."* Within the context of dialogue as an exercise in learning, the questions then were: what learning examples can be derived from the life and the message of Jesus Christ for constructive Christian–Muslim living relationships? In which way does the Qur'anic Jesus and Jesus of the Gospels espouse common values for Christian–Muslim dialogue of life and dialogue of common

---

960 Alister McGrath. *Christian Theology.* 1997, p.324.

action? It was in response to these questions that values such as: "prayer and submissiveness to God", "peace and peaceful co-existence" and the value of "solidarity with the poor and the marginalized" emerged.

In a world where secularism continues to undermine the significance of religion in society, Christians and Muslims who constitute more than 50 percent of the world's population need to work together to push back the secularist agenda through acts of common witnessing. In the Qur'an and the Gospels, while Jesus emphasized the need for humanity to submit itself to the will of God in order to attain peace and happiness, reintroducing God to all the fabrics of human society today, is now considered an ominous need than before. The visibility of God's presence in society, contributes to transforming it and re-establishing the harmony and the equilibrium in human life that have long been lost through secularism. In a world where peace is becoming a rare commodity due to the rampart conflicts and wars which are very often religious in character, Christian-Muslim concerted efforts directed to establishing peace, is a dire necessity. These could be undertaken through carefully organized and sustained Christian-Muslim interreligious prayers for peace. Working for peace and providing it was essentially part of the character of the life and the mission of Jesus in the Qur'an and in the New Testament Gospels. In a world where the devastative effects of poverty continue to threaten the very survival of the human race, Christians and Muslims are invited to work together to push back the frontiers of poverty following the examples of Jesus in the Qur'an and in the Gospels. The face of the suffering other is an authentic reminder to Christians and to Muslims, of their religious and moral obligation to respond to it in charity. Where isolated efforts fail in the sight of the multiplicity of the needs and concerns of the suffering other, Christian-Muslim collective actions may succeed where isolated actions fail.

CHAPTER EIGHT
CONCLUSION AND EVALUATION

8.1 Conclusion

At the start of this dialogical journey, we indicated that while Christology remains contentious in Christian–Muslim conversations, such contentions will continue to grow and escalate if the three traditional paradigms of dialogue continue to shape the nature of dialogue between Christians and Muslims today. As it were, not only does *exclusivism* privilege one's tradition against all others, but *inclusivism* patronises other traditions as partial versions of what is realized in only one, and *pluralism* argues for the relativization of all others including one's own.[961] We asserted that if the tripartite goals of dialogue (that is to know oneself more profoundly; to know the other more authentically; and to live ever more fully accordingly) are to be achieved, then these paradigms need to give way to new and better ways of dialoguing with the other. It was in response to this need for new and better ways of engaging the other in meaningful and beneficial dialogues, which warranted the proposed study on Christian–Muslim dialogue on Christology as an exercise in learning.

We argued in Chapter One that the interest to learn from the other implies letting the other tell me something about themselves. It implies a sense of openness to the other where one does not privilege one's views over or against other's (exclusivism); or consider the other's views as partial versions of one's own (inclusivism); or presuppose that they are more or less the same as one's own (pluralism). Dialogue as an exercise in learning is about listening to and grasping with interest the other's views or

---

961 Michael Barnes. *Theology and the Dialogue of Religions.* 2002, p.8.

beliefs about Jesus Christ within their tradition specific context. Dialogue as an exercise in learning is the mutual sharing of testimonies of faith (attestation). We argued that this orientation to dialogue removes it from the contentions and the polemics framework of "claim and counterclaim" which has often characterised Christian-Muslim relations over centuries.

It is said that theories always provide the rationale for practice. Thus, in Chapter Two, we established the theoretical foundations for dialogue as an exercise in learning following Paul Ricoeur's hermeneutics of the *self* and *the other*. This form of hermeneutics provided the framework which supported reflections on "dialogue as an exercise in learning". This is because dialogue as an exercise in learning involves the task of crossing over to another religious tradition to learn about its theological themes, belief-systems and doctrines. This act of crossing-over raises questions on the epistemological validity and the ethical allowability for such crossings. In response to these questions, we turned to Ricoeur's hermeneutics of the self (narrative identity). Through *Oneself as Another,* we demonstrated how Ricoeur's mediation of the tensions between Descartes "exulted cogito" and Nietzsche's demolition of it led to his concept of *attestation* as the equidistance between the two polarities. As the "wounded cogito" which is capable of affirming itself as oneself acting and suffering, we presented *attestation* as establishing a gesture of trust and belief-in oneself.

Understood interreligiously, *attestation* relates to the mutual sharing of testimonies of faith between the self and the other (that is, Christians and Muslims). Thus, we asserted that Christian-Muslim dialogue on Christology as an exercise in learning is likely to be constructive and positive; when it is removed from the context of argumentations and confrontations and placed within the framework of *attestation* as the sharing of mutual testimonies of faith. Here, learning takes place when one narrates or shares with the other his or her stories about the identity and the mission of Jesus Christ as they pertain to one's tradition. So, to the question what is the epistemological and the ethical legitimacy for such crossing? In response, Ricoeur shows how sometimes the narration of the stories of our lives (narrative identity) disclose the contributions others make to our narratives and we to theirs. As a result, we asserted that the possibility of narrative intertwinements serves as the epistemological basis for crossing over to learn from the traditions of the other. This is because not only do the similarities between traditions support such learning, but the potential enrichment this might bring to oneself as another encourages this form of learning. We saw that where questions of *intratextuality* were raised, Ricoeur proposed *translation* as the means of understanding texts and doctrines other than one's own.

On the ethical plane, we relied on Ricoeur's "little ethics" as the basis for reflecting on the ethical issues which arise when engaging in dialogue with other as an exercise in learning. Hence, in Chapter Three, we identified *commitment, openness, respect* and *equality* as the necessary conditions (that is, the appropriate dialogical attitudes) for dialogue as an exercise in learning. We used Ricoeur's notion of the "ethical intention" as the hermeneutic framework for reflecting on the challenges posed by the above conditions. Ricoeur's ethical intention has three components: (1) the Good life, (2) with and for others, (3) in Just institutions. While the first component provided the context for reflections on the meaning and the significance of *commitment*, the second component set the framework for the assessments of the challenge of *respect and openness* in dialogue as an exercise in learning. "Just institutions" provided the context for deliberations on the principle of *equal-partners-in-dialogue*. In the final analysis, our emphasis was that Christian–Muslim dialogue on Christology as an exercise in learning is constructive, positive, and has the potential to make meaningful contributions in the living relationships between Christians and Muslims. As an exercise in learning, not only does dialogue take seriously the "tradition-specific understandings" of the Christologies of the interlocutors' concern, it is also guided by the principles of *respect* and *openness* to learn from these tradition-specific perspectives, viewing each other as *equal-partners-in-dialogue*.

To achieve the above end, we committed Chapters Four and Five respectively as the platform for engaging the Christian and the Islamic tradition-specific perspectives on Christology. Here, we focused specifically on the Christology of Mark's Gospel and "Qur'anic Christology". By engaging these two forms of Christology, we discovered that although different, they demonstrate how the images of Jesus Christ in both traditions serve as both *bridge and barrier* to Christian-Muslim relations: that is, as a *bridge* because Christianity and Islam share similar theological concepts and themes which relate to the life and the mission of Jesus Christ; and as *barrier* because some of these concepts are understood differently in the light of the *Tawhid* and the *Holy Trinity*. Consequently, Chapter Six provided further clarity on these metaphors of *Jesus as a bridge and barrier*. Here, we explored more deeply common Christological themes such as *the Word of God, the Spirit of God, Messiah, the virginal conception, the miracles Jesus performed, the crucifixion, death and resurrection, the ascension and the second coming of Jesus.* In doing so, we discovered that although understood as a "Prophet" or a "Messenger" of Allah in Islam and the "Son of God" in Christianity, Jesus nonetheless occupies significant places in Islam and in Christianity.

The question then was: what can Christians and Muslims learn from the message of Jesus, his life, and his mission as they pertain to the Qur'an and the New Testament Gospels? What values can one derive from the message, the life, and the mission of Jesus Christ for Christian-Muslim dialogues of life and of common action? Chapter Seven responded to the above questions, eliciting and explicating values such as "prayer and submission to God", "peace and peaceful co-existence" and "solidarity with the poor and the marginalized". Reflections on these values were anchored on: how they are understood within the philosophical and the theological traditions of both faiths; their significance within the traditions; their espousals in the life of the Qur'anic Jesus and Jesus Christ in the New Testament Gospels; and how they offer common grounds for Christian-Muslim collaborative actions in response to God and to issues of human flourishing.

In the end, one could find Muslims and Christians gladly exploring a space-between them for their mutual benefits in contexts where they had hitherto been estranged by.

8.2 Evaluation

This area examines and judges as to whether or not the study fulfilled its intended purpose. This is assessed on the basis of these fundamental questions: did the study provide a new form of Christian-Muslim dialogue on Christology other than what is already known? If yes, does it provide a robust foundation on which this new approach to dialogue is situated? Does the study address without compromise, the specific Christological issues that underpin the beliefs of the two faith traditions? Does the study contribute to making Christian-Muslim dialogue more constructive and positive? What is the contribution of the study to the current debates on Christian-Muslim dialogue on Christology?

The study acknowledged that Christology is a contentious subject for Christian and Muslim relations. While most of these contentions emanate from differentials in their Christological constructions, a lot of them are also the results of the sustained prejudices that each has on the other. Consequently, while some scholars thought it impossible to engage Christians and Muslims on a constructive dialogue on Christology based on the old models of dialogue, our interest was to re-orientate Christian-Muslim dialogues from the traditional models of dialogue to dialogue as an exercise in learning. We argued that the success of the exercise of learning from and about the other creates a new form of conversation as attestations and contributes to eradicating long held and sustained prejudice. Learning always leads to enlightenment, and enlightenment liberates one from prejudices and ignorance. In this way, dialogue as an exercise in learning offers Christians and Muslims the opportunity to listen to each other and learn from what the other has to say about Jesus Christ;

thereby clarifying the underlying ideological, philosophical and theological prejudices one may hold about the other. Not only does it lead to these clarifications, but it also has the potential to unearth common values between the interlocutors.

To achieve this end, Ricoeur's hermeneutics on narrative identity that provided the hermeneutic context for reflecting on the challenges posed by dialogue as an exercise in learning from and about the other. Learning from the other always involves crossing over to a different religious tradition in order to learn and to understand them. In doing this, learning creates a tension between *commitment* to one's tradition and *respect for* and *openness* to the traditions of the other. While the whole exercise of learning involves understanding the beliefs of the other in their authenticity through narratology, Ricoeur indicates that in narrating the stories of our lives, we find that others contribute to our narratives and we to theirs. Since this possibility of narrative intertwinement establishes some form of relationship between the self and the other in contexts where they are considered estranged, we argued that this sense of intersubjectivity provides the hermeneutic framework for reflecting on Christian-Muslim dialogue on Christology as an exercise in learning.

For this form of mutual sharing to be constructive and positive, we argued that it has to be guided by what we called "the appropriate dialogical attitudes" namely: *commitment, respect, openness* and the principle of *equality*. Here, Ricoeur's "little ethics" provided the hermeneutic context for reflecting on the meaning and the significance of these dialogical attitudes. In the final analysis, the whole methodology of the thesis is centred on the argument that: for Christian-Muslim dialogue on Christology to be constructive and positive, it needs to be oriented towards dialogue as an exercise in learning from and about the other. Here, *difference* is respected at the same time that *similarities* are affirmed. In short, while we asserted that Christian-Muslim dialogue on Christology as an exercise in learning provides the best context for negotiating the impasse in their dialogical relations, Ricoeur's hermeneutics of *selfhood and otherness* provided the robust hermeneutic framework for reflecting on the significant issues which speak to the heart of this form of dialogue.

The title: "Christology in Christian-Muslim Dialogue as an exercise in learning", therefore implies a form of dialogue which engages the narrative discourses of both religious traditions, with the view to learn from and about the other. Consequently, it builds on and encourages *commitment* to one's tradition and the *openness* to listen to, learn and understand, and be enriched by the traditions of the other. To promote this dialectic of commitment and openness, Chapters Four and Five were committed to studying and understanding Christology as it pertains to the Christian and the Islamic tradition-specific contexts. This authentic approach to the subject led to the discernment of what was metaphorically identified as the *barriers* and the *bridges* in Christian-Muslim dialogue on Christology. While the concept of *barrier* underscored the question of *difference*, the idea of *bridge* highlighted the question of *similarities*. These allowed for a careful and systematic presentations of what could be authentically described as Christian or Islamic Christology based on the New Testament and the Qur'an respectively. As an exercise in learning, this form of dialogue allowed for the effective engagement between Christians and Muslims without the feisty polemics, contentions and acrimonies that have always characterised their relations on this subject.

While acknowledging that there are volumes of scholarly contributions in this area of dialogue, most of these contributions only give tangential treatments to the specific topic of Christian-Muslim dialogue on Christology. Even in contexts where specific attention is paid to the subject of Christology, few of these studies are orientated towards dialogue as an exercise in learning. In this way, there are very few scholarly contributions on Christian-Muslim dialogue on Christology as an exercise in learning – the kind of dialogue which engages the Christologies of both Christianity and Islam in conversations that are directed towards the promotion of common values inspired by the life, the messages and the mission of Jesus Christ. As an exercise in learning, its novelty lies in its attention to the promotion of common values such as: "prayer and submission to God", "peace and peaceful co-existence", and "solidarity with the poor and the marginalized."

8.3 Recommendations for Further Study

At the start of this research work, we reckoned that the entire process was a Christian–Muslim dialogical journey whose destination was not less uncertain. Just as the methodological framework provided the roadmap that guided the journey, so also the anticipated splendour of the point of destination provided the motivation to keep striving towards the goal. However, having arrived at the goal, we find that the goal of the journey has no definitive end in itself. It rather opens up new beginnings that point to other goals which beckon for further attention. As Pratt conceptualized, "I often find, in my research and thinking, that where I arrive at is where I should really begin ... The end of one journey brings me, but to the start of another."[962]

It is therefore in view of the new vistas of hope and opportunity for further research in this area that we recommend some other pressing values for further reflections on Christian–Muslim dialogues of life and of common action. These values include *sanctity of marriage and family life, human rights and gender equality, the integrity of creation and climate change, the life of chastity* in the light of prostitution and pornography. These are challenges which specifically relate to social and moral values which Christianity and Islam uphold and which the message, life and mission of Jesus Christ might help to clarify and provide common contexts for inter-faith actions. If Christianity and Islam are to be partners in the public discourse on how to make the world a better place,

---

962 Douglas Pratt. *The Challenge of Islam.* 2005, p.228.

then developing these values will not be out of place. As Ziauddin Sardar put it, Christian–Muslim actions that are "designed to generate adoptive and pragmatic intellectual responses to the problems of our age would be the most appropriate response of the believers to the postmodernist age."[963] Such collective actions are necessary more than ever today. The outcomes of such concerted actions will not only serve the needs of the two faith traditions, but also, those of the world. As Hans Küng did say some time ago, there can never be world peace without peace among the religions; and no peace among the religions, without dialogue between them; and no dialogue between them without the authentic knowledge of the other. This book offers this rare opportunity for Christian–Muslim dialogue on Christology as an exercise in learning from and about the other. Learning leads to the acquisition of knowledge; and knowledge is the gateway to enlightenment; and enlightenment not only offers the solutions to the challenges of ignorance and prejudice, but it also enriches and transforms the world of the enlightened.

---

963 Ziauddin Sardar. "The Ethical Connection: Christian–Muslim Relations in Postmodern Age." 1991, p.75.

BIBLIOGRAPHY

Abdul-Haqq, Adbiyah Akhbar. *Sharing Your Faith with a Muslim*. Bethany House Publishers, Minnesota-USA. 1980.

Abdelwahab, Bouhdiba & Muhammad Ma'ruf al-Dawalibi (editors). *The Different Aspects of Islamic Culture: The Individual and the Society in Islam*. UNESCO Publications. 1998.

Abū Ja' far Muhammad b. Jarir al-Tabari. *Jāmi 'al-bayān fí ta'wíl al_Qur'an*. Beirut, Lebanon. Vol. 1.

Afayori, Robert. Book Review: "George Dardess and Marvin L. Krier Mich. *In the Spirit of St. Francis & the Sultan: Catholics and Muslims Working Together for the Common Good*". Maryknoll: Orbis Books. 2012, p.207-208.

Agnes Michael (Editor). Webster's New World College Dictionary (4th edition). Wiley Publishing, Inc., Ohio. 2007.

Amar, Djaballah. "Jesus in Islam," in the *Southern Baptist Journal of Theology*. Vol. 8, No. 1, Spring, 2004.

Askari, Hasan. "The Dialogical Relationship between Christianity and Islam" in the *Journal of Ecumenical Studies*. Vol. 8 (1972), p.477-488.

Ata ur-Rahim, Mohammed. *Jesus the Prophet of Islam*. MWH London Publishers. 1979.

Arthur Jeffery. "The Qur'an as Scripture," in *The Muslim World*. Vol. 41 (1950), p.106-134.

Ayoub, Mahmoud. *The Qur'an and Its Interpreters*. State University of New York Press, Albany. 1984.

———. *Islam, Faith and History*. Oneworld Publications. 2004.

———. *A Muslim View of Christianity: Essays on Dialogue*. (Ed.) by Irfan A. Omar. Maryknoll, NY: Orbis Books, 2007.

———. "Towards an Islamic Christology: An Image of Jesus in Early Shi'i Muslim Literature" in *The Muslim World 66*. 1976, p.163–188.

———. "Jesus the Son of God: A study of the terms Ibn and walad in the Qur'an and Tafsir Tradition. In *Christian Muslim Encounter*. Edited by Y. Haddad and WZ Haddad. Gainesville, University of Florida Press, 1995.

Bakhtin, Mikhail, M. *Dialogic Imagination: Four Essays*. Austin: University of Texas Press. 1981.

———. *Speech, Genre and Other Essays*. Austin: University of Texas Press. 1986.

Barnes, Michael. *Theology and the Dialogue of Religions*. Cambridge University Press, UK. 2002.

———. *Interreligious Learning: Dialogue, Spirituality and the Christian Imagination*. Cambridge University Press (Electronic Publication). 2012.

Beaumont, Mark. *Christology in Dialogue with Muslims: A Critical Analysis of Christian Presentation of Christ to Muslims from the Ninth and Twentieth Century*. Regnum Books International, 2005.

Billings, Todd, J. *The Word of God for the People of God: An Entryway to the Theological Interpretation of Scripture*. Eerdmans, 2010.

Bosworth, Edmund. "Al-Tabari" in *the Encyclopedia of Islam*. New Edition, Vol. 10. BRILL 1998.

Brown, Daniel, S. Jr. (Editor). *A Communicative Perspective on Interfaith Dialogue: Living Within the Abrahamic Traditions*. Lexington Books, Plymouth – UK. 2013

Brown, Raymond. E. *The Virginal Conception and Bodily Resurrection of Jesus*. Paulist Press, New York. 1973.

———. *An Introduction to New Testament Christology*. Paulist Press, New Jersey. 1994.

Brown, Raymond, E., Fitzmyer, Joseph, A., Murphy, Ronald, E.C.O. (editors). *The New Jerome Biblical Commentary*. Prentice Hall Inc., New Jersey. 1990.

Burridge, A.R. and Gould G. Jesus *Now and Then. Society for the Promotion of Christian Knowledge.* Williams B. Eerdmans Publishing Co.: London. 2004.

Canaan, T. *Mohammedan Saints and Sanctuaries in Palestine*, in *Journal of the Palestine Oriental Sanctuaries.* iv/1–2, 1924, 1–84.

Cairns, E.E. *Christianity Through the Centuries. A History of the Christian Church.* Zondervan Publishing House, Michigan. 1984.

Campo, Juan, E. *Encyclopedia of Islam.* Infobase Publishing, New York. 2009.

Calverley, Edwin, E. "The Cross and Islam," in *The Muslim World vol. XXVII No.2.*1937.

Ceccarelli, Leah. *Shaping Science with Rhetoric: The Cases of Dobzhansky, Schrodinger, and Wilson.* The University of Chicago Press. 2001.

Cheetham David, Winkler Ulrich, Leirvik Oddbjorn, Gruber, Judith. (Editors). *Interreligious Hermeneutics in Pluralistic Europe: Between Text and People.* Rodopi B. V., Amsterdam. 2011.

Chittick, William, C. *Faith and Practice of Islam: Three Thirteenth Century Sufi Text.* University of New York Press, Albany. 1992.

Clooney, Francis, X. Clooney, Francis, X. "When Religions Become Context" in *Theology Today* 47 (1990), p.30-38.
———. *Comparative Theology: Deep Learning Across Religious Borders.* Wiley & Blackwell Publishing Corporation. 2010.
———. (ed.) *The New Comparative Theology: Interreligious Insights for the New Generation.* T & T Clark International, New York. 2010.

Cornille, Catherine. "Conditions for the Possibility of Interreligious Dialogue on God" in: Jeanrond and Lande (Eds). *The Concept of God in Global Dialogue.* Maryknoll: Orbis Books. 2005.
———. *The Impossibility of Interreligious Dialogue.* The Crossroad Publishing Company, New York. 2008.

———. "Meaning and Truth in Dialogue between Religions" in: Depoortere, Frederick and Magdalen Lambkin, Magdalene (Eds.). *The Question of Theological Truth. Philosophical and Interreligious Perspectives.* Rodopi, Amsterdam. 2012, p.137-156.

———. *The Willey- Blackwell Companion to Interreligious Dialogue.* John Willey and Sons Ltd, West Sussex – UK. 2013.

Cornille, C. & Conway C. *Interreligious Hermeneutics.* Cascade Books. Eugene and Oregon, 2010.

Cragg, Kenneth. *The Event of the Quran: Islam in its Scripture.* Oneworld Press, Oxford. 1977.

———. *Muhammad and the Christian: A Question of Response.* Oxford: Oneworld Press, 1999.

———. *Readings in the Qur'an.* Collins Liturgical Publications, San Francisco. 1988.

———. *The Call of the Minaret.* Orbis Books, Maryknoll, New York. 2000.

Cullmann, Oscar. *The Christology of the New Testament.* SCM Press Ltd. 1963.

Cumming, Joseph. "Did Jesus die on the Cross? The History of Reflection on Jesus' Death in Sunni Tafsir Literature." Yale University Press. 2001.

Dauerhauer, Bernard. "Ricoeur and Political Identity" in *Paul Ricoeur and Narrative Context and Contestation.* Edited by Morny Joy. University of Calgari Press, Calgari. 1997.

David Pellauer. "Looking for the Just" in *Etudes Ricoeuriennes/ Ricoeur Studies* vol. 2, 2012.

Dawkins, Richard. *The God Delusion.* Transworld Publishers, London. 2006.

D'Costa, Gavin. *Theology and Religious Pluralism: The Challenge of Other Religions.* Oxford: Basil Blackwell. 1986.

———. *The Meeting of religions and the Trinity.* Maryknoll, New York: Orbis Books. 2000.

———. *Christianity and the World Religions: Disputed Questions in the Theology of Religions.* Willey-Blackwell Publications, West Sussex: United Kingdom. 2009.

Deedat, Ahmed. *The Choice: Islam and Christianity* (Volumes One and Two). 1993.

DiNoia, Joseph. *The Diversity of Religions: A Christian Perspective.* Catholic University of American Press, Washington. 1992.

Dunn, James D.G. *Christology in the Making: A New Testament Inquiry into the Origins of the Doctrine of the Incarnation.* Philadelphia: Westminster, 1980.

Dupuis Jacques. *Jesus Christ at the Encounter of World Religions.* Orbis Books, Maryknoll New York, 1991.
———. *Towards a Christian Theology of religious Pluralism.* Orbis Books, Maryknoll, New York. 2001.
———. *Christianity and the Religions: From Confrontation to Dialogue.* Orbis Books, Maryknoll, New York. 2002.

Fatoohi, Louay. *The Mystery of the Historical Jesus: The Messiah in the Qur'an, the Bible and the Historical Sources.* Luna Plena Publishing Corporation, Birmingham, UK. 2007.

Fitzmyer, Joseph, A. "The Virginal Conception of Jesus Christ in the New Testament," in *Theological Studies 34.* 1973, p.541-575.

Fredericks, James, L. "A Universal Religious Experience: Comparative Theology as an Alternative to a Theology of Religion." in *Horizons* 22. 1995, p.67-87.
———. *Faith Among Faiths: Christian Theology and Non-Christian Religions.* Paulist Press, New York. 1999.

Fuchs, Lorelei, F. *Koinonia and the Quest for an Ecclesiological Ecumenism: From Foundation through Dialogue to Symbolic Competence of Communionality.* Wm. B. Eerdmans Publishing Co., Cambridge, UK. 2008.

Gadamer, Hans-Georg. *Truth and Method.* Joel Weinsheimer and Donald Marshall(editors). The Crossroad Publishing Corporation, New York.1989.

Gaudeul, M.J. *Encounters and Clashes: Islam and Christianity in History (II Text).* Pontifici Istitoto di Arabi e d'Islamistica (P.I.S.A.I.), Roma. 2000.

Ghazi bin Muhammad. *Love in the Holy Qur'an.* Kazi Publications Ltd, Chicago. 2010.

Gioia, Francesco (ed). *Interreligious Dialogue: The Official Teaching of the Catholic Church (1963-1995)* Boston Pauline Books and Media/Pontifical Council for Interreligious Dialogue. 1997.

Glassé, Cyril. *The New Encyclopedia of Islam.* Stacey International, London. 2002.

Goddard, Hugh. *A History of Christian-Muslim Relations.* New Amsterdam Books. 2000.

Graham, William. A. "Transcendence in Islam" in Dowdy, E. (ed.) *Ways of Transcendence: Insights from Major Religions and Modern Thought.* Australian Association for the Study of Religions. 1982, p.7-23.

Gregor, Brian. *A Philosophical Anthropology of the Cross: The Cruciform Self.* Indiana University Press, Indiana – United States of America. 2013.

Greisch, Jean. "Testimony and Attestation" in Paul Ricoeur. *Hermeneutics of Action.* Edited by Richard Kearney. Thousand Oaks, London. 1996.

Habet, Myk. *The Anointed Son; A Trinitarian Spirit Christology.* PICKWICK Publications: Eugene: Oregon. 2010.

Haffner, Paul, M. *New Testament Theology: An Introduction.* Gracewing Publishing Ltd: Herefordshire: England. 2006.

Haight, Roger. *The Future of Christology.* The Continuum International Publishing Group Ltd, London. 2007.

Hall, David. "The Site of Christian Ethics" Love and Justice in the Work of Paul Ricoeur" in *Paul Ricoeur and Contemporary Moral Thought.* Edited by Wall, J. Schweiker, W. & Hall, D. Routledge, New York. 2002.

Harnack, Adolf von. *What is Christianity?* (Trans.) Thomas Bailey Saunders. Fortress Press. 1986.

Hay, Lewis, S. "Son of God Christology in Mark". *American Journal of Religion.* Vol. xxxii, Issue 2. 1964, p.106-114.

Hedges, Paul. "The Old and the New Comparative Theologies: Discourses on Religion, the Theology of Religions, Orientalism and the Boundaries of Traditions." in *Religions 3:* 2012, p.1120-1137.

Hick, John. *Christianity at the Centre*. Macmillan Publications, London. 1968.

———. *God and the Universe of Faiths: Essays in the Philosophy of Religion*. Macmillan, London. 1988.

———. *An Interpretation of Religion: Human Response to the Transcendent*. New Haven: Yale University Press, 1989.

———. *A Christian Theology of Religions: The Rainbow of faiths*. Louisville: Westminster/John Knox Press. 1995.

Hick, J. & Knitter, P.F. (eds). *The Myth of Christian uniqueness: Toward a pluralistic theology of religions*. Maryknoll, New York: Orbis Books. 1987.

Hillman, Eugene. *Many Paths: A Catholic Approach to Religious Pluralism*. Orbis Books, New York. 1989.

Holland, Scott. *How Do Stories Save? An Essay with the Question of the Hermeneutics of David Tracy in View*. Peeters, Bondgenotenlaan Louvain. 2006.

Hooker, Morna. "'Who Can This Be?' The Christology of Mark's Gospel." In: Richard, N. Longenecker. *The Contours of Christology in the New Testament*. William B. Erdmann's publishing Company: Grand Rapids: Michigan. 2005.

Hurtado, Larry W. *One God, One Lord. Early Christian Devotion and Ancient Jewish Monotheism*. Philadelphia: Fortress, 1988.

Husserl, Edmund. *Cartesian Meditations: An Introduction to Phenomenology* (Trans. Darion Cairns). Kluwer Academic Publishers, Netherlands. 1999.

Gaudeul, Jean-Marie. *Encounters and Clashes: Islam and Christianity in History*. Pontifico Instituto di Studi Arabia e Islamic, Rome. 1990.

John Pontifex (Editor). *Roll Back the Stone of Fear: Prayer Poems and Letters from the Suffering Church in Sudan*. Aid to Church in Need. 2005.

John XXIII. *Pacem in Terris: Encyclical on Establishing Universal in Truth, Justice and Liberty*. Catholic Truth Society. 2002.

Kaiser, Walter, C. *The Messiah in the Old Testament*. Zondervan Publishing House, Michigan, USA. 1995.

Kaplan, David, M. *Ricoeur's Critical Theory.* State University of New York Press, Albany. 2003.

Kasper, Walter. *Jesus The Christ.* (New Edition) Burns and Oates-London and Paulist Press. New York. 1976.
———. "The Uniqueness and Universality of Jesus Christ". In: Massino Serretti (editor). *The Uniqueness and Universality of Jesus Christ; in Dialogue with Other Religions.* Wm. B. Eerdmans Publishing co. 2004, p.6–18.

Kateregga, Badru & Shenk, David, W. *Islam and Christianity.* UZIMA Press Ltd, Nairobi. 1980.

Kearney, Richard (editor). *Paul Ricoeur: The Hermeneutics of Action.* SAGE Publications Ltd. London: California: Delhi. 1996.

Kelly, J.D.N. *Early Christian Doctrines.* (Fifth Edition) CPI Antonomy Rowe. 2007.

Kendall, Daniel & O'Collins, Gerald (ed.). *In Many and Diverse Ways: In Honour of Jacques Dupuis.* Orbis Books, Maryknoll, New York. 2003.

Kerr, David A., "Christology in Muslim-Christian Dialogue" in B.F. Berkley and S. A. Edwards, (eds). *Christology in Dialogue.* Cleveland: The Pilgrim Press, 1993, p.201–220.

Kimball, Charles. *Striving Together: A Way Forward in Christian-Muslim Relations.* Orbis Books, New York. 1991.
———. "Toward a More Hopeful Future: Obstacles and Opportunities in Christian–Muslim Relations" in *The Muslim World*, 94: 2004, p.377–385.

Kingsbury, Jack, D. *The Christology of Mark's Gospel.* Fortress Press, United States of America. 1983.

Knitter, Paul. F. *One Earth Many Religions: Multifaith Dialogue and Global Responsibility.* Maryknoll, New York: Orbis Books. 1995.
———. *Jesus and the Other Names: Christian Mission and Global Responsibility.* Orbis Books. Maryknoll, New York 1996.
———. "Is the pluralist Model a Western imposition? A response in five voices," in Knitter, P. F. (ed). *The Myth of Religious Superiority: A Multifaith Exploration of Religious*

Pluralism. Orbis Books, Maryknoll, New York. 2005,
p.28-42.

Kujawa-Holbrook, Sheryl, A. *God Beyond Borders: Interreligious Learning Among Faith Communities.* Oregon: Eugene: PICKWICK Publication, 2014.

Kummel, W. G. *Introduction to the New Testament.* SCM Press Ltd. 1995.

Küng, Hans; Van Ess, Josef; Van Stietencron, Heinrich; Bechert, Heinz. *Christianity and World Religions; Paths to Dialogue.* Doubleday Dell Publishing Inc. Mary Knoll, USA. 1993.

———. *On Being a Christian.* New York: Doubleday. 1976.

———. *Islam: Past, Present & Future.* Oneworld Publications, Oxford. 2007.

Küng Hans & Moltmann, J. *Conflicts about the Holy Spirit.* The Seabury Press, New York. 1979 Lakhani, Ali, M. *The Sacred Foundation of Justice in Islam: The Teachings of Ali ibn Abi Talib.* Sacred Web Publishing, Indiana – United States of America. 2006.

Lane, Dermot, A. *The Reality of Jesus.* Veritas Press, Dublin: Paulist Press, New York. 1977.

Leirvik, Oddbjøørn. *Images of Jesus Christ in Islam.* Continuum International Publishing Group. New York. 2010.

Lejla Demiri (Editor). *A Common Word: Texts and Reflections.* The Muslim Academic rust, Cambridge – United Kingdom. 2011.

Lindbeck, George. *The Nature of Doctrine: Religion and Theology in a Postliberal Age.* Westminster Press, Philadelphia. 1984.

———. "The Gospel's Uniqueness: Election and Untranslatability" in *Modern Theology*, Vol. 13: Issue 4. 1997, p.423–450.

———. "The Unity We Seek: Setting the Agenda for Ecumenism" in *Christian Century* 121. 2005, p.28-31.

Longenecker, N. Richard. (Edited) *The Contours of Christology in the New Testament.* William B. Erdmann's publishing Company. 2005.

Machen, Gresham, J. *The Virgin Birth of Christ.* Amazon Digital Service Inc. 1987.

Mackintosh, Hugh, R. *The Person of Jesus Christ.* T & T Clark. 2000.

Marsh, Clive. & Moyise, Steve. *Jesus and the Gospels.* T & T Clark International, London & New York. 2006.

Marshal, David (Ed.). *Communicating the Word: Revelation, Translation and Interpretation in Christianity and Islam.* Georgetown University Press, Washington. 2011.

McAuliffe, Jane. *Qur'anic Christians: An Analysis of Classical and Modern Exegesis.* Cambridge University Press: Cambridge: NY. 1991,

McClintock, John. & Strong, James. *Cyclopedia of Biblical, Theological and Ecclesiastical Literature. Vol. 2.* Harper and Brothers, New York. 1894.

McGrath, Alister, E. *Christian Theology: An Introduction.* Blackwell Publishers Inc., Massachusetts, USA. 1997.

McIntyre, John. *The Shape of Christology: Studies in the Doctrine of the Person of Christ.* T&T Clark, Edinburgh. 1998.

Min, Anselm, K. *The Solidarity of Others in a Divided World: Postmodern Theology after Postmodernism.* T & T Clark International, New York. 2004.

Mohammad, Khaleel. *David in the Muslim Tradition: The Bathsheba Affair.* Lexington Books, Maryland, United State of America. 2015.

Montell, Jackson, R. *Islam Revealed.* Xulon Press, United States of America. 2003.

Moran, Dermot. *Introduction to Phenomelogy.* Routledge Publications, London. 2000.

Moucarry, George, C. *The Prophet and the Messiah: An Arab Christian Perspective on Islam and Christianity.* InterVarsity Press, Illinois. 2002.

Moule, C. F. D. (ed). *The Significance of the Message of the Resurrection for Faith in Jesus Christ.* London: SCM, 1968.

Moyaert, Marianne. "Absorption or Hospitality: Two Approaches to the Tension Between Identity and Alterity" in Cornille, C. & Conway, C. (editors). *Interreligious Hermeneutics*. CASCADE Books, Oregon, U. S. A. 2010.

———. *Fragile Identities: Towards a Theology of Interreligious Hospitality*. Rodopi B. V., Amsterdam–New York. 2011.

———. "Scriptural Reasoning as Interreligious Dialogue" in Cornille, Catherine. *The Willey- Blackwell Companion to Interreligious Dialogue*. John Willey and Sons Ltd, West Sussex. UK. 2013.

———. "On Vulnerability: Tracing the Ethical Dimension of Comparative Theology," in *Religions III. (*2012), p1144–1161: doi:10.3390/rel3041144.

Mullins, Michael. *The Gospel of John: A Commentary*. The Columba Press, Dublin. 2003.

Murata, Sachiko & Chittick, Williams, C. *The Vision of Islam*. I. B. Tauris & Co. Ltd. 1994.

Nasr, Hossein, Seyyed. *Ideals and Realities of Islam*. George Allen & Unwin Ltd. 1966.

———. "Islamic-Christian Dialogue –Problems and Obstacles to be Pondered and Overcome" in *The Muslim World*, 88: 1998, p.218–237.

Nazir, Ali Michael. *Frontiers in Muslim-Christian Encounter*. Regnum Books, Oxford. 1987.

Neal Robinson. "Sayyid Qutb's Attitude towards Christianity: *Sūrah 9.29-35 in Fī Zilāl al-Qur'ān*." in *Islamic Interpretations of Christianity*. Lloyd V.J. Ridgeon, ed. St. Martin's Press, New York. 2001, p.159-178.

———. *Christ in Islam and Christianity: Presentations of Jesus in the Qur'an and in the Classical Muslim Communities*. Macmillan Press Ltd, London. 1991.

Neusner, Jacob. *Messiah in Context: Israel's History and Destiny in Formative Judaism*. Philadelphia: Fortress, 1984.

Newman Paul. *Spirit Christology: Recovering the Biblical Paradigm of Christian Faith*. Rowman & Littlefield. 1987

Nicholson, Hughes. *Comparative Theology and the Problem of Religious Rivalry*. Oxford University Press, Oxford. 2011.

Nietzsche, Friedrich. *On the Genealogy of morals and Ecce Homo* (trans.) by Walter Kaufmann & R. J. Hollingdale. Vintage Books, New York. 1968.

Norma, Daniel. *Islam and the West: The Making of an Image.* Oneworld Press, Oxford. 1993.

O'Collins, Gerald. *Fundamental theology.* Paulist Press, New York/Mahwah. 1981.

———. *Interpreting Jesus.* New York: Paulist Press. 1983.

———. *Christology; a Biblical, Historical, and Systematic Study of Jesus.* (Second edition). Oxford University Press. 2009.

Ogden, Schubert. *The Point of Christology.* SCM Press Limited. 1982.

O'Mahony, Anthony. *Catholic Theological Perspectives on Islam at the Second Vatican Council.* New Blackfriars, 88: 2007, p.385–398.

O'Shaughnessy, Thomas. *The Koranic Concept of the Word of God.* Pontificio Instituto Biblico, Rome. 1948.

———. *The Development of the Meaning of Spirit in the Koran.* Pont. Institutum Orientalium Studiorum, Roma. 1953.

Panikkar, Raimon. *Myth, Faith and Hermeneutics; Cross cultural Studies.* Paulist Press, New York/Ramsey/Toronto. 1979.

———. "The Invisible Harmony: A Universal theory of Religion or a Cosmic Confidence in Reality?" in Swindler, L (ed), *Towards a universal theology of religion.* Maryknoll: New York: Orbis Book, 1987, p.118-153.

———. "What is Comparative Philosophy Comparing?" in: G. J. Larson & E. Deutsch (eds.) *Interpreting Across Religious Boundaries.* Princeton University Press. 1988.

———. *The Intra-Religious Dialogue.* Paulist Press, New Jersey; United States of America. 1999.

Parrinder, Geoffrey. *Jesus in the Qur'an.* One World Publications, Oxford. 1965.

Pasquini, J. *Atheism and Salvation; Atheism from the Point of View of Anonymous Christianity in the Thought of the Revolutionary Mystic and Theologian Karl Rahner.* University Press of America. 2000.

Perrin, Norma. *A Modern Pilgrimage in New Testament Christology*. Fortress Press: Minneapolis. 1974.

Phan, C. Peter. *Being Religious Interreligiously: Asian Perspective on Interfaith Dialogue*. Orbis Books, Maryknoll, New York. 2004.

Pontifical Council for Interreligious Dialogue, *Recognize the Spiritual Bonds which Unite us: 16 Years of Christian-Muslim dialogue*. Vatican City: PCID, 1994.

Pratt, Douglas. "Contextual Paradigms for Interfaith Relations." in *Current Dialogue 42* (2003), p.3-9.
———. *The Challenge of Islam; Encounters in Interfaith Dialogue*. Ashgate publishing Limited, Hampshire, England. 2005.
———. *Faith to Faith: Issues in Interreligious Engagement*. Published by OxCEPT, UK. 2008.

Rahner, Karl (editor). *Encyclopaedia of Theology: A Concise Sacramentum Mundi*. Burns and Oates, London. 1999.
———. *Foundation of Christian Faith: An Introduction to the Idea of Christianity*. Darton, Longman and Todd, London.1978.

Räisänen, Heikki. "The Portrait of Jesus in the Qur'an: Reflections of a Biblical Scholar" in *The Muslim World* 70: (1980), p.122–133.

Ratke, C. David. "The First Christian–Muslim Conversations" in: *Dialog*, 50: (2011), p8-9. Rawls, John. *A Theory of Justice*. Harvard University Press, New York. 1971.

Rāzī, Fakhr al-Dīn al-. Mafātīḥ al-ghayb: al-tafsīr al-kabīr, 2, Beirut: Dār Iḥyā' al-Turāth al- 'Arabī. 32 vols in 16. 1973.

Ricoeur, Paul. *Hermeneutics and the Human Sciences. J.B* Thompson (trans.). Cambridge University Press, New York. 1981.
———. *Time and Narrative. Volume I*. Edited by McLaughlin, K. & Pellauer, D. The University of Chicago Press, Chicago. 1984.
———. *Freedom and Nature: The Voluntary and Involuntary*. Northwestern University Press, New York. 1986.
———. "Life: A Story in Search of a Narrator" in *Facts and Values*. Edited by M. C. Doeser & J. N. Kraay. Martinus Nijhoff Publishers, Dordrecht. 1986.

———. *Time and Narrative. Vol. III.* Edited by Blamey, K. & Pellauer, D. The University of Chicago Press, Chicago–London. 1988.

———. "Explanation and Understanding" in *From Text to Action*, trans. Kathleen Blamey and John Thompson. Evanston, Ill: Northwestern University Press. 1991.

———. *From Text to Action: Essays in Hermeneutics,* II. Translated by Kathleen Blamey and John B. Thompson. Northwestern University Press, New York: London. 1991.

———. "Narrative Identity" in *Philosophy Today* 35:1 (1991), p.73–81.

———. *Oneself as Another.* Translated by Kathleen Blamey. University of Chicago Press, Chicago and London. 1992.

———. *Figuring the Sacred: Religion, Narrative and Imagination.* Translated by David Pellauer. Fortress Press, Minneapolis. 1995.

———. Ricoeur, Paul. "Pastoral Praxeology: Hermeneutics and Identity" in *Figuring the Sacred: Religion, Narrative and Imagination.* Fortress Press, Minneapolis. 1995.

———. "Naming God" in *Figuring the Sacred: Religion, Narrative and Imagination.* Fortress Press, Minneapolis. 1995, p.217-236.

———. "Reflections on a New Ethos for Europe" in *The Hermeneutics of Action* Richard Kearney (ed.). SAGE Publications Ltd. 1996.

———. *The Course of Recognition.* Translated by Pellauer, David. Howard University Press, Cambridge. 2005.

———. *On Translation.* Routledge, London 2006.

Ridgeon, Lloyd, V. J. (ed). *Islamic Interpretations of Christianity.* St. Martin's Press, New York. 2001.

Rosenthal, Franz (Trans.). *The History of al-Tabari.* (Vol. 1). State University of New York Press: Albany. 1989.

Rousseau, Richard, W. (ed). *Interreligious Dialogue (Vol. One).* Ridge Row Press. 1981.

Sacks, Jonathan. *The Dignity of Difference: How to Avoid the Clash of Civilizations.* Continuum Publications, London. 2004.

Sale, George. *The Koran* (9th edition). J.P Lippincott Company Ltd. London. 1923.

Samuel Schlorff. "The Theological and Apologetical Dimensions of Muslim Evangelization" in *Westminster Theological Journal*. Vol. 42 (1986), p.352-353.

Sardar, Ziauddin. "The Ethical Connection: Christian-Muslim Dialogue in Postmodern age" in *Islam and Christian-Muslim Relations*. Vol. 2, No. 1 (1991), p.56-76.

Saiyed Abbas Sadr-ameli (editor). *An Enlightening Commentary into the Light of the Holy Qur'an*. vol. 1, 1994.

Schlorff, Sam. "The Theological and Apologetical Dimensions of Muslim Evangelization". *Westminster Theological Journal*. Vol. 42 1986. http://www.answering-islam.org/Authors/Schlorff/schlorff1_f.html (12/04/2013).

Schwartz, Hans. *Christology*. Wm. B. Eerdmans Publishing Co. U K. 1998.

Schweitzer, Albert. *The Quest of the Historical Jesus. A Critical Study of Its Progress from Reimarus to Wrede*. New York: Macmillan, 1961 (Ger. orig. 1906.

Serretti, Massino. *The Uniqueness and Universality of Jesus Christ: in Dialogue with the Religions*. William B. Eerdmans Publishing Company. 2004.

Shellabear, Williams. "The Development of the Word 'Spirit' as Used in the Koran". 1932.

Siddiqui, Ataullah. *Christian-Muslim Dialogue in the Twentieth Century*. London: Macmillan and New York: St Martin's Press, 1997.

Siddiqui, Mona. "Being Human in Islam" in Michael Ipgrave and David Marshall (editors). *Humanity Text and Context: Christian and Muslim Perspectives*. Georgetown University Press. 2011.

———. *The Good Muslim: Reflections on Classical Islamic Law and Theology*. Cambridge University Press, New York. 2012.

———. *Christians, Muslims and Jesus*. Yale University Press, New Haven and London. 2013.

Sobrino, John. *Christology at the Crossroads*. A Latin American Approach. SCM Press Ltd. 1978.

Sonn, Tamara. *A Brief History of Islam*. Wiley and Sons Incorporated. 2004.

Sperber, Jutta, *Christians and Muslims: The Dialogue Activities of the World Council of Churches and Their Theological Foundation*. Berlin & New York: de Gruyter, 2000.

Spence, Alan. *Christology: Guide for the Perplex*. T&T Clark, New York. 2008.

Spinks, Christopher, D. *The Bible and the Crisis of Meaning: Debates on the Theological Interpretation of Scripture*. T & T Clark. 2007.

Sterkens, Carl. *Interreligious Learning: The Problem of Interreligious Dialogue in Primary Schools*. Leiden: Boston: Cologne: BRILL. 2001.

Swanson, N. Mark. *Resurrection Debates: Qur'anic Discourse and Arabic Christian Apology. Dialog,* 48: 2009, p.248–256.

Swindler, Leonard, John B. Cobb Jr, Paul F. Knitter and Monika Hellwig. *Death or Dialogue? From the Age of monologue to the Age of Dialogue*. SCM Press. London. 1990.
———. *Towards a Universal Theology of Religion. (Faith Meets Faith Series)* Orbis Books, Maryknoll. 1987.

Tabarī, Abū Ja 'far Muḥammad ibn Jarīr al-. *Tafsīr al-Ṭabarī: Jāmi 'al-bayān 'an ta'wīl ay al-Qur'ān*, ed. Maḥmūd Muḥammad Shākir and Aḥmad Muḥammad Shākir. 2nd ed. 16 vols (Incomplete). Cairo : Dār al-Ma'āri. 1955–69.

Tamara Sonn. *A Brief History in Islam*. John Wiley and Sons Ltd: Chichester, UK. 2004.

Thiselton, Anthony, C. *The Hermeneutics of Doctrine*. Wm. B. Eerdmans Publishing Co. 2007.

Thomas, a Kempis. *The Imitation of Christ*. Bruce Publishing Company, Milwaukee, Wisconsin. 1940.

Thomas, D. and Roggema, B. (edited). *Christian-Muslim Relations. A Biographical History*. Vol.1 (600–900). BRILL, Leiden and Boston. 2009.

Tracy, David. *Blessed Rage for Order: The New Pluralism in Theology.* The Seabury Press, New York. 1975.

——— . *The Analogical Imagination: Christian Theology and the Culture of Pluralism.* Crossroad Publishing Company, New York. 1981.

———. "Theology: Comparative Theology," in Mircea Eliade (ed.). *Encyclopedia of Religion,* Macmillan Publications, New York. 16 vols. 1987.

———. *Plurality and Ambiguity; Hermeneutics, Religion, Hope.* SCM Press, London. 1987.

———. "Western Hermeneutics and Interreligious Dialogue" in *Interreligious Hermeneutics.* Cornille, Catherin & Conway, Christopher (Eds). CASCADE Books, Eugene-Oregon. 2010.

Treier, Daniel, J. *Introducing Theological Interpretation of Scripture: Recovering a Christian Practice.* USA: Baker Academy. 2008.

Tsikata, Dzodzi & Sein Wayo. "Identities, Inequalities and Conflicts in Ghana" (Working Paper 5) 2004.

Vanhoozer, K. J. *The Cambridge Companion to Postmodern Theology.* (Sixth Edition) Cambridge University Press. 2009.

Vermes, Geza. *Jesus the Jew.* First Fortress Press, Philadelphia. 1973.

Waltz, James. "Historical Perspectives on 'Early Christian Missions' to Muslims" in *The Muslim World.* 61: 1971, p.170–186.

Ward, Keith. *Religion and Revelation.* Clarendon Press, Oxford. 1994.

———. *Religion and Human Nature.* Clarendon Press, Oxford. 1998.

———. *Religion and Community.* Clarendon Press, Oxford. 2000.

Webster, John (editor). *International Journal of Theology,* vol. 12 no. 2, 2010.

Wheeler, Brannon, M. *Prophets in the Qur'an: An Introduction to the Qur'an and Muslim Exegesis.* Continuum, London: New York. 2002.

Yahya, Harun. *Portents and Features of The Mahdi's Coming.* Global Publishing (Kindle Edition) 2010.

Yusuf, Ali, Abdullah. *The Holy Qur'an: English Translation, Commentary with Arabic Text.* Kitab Bhavan Publications. 2001.

Zamakhsharī, Abū al-Qāsim Jār Allāh Maḥmūd ibn ʿUmar al-. *al-Kashshāf ʿan ḥaqāʾiq al-tanzīl wa-ʿuyūn al-aqāwīl fī wujūh al-taʾwīl*, ed. Muḥammad ʿAbd al-Salām Shāhīn. 4th ed. 4 vols. Beirut: Dār al-Kutub al-ʿIlimiyya. 2006.

Zwemer, Samuel. *The Moslem Christ: An Essay on the Life, Character, Teaching of Jesus Christ According to the Koran and Orthodox Traditions.* Anderson and Ferrier Publishers, Edinburgh. 1912.

ELECTRONIC SOURCES

Aherne, Cornelius. "Son of God." The Catholic Encyclopedia. Vol. 14. New York: Robert Appleton Company, 1912. 26 Apr. 2010. http://www.newadvent.org/cathen/14142b.htm>. (03/03/2013).

Akgunduz, Ahmed. "Norms and Values in Islam: http://islam.uga.edu/norms_values.html (09/05/13).

Atkins Kim. Stanford Encyclopedia of Philosophy: "Paul Ricoeur": http://www.iep.utm.edu/ricoeur/ (02/022012).

Australian Association for the study of Religions. *Multi-faith dialogue in conversation with Raimon Panikkar:* http://dlibrary.acu.edu.au/staffhome/gehall/Hall_Panikkar.htm (28/04/11).

Cumming, Joseph. "Did Jesus die on the Cross? The History of Reflection on Jesus' Death in Sunni Tafsir Literature" (unpublished). 2001: http://www.learningace.com/doc/997971/e22490e3729b-c1bdcca5495a3f68ca09/didjesusdieenglish (09/10/14).

"Islamic Views of Hazrat Maryam." http://justsimplyinlove.wordpress.com/2012/11/18/islamic-views-of-hazrat-maryam-ra/ (09/10/14).

Irenaeus: *Against Heresies.* 3:1:3 http://www.columbia.edu/cu/augustine/arch/irenaeus/advhaer3.txt (15/01/2013).

Jason Barker. *Christian and Interreligious Dialogue.* The Watchman Expositor, Vol. 5 No. 4 1998 http://watchman.org/reltop/christiandialogue.htm (02/02/11).

John Cooper. "al-Razi Fakhr al-Din (1149-1209)" in *Routledge Encyclopaedia of Philosophy.* 1998: http://www.muslimphilosophy.com/ip/rep/H044.htm (09/09/2014).

John Paul II. "Encyclical Letter : *fides et ratio* (#31). September 15th, 1998: http://www.vatican.va/holy_father/john_paul_ii/encyclicals/documents/hf_jp-ii_enc_15101998_fides-et-ratio_en.html (16/07/2012).

Pacem in Terris: Encyclical of Pope John XXIII on Establishing Universal in Truth, Justice and Liberty. April 11, 1963: http://w2.vatican.va/content/johnxxiii/en/encyclicals/documents/hf_jxxiii_enc_11041963_pacem.html (14/04/2015).

Populorum Progressio: Encyclical of Pope Paul VI on the Development of Peoples (March 26, 1967): http://w2.vatican.va/content/paul-vi/en/encyclicals/documents/hf_p vi_enc_26031967_populorum.html (14/04/205).

Pope John Paul II: "Address to the Representatives of the Christian Churches and to the Ecclesial Communities and to the World Religions" (October 27, 1986): http://w2.vatican.va/content/john-paul-ii/en/speeches/1986/october/documents/hf_jp-ii_spe_19861027_prayer-peace-assisi-final.html (14/04/2015).

Sahih Muslim Book 001, Hadith number 0323: http://hadith-collection.com/sahihmuslim/129Sahih%20Muslim%20Book%2001.%20Faith/8461-sahih-muslim-book-001-hadith-number-0323.html (16/03/2015).

Ṣaḥīḥ Muslim, 41: 7043. Its full title is: "Al-Musnadu Al-Sahihu bi Naklil Adli": http://www.usc.edu/org/cmje/religious-texts/hadith/muslim/041-smt.php#041.7023 (27-05-2013).

The National Secular Society (NSS – Britain): http://www.secularism.org.uk/ (03/06/2013).

Samwini, Iddrisu, N. "The Need for and Importance of the Dialogue of Life in Community The Theological and Apologetical Dimensions of Muslim Evangelization" in *Westminster Theological Journal.* Vol. 42 (1986), p.335: http://www.answering-islam.org/Authors/Schlorff/schlorff1_f.html (12/04/2013).

The author

Rev. Dr. Robert Afayori was born in 1976 in
Nkawkaw, Ghana and educated at Notre Dame
Secondary School. He attended St Victor's Major
Seminary and was ordained a Catholic priest in
2005. He obtained his first degree in philosophy
in the University of Ghana in 2003 and his second
degree in education at Cape Coast University in
2009. In 2010, Robert moved to Scotland to take
a PhD in Systematic Theology at the University
of Edinburgh and a second PhD in Education at
Newcastle University whilst working as a priest in
the Archdiocese of St Andrews and Edinburgh.
He has since published several research articles on
Christology and transformational leadership effects
on schools and colleges.

"He who stops
getting better
stops being good.

This is the motto of novum publishing, and our focus
is on finding new manuscripts, publishing them and
offering long-term support to the authors.
Our publishing house was founded in 1997, and since
then it has become THE expert for new authors and
has won numerous awards.

**Our editorial team will peruse each manuscript
within a few weeks free of charge and without
obligation.**

You will find more information about
novum publishing and our books on the internet:

www.novum-publishing.co.uk